Sixth Edition

Advertising
MEDIA
Planning

Jack Z. Sissors AND Roger B. Baron

Foreword by Erwin Ephron, Founder and President, Ephron, Papazian & Ephron, Inc.

McGraw-Hill

Chicago   New York   San Francisco   Lisbon   London   Madrid   Mexico City
Milan   New Delhi   San Juan   Seoul   Singapore   Sydney   Toronto

Library of Congress Cataloging-in-Publication Data

Sissors, Jack Zanville, 1919–
    Advertising media planning / Jack Z. Sissors, Roger B. Baron.—6th ed.
       p.   cm.
    Includes index.
    ISBN 0-8442-1563-5 (alk. paper)
    1. Advertising media planning.   I. Baron, Roger B.   II. Title.

    HF5826.5 .S57 2002
    659.1'11—dc21   2002022717

McGraw-Hill

A Division of The McGraw·Hill Companies

6 7 8 9 0 DOC/DOC 0 9 8 7 6 5

ISBN 0-8442-1563-5

This book was set in Adobe Garamond and Myriad by Village Typographers, Inc.
Printed and bound by R. R. Donnelley—Crawfordsville

Cover design by Amy Yu Ng
Interior design by Village Typographers, Inc.

McGraw-Hill books are available at special quantity discounts to use as premiums and
sales promotions, or for use in corporate training programs. For more information, please
write to the Director of Special Sales, Professional Publishing, McGraw-Hill, Two Penn
Plaza, New York, NY 10121-2298. Or contact your local bookstore.

This book is printed on acid-free paper.

Contents

CHAPTER THREE

The Relationship Among Media, Advertising, and Consumers   39

CHAPTER FOUR

Basic Measurements and Calculations   57

CHAPTER FIVE

Advanced Measurements and Calculations 87

CHAPTER SIX

Marketing Strategy and Media Planning 117

APPENDIX TO CHAPTER SIX

Media-Planning Resources on the Internet   150

CHAPTER SEVEN

Strategy Planning I: Who, Where, and When   159

CHAPTER EIGHT

Strategy Planning II: Weighting, Reach, Frequency, and Scheduling 193

CHAPTER NINE

Selecting Media Classes: Intermedia Comparisons 223

CHAPTER ELEVEN

Evaluating and Selecting Media Vehicles   287

CHAPTER TWELVE
Media Costs and Buying Problems 317

Foreword

Medium is a self-effacing word. It describes something in-between—intermediate not central, a means not an end, neither rare nor well-done. For decades planning media has had an equally modest persona. It was the mailroom of advertising assigned the undemanding job of getting the message out.

In the traditional full-service agency, creative and account management, not media, attracted the talent, the salaries, and the applause. They got the stock options and became agency presidents because creating the campaign and selling it to the client made the money. Media was a cost, a base-camp support group for those highly paid troops on the front line.

That has changed. The unbundling of agency services created the independent media agency. This transformed media from a cost center to a profit center and made it one of the best career paths in advertising. Today the six largest media agencies control $40 billion in advertising spending. They are global and often more profitable than the creative agencies that spawned them. The turnip has turned into a tiger.

The media agency has come of age, but it took 30 years. It started with TV buying. In the postwar prosperity of the 1950s, the full-service agency did media planning and buying. Media options were limited and execution was phoning in the order. Then in the 1960s a major scandal hit. A media-buying service, in the person of Norman King, told advertisers their agencies were paying far too much for television and proved it. Advertisers suddenly became aware of price negotiation and other ways to buy media. Western, TBS, Botway, and a half dozen other media-buying firms were soon in business.

Buying services made their money "on-the-spread." They contracted to deliver media to an advertiser at an agreed price and kept the difference between that price and what they actually paid. It was highly profitable. Planning, which was not as lucrative, was left to the agency.

IT TOOK AN ART DIRECTOR

It took an art director to invent and bankroll the first true media independent. When George Lois left Papert Koenig Lois in the late 1960s to start a new agency, he didn't want the expense or headaches of an in-house media department. He gave those, and a contract, to Dick Gershon, who had a flair for names and started Independent Media Services. It did everything—planning as well as buying. SFM, another media independent, and others soon followed. But media services, as they were called, worked at the fringes of the business. They were associated with low media costs, not good media planning.

Years later, after Saatchi & Saatchi, a large global agency, introduced Zenith as its independent media arm, and CARAT, a media independent, won the large Pfizer media account, it was evident that independent media could compete on a skills and product basis with the best of the agency media departments. When Y&R spun off its media department as The MediaEdge, and J. Walter Thompson and Ogilvy finally handed over media responsibilities to MindShare, the media agency had arrived.

At the same time, the media business was being *transformed,* a word I do not use lightly. The explosive growth in TV channels, specialized magazines, and the Internet seemed to threaten the very idea of mass media. This led media planners to greater sophistication, experimenting with things like optimization, media mix, and data fusion to preserve advertising's cost-effectiveness. Mergers and acquisitions by agencies and media resulted in fewer, more powerful players. This led the media to package their assets in what they called cross-platform selling, while agencies concentrated their market power by consolidating buying.

Recency theory provided a new media-directed model of how advertising works. It replaced the idea of advertising as a teaching tool in favor of advertising as a timely reminder for consumers, who are in the market. This refocused media planning on weekly reach and continuity in place of the old effective frequency and flighting.

But by far the most interesting change was in advertiser expectations and the casting out of the full-service agency.

IS ADVERTISING SUPPOSED TO SELL?

Advertising agencies had long argued that since sales of a product depended on more than advertising, they could be held accountable only for building awareness, not making sales. If everything else was in place, they explained, successful advertising would increase sales in the long term. Today most advertisers expect advertising to have an immediate effect on sales. Otherwise why advertise? Remarkably, this is a new requirement. The change in advertiser expectations has had a profound effect on the historic role of the advertising agency. It has gone from a marketing partner to a service supplier.

Until the mid '60s, agencies were thought of as marketing gurus because most advertisers were manufacturers not marketers. Then came the Doyle Dane Bernbach creative revolution, and for the next 20 years agencies were creative centers. This paralleled the growing sophistication of advertisers, who began to master many of the marketing functions but still considered making ads a black art.

In the '80s, agencies went public, merged, and were taken over by one another and by the accountants who identified cost and profit centers. This cost-accounting exercise put a price on everything and unwittingly encouraged the future unbundling of agency services.

Sophisticated advertisers, now acting as their own general contractors, dissected the agency package and went here and there for what they needed. Recency theory, scanner data, and a new emphasis on advertising's immediate selling effects unraveled the old relationships. Effective creative was now deemed so important (and unpredictable) that it made little sense to be locked into a single creative source.

The simple fact was, and still is, highly successful advertising is a long shot. I recall an operation researcher, who was briefly assigned to the advertising group at a major beer brand, explaining the problem. He estimated the probability of his agency coming up with a strong campaign at about 1 in 10. Bad enough, but there was more. He suggested the probability of his management recognizing it as a strong campaign also at about 1 in 10. That made the odds 100 to 1.

Part of his solution for reducing the odds was to have more than one creative source, an important idea, which began happening more and more often. Separating the media and creative assignments makes it possible. An independent media agency can provide continuity in brand advertising management and allows the brand to look at a wider range of creative sources. A full service agency does not. That is a major reason most large advertisers use media agencies.

A DICEY MOVE

The now familiar term *creative agency* is a marker. Once it was a compliment, not a category. Most agencies were full-service. But profit goals encouraged them to spin off freestanding media groups that could spread costs and increase income by serving non-clients.

In retrospect, detaching creative from the life support of media was a dicey move. It lowered costs and broadened revenues, as planned, but it also allowed smaller creative shops to compete for large accounts, a trend richly illustrated by the successes of Arnold, Goodby, Riney, Messner, Deutsch, and many others. As David Verklin of CARAT observed, "It's really the creative agency that's been unbundled."

So in one of the great ironies of advertising, it is the central importance of creative that stripped the full-service agency and gave media its big chance to shine.

This Sissors and Baron book you are about to read is a fine entry into the exciting field of media. *Advertising Media Planning* is a remarkable work for many reasons: It explains the complexities of planning in a concise and readable text. It is state-of-the-art, covering current theory and today's best practices. It describes all of the useful planning data sources and provides their URLs for Internet access. It provides detailed real-world examples of planning problems and solutions. In fact, the book covers much of what I've learned the hard way over 35 years and a few things I confess I didn't know. Well done, Jack and Roger.

Erwin Ephron
Founder and President
Ephron, Papazian & Ephron, Inc.

Coauthor's Note

About a year and a half ago, I received a call from Jack Sissors, inviting me to coauthor the sixth edition of *Advertising Media Planning*. Like so many of us in the industry, I began learning most of what I know about media planning with this text. The early, well-thumbed copy is still in my library. Needless to say, I was flattered to be offered a chance to contribute to this classic work. My assignment was simple: update the charts and provide whatever perspective I could on changes in the industry since the last revision in 1995, when Linc Bumba served in this position.

For the next three months, Jack and I went through the book chapter by chapter, replacing old references that are no longer applicable, while keeping the seminal studies that continue to provide the foundations of our profession. Meanwhile, I added new sections that reflect the immense impact of the Internet and other developments that have occurred since the last edition.

The Internet has emerged as a medium in its own right, as well as a vast source of information for media planners. Wherever possible, I have shown the URL of research suppliers and public domain online resources where the reader can get additional information. These replace the "Selected Readings" in previous editions. I have also added material that reflects the day-to-day work of media planners: a simplistic yet representative media plan, a real-world illustration of the magazine selection process, and a more detailed discussion of the interplay between coverage and composition in all media selection.

In the last year, two significant events changed the course of the project. First, McGraw-Hill bought NTC/Contemporary Publishing Group, an old-line publisher of college textbooks. This book was an important part of that acquisition, but as in any buyout situation, work halted while the new owners reevaluated all projects under development. Work resumed this spring under the auspices of McGraw-Hill's trade division, which offers greatly increased marketing and distribution capabilities.

Jack and I had gotten about halfway through the book when, sadly, I was informed that he had suffered a stroke and would no longer be able to participate. This left me the responsibility of completing the project, while at the same time preserving the essence of this book, which has been so successful for more than 25 years. Of necessity, there will appear observations, illustrations, and points of view that I can only hope and trust Jack would have agreed with.

A few acknowledgments are in order. First to my editor, Liz MacDonell in Portland, Oregon, for gently keeping me faithful to the spirit of Jack's work and for showing me how much a good editor can contribute to a book's success. Thanks to Gary Behlow at Nielsen Media Research, Scott Turner at Mediamark Research Inc., Bill Hamm at Competitive Media Reporting, and J. P. Beauchamp at Information Resources, Inc. for reviewing the many chapters that referenced their company's products and ensuring that I got the facts right. Finally, thanks to my colleagues in the Media Department at Foote, Cone & Belding, Chicago, for their professionalism, creativity, and enthusiasm, which every day remind me why I love this business.

Above all, thanks to our wives, Dorothy Sissors and Margi Baron, for putting up with the many hours we spent hunched over the computer. This book would not have been possible without their loving support.

Roger Baron
December 2001

CHAPTER ONE

Introduction

We have all seen TV shows and movies about the advertising business—full of glamorous young people prancing around modern offices in casual clothes, shooting baskets while they think up catchy jingles to sell their client's product. Sometimes there will be a shot of the clients—a serious-looking, formally dressed group of people in a conference room, watching a presentation, then bursting out in smiles and high fives at the wonderfully creative new campaign that is going to make them all rich.

Of course, what really happens is that the client's marketing director has said something like, "This creative is great. Now I want to know how you're going to spend the $10 million I'm giving you so my customers will see it. I want to know what my competition is doing, whom you are targeting, what media you are going to use and why, where it will run, when it will run, and which particular magazines you will use. Finally, I want to know how many of the target audience will see the ad and how often they will see it. If you make a good case, I'll authorize the $10 million. So let's see your media plan."

This version is a bit overdrawn perhaps, but it is the job of the media planner to answer these questions and develop a plan that delivers the creative message to the target as effectively and as efficiently as possible. It is a fascinating job that combines marketing, psychology, show business, law, research, technology, and the planner's sensitive, creative insights into the human condition. It has the planner playing the dual roles of salesperson and client—sometimes alternating roles from one minute to the next. In the sales role, planners must convince the advertiser and his or her own agency team that they have developed the most effective media plan. Then, with a ring of the telephone, a planner becomes the client of the media sales representatives who want their magazine, newspaper, television network, or other medium included in the plan—included so they receive an order for part of that $10 million budget. These are the outward manifestations of the core job of the media planner: to make the most effective use of the advertiser's media budget.

MEDIA: A MESSAGE DELIVERY SYSTEM

Media exist primarily to deliver message content—entertainment, information, and advertisements—to a vast audience. Media should be thought of as both carriers and delivery systems. They carry advertisements and deliver them to individuals who buy or choose media first on the basis of the kind and quality of entertainment and information, and secondly on the kinds of advertisements they deliver. Advertisers find media convenient and relatively inexpensive delivery systems. It could be more expensive to deliver advertisements to a mass audience by buying media that did not carry entertainment and information.

It is important to recognize that consumers have specialized needs that media can meet, such as wanting to know more about certain kinds of products and brands. At times, audiences browse a print medium, stopping to look at or read any advertisements that seem interesting. At other times, they deliberately search a medium looking for a certain kind of product. Print media, therefore, tend to serve as catalogs for readers. Broadcast media audiences also pay attention to many commercials, but not in the same way as print audiences.

Advertisers often want to reach both mass and specialized audiences and find it is more expensive to buy media that reach specialized audiences. However, no matter which kind of audience advertisers want to reach, it is imperative that someone plan the purchase of media as far ahead of publishing or broadcast dates as possible. Advertisers cannot afford to buy media impulsively or capriciously. Therefore, the planning function is a major operation in advertising agencies and at client companies. Too much money is involved for advertisers to fail to plan. This book concentrates on the planning function.

In discussions of this subject, two words are sometimes used as if they meant the same thing: *medium* (the plural is *media*) and *vehicle*. They are not exactly the same. A medium refers to a class of carriers such as television, newspapers, or magazines. In other words, a medium is a group of carriers that have similar characteristics. A vehicle is an individual carrier within a medium. The *Chicago Tribune* is a vehicle within the newspaper medium. "60 Minutes" is a vehicle within the television medium. *Martha Stewart Living* and *People* are vehicles within the magazine medium.

MEDIA PLANNING

The process of *media planning* consists of the series of decisions made to answer the question, "What are the best means of delivering advertisements to prospective purchasers of my brand or service?" This definition is rather general, but it provides a broad picture of what media planning is all about.

Within this broad context, a media planner attempts to answer specific questions, such as the following:

- How many prospects (for purchasing a given brand of product) do I need to reach?
- In which medium (or media) should I place ads?
- How many times a month should prospects see each ad?
- In which months should ads appear?
- Where should the ads appear? In which markets and regions?
- How much money should be spent in each medium?

When all questions have been asked and decisions made, the recommendations and rationales are organized into a written document called a *media plan*. The plan, when approved by the advertiser, becomes a blueprint for the selection and use of media. Once the advertiser has approved the plan, it also serves as a guide for actually purchasing the media.

It would be a mistake, however, to think of media planning as nothing more than finding answers to a list of questions about media. Such a view is too narrow to provide the necessary perspective. Rather, it is better to assume that each question represents certain kinds of problems that need to be solved. Some problems are relatively simple, such as, "On which day of the week should television commercials be shown?" Other problems are much more difficult, such as, "In which media will ads most affect the prospect's buying behavior to result in sales?"

Media planning should be thought of as a process or a series of decisions that provides the best possible answers to a set of problems. A planner might find that a solution to a given problem does not guarantee it will work when other factors are considered. Finding the best solutions to a set of problems represents the main task of planners, and this is what makes media planning so intellectually challenging.

CHANGING FACE OF MEDIA PLANNING

Some marketers believe the traditional media forms, such as television, newspapers, magazines, and radio, are less effective in producing sales now than in the past, because markets are changing and media must reach the product's best prospects much more selectively. Traditional media are challenging because they are mass media in an era when the culture is changing—the masses are breaking up into smaller segments. Therefore, advertisers must define markets much more precisely than they were defined in the past.

During the introduction of a new product, it is sometimes easy to see that mass advertising is the way to communicate with large or small markets, as consumers flock to buy new brands that they first encountered through advertising. But today's consumers want more information about both new and established products than can be communicated with the traditional media. Because consumers expect to get this information from the Internet, marketing plans must consider how to use this new medium to build on the awareness created with mass advertising.

Traditionally, media planning has asked questions revolving around how media can reach the right persons. The "right" persons came from broadly aggregated data, such as "women aged 18–49," or "men aged 25–54." But these broad demographic characterizations obscure an almost unlimited array of lifestyles, interests, and even media habits that are relevant to marketers if they want to deliver advertising to their best prospects. Today's media planning requires planners to identify smaller groups of product users and the media that best reach them. Furthermore, as society changes, media will have to be able to alert marketers that a target group's size and composition might have changed, so marketers can reach these smaller groups with little waste.

Technology has made it economical to deliver program content that appeals to smaller and smaller groups of people. Audience fragmentation has become the dominant characteristic of media, especially television, in the early years of the 21st century. Today the average home can receive 75 television channels, up from 41 channels in 1995.[1] Cable television programs, delivered either by wire or by satellite, can now be seen in 82 percent of U.S. households with TVs.[2]

---

1. *Nielsen Television Audience* 2000.
2. Nielsen Media Research, *ADS Counts,* August 2001.

This proliferation of viewing choices has significantly eroded the audience of the traditional broadcast networks, but total hours of viewing have remained essentially constant.

The result is a splintering of the audience among channels whose content may or may not be relevant to advertisers. For example, marketers of vacation destinations will certainly advertise on the Travel Channel, but the majority of their customers never watch it. The planner's challenge is to deliver the advertising to these potential customers in other, less obvious and less targeted, but much more popular venues.

The growth of digital and interactive television is unlikely to change this picture substantially. The shape of the future can be seen today. If the average viewer can choose among 75 channels, the addition of 10 or 20 more channels is unlikely to change behavior. Digital television brings a clearer picture and the opportunity to buy pay-per-view movies, pay channels, and special events, but since these media do not accept advertising, there are no implications for consumer product marketers. Although the Internet has brought interactive salesmanship to more than half of the nation's homes, adding this capability to television is also unlikely to change behavior.

However, one technological development on the horizon has the potential to dramatically alter the media landscape. Personal video recorders (PVRs) allow viewers to create their own virtual television network by recording only the programs that interest them, regardless of the channel on which they appear. The further ability to skip through commercials threatens to undermine the economic base of the medium or, alternatively, to drive the best talent to pay services. In late-2001, penetration of PVRs was an insignificant 0.5 percent of U.S. households, and it remains to be seen whether this technology will grow to the point of affecting television advertising.

CHANGING ROLE OF MEDIA PLANNERS

As a result of technological advances and audience fragmentation, the role of media planners has changed in advertising agencies. Today, media planning ranks in importance with marketing and creative planning, but in the early days of advertising agency operations, media planning consisted of simple, clerical tasks. Fewer media were available in those days, and little research on media audiences had been done to guide planners in decision making.

Planning today is an executive function because it has become so much more complex and important than it was years ago. Today's planners must have a greater knowledge base from which to formulate media plans. The planners not only must know more about media, which have increased tremendously in number, but also must know more about marketing, research, and advertising than did their predecessors. Most important, planners are called upon not only to make decisions, but also to defend those decisions as the best that could be made after considering the many alternatives.

What brought about this change? Foremost was the rise of the marketing concept, which changed media planning from an isolated activity to one closely related to marketing planning. In fact, one way to evaluate a media plan is to measure how effectively it helps to attain marketing objectives. Another cause of the change was the development of new and more definitive media audience research techniques. As a result, there are more research data available to help planners choose from among myriad alternatives.

The change is also due to the universal availability of the Internet and low-cost, high-speed computers that make routine the physical acquisition and manipulation of vast amounts of data. The computer is the workbench planners use to compare and cost out media alternatives. And finally, it is used to develop the presentation that will ultimately sell the plan to the client.

Media planning, then, is not so much a matter of being able to answer such relatively simple questions as where to place advertisements or how many advertisements to run each week. It is a matter of proving that optimal decisions were made under a given set of marketing circumstances. Advertisers demand such explanations, and media planners must be able to provide them. Today's media planners have changed as requirements for planning have changed. The new planner must have breadth of knowledge, marketing understanding, research familiarity, computer literacy, creative planning awareness, and media acumen to do the job competently. It is within this framework that media planning now takes place.

CLASSES OF MEDIA

Media are often separated into different classes and categories. Some important classifications include traditional mass media, nontraditional media, and specialized media. This section distinguishes these classifications and describes types of each.

Traditional Mass Media

Mass media such as newspapers, magazines, radio, and television are especially well suited for delivering advertisements—as well as news, entertainment, and educational content—to a widespread general (or mass) audience. Mass media are valuable to advertisers because they offer several advantages:

- Such media are able to deliver large audiences at relatively low costs.
- They can deliver advertisements to special kinds of audiences who are attracted to each medium's editorial or programming.
- They tend to develop strong loyalties among audiences who return to their favorite medium with a high degree of regularity.

If a planner wants to reach a special kind of audience repeatedly within a certain time period, some media vehicles will be better suited for this purpose than others. Recent research suggests, for example, that certain types of broadcast programs create higher degrees of viewer interest than other program types, thus offering better environments for commercials.

Like other media, however, mass media have limitations in delivering advertising messages. The most serious is that mass media audiences do not see, hear, or read a medium solely because of the advertising content. Media also vary in their ability to expose both editorial and advertising material.

Newspapers offer their readers news, entertainment, information, and catalog values. A newspaper generally has excellent readership of local news, editorial, and advertising material, serving as a buying guide for readers who are looking for many different kinds of products. People often check newspaper ads immediately before their regular food-shopping day to find the best grocery bargains. For frequently purchased products, where prices are prominently displayed, newspapers can be a very effective selling medium.

Magazines, on the other hand, are much different in their ability to expose ads. Some, such as fashion, home, and special-interest publications, are bought as much for their advertising as for their editorial matter. General-interest publications, such as newsweeklies and personality and sports magazines, appeal to readers who are looking for interesting articles and stories, rather than product information.

Consumers are least likely to turn to broadcast media, such as radio and television, for the advertisements alone. Broadcast commercials have an intrusive character, breaking into the play or action of a program and compelling some attention to the advertising message. Whether any given viewer will or will not watch a particular commercial depends more on the ingenuity and value of the message than its appearance on an interesting program.

The Internet is primarily an information-delivering medium. People go to the site that contains the information they are looking for, whether that is weather, sports, news, airline schedules, or the fact sheet on a late-model automobile. This makes the Internet a highly efficient medium for delivering sales information to consumers who are planning to buy, as well as offering the ability to place an order directly online.

Obviously, the effectiveness of the advertisement to communicate affects its impact on the consumer and the number of consumers who will read, see, or hear it. This is true regardless of which medium is used.

Nontraditional Media

Traditional mass media all engage in one-way communication—from the source to the viewer, listener, or reader. Almost any other innovative way of delivering ad messages to consumers is considered a *nontraditional medium*. These media disseminate advertising messages through means not usually called media. For example, the combination of magazines and sales promotion is sometimes called nontraditional media, even though sales promotion has not historically been categorized as a medium. Similarly, Internet advertising, though certainly not traditional, is generally viewed in its own category as a new electronic medium.

Nontraditional media can fill an advertiser's need to find alternative ways of reaching customers in venues where advertising will stand out from the advertiser's competition. They also satisfy the need for additional revenue from companies that have exposure to the public and feel that their unique location offers an opportunity to sell advertising. The most commonly used nontraditional media include television screens in airport waiting areas and doctors' offices, and posters in health clubs, on golf courses, and at public events. Placement of advertising in other locations, such as the walls of public rest rooms, the floor of grocery stores, and overhead luggage bins of commercial airliners, may be driven more by a proprietor's desire for additional income than by the advertiser's need for an alternative venue.

Many media planners recommend that their clients use nontraditional media, but there have been some problems in determining what the advertiser receives for the money. The problems are caused by not having any continuing measurements of the audience sizes delivered by these less established media. In addition, what information does exist is typically provided by the media themselves, raising questions about its accuracy and objectivity. In most instances, planners have to "guesstimate" the sizes of audiences. Without independent measurements, it is difficult to calculate a cost per thousand exposures that represents the value of the money spent for advertising related to the number of audience members delivered.

Specialized Media

Special-interest consumer magazines appeal to specific reader interests such as skiing, money management, photography, or antiques. These magazines are read as much for their advertising as they are for their editorial content. Therefore, these magazines often attract readers who purchase the magazine not only for the editorial material, but also for information on the kinds of products advertised. Such media are often referred to as *niche media* because of their special-interest focus.

A large category of media also exists to meet the specialized needs of industrial manufacturers, service companies, wholesalers, retailers, and professional workers such as physicians, attorneys, and teachers. These media take the form of publications that contain editorial matter as well as advertising pertaining to the specialized market, but they also include films, trade shows, convention exhibits, and cassette tapes. These magazines are often provided free to the readers, paid for entirely by advertisers who want to reach a specialized audience. Business-to-business advertisers are typically the advertisers most interested in these publications.

Other specialized media exist exclusively for delivering advertising messages. They carry no editorial matter and are not sought after by readers as are other forms of media. Such advertising-oriented media include handbills, direct mail, outdoor billboards, car cards that appear on buses or trucks, and free-standing inserts (FSIs) in newspapers.

Another specialized medium is the catalog. Although consumers often request catalogs, they look at catalogs less frequently than mass media. At the same time, many advertisers find catalogs productive because consumers use them as shopping guides. One form of catalog is the telephone book, which carries advertising but also carries editorial matter—telephone numbers. Plumbers, for example, might justifiably use telephone book advertising exclusively, because plumbers are not usually called until an emergency arises. On such occasions, the consumer will search ads in the *Yellow Pages* to find a plumber but probably will not notice such ads at any other time.

GENERAL PROCEDURES IN MEDIA PLANNING

Marketing considerations must precede media planning. Media planning never starts with answers to such questions as, Which medium should I select? or Should I use television or magazines? Planning grows out of a marketing problem that needs to be solved. To start without knowing or understanding the underlying marketing problem is illogical, because media are primarily a tool for implementing the marketing strategy.

As you will see in the hypothetical media plan that is presented in Chapter 2, the starting point for a media plan should be an analysis of the marketing situation. This analysis gives both marketing and media planners a bird's-eye view of how a company has been operating against its competitors in the total market. The analysis serves as a means of learning the various details of the problem, possibilities for its solution, and sources of advantage over the company's competitors.

After analyzing the marketing situation, marketing and media planners devise a marketing strategy and plan that state marketing objectives and spell out the actions to accomplish those objectives. When the marketing strategy calls for advertising, the usual purpose is to communicate to consumers some information that helps attain a marketing objective. Media are the means whereby advertisements are delivered to the market.

Once a marketing plan has been devised, an advertising creative strategy must also be determined. This consists of decisions about what is to be communicated, how it will be executed, and what it is supposed to accomplish. A statement of advertising copy themes and how copy will be used to communicate the selling message is also part of that strategy. Media-planning decisions are affected by advertising creative strategy, because some creative strategies are better suited to one medium than to any other. For example, if a product requires demonstration, television is the best medium. If an ad must be shown in high-fidelity color, magazines or newspaper supplements are preferable. Creative strategy also reflects the prospect profile in terms of such demographic variables as age, sex, income, or occupation. These prospects now become the targets that the planner will focus on in selecting media vehicles.

Up to this point, persons other than the media planner have been making decisions that will ultimately affect the media plan. The marketing or marketing research people are responsible for the situation analysis and marketing plan, although media planners are sometimes involved at the inception of the marketing plan. Copywriters and art directors are generally responsible for carrying out the creative strategy. Sometimes a marketing plan is as simple as a memorandum from a marketing executive to the media planner or even an idea in an advertising executive's mind. In such informal situations, media planning begins almost immediately, with little or no marketing research preceding it. Exhibit 1-1 summarizes the preplanning steps.

The media planner begins work as soon as a marketing strategy plan is in hand. This plan sets the tone and guides the direction of the media decisions that will follow.

The first item to come out of such a plan is a statement of *media objectives.* These are the goals that a media planner believes are most important in helping to attain marketing objectives. Goals include determination of which targets (persons most likely to purchase a given product or service) are most important, how many of those targets need to be reached, and where advertising should be concentrated at what times.

Objectives form the basis for media strategies. A *media strategy* is a series of actions selected from several possible alternatives to best achieve the media objectives. Media strategies will cover such decisions as which kinds of media should be used, whether national or spot broadcast advertising should be used, how ads should be scheduled, and many other decisions.

EXHIBIT 1-1

Scope of Media Preplanning Activities

<table>
<tr>
<td colspan="3">

Marketing Problem

All media planning starts with a problem in the context of national, local, or business-to-business marketing/advertising. Examples of the kinds of problems could be how much to spend for advertising next year, how to increase sales volume, or how to stop eroding market share.

</td>
</tr>
<tr>
<td>

Situation Analysis

Purpose: To understand the marketing problem. A company and its competitors are analyzed on the basis of:
1. Size and share of the total market
2. Sales history, costs, and profits
3. Distribution practices
4. Methods of selling
5. Use of advertising
6. Identification of prospects
7. Nature of the product

</td>
<td>

Marketing Strategy Plan

Purpose: To plan activities that will solve one or more of the marketing problems. Includes the determination of:
1. Marketing objectives
2. Product and spending strategy
3. Distribution strategy
4. Which elements of the marketing mix to use
5. Identification of "best" market segments

</td>
<td>

Creative Strategy Plan

Purpose: To determine what to communicate through advertisements. Includes the determination of:
1. How product can meet consumer needs
2. How product will be positioned in advertisements
3. Copy themes
4. Specific objectives of each advertisement
5. Number and sizes of advertisements

</td>
</tr>
<tr>
<td colspan="3" align="center">

Media Planning

</td>
</tr>
</table>

After the strategy is determined, the implementation of the media plan begins. Some planners call all these subsequent decisions tactics. Whatever they are called, many decisions still have to be made before tactics culminate in a media plan. As indicated in Exhibit 1-2, these decisions might include the selection of vehicles in which to place ads, the number of ads to be placed in each vehicle, the size of each ad, and the specific position within each vehicle that an ad will occupy.

EXHIBIT 1-2

Kinds of Questions That Lead to Decisions About Media Objectives and Strategies

The following is an overview of some of the many questions that lead to media objectives and strategies. Note that strategies grow out of objectives.

Media Objectives	Media Strategies
What action should we take as a result of media used by competitors?	Should we use same media mix as competitors? Should we allocate weight the same way as competitors? Should we ignore competitors?
What actions should we take as a result of our brand's creative strategies?	Which media/vehicles are best suited? Any special treatments (gatefolds, inserts)? Which dayparts?
Who should be our primary and secondary targets?	Which product usage patterns should we consider? Heavy/medium/light users? What distribution of strategic impressions? Which dayparts?
What balance of reach to frequency is needed?	What levels of reach and frequency? What levels of effective reach/frequency?
Do we need national and/or local media?	What proportions should go into national media? What proportion in local media?
What patterns of geographical weighting should we use?	Should we weight by dollars or GRPs? Where should we place weights? When should we weight (weeks/months)? What weight levels for each market?
What communication goals (or effectiveness goals) are needed?	Which criteria of effectiveness should we use?
Which kind of scheduling pattern suits our plans: continuity, flighting, or pulsing?	Should we use one or more? When should we weight more heavily?
Do media have to support promotions? Why?	What proportion of the budget should be used? What media mix?
Is media testing needed? How should it be used?	How many tests and in which markets? How should we translate (Little USA or As Is)?
Is budget large enough to accomplish objectives?	Do we need to set priorities? Which must we achieve, and which are optional? Do we need more money than is available?

A media plan is custom tailored—designed expressly to meet the needs of an advertiser at a given time for specific marketing purposes. Today's media plan is usually not a copy of last year's plan, nor is it simply a blank form with spaces that can be filled in quickly with selected dates or times for running ads. Each media plan should differ from preceding ones for the same product.

Plans are custom tailored because the marketplace is rarely the same from year to year. Competitors rarely stand still in their marketing activities. They change their messages, change their marketing expenditures, introduce new brands, or discontinue distribution of old brands. Consumers also change, mov-

---

EXHIBIT 1-3

Is There a *Best* Media Strategy?

Competitive Media Expenditures for Vacuum Cleaners (Annual Percentages)

	BRAND A	BRAND B	BRAND C	BRAND D
Consumer magazines	—	—	16.4%	—
Sunday magazines	—	—	7.0	0.2%
Local newspapers	—	0.8%	—	39.4
Network TV	40.4%	11.5	33.5	0.9
Spot TV	31.1	2.2	2.6	1.7
Syndication TV	0.5	3.0	23.2	0.2
Cable TV	28.0	82.5	17.3	—
Network radio	—	—	—	57.6
Total	100.0%	100.0%	100.0%	100.0%

COMMENTS

1. Media expenditures often provide more insight into strategy than any other data.
2. From the data, one can conclude that there is no one best media strategy for all advertisers, because each perceives the market in slightly different ways based on its own marketing needs. Some marketers want to increase market share; others want simply to maintain their present position. Such differences play a major role in media selection. Also, some advertisers see one medium as being more effective than others.
3. In this case, all four vacuum cleaner brands use television, but Brand A places almost a third of its budget in spot TV, while Brand B concentrates in national TV, primarily cable and network. Brand C supports TV with a strong consumer print campaign, while Brand D uses almost no TV, splitting its budget between local newspapers and network radio.
4. Occasionally, one sees all competitors using the same media, but the competitors in this seemingly routine product have widely differing views of the value of alternative media.

SOURCE: CMR Taylor Nelson Sofres.

ing to different geographical areas, getting new jobs, retiring, getting married, adopting different leisure-time activities, or buying new kinds of products. As a result, each marketing situation presents new opportunities as well as new problems.

Because marketing situations change, new approaches to planning are constantly needed to keep up with, or ahead of, competitors. Media planning is also affected by the new kinds of research or analysis needed to keep abreast of a changing business world. Media planning requires a great sensitivity to change. For this reason, even direct competitors may decide on very different media strategies. Exhibit 1-3 illustrates this point.

PRINCIPLES FOR SELECTING MEDIA VEHICLES

Of all the media decisions, one of the most important is selecting individual vehicles. Planners tend to select one or more vehicles that effectively reach an optimum number of prospects (1) with an optimum amount of frequency (or repetition), (2) at the lowest cost per thousand prospects reached (cost efficiency), (3) with a minimum of waste (or nonprospects), and (4) within a specified budget.

These principles apply most when selecting vehicles for mass-produced and mass-consumed products such as food, clothing, or automobiles. Yet even though they are more difficult to execute, the principles should be the same in selecting vehicles for such products as noncommercial airplanes or yachts, where prospects are distributed unevenly throughout the population. It may be less cost-efficient to reach those prospects than to reach prospects for mass-consumed products, because reaching such selective markets requires vehicles that contain large amounts of waste. There are other times when the principles have to be modified. For example, if a creative strategy calls for certain kinds of media, such as those that produce ads in high-fidelity color, then cost or waste must be disregarded in favor of meeting creative goals. Most often, however, plans follow these principles consistently.

When planners apply media selection principles, they use media delivery statistics as one piece of evidence that they have achieved the reach required. *Delivery* means simply the number of audience members reached by, or exposed to, a vehicle or a combination of media vehicles.

With the goal of obtaining the highest possible exposure, the planner starts by looking among the many media alternatives that will reach prospects. A planner does this using media audience research data for individual vehicles. The data are in the form of numbers classified by audience types, and the numbers listed for each medium can be used as proof of audience delivery. In other words, the planner uses this statistical evidence to prove that a plan uses the best vehicle(s) for reaching the targeted prospects. Obviously, there are other considerations in making this decision. Costs of media might be so high per prospect reached that the planner has to reject the first choice in favor of other media that reach smaller numbers of prospects but at lower costs.

Once audience delivery numbers have been found, they are related to the total number of prospects in the market. If a market consists of 35 million women in the United States who purchased a given kind of product within the last month, then the size of the market is 35 million. The planner selects certain magazines that reach 17.5 million purchasing women, or 50 percent of the market. Is 50 percent enough? It depends on the marketing objectives. If that percentage isn't enough, the planner selects one or more other media vehicles to increase the percentage reached. Because no decision is made in a vacuum, the planner must also consider the creative, promotional, and executional goals of the marketing strategy while evaluating the vehicle's ability to deliver prospects.

The decisions described so far apply primarily to the traditional mass media. Selection of websites to carry Internet advertising is based on some of the same criteria, plus additional measures that are unique to the Internet. Planners look at the number of prospects who visit the site, the concentration of those prospects among all the site's visitors, the site's charges for each thousand impressions delivered, and historical records of the number of visitors who click through the banner to the advertiser's own website. This represents a major change from traditional planning. Thus, it is necessary for the media planner to understand not only the traditional media planning techniques, but also the new ones that are now emerging.

PROBLEMS IN MEDIA PLANNING

Although media planning has become very important within advertising agency operations, it is not performed as efficiently as one might suppose. The planner is faced with many different kinds of problems that make it difficult to arrive at objective decisions.

Insufficient Media Data

Media planners almost always require more data about markets and media than are available. Some data never will be available, either because audiences cannot be measured or the data are too expensive to collect. For example, no complete and inclusive research service measures the audience exposure to outdoor advertising, or to television viewing in hotel rooms and college dorms, or to portable-television viewing. Why? Because such services are too costly to provide and because there is no adequate way of measuring these audiences. Both outdoor exposure and out-of-home TV viewing have been measured, but not on a continuous basis in all cities. There are also inadequate research data on the amount of money that competitors spend yearly for outdoor advertising, for local radio advertising, and for newspaper ads. In television planning, measurements of the audience size for commercial messages are not available.

Most television rating services measure the audience size only in terms of individuals or homes tuned in to *programs.* This is not an advertising exposure measurement because there is no assurance that those who press people meter buttons are paying attention to a program. Even if people are in front of the television set watching a given program, there is no guarantee that they are watching the commercials. Furthermore, while it might be possible to estimate the size of the audience for a given commercial, there is no way to measure the degree of attention audiences pay to that commercial.

Another problem in television planning is that decisions about the future performance of television programs must be based on data that represent past performance. If the future is radically different from the past, then the data on which a decision is based may be worthless.

Although advertising impressions delivered on the Internet are counted with extreme precision, it takes a special effort to know whether a banner ad actually appeared on the user's screen or the viewer clicked away before it had a chance to come up. Even then, it is impossible to know if the user paid any attention to the ad. With click-through rates typically below 1 percent, planners are questioning the value of the Internet as an advertising medium for products used by mass targets.

The problem of obtaining sufficient information is especially acute for small advertisers, many of whom cannot afford to buy research data. These companies often do not know how large their own retail sales are because they sell only to distributors or wholesalers. The media planner, then, must guess at the client's sales position in any given market.

Another problem involves measuring how people read newspapers and magazines. How much of any given magazine or newspaper is read? How many advertisements are read? How thoroughly are they read? What is the value of placing an advertisement in one vehicle versus another? How does each vehicle affect the perception of an advertisement that it carries? Answers to these and many other questions are not available on a continuing basis, so the media planner must make decisions without knowing all the pertinent facts.

Time Pressures

A problem that affects media planning in an entirely different way is that of the time pressure involved in making decisions. When the agency and advertiser are ready to start their advertising program, the planner often is faced with a lack of sufficient time to solve problems thoroughly. For example, in many cases the planner requires competitive media expenditure analyses showing how much each competitor spends in major markets throughout the country. Although modern systems can deliver masses of raw data in a few hours, analyzing thousands of pieces of information is time-consuming, so the planner often bypasses this investigation in order to write a media plan quickly.

Another time-related problem is the limited number of broadcast times and programs available to be purchased by advertisers at any given time. This problem is compounded if the client is slow to approve the budget. In that case the most desirable broadcast time periods and/or programs might be sold before the advertiser enters the marketplace.

External Influences

There are at least two external influences on media planning decisions besides the directions that numbers provide. The two influences are the pressure to produce "creative" media plans and institutional influences. Whether these influences result in better media plans is not clear. But because of their subtle nature, there is a danger that they can impair the best judgments of planners. Those who favor these kinds of influence think otherwise.

Pressure to Produce "Creative" Media Plans   In the media departments of most advertising agencies, it is an established tradition to give clients statistical proof that media decisions are the best alternative possible under budget and other constraints normally required for media planning. Therefore, clients usually receive media plans in statistical formats, composed of many pages of numbers.

A growing number of planners are developing an antagonism toward these kinds of plans. Some people believe that media plans for brands within the same product category look too much alike. Media plans that are similar might tend to nullify each other's best efforts at reaching and communicating with consumers. Therefore, a brand might suffer.

Alan Goldin, media director, House of Seagram, and Kathy Neisloss, advertising director of *Vanity Fair,* wrote about young assistant media planners who are expected to limit their plan to just the most cost-efficient media. They grow weary of numbers-only recommendations and look for opportunities to accelerate their rise in the profession by standing out and supporting some unusual media opportunities. But their motivation might be further inspired by agency and account managers who dread the typical, mundane media plans. They "continually encourage something new in the name of imagination, creativity, or innovation."[3]

A better way to proceed, Goldin and Neisloss suggest, is to make media plans "creative." This approach suggests that quantitatively based plans are not creative, which is questionable. The definition of *creative,* however, is not universally agreed upon. There are at least two approaches to achieving a creative media plan. Some planners prefer a media plan that starts with a basic set of quantitative data and then proceeds beyond the data intuitively, at no extra cost. Placing a pet food commercial within a TV program that features pets

---

3. Alan Goldin and Kathy Neisloss, "Evaluating Print Qualitatively: A No-Nonsense Guide," *Inside Print* (November 1986): 27–29.

might be one example. Other planners think that the numbers are relatively unimportant and that decisions for or against vehicles simply have to be innovative. These people might want a plan that is much different from plans for other products in the category, one that stands out because it represents an innovative way to communicate with people.

Another reason for a call for creativity is the feeling that media numbers are not as precise as many people assume them to be. Numbers such as ratings and audience sizes are not measures of everyone in the universe; they are projections based on samples. But once numbers get printed on paper, or appear in plan reports, they seem to have a credibility that might not be warranted. In the last analysis, they are only estimates, and perhaps rough estimates at that.

In addition, advertisers and their agencies use creative media plans in an attempt to reach increasingly fragmented and difficult-to-target audiences. Plans that target working women, for example, might force more creative and selective daypart/program selection or add a nontraditional publication to a "women aged 25–54" schedule.

The call for creativity in planning also comes from some media salespeople who do not have the largest or most acceptable media audience numbers for their vehicles as compared to their competitors. They may compensate by asking planners to make decisions on a subjective rather than objective basis. Perhaps the vehicle they are selling has a "something" that can't be measured very well. Therefore, these people tend to be among the groups advocating more planning on a subjective and creative basis.

Institutional Influences on Media Decisions   One of the less obvious external sources of influence on media decisions is client pressures to use or not use certain media vehicles, or to use them in certain ways. Often these pressures are well known by everyone working on a client's account; the client continually reminds everyone of the restrictions. At other times these influences are known by relatively few persons, perhaps only those who regularly visit the client and are constantly communicating directly with him or her. Besides the client, other subtle influences affect planners. Directors or assistant directors in the media department, or in account executive positions, often influence decisions.

The problem with these institutional influences is that little or no information is available concerning the extent to which they exist, or how much they

CHAPTER TWO

Sample Media Plan Presentation

A *media plan* is the blueprint for how the advertising message will be delivered to the target audience. It is also a persuasive document that communicates the rationale behind a recommendation to spend significant amounts of money. To provide a broad overview of the media-planning process and the topics of this book, this chapter presents a hypothetical plan along with explanations about why particular decisions were made.

Typically presented by the planner at a meeting with the advertiser, a media plan summarizes weeks or months of behind-the-scenes work. Preparing a media plan entails evaluating alternatives, meeting with media representatives, and developing the understanding of the consumer and marketplace that is necessary to produce the most effective media plan.

Because a media plan is a blueprint for action, it must be organized so the presentation flows smoothly in the readers' minds. Media plans have two main audiences: the clients (including the account executives) and the media buyers. Most likely, the clients will be the first persons outside the agency to see the plan. The clients will probably pay most attention to determining whether the recommended media plan can do what it is supposed to do in solving the original marketing problem.

The plan should also enable the buyers—who eventually have to implement the strategies—to proceed quickly and accurately. The media plan can help all this by being well organized, well written, and simply presented.

Although there is extensive backup documentation in a "leave-behind," the presentation itself is relatively straightforward and not especially long—often only 10 to 15 minutes. It talks in human terms about the people the advertiser is trying to reach. The following pages show a typical (but hypothetical) media plan as it might be presented to a brand's marketing director. It is a simple, plain-vanilla plan, yet it illustrates and introduces concepts that will be discussed in greater detail in the following chapters.

At the barest minimum, a media plan should include (possibly, but not necessarily, in this order) the following elements:

- Media objectives—what tasks the media are expected to carry out
- Competitive analysis—spending levels, media used, timing
- Target audience analysis and recommendation
- Media habits of the target audience
- Rationale for media selection—reasons for selecting the various media elements and vehicles
- Media strategy—how the media plan will accomplish the stated objectives
- Flowchart, budget, and expected reach and frequency

Depending on the particular situation, the media plan may also contain the following topics:

- Rationale for magazine selection—cost, coverage, composition, and cost per thousand (CPM) of publications that were recommended and those considered but not recommended
- Spot market list and rationale for media dollar allocation
- Product seasonality
- Detailed broadcast cost estimates
- Other media considered but not recommended
- Alternative print and broadcast plans considered but not recommended
- Detailed newspaper list
- Alternative plans at varying budget levels above and below the established level
- Decision dates/cancellation flexibility
- Responses to earlier client questions
- Anything else the planner thinks may become a question or an issue during the presentation, based on earlier discussions with the client and account group (either incorporated into the presentation or held in reserve in case the question comes up)

BACKGROUND TO HYPOTHETICAL PLAN

The fictitious RBB Sporting Goods Company has been a leading producer of sporting products for more than 20 years. In anticipation of baby boomer retirements, the company plans to expand into products for golfers, beginning with Power Flight golf clubs. These newly engineered clubs promise to improve the average golfer's game. The Power Flight's core is made of titanium dioxide, making it more flexible than other clubs. It is also lighter and stronger than other models. The product will be in full national distribution in time for golf season.

RBB is considering hiring a new advertising agency to handle the Power Flight golf club introduction. The company has told the agency to assume a total advertising budget of $11 million, of which $10 million is for working media, and has asked for a recommended media plan. The account group says the creative department is working on 30-second television commercials and page-four/color magazine ads.

MEDIA OBJECTIVES

Media plans typically begin with a statement of the *media objectives*—that is, what goals the media are expected to accomplish. In this case, the first and most important objective is to create awareness of the new golf clubs and then sustain that awareness throughout the golf season.

Because the product will be sold nationally, there must be advertising everywhere in the United States. If the client had said the launch needed additional weight in certain cities, that goal would be included as an additional objective. Similarly, if RBB had planned for a professional golfer to demonstrate the product at a local country club, a media objective would be to announce this event with local media. The media objectives reflect the advertiser's marketing objectives.

Media objectives specifically identify the marketing target and how many times those people should see the advertising message during the introductory and sustaining periods. This reflects a balance between how many people will see each ad and how many times they will see it (i.e., a few people many times or many people a few times). The need to balance trade-offs is a key and recurring theme in media planning.

EXHIBIT 2-1

Media Objectives

- Within the $10 million budget, create national awareness of RBB Power Flight golf clubs before the start of golf season.

- Following introduction, provide sustaining support through the remainder of the warm-weather months.

- Target advertising to regular golfers who play at least once a month.

- During the introductory period, reach 80 percent of target golfers an average of five times, and 50 percent three or more times.

- Following the introduction, sustain awareness by reaching 30 percent of golfers at least once a month.

- Utilize media that can create awareness and effectively communicate the technical advantages of the Power Flight clubs.

Finally, the client has indicated there is a strong technical story that explains how the Power Flight clubs improve golfers' accuracy. In addition to creating awareness, the media plan must effectively communicate this relatively complex message. The media objectives for the introduction of the Power Flight golf club are listed in Exhibit 2-1.

COMPETITIVE ANALYSIS

Knowledge of the competitive environment is critical to any media plan. The competitive analysis includes budgets, media selection, and timing of media delivery.

Budgets

First, knowing the planner has $10 million to work with is meaningful only when compared to the spending levels of RBB's competitors. Exhibit 2-2 shows how much money the leading brands spent in the previous year. It indicates that the budget should be adequate to do the job, but RBB will still trail the Callaway, Adams, and Taylor Made brands. The introductory $10 million will have to work hard to overcome this competitive noise.

EXHIBIT 2-2

Competitive Environment

Leading Golf Club Competitors

BRAND	TOTAL ANNUAL EXPENDITURES $(000)
Callaway Golf Clubs	$14,382.0
Adams Golf Clubs	11,647.8
Taylor Made Golf Clubs	10,466.1
King Cobra Golf Clubs	8,103.7
Odyssey Golf Clubs	6,813.7
Armour Golf Clubs	5,758.0
Wilson Golf Clubs	3,274.6
Total	$60,445.9

SOURCE: CMR Taylor Nelson Sofres, 1998.

Media Selection

The amounts that competitors spent are only part of the story. The planner also needs to know which media the competitors used. Exhibit 2-3 indicates that the majority of the dollars were in network television and magazines. Backup charts show spending by medium for each advertiser. They show which television programs were used (mostly weekend golf tournaments) and which cable networks (mostly ESPN). Backup charts also show which magazines were used and other details about competitors' plans.

Timing of Media Delivery

Timing of media delivery is critical as well. In the case of golf, it naturally follows the seasons, as shown in Exhibit 2-4. Note the peak spending in March, as the weather turns warmer and golfers start to think about the clubs they will use when the golf courses open for business. But also note that money is spent throughout the year, even in winter. This reflects the need to maintain awareness among golfers on warm-weather vacations. The bump in December suggests advertising to support the gift of golf clubs for the holidays.

EXHIBIT 2-3

Leading Competitors' Media Use

Leading competitors concentrate spending in network television and consumer magazines.

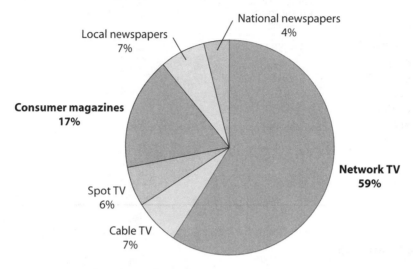

SOURCE: CMR Taylor Nelson Sofres, 1998.

TARGET AUDIENCE ANALYSIS

Another part of every media plan is an analysis of the target audience. RBB has said it believes its best prospects are "frequent golfers—those who play more than 12 rounds of golf a year." This reflects the advertiser's marketing research, but their studies typically provide little useful information about consumers' *media* habits. For this purpose, ad agencies purchase syndicated research (one study that is sold to many different buyers, as distinguished from custom research tailored to a single company). This research provides information on product usage, demographics, and media behavior.

For example, Mediamark Research Inc. (MRI) asks respondents about their personal participation in more than 50 sports, ranging from aerobics to white-water rafting, and including golf. Respondents are asked how often they engage in each activity: "two or more times a week, once a week, two to three times a

EXHIBIT 2-4

Leading Competitors' Timing of Delivery

Competitors focus weight in the warm-weather months.

$ (Millions)

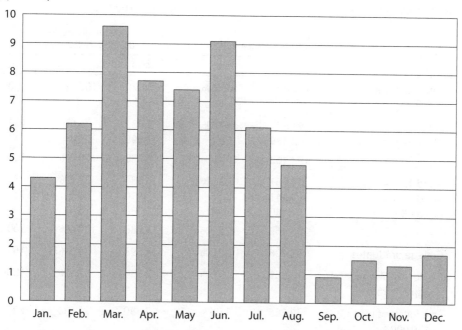

SOURCE: CMR Taylor Nelson Sofres, 1998.

month, once a month, less than once a month, or never." The planner makes the judgment that "once a month or more" is comparable to the client's "frequent" golfer. As detailed in Exhibit 2-5, this definition yields a group that accounts for 6.6 percent of all adults—a small enough target to be selective, but large enough to be statistically valid.

MEDIA HABITS

In addition to demographics, MRI tells planners which television programs regular golfers watch. Although MRI data are not as timely or as detailed as the

EXHIBIT 2-5

The Target Audience

Thirteen million (6.6 percent) adults are regular golfers (play 1+ times/month); 75.6 percent of them are men. They tend to be 35–64 years old, college graduates, work in executive/administrative jobs, and earn more than $50,000/year.

	U.S. POPULATION		REGULAR GOLFERS (PLAY 1+ TIMES/MONTH)		
	(000)	(%)	(000)	(%)	INDEX
Total adults aged 18+	197,462	100.0%	13,079 (6.6%)	100.0%	100
Men	94,827	48.0%	9,882	75.6%	157
Women	102,635	52.0	3,198	24.4	47
	197,462	100.0%	13,080	100.0%	100
Aged 18–34	64,961	32.9%	3,584	27.4%	83
Aged 35–64	100,241	50.8	7,410	56.7	112
Aged 65+	32,260	16.3	2,086	15.9	98
	197,462	100.0%	13,080	100.0%	100
College graduates	43,406	22.0%	4,693	35.9%	163
Executives/managers/ administrators	18,969	9.6%	2,330	17.8%	185
Employment income $50,000+	22,865	11.6%	3,380	25.8%	223

SOURCE: Mediamark Research Inc., Spring 1999.

Nielsen ratings, they offer insights into the kind of programs that this group enjoys.

Exhibit 2-6 illustrates the concept of media selectivity. *Composition* (or *comp* for short) represents the percent of adults or program viewers who are regular golfers. As noted before, 6.6 percent of all adults are regular golfers. If the viewers of the Kapalua International Golf Tournament were the same as all adults, we would expect 6.6 percent of them to be regular golfers. But the MRI research shows that 58.3 percent of the tournament's viewers fall in this group.

EXHIBIT 2-6

Target Audience's Media Habits: Watching Golf on TV

They are avid fans of golf tournaments on television.

	ADULTS (000)	REGULAR GOLFERS (PLAY 1+ TIMES/MONTH)		
		(000)	COMP	INDEX
Total adults	197,462	13,079	6.6	100
Kapalua International	3,551	2,068	58.3	879
Honda Golf Classic	4,331	2,428	56.1	846
Sprint International	2,759	1,542	55.9	844
Wendy's Three Tour Golf Challenge	2,722	1,381	55.3	834
Motorola Western Open	2,499	1,503	55.2	834
Lexus Challenge	2,721	1,479	54.4	821
Memorial Tournament	4,122	2,210	53.6	810
Nissan Open	4,170	2,221	53.3	804
The Tour Championship	5,798	3,052	52.6	795
Federal Express St. Jude Classic	3,266	1,716	52.6	794
Shell Houston Open	3,081	1,614	52.4	791
Doral Ryder Open	5,730	2,988	52.1	787
Andersen Consulting World Championship	3,100	1,614	52.1	786
Liberty Mutual Legends of Golf	2,786	1,445	51.9	783
NEC World Series of Golf	3,845	1,990	51.7	781

SOURCE: Mediamark Research Inc., Spring 1999.

Comparing these as a proportion, $58.3/6.6 = 8.79$, and multiplying by 100 gives us an index of 879. By convention, the planner would say that the program's viewers are 779 percent (or 7.8 times) more likely to be regular golfers than the average adult. (Note that 58.3 and 6.6 are rounded numbers, while the 879 index was calculated by the computer from the unrounded percentages. These minor rounding differences occur throughout media planning and have no practical significance.)

EXHIBIT 2-7

Target Audience's Media Habits: Other Sports on TV

They also like other sports programs on television.

	ADULTS (000)	REGULAR GOLFERS (PLAY 1+ TIMES/MONTH)		
		(000)	COMP	INDEX
Total adults	197,462	13,079	6.6	100
Football bowl games—specials	14,757	2,368	16.1	242
Tennis	9,619	1,523	15.8	239
Basketball specials—college	20,248	2,959	14.6	221
Baseball specials	37,403	5,003	13.4	202
Football specials—pro	32,387	3,928	12.1	183
Basketball—weekend—college	6,382	759	11.9	180
Basketball specials—pro	38,954	4,393	11.3	170
Auto racing—specials	8,178	901	11.0	166

SOURCE: Mediamark Research Inc., Spring 1999.

The media behavior analysis continues in Exhibit 2-7 by showing regular golfers' selectivity to other sports programs on TV. These analyses show which programs have concentrations of the target audience (regular golfers), and guide the planner in selecting the best media to reach them.

The same concept applies to golfers' readership of consumer magazines. Readers of *Golf Digest* are 533 percent more likely to be regular golfers than the average adult; readers of *Newsweek* are 64 percent more likely to be regular golfers.

Although composition is important, planners must also consider *coverage*—the percent of the target that reads a magazine, watches a TV show, or uses other media. *Golf Digest,* for example, is read by 2,530,000 regular golfers. Expressing numbers in thousands, 2,530m readers/13,079m golfers = 19.3 percent. We say that *Golf Digest* "covers," or is read by, 19.3 percent of regular golfers. *National Geographic* covers virtually the same number of golfers, but its low 8.6 percent composition indicates there would be a great deal of waste if this maga-

EXHIBIT 2-8

Target Audience's Media Habits: Magazines

They read golf magazines and newsweeklies.

	AUDIENCE (000)	COMP	COVERAGE	INDEX	4C COST	4C CPM
			REGULAR GOLFERS (PLAY 1+ TIMES/MONTH)			
Regular golfers	13,079	6.6%	100.0%	100	—	—
Golf Digest	2,530	41.9	19.3	633	$111,930	$44.24
Golf Magazine	2,191	38.0	16.8	574	88,070	40.20
Golf World	609	33.7	4.7	508	21,260	34.91
U.S. News & World Report	1,130	11.1	8.6	167	108,675	96.17
Newsweek	2,004	10.8	15.3	164	160,940	80.31
Sports Illustrated	2,425	10.6	18.5	161	180,000	74.23
Popular Mechanics	931	10.6	7.1	159	75,060	80.62
Field & Stream	1,098	10.3	8.4	156	88,870 .	80.94
National Geographic	2,526	8.6	19.3	130	175,675	69.55
Men's Fitness	419	8.0	3.2	121	24,640	58.81
Life	1,135	7.4	8.7	112	71,630	63.11
Reader's Digest	3,251	7.1	24.9	107	183,800	56.54
People	2,336	6.6	17.9	100	138,000	59.08

SOURCE: Mediamark Research Inc., Spring 1999; *Marketer's Guide to Media,* 2000.

zine was selected. (Because 91.4 percent of its readers are not regular golfers, they would have little interest in ads for the new Power Flight clubs.) This need to find a balance between coverage and composition is a recurring theme in media planning.

Planners must also consider the cost-efficiency of the media they select. This is typically evaluated as *cost per thousand* target people exposed, or CPM. A page in *Golf Digest* costs $111,930 and is read by 2,530,000 regular golfers. To find the cost per thousand, divide the cost by the number of target readers: CPM = $111,930/2,530 = $44.24 per thousand golfers.

Exhibit 2-8 illustrates the trade-offs that media planners must make among coverage, composition, and media cost-efficiency.

MEDIA SELECTION RATIONALE

Planners are theoretically free to choose any mass medium (television, radio, magazines, newspapers, outdoor, Internet), but in practice the choice reflects a general understanding of the category by the advertiser, the agency's account team, and media management. Because the decision in this example has been made to start the creatives working on 30-second television commercials and four-color page magazine ads, the plan is expected to reflect these media. To a large extent, the rationale for selecting the primary media is obvious and reflects the media/marketing objectives and the competitive practices of the product category.

Although the broad media to be used may be predetermined (in this case, TV and consumer magazines), the planner needs to show the rationale for selecting different vehicles and components. For television, this includes program types, dayparts, cost-efficiencies, the reach and frequency of alternative weight levels, and the scheduling options considered. In the stand-up presentation, the media planner will provide this rationale by referring to the preceding charts on media habits as well as more detailed analyses.

For magazines, the plan needs to show publications that were considered and those that were and were not recommended. This latter information can be useful to the advertiser and agency management if they need to explain to sales representatives why a given magazine did not get the order. This information is provided by the chart (Exhibit 2-8) that shows the target's readership and cost efficiencies of the candidate and selected magazines. (Note that an actual plan would show many more publications than this sample and would probably be ranked by CPM.)

Creative Media Options

In the Power Flight example, television and print are the meat-and-potatoes media that—in an academic setting—would earn a grade of C. But advertisers expect something more: a creative fillip that will separate them from their competitors. This is an opportunity for planners to show their initiative and imagination. They might recommend an unusual use of conventional media, such as, in this case, a multipage insert in golf magazines to give a detailed explanation of the new club's technical advantages. Or, because one of the objectives of the Power Flight media plan is to create awareness, planners might recommend placing introductory ads on the hood of golf carts or in the hitting area of practice facilities. See www.pinpointgolf.com for a broad range of media directed to golfers. A full listing can be found in the Out-of-Home SRDS.

Creative media are generally less expensive than mainstream media, and they add interest and excitement to the plan. Also, they mark the planner as a person who gives more than just what is expected.

MEDIA STRATEGY

The plan now draws on the background material presented to lay out the proposed strategies that will accomplish the stated media objectives, as shown in Exhibit 2-9. Television will be the primary medium to create awareness. A media objective is to direct advertising to regular golfers, but the Nielsen program ratings that are needed by time buyers merely count audiences in terms of age and gender. From the targeting analysis, it is clear that the most selective tar-

EXHIBIT 2-9

Media Strategy

- Use television as the primary medium to create awareness.
  —Target men 35–64 years of age.
- Use network and cable television golf and weekend sports programs to achieve broad national reach of target regular golfers.
- Concentrate introductory weight in February/March to lead the golf season.
  —Purchase TV golf tournament sponsorships to achieve high frequency during the introduction.
- Provide sustaining support in cable and network weekend sports programs throughout the warm-weather golf season.
- Use golf-oriented consumer magazines and selective newsweeklies to communicate the technical advantages of Power Flight golf clubs and to maintain awareness during the holiday season.
- Use RBB's website to provide additional technical details about the Power Flight clubs. Highlight the site's Internet address in print and TV.

get is men 35 to 64 years old. The strategy identifies the recommended day-parts and program types. It indicates the general timing of the introductory and sustaining weight, but specifics will be presented later in a flowchart. Finally, the strategy identifies consumer magazines and RBB's website as the recommended media to deliver the technical information about the Power Flight golf clubs.

FLOWCHART AND BUDGET

The last key element of a media plan is the flowchart. This single document, shown in Exhibit 2-10, summarizes the action elements of the media plan. It shows the media to be used, the schedule for the ads, the amount of weight to be given to each, the reach and frequency of the plan, ad sizes, and the cost of each element that adds to the total budget. Each cost is an *estimate* and will not become final until the negotiations are complete. Buyers are expected to purchase each medium for the stated cost, plus or minus 10 percent, but the bottom-line total can never exceed the $10 million budget authorized by the advertiser.

POST-BUY EVALUATION

At some time after the advertising has run, the planner and buyer prepare a post-buy evaluation that reports the number of television rating points that were actually delivered according to the Nielsen ratings, and the final price that was paid. These numbers are then compared to the original goals. The post-buy evaluation is generally prepared as a top-line report, but may include detail down to the level of individual telecasts if the buy greatly over- or underdelivered and an explanation is required.

For magazines, the post-buy report shows on what page each ad appeared (to ensure that the advertiser got a fair rotation when there was more than one insertion in a given magazine), presence of any neighboring competitive advertising, right-hand or left-hand page, adjacency to compatible editorial material, and other characteristics that the advertiser and agency consider important. In addition to advising the client, this report is used as background for future negotiations with the publications.

EXHIBIT 2-10

Media Plan Flowchart

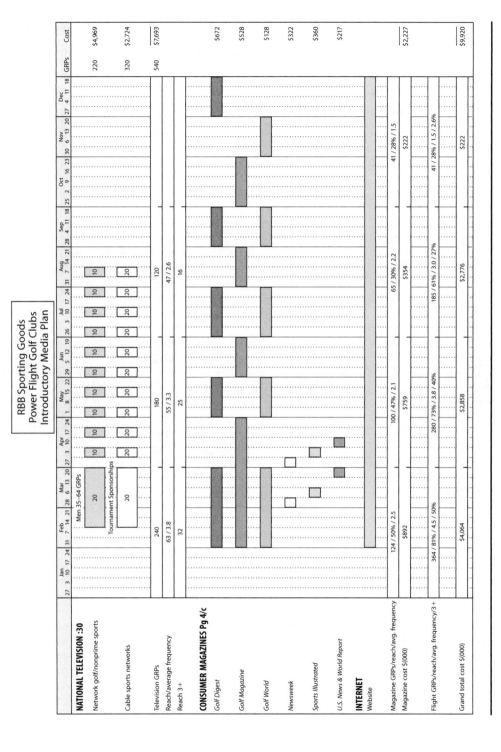

RBB Sporting Goods
Power Flight Golf Clubs
Introductory Media Plan

Note that the media post-buy evaluation is a numerical analysis of the way the media buy was executed versus what was planned. It typically does not deal with the larger issues, such as whether awareness was actually created or the campaign was successful. These relate to the effectiveness of the whole advertising program, which is the responsibility of the entire marketing team.

CHAPTER THREE

The Relationship Among Media, Advertising, and Consumers

This chapter addresses the relationship among media, advertising, and consumers. This relationship affects the manner in which consumers perceive media as well as advertising. It also affects the manner in which media are measured, planned, and delivered. This chapter sets the stage for Chapter 4, "Basic Measurements and Calculations."

HOW CONSUMERS CHOOSE MEDIA: ENTERTAINMENT AND INFORMATION

Most advertising is delivered to consumers by mass media such as newspapers, television, magazines, or radio. Audiences are not, however, waiting for mass media to come to their doors. They have many other activities that compete for their time and interest, such as business, family, church, and leisure.

Audiences become interested in certain subjects because a need or want is developed. They choose the television programs they watch and the magazines they read because they expect to see certain subjects that satisfy their interests quickly. Sometimes they are willing to waste a bit of time by watching television programs of little interest while waiting for their favorite programs to come on or by leafing through a newspaper or magazine casually as they wait to go on to some other activity. However, they probably pay less attention to these intervening media than they do to their favorites.

What audiences usually want from media is either entertainment or information. To what extent does any media vehicle provide what audiences want?

The degree of intensity among audiences in evaluating media content depends on several variables, including those discussed below. This difference in intensity will most likely affect the degree of attention paid to the medium itself or to advertising placed therein.

Strong Feelings

Many audience members have strong or weak feelings about a medium. Some of the feelings are expressed by adjectives that describe traits of the medium, such as being a leader, authoritative, provocative, warm, cold, strong, or weak. Some media are difficult to describe, suggesting that the relationship between audience members and the media is confusing, negative, or indifferent.

When researchers measure media images, feelings often show up for some media. Media that take political stands are usually perceived to have clear images. An image represents feelings, attitudes, opinions, and facts about a medium.

Loyalty

Audiences often like some media vehicles so much that they develop loyalties that go beyond economic constraint. If they favor newspapers or the Internet, for example, they will cut back expenses somewhere else in their budgets to afford their favorite medium.

Loyalty to media vehicles, however, does not necessarily mean that the loyal audience will perceive media advertisements similarly or buy more of the advertised products. Buying depends on other factors, including the need to have more information about a brand. If the audience already has a great deal of brand knowledge, the audience might respond to the advertising. Generally, when changes have been made in the brand or in the content or creative style of advertising, then the message will influence buying behavior to some extent.

Media Usage and Subsequent Behavior

Advertisers who buy space in a magazine generally assume they are reaching all readers of that periodical, but some subscribers do not read each issue immediately, and many have back issues of the magazine that they have not even opened. If asked why they have not read magazines they are paying for, the non-readers might respond that they do intend to read them when they have some free time. The potential for reaching these people exists, but the audience never fulfills its ultimate potential.

The same can be said for television: There is a widespread assumption that television sells better than print media because television is intrusive and its audiences tend to react to the medium more regularly than they read magazines. Television programs featuring famous persons or interesting national events do draw huge audiences. Yet audience response to ads carried in these programs varies greatly. Some advertisers seem to sell their products well; others don't.

For example, the 2000 Super Bowl featured 19 dot-com advertisers—accounting for almost one-third of all the commercials in the game. A year later, the majority of these companies were bankrupt due to poorly thought-out business plans and the general decline of the technology sector. Only four online companies placed ads in Super Bowl 2001.[1] All of this suggests that there is more to a successful advertising campaign than selecting media vehicles that deliver large audiences.

It is difficult, however, to assess the effectiveness of one media vehicle's ability to sell the advertised products on the basis of the number of advertisements carried by the vehicle. Large audiences do not automatically buy more than smaller audiences. In the end, an ad's ability to sell products is more influenced by the quality and memorability of the creative message than by any inherent qualities of the medium that delivers it.

Consumers simply do not pay attention to commercials if they do not need the product or already know a lot about the brand. They have developed the ability to see and hear a message and then forget it. Perhaps this is caused by an overload of communication, known as *semantic satiation*. Furthermore, sometimes audiences pay attention to commercials or print ads but don't respond immediately. In one study of response to a retailer's coupon promotion, some buyers came to the store with their coupons a month after the ad had appeared.

---

1. CMR Taylor Nelson Sofres, 2001.

Varied Relationships Between Audiences and Media

Relationships between audiences and media run the gamut from casual to intense. When sports teams are playing, the reason for watching any game depends on how much of a chance a team has of making the playoffs. If there is a good chance, an audience will return each week with a sense of loyalty and anticipation for the game. If a team has a losing record, however, then the number of viewers will most likely drop, because the relationship with the event is not as strong.

Even if a vehicle has a large and interested audience, the numbers might not be the critical determinant of its effect. Relationships today are not strong, especially among certain demographically defined audiences. For example, teenagers seem uninterested in reading newspapers, and all the techniques that have been used to attract them still have not changed the very loose relationship between the two.

Nowadays, some media planners tend to reject mass media in favor of more specialized media with smaller, more selective audiences. Data from single-source research often indicates that small market segments account for a large proportion of sales. This kind of data might not be accurate. The relationship between audiences and media, however, is more important: If it is casual, then advertising may be less effective. If the relationship is close, then smaller audiences will account for a large proportion of sales, although it is usually impossible to quantify this relationship accurately enough to influence media planning and buying decisions.

HOW CONSUMERS PERCEIVE INTERNET ADVERTISING

The Internet has greatly expanded the ability to sell products by providing virtually unlimited information to the prospective buyer. It has blurred the line between advertising as pure salesmanship and as a provider of product information. This is especially valuable for high-cost, considered purchases such as automobiles, travel services, computer systems, and financial services, where consumers need a vast amount of information to make a reasoned decision. Even advertising for food products can include detailed recipes and nutritional values. The Internet can then go beyond salesmanship to take the order, collect payment, and arrange shipping. According to Mediamark Research Inc., by the fall of 2001, 70 percent of adults had access to the Internet, and 15 percent had bought something online in the last 30 days for personal or business use. This behavior is expected to increase as more homes become connected and online shopping opportunities expand.[2]

HOW AUDIENCES PROCESS INFORMATION FROM MEDIA

Much of the information received from media is stored in people's short-term memory. Such information, like the last few words of a sentence just heard or read, or a telephone number found in the phone book, can be recalled for only a short time. Advertisers have observed that audiences who want to remember some part of an advertising message can do so by spending time and effort in rehearsing the message. They can repeat it mentally until it is learned. Then the message is remembered longer, because it has been transferred to long-term memory.

The point is that media often do not do any more than deliver advertising to consumers. Media planners are sometimes called on to help consumers remember a message by buying media vehicles repeatedly within a given period. If audiences are not interested, they will not pay attention and the repetitions will be wasted. Audiences can be very selective in what they hear or see.

Can a media planner do any more to deliver advertising messages? There is widespread disagreement among media professionals about this question. Some say much can be done by strategic media planning. By careful media selection and timing, by placing ads in markets where sales opportunities are best, by repeating the advertising, and by other strategic activities, a planner can help the advertisers achieve their goals. Others say that a media planner's job is done when the message is delivered to the right targets, at the right time, and in sufficient quantities.

It is clear that media work with the creative message and the appeal of a product to get the message through to consumers. When audience members want or need a product for any reason, they tend to pay attention to an ad for

---

2. Mediamark Research Inc., Fall 2001.

that product. They may not notice an ad the first time it is broadcast or printed, but their attention will presumably alert them to eventually notice the ad. Audiences are not waiting for an ad to appear; however, creative effort can take ordinary ideas and dramatize them to such an extent that the audience will pay attention to the ad for a short time at least.

Yet great creative efforts do not necessarily translate into positive results in the marketplace. For example, in the late 1990s, widely viewed advertising for the Taco Bell restaurant chain featured a talking Chihuahua whose signature *"Yo Quiero!"* became a national icon. The campaign was dropped in 2001 after marketers realized that it was not effectively driving customers into the restaurants. It was a popular and creative success, but a marketing failure. This runs counter to the general belief that any product can be sold by clever advertising.

MEDIA'S IMPORTANCE IN THE BUYING PROCESS

It is assumed that the power of media to deliver influence and impact for advertising messages also depends on where in the purchasing process a consumer happens to be. The classic Engel/Kollats model of the buying process tells us that the order of purchasing is as follows:[3]

1. *Problem recognition*—For example, an auto needs new tires, or an individual wants a new suit of clothes.
2. *Search for alternatives* to solve a problem—For example, a consumer reads, hears, or sees advertising; talks to a friend about the problem; or goes shopping for a product or brand.
3. *Alternative evaluation* of different brands—A consumer has found two or three brands that could solve a problem. The consumer is deciding which one to choose.
4. *Purchase made* through a choice of a brand—This is the buying action.
5. *Postpurchasing evaluation*—After buying, the consumer evaluates whether the product and brand meet his or her expectations for solving the problem.

---

3. J. F. Engel, R. D. Blackwell, and P. W. Miniard, *Consumer Behavior,* 8th edition (Hinsdale, IL: Dryden Press Series in Marketing, 1997).

6. *Feedback* about how satisfying the purchase was—Unsatisfactory purchases can be returned, or the consumer might keep the product and look for confirmation that he or she made a good buying decision. Frustration over the quality of the purchase can result in anger against the brand or the store where the product was purchased.

If consumers do not perceive that they have a problem, then presumably they will not react much to either media or advertising. In contrast, when consumers do have a problem, they are receptive to both. Some problems are simple, such as finding that there is no ketchup in the house when hamburgers are being served. Others, such as buying a new home, are complex.

MEDIA PLANNING AND THE MARKETING MIX

Anyone studying media planning needs to understand the relationship between media planning and the marketing mix. The *marketing mix* is a group of elements that a firm uses to sell a product. This mix was once called the "four *P*s": product, place (or distribution), price, and promotion. It has been suggested that the four *P*s are dead, but the marketing mix is as important as ever. Marketers always did have more elements than the four *P*s to use in marketing. A fuller account of the four *P*s is listed in Exhibit 3-1.[4] Marketing strategy is discussed more fully in Chapter 6, "Marketing Strategy and Media Planning."

Although media are not always considered to be a fundamental element of the marketing mix, they play a significant role in the selling process when advertising is required. The key to understanding the relationship between media and the marketing mix is that media do not work alone; they are part of a team of selling variables. Planners often get so involved with the complexity of their work that they forget this. In addition, media's role is important because they control the efficient delivery of advertisements to those who will probably buy.

Therefore, targeting prospects correctly is one way to fulfill the marketing–media team effort. Inefficient targeting means wasted effort and money. Media add a qualitative value to an advertisement because of some quality in each

---

4. Modified from Philip Kotler, *Marketing Management* (Englewood Cliffs, NJ: Prentice-Hall, 1984): 69.

EXHIBIT 3-1

The Four *P*s of Marketing

PRODUCT	PLACE	PRICE	PROMOTION
Quality	Distribution channels	List price	Advertising
Features	Coverage	Discounts	Copy and art
Options	Locations	Allowances	Media
Style	Inventory	Payment period	Personal selling
Brand name	Transportation	Credit terms	Sales promotion
Packaging			Public relations
			Direct marketing
			Integrated marketing
			Event marketing
			Local-area marketing

medium. An example is *Good Housekeeping*'s "Seal of Approval," which helps consumers make better buying decisions. Other qualitative values exist for specialized media that contribute to the medium's integral role in the advertising message.

EXPOSURE: THE BASIC MEASUREMENT OF MEDIA AUDIENCES

Industry leaders have chosen a measurement of media audiences—exposure—that is less than perfect, but that can differentiate media vehicles on the basis of their audience sizes. Audiences also can be measured and compared with competitive media at a reasonable cost. Exhibit 3-2 shows many other means of measuring media audiences.

Technically, *exposure* means "open eyes (or listening ears) facing the medium." Practically (as will be explained in detail in Chapter 4), it is a measurement of people who either say they are sure they have looked into or read a vehicle within a given period (yesterday for newspapers; within the last 30 days for a monthly magazine) or identify themselves as having watched TV or listened to the radio when a specified program was being broadcast.

Exposure measurements are different for each medium. In magazines, for example, persons exposed to a publication are counted if they say they read the

EXHIBIT 3-2

Ways That Media Audiences Could Be Measured

MEDIA MEASUREMENT	WHAT IT MEASURES	WHAT IT MEANS
Vehicle exposure	Exposure to TV or print media (not ads)	Open eyes facing a vehicle (or opportunities to see ads)
Print media circulation	Number of copies distributed	People or families receiving newspaper vehicles (no exposure counted)
Advertising exposure	Number of ads exposed per issue or per TV program	A gross (or crude) counting of total number of ads exposed in a vehicle
Advertising perception	Number of ads that consumers remember having seen in a vehicle	The smallest amount of communication remembered of ads in a vehicle
Advertising communication	The total amount of recalled material from ads in a vehicle	Feedback from ad messages in vehicles
Response function: media effectiveness	The number of responses to specific advertising in a vehicle	The effects of advertising on consumers (responses such as sales, brand awareness, attitude change, and recall of messages)

publication. But persons exposed to a television program are counted only if they consider themselves to be "watching" TV and press a button on a measuring device known as a people meter. Of course, not every home has such a device, and even when the device is available and a person is watching a program, the failure to press a certain button on the device will mean that a viewer is not counted. Local television viewing and radio listening are reported by people who fill in a diary. However, the growth of push buttons on portable radios and rapid channel surfing with television remote controls have caused industry leaders to question the diary's validity. On the Internet, exposure occurs when the user is served an ad banner, pop-up ad, or page of content from a website.

People who are not acquainted with measurements of media audiences are surprised when they learn that audience numbers obtained from media research such as Simmons Market Research Bureau, Mediamark Research Inc. (MRI), or Nielsen Media Research do not count the number of people or households exposed to advertisements in the vehicles. Even some experienced professionals forget or never knew that media exposure measurements do not show how many persons have read advertisements. And it cannot be assumed that a large audience for a media vehicle automatically indicates that a large number of individuals saw a client's advertisement.

Even if the industry did start measuring readership of ads rather than exposure to vehicles, the numbers would be inaccurate. Such data would miss people who actually saw many ads but forgot them. Therefore, the numbers produced by such measurements would underestimate the true audience size of a media vehicle. However, media exposure measurements are related to advertising in a certain way: It is necessary to be exposed to a vehicle before anyone can see an advertisement.

Therefore, media exposure measurements represent an opportunity to see advertisements. In practical terms, exposure to a TV ad campaign means that a person saw one or more of the TV telecasts that contained an ad. But here the research is limited. It does not tell us if they saw the actual commercial, only that they saw at least one of the programs that contained it. (For more information about how TV ratings are produced, go to www.nielsenmedia.com/whatratingsmean. Additional information about print measurement is available at www.mediamark.com.)

NEED FOR BETTER MEDIA VEHICLE MEASUREMENTS

Planners need a better measurement that can help them find the best medium or vehicle to help sell a client's product or service. If it could be shown that one medium sells more of a brand than any other medium, and if the cost were not prohibitive, then that medium would be the one in which to place advertising.

Unfortunately, no measurement available today can provide precisely that kind of information. There are planners who have conducted customized research to guide them in finding a medium that has the greatest sales potential. The problem with that kind of research is that it is difficult to parse out a medium's contribution to a sale, because, after all, media are not the only factors contributing to sales. Every element of the marketing mix contributes a little, and some contribute a great deal. For example, sometimes the factor that is most responsible for selling a product is a reduced price. In that case, media that carry news of the price reduction in an ad play a secondary role in the sale. Other marketing mix factors that contribute to a sale are distribution, positioning, personal selling, sales promotion, public relations, and packaging. And the most important elements in the selling of a brand generally are its product quality and uniqueness.

Many planners are dissatisfied with using exposure as the basis for media comparison. They argue that media are not passive carriers of ads. Rather, each medium has some power to affect an audience in some way, and this power should be measured.

However, advertisers have been unable to separate the effect of the medium from the effect of the quality of the creative message. Research companies can measure the persuasive power of individual commercials and compare the results to the average (norms) of all the commercials that they have ever measured. But these tests are conducted after the commercials have been created. Some score high; some score low. In the end, developing persuasive advertising is far more an art than a science.

To be effective, a commercial must be seen—it must reach the target. But seeing an ad only once is not enough. To be effective, a commercial or magazine ad must be seen a number of times. Determining how many times a person needs to see an ad for it to elicit the desired response is one of the basic challenges of media planning.

RESPONSE FUNCTION

A *response function* quantifies the perceived ability of multiple exposures of an ad to elicit a response from the viewer. If we broadcast a commercial 20 times, some people will see it only once, others will see it 5 times, others 8 times, and a few might even see it all 20 times. The response function shows what percent of the people who are exposed to an ad varying numbers of times are expected to respond to that ad. For instance, we might say that only 10 percent of the people who see a commercial once will respond, but 50 percent of the people who see it 8 or more times will respond. Exhibit 3-3 illustrates a sample response function. It means, "10 percent of the people exposed to the ad once

EXHIBIT 3-3

Sample Response Function

NUMBER OF EXPOSURES	PERCENT RESPONDING
1	10%
2	25
3	35
4	40
5	44
6	47
7	49
8+	50

will respond; 25 percent of the people exposed to the ad twice will respond," and so on.

Media research can tell the planner with great accuracy how many people are exposed to a campaign different numbers of times. But deciding what percent of those people will respond is a subtle judgment that depends on the product being sold, the ad's creative quality, the medium in which the ad appears, and a variety of other factors. We will go into this subject in more detail in Chapter 6.

It is important to note that media planning should not be a mechanistic activity limited only to delivering media. Good media planners perceive consumers' needs and wants and the way consumers view advertising as an aid in helping them make buying decisions. As time goes on, media planners will expend additional efforts to better know and understand consumers. (See Case Study 3-1.)

MEASURING AUDIENCES TO ADVERTISING IN VEHICLES

Some media planners believe that vehicles are nothing more than passive carriers of ads to consumers. These planners therefore consider a simple measurement such as exposure to be adequate for comparing audience sizes of media vehicles. In other words, the vehicle (or vehicles) that delivers the largest num-

CASE STUDY 3-1

How Consumers Could React to Media and Advertising

How can a planner think about the effect of a media plan in terms of the ultimate sales response? One answer is to estimate what happens after the ads appear in the media vehicles. The following is a hypothetical example of such an estimate:

		TARGET AUDIENCE
Number of targets in the United States		10,000,000
Percent of U.S. targets exposed to media vehicles	50%	5,000,000
Percent of those reached who saw any ad in vehicles (ad exposure)	25	1,250,000
Percent of targets who saw any ad who read our ad(s)	25	312,500
Percent of those who read our ad(s) who bought our brand because of our ad(s)	10	31,250
Percent of those who bought our brand once and bought it a second time (a rough measure of brand loyalty)	10	3,125

ber of exposed targets at the most efficient cost is a good enough criterion for selecting media.

But the other portion of the principle is equally important. This requires that the media selected reach the largest number of prospects at the most efficient cost. *Cost-efficiency* simply means that audience size must be related to media costs. Measuring this efficiency is done through cost per thousand and/or cost per rating point.

Cost per Thousand

Just as the statement "Potatoes: $2.00" becomes meaningful when expressed as "Potatoes: $2.00/pound," in advertising media, for comparison with other options, the cost of an ad is expressed in terms of the cost per thousand targets exposed. Specifically, *cost per thousand (CPM)* is the cost to deliver 1,000 people or homes. It is calculated by dividing the cost by the audience delivery and multiplying the quotient by 1,000. The audience base can be either circulation, homes reached, readers, or number of audience members of any kind of demographic or product usage classification.

Cost per thousand is a comparative device. It enables planners to compare one medium or media vehicle with another to find those that are the most efficient. It can be used for either intramedia or intermedia comparisons.

Following are various formulas that can be used to compare vehicles or media on the basis of cost per thousand:

1. *For print media (when audience data are not available):*

$$CPM = \frac{\text{Cost of 1 page} \times 1{,}000}{\text{Circulation}}$$

CPM circulation tells planners how much it costs to deliver 1,000 copies of the print ad, but it tells them nothing about the people who read those copies. It is used as a fallback measure to evaluate publications that do not have audience research.

2. *For print media (when audience data are available):*

$$CPM = \frac{\text{Cost of 1 page} \times 1{,}000}{\text{Number of prospects (readers) reached}}$$

3. *For broadcast media (based on homes or audience reached by a given program or time):*

$$CPM = \frac{\text{Cost of 1 unit of time} \times 1{,}000}{\begin{array}{c}\text{Number of homes or persons}\\\text{reached by a given program or time}\end{array}}$$

4. *For newspapers:*

$$CPM = \frac{\text{Cost of ad} \times 1{,}000}{\text{Circulation}}$$

Wherever precise demographic classifications of the audiences are available, these data should be used in the denominator of the formula.

The procedure for using any of the preceding formulas is to compare media on the basis of the two variables: audience and cost. The medium with the lowest cost per thousand is the most efficient, other things being equal. Since each medium is measured differently, CPM analysis is most typically applied to vehicles within a single medium, that is, one magazine versus another, or one television program versus another.

Media planners should be cautious about automatically accepting or rejecting media vehicles on the basis of the lowest cost per thousand. A difference of 10 percent one way or another is meaningless. Furthermore, David Poltrack, director of research at CBS, and others note that the range of error in television sample audiences is so great that a true calculation of the room for error would tell us that even a CPM variation of a dollar or more might not be real.[5] Unfortunately, planners often ignore this advice in day-to-day practice.

Although the general principle is to select the media vehicle with the lowest CPM, other criteria may be more important. If the advertiser requires a special kind of target audience, and few or no media reach that audience exclusively, then the costs per thousand are ignored. Instead, media are selected on the principle of reaching the largest number of targets, regardless of cost.

For example, the target audience is sometimes individuals with annual incomes of more than $100,000. A few media vehicles reach a small proportion of these audiences, but even if many such vehicles were used, the total number of persons reached might be relatively small. On the other hand, a very large number of these persons might be reached with mass media such as a network television program or a national magazine. It is obvious that either of these two media would also include a large amount of waste because of the low target audience composition. Therefore, when the CPMs are computed, they will seem unduly high. Yet the waste and the high CPM might have to be ignored in order to maximize the size of target audiences reached.

To reach the target audiences for mass-produced and mass-consumed products, such as fast-food restaurants, breakfast cereals, and automobiles, media usually are selected primarily on a CPM basis. Specialized products such as yachts, private airplanes, and classical recordings have specialized target audiences. Selecting media to reach them requires less attention to cost-efficiencies and more to audience sizes. The concepts of coverage (the percent of target people who are exposed to the medium) and composition (the percent of all exposed people who are in the target) will be discussed in more detail in Chapter 4.

---

5. Erick Larson, "Watching Americans Watch TV," *Atlantic Monthly* (March 1992): 72.

Cost per Rating Point

Another method of comparing the cost-efficiency of radio and television vehicles is the *cost per rating point (CPP)*. Essentially, CPP measures the cost of one household or demographic rating point in a given market. It is calculated by dividing the cost per commercial, or spot, by the rating. In television, a *rating* is the percent of the target audience in a market that is tuned in during the average minute of a program. A *market* is the geographic area that can receive the program; it can range from the entire United States down to a local market called a *Designated Market Area (DMA)*. This will be discussed in more detail in Chapter 4. Both CPM and CPP are measurements of relative value, but each uses a different base. The formula for calculating CPP is as follows:

$$CPP = \frac{\text{Cost of a commercial}}{\text{Rating}}$$

For example, if the cost of a prime-time network TV commercial is $200,000 and the national women 25–54 rating for that announcement is 10 (that is, 10 percent of all the women aged 25–54 in the United States were watching during the average minute of this program), then the CPP would be $200,000/10 = $20,000.

How does a CPP compare with a CPM for the same station and commercial? The following example shows the differences as they might relate to a local market:

CPM
Cost of 30-second commercial: $1,100
Number of households delivered at 2:00 P.M.: 77,000
$1,100 × 1,000/77,000 = $14.29

CPP
Cost of 30-second commercial: $1,100
DMA rating at 2:00 P.M.: 8
$1,100/8 = $137.50

Is there any preference for using one measurement method over the other? Generally, CPM is used to compare the efficiency of individual vehicles. CPP is the tool most often used to calculate the cost of an entire broadcast plan.

Is There a Better Way?

We use CPM to compare media efficiency because we have to. Advertisers would much prefer to compare media on the basis of their ability to generate sales. Unfortunately, no one has been able to correlate the size of a medium's audience with the number of additional sales that an ad produces, because advertising is only one of many factors that determine how much of a product will be sold. Media researchers cannot measure sales, but they can measure the number of people exposed to the ad, allowing planners to evaluate the cost per thousand people exposed.

The Internet provides a much more direct link between exposure and action. Researchers can report to the advertiser the number of people who are exposed to the banner ad, as well as the number who click through a banner to the advertiser's website. The Internet also allows an advertiser to know exactly how many sales were generated for products and services that can be sold online. This is a dramatic leap forward, but for the majority of day-to-day low-interest products, advertisers will continue to evaluate media in terms of CPM.

CHAPTER FOUR

Basic Measurements and Calculations

This chapter describes and explains the basic measurements and calculations used in media planning. These explanations serve as the foundation for understanding media strategy decisions, which will be discussed in Chapter 6, "Marketing Strategy and Media Planning." The measurements and calculations discussed in this chapter are by no means all that are available. They represent only those used most often.

It is vital to understand how media audiences are measured and what those measurements mean. Media planners can, and sometimes do, make strategy decisions without using measurement data as a guide, but such decisions are difficult to defend because they tend to be too subjective. Measurement data, on the other hand, provide a degree of objectivity that is hard to refute.

HOW MEDIA VEHICLES ARE MEASURED

Most media audiences are measured through sample surveys, using data about a small group to find out about a larger universe's exposure to a particular medium. Sample sizes can vary from as few as 200 to as many as 26,000 individuals. Measurements are usually made at specified intervals, not every day of the year. The chief reason for measuring samples rather than a vehicle's entire audience is that samples are less expensive. But even if a vehicle's entire audience could be measured, it is doubtful that the effort would produce data that would justify the extra cost and time.

Measurement technology is continually being changed as new ideas or methods are developed, and planners are always looking for better ways to measure audiences. The methods presented in this chapter simply represent those used most often today.

Television and Radio

Network television audiences are measured through national samples of households whose program preferences are recorded by an electronic *people meter*. Nielsen Media Research (www.nielsenmedia.com) employs a single sample of 5,000 people-meter homes to produce all national (network, cable, and syndicated program) television ratings. These meters automatically record the time of day, day of week, and channel numbers tuned in. Audience composition is collected when household members indicate they are watching TV by pushing a button on the people meter or on a handheld remote device. Local television viewing is measured in 210 television markets, called *Designated Market Areas (DMAs)*. In 53 of these markets, audiences are measured with a combination of meters and diaries. Meters provide continuous household data, and the diaries provide demographic data. The two samples are "wedded" four to seven times each year. The 53 metered markets cover about 68 percent of the U.S. population. The remaining 157 local markets are measured by diary method only.

In 2002, Nielsen began using the people meter to measure local market ratings, starting with Boston. Although methodologically superior to the traditional meter/diary, the people meter has faced resistance from television stations, which fear it will be more expensive to operate and may give lower ratings. Even if it is accepted in Boston, the people meter is likely to be feasible only in the largest markets.

Local radio measurements are also made through the use of diaries. There are more than 270 radio markets in the United States because the geographic areas measured are smaller than television DMAs. Furthermore, only large markets are measured relatively often.

Although the diary has been used to measure both local television and radio audiences for more than 50 years, researchers have long recognized that this method has severe shortcomings, especially with the expansion of cable and today's nearly universal channel surfing with remote controls. Its only advantage is low cost.

The Arbitron Company (www.arbitron.com), in cooperation with Nielsen Media Research, is experimenting with a pager-size personal meter that responds to special codes in a radio or TV station's audio signal. This passive meter will greatly improve audience measurement at far lower cost than the push-button people meter, but it will also change the definition of an "audience." Traditional methods count the audience as people who consider themselves to be "watching TV" or "listening to the radio," whereas the personal meter counts people who are within hearing distance of the set, regardless of whether they are paying attention. Preliminary indications from a 2001 test in Philadelphia indicate the meter works from a technical standpoint, but there is a long way to go before it can replace the diary.

Magazines and Newspapers

At least three different techniques commonly have been used to measure magazine and newspaper audiences: recent-reading and frequency-of-reading techniques for magazines, and the yesterday-reading technique for newspapers.

Recent Reading   The *recent-reading technique* is used by Mediamark Research Inc. (MRI, at www.mediamark.com) and is the most widely used source of magazine audience estimates today. In this method, an interviewer visits a sample of respondents and uses a specially designed procedure to elicit responses. The interviewer has a set of well over 200 cards, with the logotype of a different magazine printed on each. These are screened to about 12 to 15 magazines that the respondent claims to have read within the last six months. For these magazines, the interviewer shows each respondent the cards one at a time and asks if the respondent has read or looked at the magazine within the last month, week, or other publication period. Respondents who say they are "sure they have" done so are considered readers of the publication. After this questioning, respondents are asked for demographic information about themselves and their family. The interviewer also leaves behind a 96-page questionnaire that asks respondents to fill out details about various products they have used and how often they used them. The interviewer returns several weeks later to pick up the questionnaire.

This technique has the advantage of providing rapid information for a large number of publications with a reliability that has been proven in more than 20 years of practice. But there are several disadvantages. First, because the interviewer shows just the logo, respondents may become confused about which magazines they have read, especially if a title is similar to that of another magazine (as in the case of *Parents* versus *Parenting*). This technique is also more costly than mailed surveys because it must be administered in person by the interviewer.

Frequency of Reading   The *frequency-of-reading technique* is the most commonly used method for determining the number of people who read a magazine. In this procedure, the respondent is shown a list of magazine logotypes or cover pictures and is asked to record the number of copies of each that he or she has read out of the last four issues—one out of four, two out of four, and so on. It is the least expensive methodology because the survey can be conducted through the mail. However, it is limited to about 50 titles due to respondent fatigue, and it lacks the validity of the other methodologies because respondents have difficulty remembering how many copies of a magazine they have read.

Yesterday Reading   In the *yesterday-reading technique,* interviewers contact respondents in a selected sample and ask which newspapers they read yesterday. The procedure is much the same as the recent-reading technique for magazines. Because relatively few newspapers are read in any given market, this interview is quite short.

Internet

The most widely used company that measures the number of visitors to Internet websites is Nielsen//NetRatings (www.nielsennetratings.com). This service maintains a nationally representative sample of about 60,000 respondents in the United States. These respondents allow the researchers to place software on their computers to record every site visited. In addition to the number of unique visitors, the services can tell how long people stay with each page, how deeply they go into a site, and how many times they return.

This service is considered to provide "passive" measures because the data are collected automatically, without any conscious effort by the respondents. This allows Nielsen//NetRatings to report on many more sites than would be possible in a survey that relies on respondents' memories.

Out-of-Home

Outdoor audiences are measured by the Traffic Audit Bureau (www.tabonline. com), which counts the number of cars passing each billboard on the average day. This number is translated into "daily circulation," which is the basis for media sales.

Other out-of-home media, such as ads on buses, airport posters, signage in baseball stadiums, and mass-transit advertising, estimate their audience with a variety of techniques that range from ticket sales to proprietary surveys. Because these studies generally are conducted by the media themselves, they are considered less reliable than research conducted by independent companies such as the Traffic Audit Bureau, Nielsen, and MRI.

HOW THE DATA ARE INTERPRETED

All audience measurement techniques involve interacting with a sample of people who live in the geographic area being measured—whether that is a local market, such as Hartford, or the entire United States. To get the percent exposed, researchers divide the number of sample respondents who read a magazine, watched a TV show, or were exposed to an Internet banner by the total number of people in the sample. Then they project this percentage to the total population by simple multiplication.

For instance, if the national people meter sample has 5,000 households, and if 750 of those homes watched "ER" on a given Thursday night, the percentage is 750 divided by 5,000, which equals 15 percent. This is the *household rating* of the program. To find out how many households this represents nationwide, multiply the 105,500,000 U.S. households by 15 percent to get 15,825,000 households. This same process is used for demographics. The researcher simply substitutes the appropriate number of viewers and population base for the selected demographic group.

GENERAL USES OF VEHICLE AUDIENCE MEASUREMENTS

One of the most significant problems facing media planners is choosing the medium in which to place advertisements, because there are so many options—

and the numbers available are growing. The size of the audience and the cost to reach them in these alternative media are important measurements for comparison purposes.

All these attempts at measurement result in a large volume of numerical data, produced at regular intervals. However, such a quantity of data can have the unintended effect of giving media planners and others involved in marketing/media operations a sense of confidence that is perhaps unwarranted. Despite the quantitative aspect, media planning is not scientific in the same manner that, say, physics is.

Media audience numbers are the best that can be attained at a reasonable cost, but they do not represent the kind of measurement data planners would ideally like to have. Under ideal conditions, planners would prefer information about which media vehicle produces the most sales. Because the more commonly used numbers often take on undue importance, users of measurement data are warned that the numbers are only rough estimates for interpretive purposes, not absolutes.

Planners use audience measurement and product usage data for the following comparative purposes:

- To learn the demographics of product or brand users
- To learn the audience demographics of various kinds of media vehicles— who reads, sees, or hears the vehicles
- To learn the way purchasers use a product or brand (How many are heavy, medium, or light users?)
- To learn whether audience members of a particular media vehicle are heavy, medium, or light users of the product
- To learn how many people were exposed to vehicles

All of this information has one basic goal: to help planners and buyers match media with target markets. The market for any product, from margarine to automobiles, can be identified in terms of certain demographics. What the planner wants is to find media vehicles that best reach the demographic target.

Two main concepts guide planners in their use of measurement data. The first is to find vehicles that reach the largest numbers of prospects for a product category or a brand within that category. But planners do not always select the vehicle that delivers the largest number of prospects. Sometimes they choose a second concept, which is finding the vehicle that delivers the greatest concentrations of prospects, even if there are relatively few of them.

VARIOUS CONCEPTS OF AUDIENCE MEASUREMENTS

One difficulty in matching markets with media is that no single measurement can be used to determine the audience sizes for all media. Therefore, it is difficult to make intermedia comparisons (such as comparisons between the audience sizes of a television program and a magazine). Audience size numbers do not mean the same thing from medium to medium, even when they are measured on the same base. A *base* is a demographic group, such as total women or men aged 35–49. All media can be properly measured against the same base, but the audience numbers mean different things because the measurement methodology is different.

Actual or Potential Audience Size Measurements

Those who use media audience research should be careful not to confuse data that show the actual size of a vehicle's audience with other data that look similar but show only potential audience size. The division of audience measurement data into classifications of *actual* versus *potential,* or *vehicle distribution* versus *vehicle exposure,* depends on how the audience is measured.

Before statistical sampling was widely accepted, media owners simply used distribution counts of their vehicles as evidence of audience size. Circulation of print media is one of these older measurements. It represents only potential audience size of the measured vehicle, because it does not measure how many people will actually read a given copy of the periodical. In the last 30 years, as media research techniques have become more scientific, print media have been able to define their readership in terms of numbers of people who actually read the publication, in addition to pure circulation or distribution counts.

Print Circulation Measurements   Circulation measurements are available for most newspaper and magazine vehicles, but these data are of limited use in selection decisions. As stated previously, they do not provide the planner with information about the number of readers in a vehicle's audience. One unit of circulation means one copy of a periodical distributed, but for every copy distributed, there could be as many as six different readers. Needless to say, this can be confusing. Furthermore, circulation data tell the planner nothing about the demographics of the audience, such as readers' age, sex, household income, education, and other crucial pieces of information that are needed to select vehicles that will reach precise marketing targets.

As a result, circulation data are seldom used alone in selecting magazines in which to place ads. However, such data are often used in making decisions about newspapers, because little other audience data are available. Circulation data, while admittedly limited, are still valuable.

When circulation data must be used, the most reliable are measurements verified by the Audit Bureau of Circulations (ABC) (www.accessabc.com). The accuracy of ABC audits is widely accepted throughout the advertising industry. The ABC is a nonprofit, cooperative association of about 1,100 advertisers and advertising agencies and 3,400 daily and weekly newspapers, business publications, magazines, and farm publications in the United States and Canada. It audits and reports the circulation of these publications at regular intervals.

ABC data include paid circulations categorized for newspapers by city zone, trading zone, and outside areas. In addition, circulation is categorized for newspapers by Metropolitan Statistical Areas (MSAs) and television DMAs, making it possible to determine how the distribution of circulation matches selling and marketing areas of advertisers.

Magazine data from ABC show circulation categorized by size of metropolitan areas, by states and regions of the United States, and by other geographic divisions, all aimed at helping the planner choose the medium that best reaches geographic targets. No demographic data about the reading audience are available from ABC.

Print Audience Measurements   Actual audience measurements for print vehicles can be made with the magazine measurement techniques discussed earlier in this chapter. Most media planners are not interested in the total audience per se, but rather only in the numbers of those demographic targets who are the best prospects to purchase their products.

Audience Accumulation

Audience accumulation is the buildup of total audiences over time (usually a month). A major part of the accumulation concept is that audience members are counted only once, no matter how many additional times they are exposed to a particular vehicle or commercial. The number of different people who see an ad at least once is called *reach*. Some people who are reached will see an ad only once; others will see it many times. The number of times the average person sees the ad is called *frequency*. Both reach and frequency will be discussed in more detail in Chapter 5.

It is of utmost importance to know that the vehicle exposure is not about advertising, per se. Its main purpose is to learn how many persons looked at something inside the magazine. When the planner wants to know how many saw advertisements, then a different measurement, called *advertising page exposure,* can be used, although there is disagreement among planners about the validity of the estimates. So exposure is a broad measurement of the vehicle. The point is that when a vehicle is seen, it has potential for selling through ads.

Audience Accumulation in Magazines   In magazines, audience accumulates in three ways:

1. When advertising is placed in successive issues of the same magazine
2. When advertising is placed in the same month's issue of different magazines
3. Over the issue life of the publication, as the magazine is read by more and more people, passing it along from one reader to another

In 2000, MRI released the first modern study of how quickly a single issue of a magazine accumulates readers. As expected, the study revealed that a time-sensitive magazine such as *TV Guide* accumulates virtually all of its audience within a week, while newsweeklies such as *U.S. News & World Report* take almost a month to reach 90 percent of their total readership. Monthly magazines take almost three months to accumulate the same readership level.[1]

---

1. Mediamark Research Inc., "Magazine Audience Accumulation: Development of a Measurement System and Initial Results," 2000.

Within a magazine's total audience, researchers distinguish between *primary readers* (those who either have purchased the magazine themselves or are members of the purchaser's household) and *secondary,* or *pass-along, readers* (those not in the purchaser's household). Typical pass-along readers are the purchaser's friends and people reading in doctors' offices, in barbershops, or on airplanes.

In addition to the type of reader, syndicated research companies also provide data showing where people read magazines. MRI cites in-home and out-of-home readership for all the publications in its reports. Several isolated research studies have indicated that the in-home reader, whether a primary or pass-along reader, reads more pages of a magazine and spends more time reading than the person outside of the home. Media planners sometimes use this information to give different values, or weights, to each type of reader in order to compare one media vehicle to another.

Audience Accumulation in Broadcast   Although the concept of reach accumulation is the same in broadcast as with magazines, the mechanics differ widely. This is because once a TV or radio program is broadcast, it is finished (unless it is recorded). The people who viewed or listened to the show are the only audience the program will have; there is no pass-along audience as with magazines. Time is a major element in broadcast accumulation.

Nevertheless, TV and radio programs do accumulate audience in three ways:

1. Within the program audience while it is being broadcast
2. With successive airings of the same program within a four-week period
3. With the airing of different programs within the same four-week period

TV viewers are counted by people meters if they press the buttons designating themselves as viewers of a given program. If new viewers watch a program after the first telecast, they are added to those who viewed it previously. Radio listeners are so designated if they write in a diary that they listen to five minutes or more of the program. Each week that a program is aired, new audience members will tune in for the first time, and thus the program's reach grows. Another way accumulation grows is by advertising on different programs that appeal to the same audience, such as women aged 18–49.

EXHIBIT 4-1

Comparison of Program Ratings: Average Minute Versus Total for Entire Program

PROGRAM	PROGRAM LENGTH	DAY OF TELECAST	HOUSEHOLDS VIEWING (%)	
			AVERAGE MINUTE	TOTAL PROGRAM
"NYPD Blue"	60 min.	Tuesday, March 7	10.9	13.4
"Friends"	30 min.	Thursday, March 9	13.9	16.6
"60 Minutes"	60 min.	Sunday, March 12	14.7	20.4

SOURCE: Nielsen Media Research, *NTI Pocketpiece,* March 6–12, 2000. Reprinted with permission.

In the real world, people tune in and tune out programs at different times during the program broadcast. Ten people might tune in a particular program in the first five minutes, but some of them will tune out, and some new people will tune in. This phenomenon occurs throughout the program. Exhibit 4-1 shows how the accumulated total audience of a single episode varies for several programs, compared with the audience who viewed the program during an average minute. In every case, the size of the tuned-in audience is larger than the number who tuned out. In other words, the bucket was being filled faster than it was being emptied. This pattern results in a gradual buildup of audience over the entire program.

Coverage

Audiences can be analyzed in two broad ways: in total numbers of people (for example, the evening news audience) and as a percentage of the demographic universe of which they are a part (say, all women aged 35–49). One might compare the audience size of 10 magazines or television programs on the basis of which delivers the most people in a target audience or which delivers the highest percentage of the total population in that target audience. Either method will reveal the same relative differences between the media vehicles.

Coverage is a convenient statistical term used to assess the degree to which a media vehicle delivers a given target audience. The higher the coverage, the greater the delivery. Coverage is usually expressed as a percentage of a market population reached.

To calculate coverage, the researcher divides a given vehicle's delivery of a specific demographic group (or target audience) by the total population of that demographic group (the market size, or *universe*). For example, suppose a magazine is read by 2.5 million women aged 35–49, and the total population of women aged 35–49 is 25 million. The magazine has a 10 percent coverage of that target audience (that is, 2.5 million divided by 25 million).

Unfortunately, the term *coverage* can be confusing, because it is used in different ways for different media forms (see Exhibit 4-2 on pages 70–71 for a summary). In magazines, *coverage* is used as just described. For example, if 12 million households in the United States own cats and Magazine A reaches 6 million of them, then Magazine A's coverage is 50 percent. This 50 percent represents actual exposure to the vehicle. But in newspapers and television, coverage represents only the potential for exposure, not actual exposure (or reach). Because *coverage* can mean a number of different things, it is important for anyone who uses this term to know and understand its alternative meanings. Following is a discussion of how coverage is defined in specific media.

Newspaper Coverage   *Newspaper coverage* is the number of copies circulated compared to the number of households in the circulation area. Most newspapers measure the number of copies sold or distributed and call this number *circulation.*

If the circulation of a newspaper is 500,000 and the number of households in the area (the household universe) is 2,000,000, then the coverage is 25 percent. The assumption is that each unit of circulation equals one household covered. Newspaper coverage represents potential rather than actual exposure, because not everyone who receives a copy of a newspaper reads it; no exposure to the medium is necessarily assumed. Therefore, coverage based on circulation is only a rough comparison of newspaper audience size related to the market size as measured by the total number of households in that area.

When using newspaper coverage, planners sometimes suggest that the coverage level in any individual market should be at least 50 percent. If it can be assumed that not all persons in all households will be exposed to any given edition of a newspaper, then 50 percent is the lowest level that seems practical. Perhaps only two-thirds of that 50 percent will be exposed. Some media planners set much higher limits on local market coverage, such as no less than 70 percent. In such situations, it may take two or even three newspapers in that community to attain 70 percent unduplicated coverage.

When a newspaper has research of its readership and provides a breakdown of that audience by demographic segments, then coverage will mean something different. In this case, it will mean the number of individuals exposed to newspapers compared to the total number of individuals (rather than households) in the market. Because such measurements are not always available on a regular basis, newspaper coverage usually means potential exposure.

Magazine Coverage   As described earlier in this section, *magazine coverage* is simply the number of prospects who read a publication divided by the size of a target market. This is sometimes referred to as a magazine's *average issue audience.* The concept is directly comparable to a broadcast rating.

Another way to look at magazine coverage is to look at total users of a given product class. For example, as shown in Exhibit 4-3 on page 72, MRI reported that 31,184,000 adults were dieting to maintain their weight or physical fitness. This figure represents the size of the total market of such consumers. If 6,630,000 readers of *People* magazine are controlling their diet, that number represents 21.3 percent market coverage by *People* (6,630,000 divided by 31,184,000).

Earlier in this chapter, we discussed the various ways in which researchers determine how many people read a given magazine. However, the number of readers, as a number by itself, is of very little value until it is put into context as a percent of both the target (coverage) and of the medium's total audience (composition).

Exhibit 4-4 on page 73 illustrates the concept. Mass magazines, such as *People,* are read by such a large percent of the whole country that they can't help also being read by a large percent of target dieters. They offer high coverage, but there is a great deal of waste; more than half the circle of *People* readers is outside the target audience. In this case, we would say that *People* has high coverage of our target but low composition.

EXHIBIT 4-2

Different Meanings of the Term *Coverage*

KIND OF COVERAGE	MEANING	USES
General concept (more accurately called "market coverage")	The number of prospects delivered (exposed) by a given medium. Coverage expressed as a percentage of the universe of prospects.	Serves as a goal in planning. Used to determine whether media selected are delivering enough prospects.
Newspaper coverage	The number of circulation units as a percentage of the number of households in an area. If the readers of newspapers in a local market are measured, then coverage is the number of readers in a demographic segment (such as men aged 18–24) as a percentage of all men 18–24 in the local market.	For local markets. A goal to determine whether enough households are reached with one or more newspapers. This represents potential audience size.
Magazine coverage (sometimes called "reach")	Same as the general concept. Prospects are demographically defined.	Same as the general concept. This represents estimated actual audience size.
Spot TV and radio coverage (local market)	The number of TV (or radio) homes within the signal area of station that can tune in to that station.	Serves as a basis for potential delivery in planning. Indicates the maximum size of the potential audience of radio or TV homes.
Spot TV coverage for a national campaign (also for spot radio)	Total number of TV homes in selected markets that are part of a campaign, that can tune in (or can be reached).	It can show the percentage of U.S. TV homes that may be potentially delivered by a spot plan. Maximum number and percentage of potential exposure.

EXHIBIT 4-2 (*continued*)

Different Meanings of the Term *Coverage*

KIND OF COVERAGE	MEANING	USES
Network TV program coverage	The number and percentage of U.S. TV homes for all stations in a network carrying a given program, compared to total TV homes in the United States.	An indication of the maximum potential of TV homes that a TV program can reach.
Outdoor advertising and transit coverage	The number of people who pass and are exposed to a given showing of billboards in a local market, expressed as a percentage of the total people in the market.	To determine the size of an audience that might look at each showing of billboards.
Cable TV channel coverage	The number and percentage of U.S. TV homes that can receive a given cable channel from any source: wired cable, direct broadcast satellite, apartment cable system, or other system.	An indication of the maximum audience that can be reached by an individual cable network.
Internet coverage	All members (two years of age or older) of U.S. households that currently have access to the Internet. Some services define coverage as the percent of persons who used the Internet or other digital media at home, work, or college in the last 30 days.	Provides the maximum number or percent of persons who can be exposed to an Internet ad campaign.

EXHIBIT 4-3

Magazine Coverage and Composition

Persons Dieting to Maintain Weight or Physical Fitness
Population: 31,184 (000)

	NUMBER (000)	COVERAGE	COMPOSITION	INDEX
Total dieting adults	31,184	100.0%	15.7%	100
High-Coverage Magazines—Low Composition				
People	6,630	21.3	18.9	120
Parade (Sunday magazine)	14,149	45.4	18.1	115
Reader's Digest	7,510	24.1	16.8	107
TV Guide	5,124	16.4	14.9	95
High-Composition Magazines—Low Coverage				
Shape	1,354	4.3	31.5	200
Self	1,141	3.7	26.9	171
Fitness	1,652	5.3	25.4	161
New Yorker	631	2.0	23.7	151
Glamour	2,529	8.1	23.3	148

SOURCE: Mediamark Research Inc., Fall 1999.

Small, selective magazines such as *Fitness,* on the other hand, cover only a relatively small part of the target, but a larger percent of the magazine's (few) readers fall within the target. There is far less waste. We would say *Fitness* has low coverage but high composition.

Exhibit 4-3 shows the differences in coverage and composition for magazines that might be used to reach this dieting target audience. The indices quantify the target audience selectivity of each magazine.

Planners must be careful to avoid either extreme. Using only high-coverage mass magazines will certainly reach the target, but a significant part of the budget will be wasted on people who have no interest in the advertised product. Using only high-composition magazines, on the other hand, risks missing people who buy the product but do not happen to be readers of the highly selective publications. Planners typically use a mixture of high-coverage and high-composition magazines to ensure adequate reach while minimizing waste.

EXHIBIT 4-4

Coverage Versus Composition

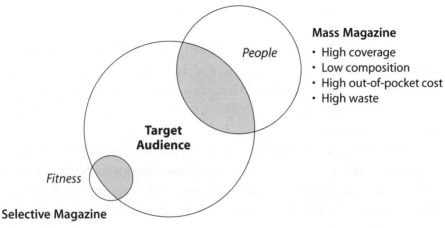

Mass Magazine
- High coverage
- Low composition
- High out-of-pocket cost
- High waste

People

Target Audience

Fitness

Selective Magazine
- Low coverage
- High composition
- Low out-of-pocket cost
- Little waste

Local Television and Radio Coverage   For local radio and television, coverage means the number (or percentage) of homes with radio or television sets within the signal area of a given station. These receivers can tune in to that station because they can pick up the station's signal. Whether or not the households choose to tune in depends on a number of factors:

- The programming of the station (whether it is interesting enough to attract them)
- The power of the station (more powerful stations can cover more homes than weaker stations)
- The height of a station's antenna and the pull of the home's antenna, which affect reception of signals
- The number and nature of obstructions that might prevent the broadcast signal from being received, such as mountains, tall buildings, or bridges

- The service area of cable systems that carry a station's signal (By law, cable systems must carry every station that is licensed to the market they serve. This can greatly extend the coverage area of stations whose over-the-air signal serves only a small portion of a market.)

Television stations produce an engineering contour map based on their signal strength in a market to indicate how wide an area the station's signal covers. The strongest signal is designated Grade A (or one that covers the primary market area surrounding the station). The next strongest signal is Grade B (or secondary area coverage).

Although signal contours are important for the licensing of broadcast stations, media planners must recognize that homes outside of the A or B areas can also receive certain stations whose signal comes in on cable or satellite television. For this reason, the DMA television market is defined by viewing patterns, not signal coverage.

Spot Radio or Television Coverage in Multiple Markets   An advertiser who buys spot announcements in a number of markets located in various geographic regions of the United States will be interested in knowing what percentage of all television (or radio) homes in the country the commercial could potentially reach. Perhaps a planner has selected 50 of the largest markets in the country in which to advertise. To determine the percentage of coverage, it is only necessary to add the percent of the United States represented by each of the 50 markets. Exhibit 4-5 lists the percentage coverages for the largest U.S. markets.

For example, by buying spot announcements in the largest 50 markets, planners can potentially reach nearly 70 percent of the television homes in the country. The planner knows, then, that the maximum audience size (expressed in terms of homes that can tune in to a station's signal) is no larger than 70 percent. Because not everyone in those 50 markets will see the commercials, the exposure will be lower than 70 percent.[2]

Network Television Coverage   In network television, coverage is defined as the number and percentage of all U.S. television households that are able to

---

2. See www.nielsenmedia.com for a list of the 210 television DMAs and their populations.

receive a given program. Generally speaking, the degree of coverage is affected by the number of stations in a network lineup. The more stations, the more coverage. Exhibit 4-6 indicates the coverage of several network programs. Although these statistics are of interest to the television networks, which want to see their programs carried on as many stations as possible, buyers and planners are typi-

EXHIBIT 4-5

Coverage of Top U.S. Markets Using Spot TV

MARKETS	U.S. COVERAGE
Top 10	30%
Top 20	44
Top 30	54
Top 40	61
Top 50	67
Top 60	72
Top 70	76
Top 80	80
Top 90	83
Top 100	86

SOURCE: Nielsen Media Research, *U.S. TV Household Estimates,* September 1999.

EXHIBIT 4-6

Network Program Coverage

NETWORK	PROGRAM	HOUSEHOLD COVERAGE	NUMBER OF STATIONS IN NETWORK LINEUP
ABC	"Dharma & Gregg"	99%	222
NBC	"Friends"	99	217
CBS	"Nash Bridges"	98	202
FOX	"King of the Hill"	99	228
WB	"Felicity"	86	209
UPN	"Malcolm & Eddie"	81	158

SOURCE: Nielsen Media Research, *NTI Pocketpiece,* March 6–12, 2000. Reprinted with permission.

cally not concerned with such data, because coverage is automatically reflected in a program's rating.

Cable Television Coverage   Cable coverage is defined as the percent of U.S. households that can receive a cable network by any means, including cable, large satellite dish, direct broadcast satellite, microwave, and other distribution methods. In January 2002, 83.7 percent of all homes could receive cable channels.[3]

Unlike network television signals, which are carried by broadcast stations that can reach all television households, individual cable networks must secure clearance on thousands of local systems. Although some can offer hundreds of channels, others are limited to a few dozen, resulting in strong competition to secure clearance. Large, established channels, such as ESPN, CNN, and USA Network, are carried by virtually all cable systems (and so report near 83 percent coverage of U.S. television households). Newer channels must fight for every household, and many cover less than 25 percent of the United States.

Because cable channels must compete with the broadcast networks for advertising dollars, they prefer to report their ratings as a percent of their coverage area, instead of total United States. For example, a cable channel that can be seen in 20 million homes may have a program that is seen in 500,000 households. This is only 0.5 percent of the 105.5 million U.S. households. It makes a stronger sales story to say that the program has a 2.5 percent rating (to the base of the 20 million coverage area households).

Internet Coverage   By the fall of 2001, 70 percent of all adults had access to the Internet at home or at work. Like cable networks, Internet websites prefer to express their audience as a percent of these active Internet users, rather than the larger total U.S. population.[4]

Out-of-Home Media Coverage   Out-of-home media include all media that are located outside a person's home, such as billboards, posters in shopping malls, advertisements in and on buses, and so forth. Coverage for out-of-home

---

3. Nielsen Media Research, 2002.
4. Mediamark Research Inc., Fall 2001.

EXHIBIT 4-7

Reach and Frequency of Outdoor Showings

100 SHOWING		50 SHOWING		25 SHOWING	
REACH	FREQUENCY	REACH	FREQUENCY	REACH	FREQUENCY
91.5%	27.9	90.6%	14.3	87.4%	7.7

SOURCE: Simmons Market Research Bureau, 1991. Reprinted by permission.

media is the percentage of the population that passes one or more of these out-of-home media in a given period of time. Coverage for out-of-home media, therefore, represents the potential for advertising exposure.

Out-of-home media are generally purchased by advertisers on the basis of daily gross rating points, also expressed as a "showing." A *gross rating point* is a measure of the total (duplicated) weight delivered by an advertising vehicle or vehicles. Suppose a market has 100 different billboards erected in and around the city, each of which is passed by an average of 1,000 people each day. If an advertiser purchases 50 of these billboards, a total of 50,000 people will pass these boards. If the market has a population of 100,000, then these 50 boards would deliver 50 GRPs/day, or a 50 showing. We call the data "gross" or "duplicated" because a person who passes 2 of the 50 boards will be counted twice. Other showing sizes can also be purchased, such as a 100 showing (meaning twice as many exposures as in a 50 showing), a 25 showing (half as many exposures), and so on. These measures can also be expressed as 100, 75, 50, and 25 GRPs per day.

An outdoor medium is able to generate very high coverage, and therefore high reach, over time. Exhibit 4-7 shows the accumulated reach over a 30-day period for outdoor showings of different sizes.

Households Using Television (HUT)

One important television measurement that is frequently used in planning is *households using television (HUT)*. This represents the total percentage of homes in a market that are watching television at a given point in time. Because it

EXHIBIT 4-8

Variations in Viewing by Daypart and Season

DAYPART	TOTAL TV HOUSEHOLDS USING TELEVISION (%)			
	SPRING	SUMMER	FALL	WINTER
Daytime (Mon.–Fri.)	27%	28%	27%	29%
Early fringe (Mon.–Fri.)	40	40	43	45
Prime time (Mon.–Sun.)	57	54	61	62
Late fringe (Mon.–Fri.)	32	32	32	32

SOURCE: Nielsen Media Research, *Households Using Television Summary Report,* January–March 2000.

includes a time consideration, HUT can be classified as a measurement of net potential audience size.

Remember that coverage data in television represent only audience potential. If a station covers 1,410,000 TV homes, this does not mean an advertiser will reach all of those homes with a commercial on that station. But what determines how many homes will be reached? To a great extent, the HUT at any time of day provides a clue to the possible tune-in. As a measure of the net potential audience, HUT indicates what percentage of households with a television set have it turned on at any given time of day, such as morning, early afternoon, late afternoon, prime time, or late evening.

Television viewing is affected by living habits. In the morning, tune-in (HUT) tends to be low, with many men and women at work and children in school. Primary viewers are retirees, unemployed workers, and stay-at-home parents with small children. When children return home from school about 4:00 P.M., the tune-ins rise dramatically. After 6:00 P.M., when many people have returned home from work, the rise in tune-ins is even greater. After 11:00 P.M. (eastern time), viewing drops again. Exhibit 4-8 indicates the variations in viewing for different time periods, as well as by seasons of the year.

Media planners can study HUT data and estimate potential audience size better than by studying coverage figures alone. In the evening hours, more viewers are available than at any other time of day, because both children and adults are usually at home. But there are variations in viewing not only during a single

EXHIBIT 4-9

Average Number of Homes Reached at Least Once by Chicago-Area TV Station

DAYPART	DAY/TIME*	HOMES REACHED
Morning	Mon.–Fri., 9 A.M.–noon	648,000
Afternoon	Mon.–Fri., noon–3 P.M.	396,000
Early evening	Mon.–Fri., 5–7 P.M.	717,000
Prime time	Mon.–Sun., 7–10 P.M.	1,875,000
Late news	Mon.–Fri., 10:00–10:30 P.M.	749,000
Late fringe	Mon.–Fri., 10:30 P.M.–midnight	598,000

*Central standard time.
SOURCE: Nielsen Media Research: Station Index, *Chicago Viewers in Profile,* May 1999.

day, but also during a given week and month. During the summer, for example, when people spend more time outdoors, television viewing is much lower in some viewing periods than it is in winter. These variations affect the size of the audience that can be obtained.

From Nielsen, it is possible to determine how large the net potential audience is. Exhibit 4-9 shows these data for a hypothetical Chicago-area TV station. As noted above, these figures would probably be lower if the planner were studying data for the months of July or August, because fewer people watch television during these months. Furthermore, there are differences between the net potential audience of this station and other Chicago stations. In any case, these figures help the advertiser learn about the potential audience size. After potential audience sizes are examined, program ratings are used to learn the estimated audience size for a given program.

Broadcast Ratings

A *broadcast rating* (television or radio) represents an estimate of the audience that has viewed a program or has tuned in during a specific time period. This rating is determined through sampling procedures. It is financially and physically impossible to measure the viewing habits of every person in the United

States, but it is possible to measure a small sample of viewers. This information, however, is only an estimate of the size of the actual viewing audience.

These estimates are reported in the form of percentages of the demographic universe being considered. For households tuned in to a network television program, the base figure usually includes all households in the United States that have at least one television set. The geographic area for local television stations is based on counties that are grouped together to form television markets, or DMAs.

The Nielsen County Coverage Study shows which city (and which TV stations) the residents of each county spend most of their time watching. For example, this research shows that the residents of Cook County, Illinois, spend 78 percent of their weekly viewing hours watching stations that are licensed to the Chicago television market. Accordingly, Cook County is assigned to the Chicago DMA. De Kalb County spends 46 percent of its time watching Chicago stations and 18 percent of its time watching stations in neighboring Rockford. Because the majority of its viewing is to Chicago stations, De Kalb County is also assigned to the Chicago DMA. Boone County, however, spends 56 percent of its time watching Rockford but only 10 percent watching Chicago. Thus, it is assigned to the Rockford DMA. Nielsen uses this procedure to assign every county in the United States to one DMA or another. Exhibit 4-10 shows the counties of the Chicago DMA.

Ratings are made for both households and individuals. The universe for network, cable, and syndicated programs consists of all persons of a given age group living in national television households. For example, for women aged 18–49, the network program base would be all women aged 18–49 in television households in the United States. A rating for women 18–49 in the Chicago DMA would be based on the women of that age who live in any of the counties that make up the Chicago DMA.

A local radio rating is usually expressed in the form of an average quarter-hour tune-in and as a percentage of the people in a special metro area created by Arbitron that reflects radio listening patterns. These counties are also identified in Exhibit 4-10.

Rather than talk about a rating of 18 percent, it is common practice to talk about a program having an 18 rating. This custom assumes the understanding that a rating is a percentage.

EXHIBIT 4-10

Counties of the Chicago DMA

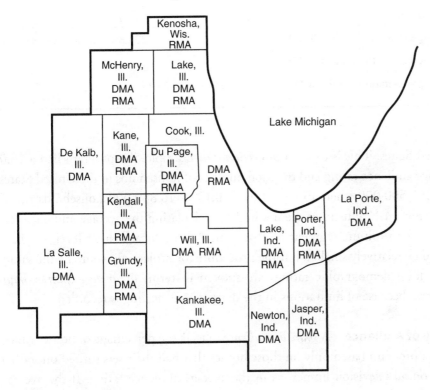

Kenosha, Wis. RMA

McHenry, Ill. DMA RMA

Lake, Ill. DMA RMA

Lake Michigan

Kane, Ill. DMA RMA

Cook, Ill.

De Kalb, Ill. DMA

Du Page, Ill. DMA RMA

DMA RMA

La Porte, Ind. DMA

Kendall, Ill. DMA RMA

Porter, Ind. DMA RMA

La Salle, Ill. DMA

Will, Ill. DMA RMA

Lake, Ind. DMA RMA

Grundy, Ill. DMA RMA

Kankakee, Ill. DMA

Newton, Ind. DMA

Jasper, Ind. DMA

TV DMA—16 counties
Radio Metro Area (RMA)—11 counties

SOURCE: *The Chicago DMA Television Market.* Copyright: Nielsen Media Research, 2002.

Average Audience Rating   For national broadcasts on network, cable, and syndicated programs, Nielsen Media Research provides an *average audience rating,* obtained through a people meter. This rating represents the percentage of homes (and people) tuned in to the average minute of a program. Data provided in the *Nielsen Television Index Pocketpiece* show average audience ratings tuned in for each half-hour or quarter-hour segment.

To learn how many households (or people) have tuned in to a program, one need only multiply the rating by the total number of TV households in the

EXHIBIT 4-11

Computing an Average Audience Rating

MINUTES IN A PROGRAM	1	2	3	4	5	6	7	8	9	10	11	12	13	14	15
Percentage tuned in	30	30	30	31	31	31	31	32	32	32	33	33	33	33	33

Total tuned in for 15 minutes = 475

Average percentage tune-in for 15 minutes = 475 ÷ 15 = 31.7

United States. This is called a *projection.* For example, if a program had a 16.0 average audience rating and the total number of households in the United States was 105,500,000, then 105,500,000 × 0.16 = 16,880,000 households tuned in. Exhibit 4-11 illustrates the method for calculating the average audience rating for a 15-minute segment of a program.[5] On a local market level, the base would be relatively smaller, but the procedure for projection would be the same. Also, local demographic ratings are spoken in terms of *average quarter-hour audience* because of limitations in the diary where viewing is recorded.

Share of Audience   A *share of audience* reflects the percentage of homes tuned in to a program based only on those homes that had their sets turned on, rather than on all television homes, as in the average audience rating. If the average audience ratings for every station that was on the air in a 15-minute period were added together, the sum would represent the HUT, which always is a proportion of all television homes and is always less than 100 percent. But the sum of the audience shares represents only those homes tuned in at a particular time and theoretically equals 100 percent, because homes that had their sets turned off are never figured in the base. The formula for computing share is as follows:

$$\text{Share} = \frac{\text{Rating}}{\text{HUT}}$$

---

5. See www.nielsenmedia.com for a complete description of broadcast rating terms and methodology.

EXHIBIT 4-12

Difference Between Average Audience Rating and Share

PROGRAMS BEING BROADCAST DURING SAME 15-MINUTE PERIOD	AVERAGE AUDIENCE RATING	SHARE OF AUDIENCE
A	20%	33.3%
B	10	16.7
C	30	50.0
Total	60% (HUT)	100.0%

A comparison of share data with average audience ratings is illustrated in Exhibit 4-12. According to the data, 40 percent of the sets were not turned on. When this 40 percent is added to the HUT, the total is 100 percent. Share was computed by dividing the average audience rating by the HUT. The sum of all average audience ratings equals the HUT, or 60 percent. But the sum of shares is 100 percent. The share statistic enables the media planner to compare the relative popularity of two programs that compete for viewers at the same time of the day.

In this example, Program C, with a 50 percent share of viewers, is the most popular—a conclusion that would be valid regardless of changes in the HUT level over different times of the year. Note that this exhibit is just for illustration; actual ratings are much lower. In April 2001, for instance, the average prime-time program was watched in only 5 percent of homes, and many programs on the newer broadcast networks (PAX, UPN, and WB) were seen in less than 2 percent of homes. Most cable programs are viewed in less than 1 percent of homes.[6]

Exhibit 4-13 illustrates another use of share data. It shows ratings for a sample program and its shares at different times of the year. If media planners had made decisions about Program X based only on the average audience rating,

---

6. Nielsen Media Research, April 2001.

EXHIBIT 4-13

Program X, Ratings Versus Share

MONTH	AVERAGE AUDIENCE RATING	HUT	SHARE OF AUDIENCE
January	15.2	66.5	22.9
April	14.6	63.6	23.0
July	12.5	49.8	25.1

they might have concluded that this program was losing its audience; after all, ratings were declining. But a study of HUTs shows that they, too, were declining, as might be expected when comparing HUTs for January and July. When shares were computed, the numbers showed that the program was not only doing well, it was actually improving from January to July.

Exhibit 4-14 shows sample pages from *Nielsen Television Index* to illustrate the various kinds of ratings used by media analysts. Note the average audience and share for each program listed.

It is important to remember that although ratings can be reported for households, planners most often use ratings for people viewing programs. Such ratings usually are broken down by the viewer's age and sex cross-tabulated with other demographics such as household income, head-of-household education, and number of children. These cross-tabulations allow a media planner to have a better understanding of who views each program so that it is possible to better match markets with media.

Although ratings, HUT, and share help planners understand broad patterns of television usage, these audience statistics are used most commonly by media buyers who must decide on which specific program to place the ads. In this context, the ratings provide a critical measure of the media value received for the cost of the ad. In essence, ratings are the "currency" of broadcast negotiation and buying worth over $40 billion per year. To ensure the quality of these estimates, the survey methodology and execution are closely scrutinized by an independent industry organization, the Media Rating Council, which reports its findings to the users.

EXHIBIT 4-14

Sample National Nielsen TV Audience Estimates

NATIONAL *NielsenTV* AUDIENCE ESTIMATES — **EVE.THU. JUL.12, 2001**

TIME	7:00	7:15	7:30	7:45	8:00	8:15	8:30	8:45	9:00	9:15	9:30	9:45	10:00	10:15	10:30	10:45
HUT	45.5	46.4	47.4	48.9	49.5	50.8	52.0	53.8	55.8	57.3	58.2	59.1	57.2	56.8	55.8	54.4

ABC TV

WHOSE LINE IS IT ANYWAY? (R) — WHOSE LINE ANYWAY-8:30PM (R) — MILLIONAIRE-THU — PRIMETIME THURSDAY →

HHLD AUDIENCE% & (000)					3.9 4,010		4.6 4,660		8.6 8,840		9.0 9,230		9.7*
74% AVG. AUD. 1/2 HR %					5.7		5.9 5.5		12.4		13.4		18*
SHARE AUDIENCE %					6		10 15		15 15*		16 15*		18*
AVG. AUD. BY 1/4 HR %					4.0 3.8		4.3 4.9		7.8 8.7		9.3 8.7 8.1		8.4 9.4 8.7 9.9

— BIG BROTHER II — / 48 HOURS →

CBS TV

CSI (R)

HHLD AUDIENCE% & (000)					6.1 6,280		6.4*		7.5 7,700				6.2 6,310		6.2*
74% AVG. AUD. 1/2 HR %					9.7 5.9*		6.4* 12*		10.4 7.3*		7.7* 7.3*		10.3 6.1*		6.1* 11*
SHARE AUDIENCE %					12 12*		12* 6.6		13 7.3		13* 7.3		11 6.0		11* 6.4
AVG. AUD. BY 1/4 HR %					6.1 5.7		6.2		7.3		7.7 7.8		6.2 6.1

NBC TV

FRIENDS — SPY TV — WILL & GRACE (R) — JUST SHOOT ME (R) — E.R. (R) →

HHLD AUDIENCE% & (000)					5.9 6,070		5.2 5,290		5.5 5,660		5.4 5,470		5.1 5,190		5.2*
74% AVG. AUD. 1/2 HR %					7.6 5.9*		6.7 10		7.0 10		6.9 5.0*		8.1 5.0*		9*
SHARE AUDIENCE %					12 12*		10 5.3		10 5.3		9*		9*		9 5.3
AVG. AUD. BY 1/4 HR %					5.7		5.3 5.0		5.3 5.8		5.5 5.2		4.8 5.1		5.1

[NIGHT VISIONS SPECIAL] — NIGHT VISIONS →

FOX TV

HHLD AUDIENCE% & (000)					3.6 3,650		3.5*		3.3 3,330		3.2*		3.2*
74% AVG. AUD. 1/2 HR %					5.4 3.6*		3.7*		4.7 3.3*		3.6*		3.6*
SHARE AUDIENCE %					7		7*		6 3.2		3*		3*
AVG. AUD. BY 1/4 HR %					3.7 3.5		3.6 3.5		3.4 3.2		3.2 3.3

WB TV

— GILMORE GIRLS - WB (R) — CHARMED - WB (R) →

HHLD AUDIENCE% & (000)					1.8 1,870		1.9*		1.9 1,990		2.0*
74% AVG. AUD. 1/2 HR %					2.9 3.6*		1.7* 3*		3.0 1.9*		2.0*
SHARE AUDIENCE %					4 3*		4*		3 3*		3*
AVG. AUD. BY 1/4 HR %					1.8 1.7		1.8 2.0		1.8 1.9		2.0 2.1

— WWF SMACKDOWN! →

UPN TV

IT'S A MIRACLE (R) — TOUCHED BY AN ANGEL-THU — DIAGNOSIS MURDER-THU → (R)

HHLD AUDIENCE% & (000)					4.0 4,130		3.8*		4.2*		4.5*
74% AVG. AUD. 1/2 HR %					7.2 3.8*		3.9*		1.9*		4.8*
SHARE AUDIENCE %					8 3*		3*		3*		4.8*
AVG. AUD. BY 1/4 HR %					3.5 3.8 3.7		3.9 4.2		4.3 4.4		4.8

PAX TV

HHLD AUDIENCE% & (000)					0.7 760		0.8*		0.8 800		0.9*		1.6 1,640		1.7*
74% AVG. AUD. 1/2 HR %					1.2 0.7*		1*		1.4 0.6*		0.2*		2.2 1.5*		1.3*
SHARE AUDIENCE %					1 1*		1*		1 1*		1*		3 1*		1.7
AVG. AUD. BY 1/4 HR %					0.6 0.8		0.8 0.8		0.6 0.7		0.8 1.0		1.5 1.6		1.7

U.S. TV Households: 102,200,000

For explanation of symbols. See page B.

For SPANISH LANGUAGE TELEVISION audience estimates, see the Nielsen Hispanic Television Index (NHTI) TV Audience Report.

SOURCE: Nielsen Media Research, 2001.

CHAPTER FIVE

Advanced Measurements and Calculations

The preceding chapter introduced the concept of audience accumulation, along with other measurements of a single telecast or print insertion. But broadcast commercials and print ads are repeated many times in order to develop sufficient weight to achieve the advertiser's marketing goals. This chapter introduces the more advanced numerical tools used to manage this weight and develop media plans: gross rating points, gross impressions, reach, frequency, and effective frequency. These tools answer the most commonly asked questions about a media plan, such as the following:

- How many people will see the ad? (Reach)
- How often will they see it? (Frequency)
- How many people will see it at least three times? Four times? *N* times? (Effective reach)

Reach and frequency are parts of strategy planning and can be manipulated to help attain certain marketing and media objectives. Generally, when the advertiser needs broad message dispersion, high levels of reach will be planned. To achieve a great deal of repetition, the plan will call for high frequency or effective frequency levels. Sometimes planning will have to attain both high reach and high frequency.

GROSS RATING POINTS

Recall from Chapter 4 that when planners want to know the audience size for a single TV program, they use either a program rating or a calculation of the number of viewers exposed to the program. For a single ad in a magazine, they use either a target audience measurement or a percentage that represents coverage of the market. Internet planners want to know how many different people will be exposed to a banner or pop-up ad that is presented on a given website.

Planners often want to discuss audience sizes for more than one program. To do that, they simply add ratings or audience size numbers from each time the commercial is broadcast and disregard the duplication that results. The sum of ratings (percentages) is called *gross rating points (GRPs)*. The sum of audience sizes is called *gross impressions*. Both numbers are duplicated—that is, they are sums of measurements that can overlap.

Using gross rating points or gross impressions enables the planner to use a single number to describe the quantity of message weight. *Message weight* is a number that quickly tells the planner the duplicated audience for many programs within a given time period. Planners often deal with the number of gross rating points per week or per month. But one also can discuss the message weight of an entire year, using either gross rating points or gross impressions. The user of these numbers, however, must always remember that they represent duplicated audiences.

GRPs in Broadcast Media

In planning for television, gross rating points are often used to describe the message weight delivered each week or month, although they could be used for any number of weeks or months. Following is an example of commercials that constituted 90 gross rating points a week:

Two commercials each with a 15 rating	= 30 GRPs
Five commercials each with a 10 rating	= 50 GRPs
Two commercials each with a 5 rating	= 10 GRPs
Total weekly GRPs	= 90

For television planning, one might also want to know how many GRPs per month would be needed to attain a 70 reach. Appropriate tables and formulas are available for making such reach estimates once the number of GRPs is known.

GRPs in Other Media

In recent years, planners have extended the GRP concept to other media such as magazines, newspapers, and outdoor. In magazines, for example, gross rating points equal the percentage of market coverage of a target audience times the number of ad insertions, as in the following example:

People magazine's target reach of dieters: 21.3 percent
Number of ads to be placed in *People:* 5
Gross rating points (21.3 × 5): 106.5

Another way to use gross rating points for magazines (or newspapers) is to add the target coverage for one insertion in a number of magazines:

Women 25–54 coverage of *People*	26.1
Women 25–54 coverage of *Reader's Digest*	23.2
Women 25–54 coverage of *Shape*	5.3
Women 25–54 coverage of *New Yorker*	1.6
Total women 25–54 GRPs	56.2

One last way to calculate GRPs is to multiply reach times frequency for a given time period. For example, a schedule that reaches 60 percent of the target an average of five times will have 300 GRPs (60 × 5).

For outdoor, the Outdoor Advertising Association of America adopted as its basic unit of sale the term *100 gross rating points daily.* This basic standardized unit of poster sales is the number of poster panels required in each market to produce a "daily effective circulation" equal to the population of the market. Other units of sale are expressed as fractions of the basic unit: 75 gross rating points daily, 50 gross rating points daily, and 25 gross rating points daily. This change in no way alters the 30-day period of sale and measurement.

GROSS IMPRESSIONS

Gross impressions (or gross weight of media) are the raw numbers of media audiences, in duplicated form—that is, the same person can be counted more than once. The purpose of gross impression analysis is to get a quick look at the total audience size of one or more media, thus the gross weight of a plan. With this one number, a planner can make comparisons with other plans and other groups of vehicles that might have been selected. Gross impressions are an alternative to accumulated audience data, or reach, which shows the unduplicated audience size. Thus, gross impressions represent the weight of a select group of media vehicles.

There are two methods of finding gross impressions. One method is to multiply GRPs by a target audience base. For example, if a planner intended to buy 130 target GRPs a month (for men 18–49 in the United States), the planner would then multiply 1.3 by 61 million (the total U.S. universe of men 18–49). The product of these numbers is 79.3 million gross impressions.

The other method of calculating gross impressions is to add the target audience sizes delivered by each vehicle, as follows:

Program A	5,160,000	exposures
Program B	6,990,000	
Program C	4,320,000	
Program D	6,180,000	
Gross impressions	22,650,000	exposures (duplicated)

Another use of broadcast gross impressions might occur when someone wants to know the weight of nine commercials to be purchased on any one program. To calculate the gross impressions for nine commercials on Program A, multiply the number of commercials by the exposures for each. Using the previous example of Program A, the gross impressions for nine commercials would be $9 \times 5,160,000 = 46,440,000$.

In short, gross rating points or gross impressions are the simple sum of the ratings or impressions each time the ad appears. Because they do not account for duplication, gross rating points can, and frequently do, exceed 100. Heavy campaigns for fast-food restaurants, movies, and political campaigns often run well over 500 GRPs per week. The rating each time the commercial appears is added to the total points for the week.

The concept of GRPs is central to media planning because it is the basis for determining the cost of a broadcast campaign. In this example, if a planner wishes to run 100 GRPs per week, and if the cost is $2,000 per GRP, the cam-

EXHIBIT 5-1

Total Gross Impressions for Three Magazines

MAGAZINE	NUMBER OF TARGETS REACHED AT LEAST ONCE		NUMBER OF ADS TO BE PURCHASED		GROSS IMPRESSIONS
A	5,000,000	×	5	=	25,000,000
B	2,100,000	×	3	=	6,300,000
C	7,000,000	×	2	=	14,000,000
Total gross impressions					45,300,000

paign will cost the advertiser $200,000 per week (100 × $2,000). This will be discussed in more detail in Chapter 6.

The use of gross impressions for print media is much the same as it is for broadcast. Exhibit 5-1 shows how total gross impressions would be calculated for three magazines with varying numbers of ads to be purchased. The number of impressions delivered by a media plan usually runs into the millions. Because the number is so large, it is called a *boxcar figure*. (This expression is used from time to time to indicate that we are using big, coarse, crude measures of media "tonnage"—numbers so large as to be almost meaningless in human terms but impressive to the unsophisticated—like Carl Sagan's "billions and billions of stars.") Alone, gross impressions have limited meaning. But if they can be related to some measure of campaign effectiveness such as sales volume, brand awareness, or competitive media plan effectiveness, they can be used to compare media.

Gross impressions also are useful in comparing the weight given to geographic areas or demographic segments of a market. For example, if the planner wants to be sure a given media plan reaches a number of different geographic areas in the correct proportions, the gross impressions could be added for each vehicle in the plan, and then the proportions of each could be compared with a weighted goal. Exhibit 5-2 shows an example of how this works. This table indicates that the gross impression distribution of the vehicles selected comes fairly close to the goals set for the plan. It might not be worth the extra effort to make the gross impression totals come any closer to the stated goals.

Other impression analysis could have been made for targets by age, gender, income, or any other demographic segment desired.

EXHIBIT 5-2

Distribution of Gross Impressions in Media Plan for Brand X

COUNTY SIZE	GROSS IMPRESSIONS DELIVERED (000)				TARGET	GOAL FOR PLAN
	VEHICLE 1	VEHICLE 2	VEHICLE 3	TOTAL		
A	308,582	246,972	471,342	1,026,896	47.0%	51.0%
B	276,980	151,370	153,981	582,331	26.7	24.1
C	187,752	72,764	78,796	339,312	15.5	17.3
D	156,150	60,016	18,796	234,962	10.8	7.6
				2,183,501	100.0%	100.0%

REACH

Reach is a measurement of audience accumulation. Reach tells planners how many different prospects or households will see the ad at least once over any period of time the planner finds relevant. Reach is usually expressed as a percentage of a universe with whom a planner is trying to communicate. If the universe is women aged 18–49, then all women aged 18–49 represent the universe.

Note also that reach differs from GRPs because it is an unduplicated number—each person is counted only once. To understand the difference between GRPs and reach, consider that a popular weekly television program might have an average weekly rating of 30. Its four-week gross rating points are 120 (30 × 4 = 120). But the GRP statistic double-counts people who see the program several times. Reach takes out duplication to tell the planner how many *different* people will see the program at least once. The same television program could have a four-week reach of 65 percent (or 65). Reach, as a percent of the target, can never exceed 100 percent, while GRPs can continue building without limit.

Why Audience Is Counted Only Once

The reason audience members are counted only once in a reach measurement lies in the history of media research. When early planners were trying to decide which kind of measurement to use to count the size of a vehicle's audience, some believed an audience member would have to be exposed several times to a vehicle before ads would have any effect. Other planners disagreed, saying it could not be known how many exposures would be required. Planners decided to compromise and count one exposure to a vehicle as evidence of reach, because whether or not the ad was seen, there was a significant difference between being exposed and not being exposed. To be exposed at least once means that audiences then had an opportunity to see ads within the vehicle. There obviously would be no opportunity to see ads if there were no exposure.

Another historical reason for the development of reach concerned the invention of a statistic for radio and television that would parallel the audience reach of a monthly magazine. Planners realized it would be unfair to compare a one-week broadcast rating with the reach of a monthly issue of a magazine. Obviously, the magazine reach would be higher, but by using a four-week reach for broadcast media, the planner now had a statistic that was fairly comparable to that of a monthly magazine in terms of audience size.

Exhibit 5-3 illustrates the measurement of reach using a sample of 10 persons. The sample size for measuring reach is actually much larger, but using 10 simplifies the concept. Four weeks is the usual measuring period, but reach can be measured for almost any period of time. Four weeks happens to have become a standard measuring unit, easily conforming to a monthly accounting period.

Exhibit 5-3 is interpreted this way: Viewers 3, 5, 8, and 9 saw the program in week 1, so the one-week rating is 40 percent (4 out of 10). Because viewers are counted only once, the one-week reach is the same as the one-week rating. In week 2, only one new person was added to the audience (Viewer 7), so the second-week rating was 10 and the two-week reach was 50 (or 40 for week 1 and 10 for week 2). In week 3, only one new viewer was added (Viewer 6), so the rating was 10, but the three-week reach was 60. In week 4, again, only one new viewer was added (Viewer 10), and the four-week reach was 70. Note that Viewers 3, 5, 6, and 9 viewed the program more than once in the four-week period but were counted only once for the purpose of calculating reach. Also note that the one-week rating is unduplicated, so it would be correct to call that rating the one-week reach, although common practice usually refers to it as a rating.

EXHIBIT 5-3

A Four-Week Reach Measurement for Program X

VIEWER	WEEK 1	WEEK 2	WEEK 3	WEEK 4
1	—	—	—	—
2	—	—	—	—
3	$\oplus$	×	—	×
4	—	—	—	—
5	$\oplus$	—	×	—
6	—	—	$\oplus$	×
7	—	$\oplus$	×	—
8	$\oplus$	—	—	—
9	$\oplus$	×	—	×
10	—	—	—	$\oplus$
Ratings each week	40	30	30	40

For a weekly evening program: × = Viewed the program;
$\oplus$ = Counted only in reach measurement.
GRPs = 140, reach = 70, frequency = 2.

Kinds of Reach

There are two ways of looking at reach in broadcast planning:

1. The four-week reach of an individual vehicle, such as a television program
2. More commonly, the combined reach of four or five television programs that would be bought as a single package in an ad campaign

No matter which kind of reach the planner is interested in, the same principle applies, namely, that audience members are counted only once, no matter how many times they see the vehicle within a four-week period. If four television programs are being considered for one campaign package, some audience members will be exposed three or four times to only one television program, and other audience members will be exposed to all four television programs a different number of times. But if they see any one of the four programs at least once, they are counted as having been reached in a four-week period. In either case, the concept of exposure is the same. We don't know whether those exposed to the vehicle saw the ads (or our ads), so we can only say that *reach* means "opportunities to see" ads, not ad exposure.

Suppose, for example, the reach of four programs was 35 million men aged 18–34. If the planner places a commercial in each of the four television programs, it is estimated that 35 million men aged 18–34 will have an opportunity to see at least one of those four vehicles and, the planner hopes, one of the four commercials within the vehicle. The word *hope* is a reminder that reach is concerned only with vehicle exposure, not ad exposure. Other measurements can provide ad exposure, but they are not yet available on a syndicated basis.

Exhibit 5-4 shows how to calculate the reach of four television programs. Six homes viewed one of the four programs at least once in the measured week.

EXHIBIT 5-4

Reach/Frequency of a TV Schedule

	"WHO WANTS TO BE A MILLIONAIRE" 12/17 8:05 P.M.	"JUDGING AMY" 12/18 10:14 P.M.	"SURVIVOR: AFRICA" 12/20 8:23 P.M.	"ER" 12/20 10:45 P.M.	TOTAL IMPRESSIONS
🏠		✓	✓		2
🏠					0
🏠				✓	1
🏠	✓	✓	✓		3
🏠	✓			✓	2
🏠			✓		1
🏠					0
🏠	✓		✓		2
🏠					0
🏠					0
Rating	30%	20%	40%	20%	0 × 40%
GRPs	30	50	90	110	1 × 20%
Reach	30%	40%	50%	60%	2 × 30%
Frequency	1.0	1.25	1.8	1.8	3+ × 10%

A home or person is counted only once, regardless of how many programs were viewed. Therefore, the first home has received two impressions (one from "Judging Amy" and one from "Survivor: Africa") but is counted only once toward reach. The second home didn't see any of the telecasts. The third home was exposed once, the fourth home three times, and so on. At the end of the one-week schedule of four telecasts, 6 of the 10 homes have been reached one or more times. Other terms that are sometimes used to describe the net reach of four television programs are *cumulative audience, audience accumulated by four television programs,* and *net unduplicated audience.* Each term is correct, but in popular usage people are more likely to say, "The reach of these four programs is 60 percent." Note how GRPs and reach increase with each telecast. *Average frequency* (the number of times the average home saw a commercial) is calculated as GRPs/reach.

Relationship of Reach to Coverage

It can be confusing to know whether to use the term *coverage* or *reach* when referring to audience accumulation data. The terms can be interchangeable because coverage sometimes is synonymous with reach. A better answer is that coverage and reach are quite different, because coverage could mean potential to be exposed to the advertising, and reach refers to those people who actually are exposed.

Popular usage of these terms provides the basic answer. Coverage usually refers to potential audience for broadcast media and to actual delivered audience for print media. Reach always refers to the audience actually delivered by any advertising vehicle. Exhibit 5-5 summarizes the distinction.

How Reach Builds over Time

Reach for television programs accumulates, or builds, in a fairly consistent pattern over time as a commercial is broadcast over and over again. The first time a commercial is telecast, it accumulates the largest number of viewers. The second time it is telecast, most of the viewers are repeat viewers, although some new viewers are added. The third and subsequent telecasts accumulate even fewer new viewers. Exhibit 5-6 shows the classic pattern of diminishing returns in accumulation of reach as a commercial is repeated and GRPs are added.

EXHIBIT 5-5

How to Use the Terms *Reach* and *Coverage*

Use *Reach* to express a whole number or percentage of different people actually exposed only once to a media vehicle or combination of vehicles.

EXAMPLE: Television program X reaches 9 million men aged 18–34 within a four-week period.

EXAMPLE: Magazine Y has a reach of 25 percent of men aged 18–34 with an average issue.

Use *Coverage* to express the potential audience of a broadcast medium *or* the actual audience of a print medium exposed only once.

EXAMPLE: A network television program has a coverage of 95 percent of TV homes in the United States.

EXAMPLE: Magazine Y has a 25 percent coverage of men aged 18–34. (Means the same as *reach*.)

EXHIBIT 5-6

Relationship Between GRPs and Reach in Prime Time

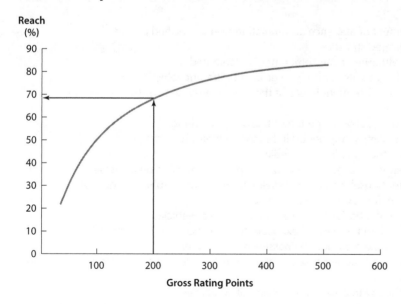

SOURCE: True North Communications, Reach-2000.

In this illustration, after 200 GRPs have been delivered, approximately 68 percent of viewers will have seen the commercial at least once. Does reach ever level out over a year? No. The curve is never perfectly horizontal, but it comes close after about 3,000 GRPs.

Reach in Print Media

Whereas time is the basic measuring unit for reach in broadcast media, in print media the basic unit of reach is an issue of a magazine or newspaper. One does not usually speak of the four-week reach of a magazine, although there are measurements that estimate audience accumulation over time for an average issue of a magazine. Generally speaking, monthly magazines have a longer issue life than weeklies, and general-content magazines have a longer life than news-oriented magazines.

EXHIBIT 5-7

Meaning of *Reach,* Summarized

Reach is
 1. A measurement of audience accumulation over a specified period
 2. An unduplicated statistic
 3. Measured, although it can sometimes be estimated
 4. Measured for a single vehicle or a group of different vehicles
 5. Measured for subsequent issues of the same magazine (e.g., the seven-issue reach of *TV Guide* is . . .)
 6. Reported for a four-week period of television watching
 7. Reported for almost any period in broadcast measurements
 8. Reported by the issue in print media
 9. Reported either as a raw number or as a percentage of some universe
10. Reported for households or for individuals in a demographic category
11. Another term for *coverage* in print media
12. Measured on the basis of exposure to a vehicle or vehicles
13. Not measured on the basis of exposure to ads in vehicles, but commercial exposure is expected to be measured by passive people meters
14. A measurement that tells how many different people had an opportunity to see ads in vehicles
15. A media strategy that shows dispersion of audiences

Magazine reach can be expressed in a number of ways:

- Audience reach of one issue of a magazine (e.g., reach of the July 1 issue of *Newsweek*—also called the *total audience* of *Newsweek*)
- Target audience reach of multiple issues of the same magazine (e.g., the reach—or *net unduplicated audience*—of the July 1, July 8, July 15, July 22, and July 29 issues of *Newsweek*)
- Target audience reach of single issues of different magazines within the same month (e.g., the reach—or net unduplicated audience—of July issues of *Redbook, Ladies' Home Journal, Reader's Digest,* and *TV Guide*)
- The reach of single or multiple issues of different magazines occurring throughout the advertising campaign (e.g., the reach of *Popular Mechanics* in June and August, *Field & Stream* in July and August, and *Sport* in June and July)

Because a reach measurement can express many qualities, knowing them all becomes important. Exhibit 5-7 summarizes these qualities.

FREQUENCY

Frequency is a companion statistic to reach. It tells the planner the average number of times that audience members were exposed to a broadcast program within a four-week period or were exposed to issues of different print media. Reach is a measure of *message dispersion,* indicating how widely the message is received in a target universe. Frequency is a measure of *repetition,* indicating to what extent audience members were exposed to the same vehicle or group of vehicles. Both reach and frequency are valuable decision-making tools, because they give the media planner different options for arranging message delivery in a media plan.

Frequency is usually calculated from measurement data. The formula is the same for broadcast and print media:

$$\text{Frequency} = \frac{\text{GRPs or total duplicated audience}}{\text{Reach}}$$

Let's apply this to an example in broadcast. Suppose a commercial is telecast once each week on a program that has an average rating of 20 for each week. It has a four-week reach of 43. (Note that this number comes from Nielsen research or computer models; it cannot be calculated by hand.) The average frequency is calculated by finding GRPs and using that value in the equation:

$$GRP = rating \times number\ of\ telecasts$$

$$GRP = 20 \times 4 = 80$$

$$Frequency = \frac{80\ GRPs}{43\ reach} = 1.9$$

This means that some people saw only one of the four telecasts, other people saw all four of them, and the average person saw the commercial 1.9 times, or almost twice.

For print, the calculations are similar. Suppose Magazine Y has a reach of 54 for six consecutive issues. Its one-issue reach (average issue audience) is 29.5. First calculate GRPs, then use that value to find average frequency:

$$GRP = 29.5 \times 6 = 177$$

$$Frequency = \frac{177\ GRPs}{54\ reach} = 3.3$$

Again, the average issue audience (29.5) and the six-issue reach (sometimes called "cumulative audience" or "cume") (54) come from computer models and cannot be estimated by hand. Also, because reach is an estimate, it is usually displayed as a whole number.

Frequency Distribution

Media planners who use measurement data sometimes forget that frequency is an average, not an absolute number. It is subject, therefore, to the characteristics of all statistical averages. Averages, for example, are affected by extreme scores in a distribution. A few very high numbers can bring up the average of the scores, and a few very low ones can drag down the average. The only way to guard against being deceived by a frequency statistic is to look at a frequency distribu-

EXHIBIT 5-8

Quintile Analysis of Tune-Ins for Program X

DIVISIONS OF VIEWER SAMPLE	REACH	FREQUENCY	GRPs
Heaviest 20%	17%	11	187
Next 20%	17	6	102
Third 20%	17	5	85
Next 20%	17	3	51
Lightest 20%	17	1	17
Totals*	85%	5.2 avg.	442

*Reach of entire sample, 85; frequency of entire sample, 5.2; gross rating points, 442.

tion and see whether some segments of a sample are getting disproportionately more frequency than others.

Exhibit 5-8 shows a sample divided into fixed quintiles and each group's reach and frequency. (*Fixed quintiles* means that the sample of audience members exposed was divided into five equal groups, each with 20 percent of the total number exposed.) The distribution of frequency is obviously unequal in Exhibit 5-8. Some of the quintiles received much more frequency than others. This phenomenon is known as *skew*.

Exhibit 5-9 dramatizes the skew by showing the frequency distribution in graphic form. Daily Program X had a 5.2 average frequency, but some segments were receiving more frequency than others. The average frequency of 5.2 does not indicate the disparity. The planner could be deceived by the average frequency level of Program X, thinking every home in the sample tuned to the program 5.2 times during a four-week period. The illustration shows otherwise. Frequency distributions with a large skew are called *unbalanced*.

Frequency distributions can be arranged according to quintiles, but they can also be arranged according to single increments of exposure, giving the planner a more detailed picture of exposure. Exhibit 5-10 shows a frequency distribution of exposure for all media in a given plan. Subtracting the number reached from the universe size shows that 8,227,000 of the universe of 29,356,000 did not see any of the vehicles used. Some 3,125,000 were exposed only once out of the 12 opportunities for exposure, and 2,269,000 were exposed

EXHIBIT 5-9

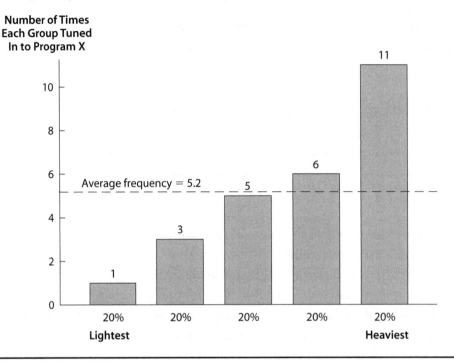

Frequency Distribution for Program X

**Number of Times
Each Group Tuned
In to Program X**

to any 2 out of the 12 exposures. The number exposed at any frequency is un-duplicated, meaning that these people are counted only once. A person receiving 12 exposures would not be counted at any other frequency level.

Frequency distributions therefore provide planners with a method of determining the pattern of repetition that the plan provides. Alternative plans will provide more or fewer repetition patterns. More important, however, is that the distribution will show whether repetition is spread widely or among only a very few prospects.

The example in Exhibit 5-11 shows how a frequency distribution can help a media planner decide among alternative plans. Plan A has a 4.0 average frequency, and Plan B a 3.6. If the frequency is important, then Plan A would seem to be the better plan.

EXHIBIT 5-10

Frequency Distribution of a Media Plan

		FREQUENCY OF EXPOSURE	NUMBER EXPOSED (000)
Reach	72%	0	8,227
Frequency	4.01	1	3,125
Gross impressions	84,749	2	2,269
Number reached	21,129	3	3,632
Universe	29,356	4	5,236
		5	2,474
		6	1,201
		7	1,462
		8	771
		9	622
		10	135
Calculations		11	104
$21,129 \div 29,356 = 72\%$		12	98
$84,749 \div 21,129 = 4.01$			21,129

EXHIBIT 5-11

Four-Week Reaches and Frequencies of Two Media Plans

FREQUENCY OF EXPOSURE	PLAN A	PLAN B	
1	24%	20%	
2	16	15	
3	9 ⎫	12 ⎫	
4–5	6 ⎪	13 ⎪	
6–8	5 ⎬ 30%	10 ⎬ 40%	3+ reach
9–12	5 ⎪	4 ⎪	
13+	5 ⎭	1 ⎭	
Average frequency	4.0	3.6	
Total reach	70%	75%	
Reach at 3+ frequency	30%	40%	

Upon studying a frequency distribution such as the one in Exhibit 5-11, however, the planner learns something that could change the decision: Plan A delivers more audience members at exposure levels 1 and 2, but for exposures 3 through 8, Plan B is superior. Plan B reaches more persons than does Plan A at the 3-or-higher exposure level. If the advertising effort requires that people receive high levels of exposure (higher frequency), then Plan B is the obvious choice. Approximately 75 percent of the target will see the commercial at least once, while 40 percent will see it three or more times.

Relationship of Reach to Frequency

It is necessary to understand that reach and frequency occur at the same time but at different rates and in an inverse relationship. Within a given number of gross rating points, as one goes up, the other goes down. To understand how these companion terms relate to each other, let us first look at the mathematics:

$$\text{Reach} \times \text{Frequency} = \text{Gross Rating Points}$$

According to this equation, an advertising schedule composed of a 50 reach with a 2.0 frequency yields 100 GRPs. If these same 100 GRPs were obtained in a different mixture of media, the reach might increase, but the frequency would decline. Conversely, a 100 GRP schedule in still other media mixtures might produce higher frequency, but less reach.

In a classic explanation, Seymour Banks, formerly vice president of Leo Burnett Company, discussed the dynamics of reach and frequency relative to rating size and number of telecasts:

> Reach is not directly proportional to either ratings or the number of telecasts. Rather, as ratings increase or as the number of telecasts used increases, reach also rises but at a decreasing rate. This is more easily understood when we consider that the companion of reach is frequency. And when the rating or the number of telecasts increases, some of this increase goes towards boosting reach, while some of it contributes to an increase in frequency.[1]

---

1. Seymour Banks, "How to Estimate Reach and Frequency" (Leo Burnett Company, 1960): 5.

Up to a certain point, it is relatively easy to build reach. By selecting different dayparts in which to place commercials, it is possible to reach different kinds of people. But there is a point of diminishing returns, where each attempt to build more reach by selecting more and different kinds of programs results in reaching the same persons over and over again, with an increase in frequency rather than in reach. Some homes may never tune in their television sets over an entire month, so they are impossible to reach with TV in that month. Reach will increase as ratings and number of telecasts increase, but it will begin to decline in rate (not total) over time.

The point of diminishing returns can be seen in Exhibit 5-12, which illustrates reach accumulation among women 25–54. It shows, for example, that when 500 GRPs are split evenly among prime time, late fringe, cable, and syndication, the plan will reach 85 percent of target women one or more times.

EXHIBIT 5-12

Effective Reach Versus GRPs and Cost

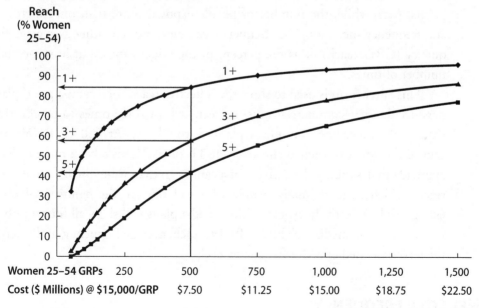

Women 25–54 GRPs	250	500	750	1,000	1,250	1,500
Cost ($ Millions) @ $15,000/GRP	$7.50	$11.25	$15.00	$18.75	$22.50

SOURCE: True North Communications, Reach-2000.

This includes 59 percent of target women who are reached three or more times, and 42 percent five or more times. We see that 1+ reach rises rapidly until about 400 GRPs (80 percent reach), and that additional weight beyond this point produces proportionately less reach and more frequency. The percent exposed 3+ and 5+ times continues to rise, but at some point, these curves too will flatten out in the same manner as the 1+ curve.

The challenge for planners comes when they must relate the desired reach to the cost of buying the GRPs necessary to achieve that reach. In Chapter 3 we discussed the concept of cost per rating point (CPP). In this example, the average cost per women 25–54 rating point is $15,000, with weight split equally among prime time, late fringe, cable, and syndication. Using this price, it will cost $15 million to buy 1,000 points. Note that the CPP and the shape of the reach curves are different for each demographic target and daypart.

To summarize, reach and frequency are inversely related, but at a changing rate. When a campaign starts out, very few people have seen the advertising. Each new telecast reaches mostly people who have never seen it before, and reach rises quickly. As the campaign becomes more mature, there are fewer and fewer new prospects to expose. Reach rises more slowly with additional rating points. Meanwhile, the number of people exposed more than once increases, and frequency increases. That frequency can be expressed either as average frequency (GRPs/reach) or as the percent of the target exposed at least a certain number of times.

This latter form is used to show the "effective reach" of a campaign. If planners decide their commercial must be seen at least three times to be effective, then in the preceding example, a planner would say, "At 500 GRPs, 59 percent of the target is reached effectively at 3+ times." This takes a more realistic approach to describing the delivery of a campaign than using the 85 percent 1+ reach, which includes many people who will not see the commercial often enough to be effectively exposed. Most media plans will show all four numbers when describing media weight: GRPs, 1+ reach, average frequency, and reach at the recommended effective frequency level.

EFFECTIVE FREQUENCY

Effective frequency can be defined as the amount of frequency (or repetition) the planner judges to be necessary for advertisements to be effective in communicating. The underlying assumption, of course, is that the average frequency statistic used in most media plans does not tell enough about a plan's delivery to be useful. Therefore, effective frequency can represent a great improvement over ordinary reach and frequency numbers used in traditionally created media plans.

The problem with ordinary reach and frequency is that they are not directly related to the effects that media plans produce. They do not help a planner determine the adequacy of alternative plans. An ordinary reach number simply represents opportunities for audiences to see advertisements. There is no guarantee that those who are reached actually see any of the ads, because exposure measurements used to compare media do not cover exposure to ads. Furthermore, even if audiences see ads in a vehicle, the reach of a media plan does not provide a way to know whether the ads were effective. Ordinary frequency generated by a plan is the average number of times the target audience is exposed to the media vehicles selected. Average frequency, too, is not related to the plan's effectiveness.

But planners who use effective frequency attempt to correct both situations by estimating the number of repetitions that are needed to attain communication goals. Those goals might be achieving brand awareness, attitude changes, brand switching, and recall of messages, to name a few. If, for example, someone sets a communication goal of building 70 percent brand awareness, a media planner should ask, "How much repetition will help accomplish the task?" Through test marketing or studying responses to advertising done in the past, the planner can estimate the vehicle frequency level needed. One unusual aspect of estimating effective frequency is that this technique for media planning differs from those used in the past.

In the first place, building brand awareness is usually thought to be a communication goal, not a media goal. Therefore, by using effective frequency, planners are enlarging the scope of their work, combining media and creative activities. That combination in itself is a relatively new idea in media planning.

Second, planners rarely have data by which to determine objectively how much repetition is necessary to accomplish the task. As a result, the planner might have to base decisions on either experience or specialized research. If experience is the basis for the answer, then it will be rather subjective, because it is difficult to parse out a media vehicle's contribution to building brand awareness. If research is used to find the answer to the awareness problem, then the effort will take time and money. Furthermore, the result might not be conclusive, because it is difficult to prove that research findings apply to all plans equally.

The key point is that it is difficult to prove the relationship between effective frequency and a goal of 70 percent brand awareness. The relationship is subtle, not a simple cause-and-effect relationship.

Response Curves and Effective Frequency

The number at which frequency can be called "effective" depends on ideas of how much repetition is needed to communicate with consumers. Media planners find or estimate this number by observing what happens at varying repetitive levels. The analysis is common for Internet advertising, where the number of exposures delivered to a given computer and the resulting click-throughs are easy to track. It is much more difficult to observe for traditional media.

Over many years, practitioners have hypothesized about how advertising works. Most believe that advertising does not work immediately. According to Herbert Krugman, author of the "three hit" theory, audiences may respond to their first perception of an advertisement by raising questions about the brand, such as, "What is it?" After audiences have perceived the same ad a second time, they will ask, "What of it?" On the second exposure, then, consumers react to the commercial and begin to compare alternative brands. The third exposure is a reminder of the other two and the beginning of a time where consumers pay little or no attention. Krugman hypothesized that when audiences are in the market to buy a product, they will respond to that second repetition. Therefore, effective frequency begins after the second repetition, but only when a consumer is ready to buy a given product. Many other practitioners have hypothesized that audiences begin to respond to advertising at about the third repetition. Beginning with the third repetition, the number of responses begins to grow with each additional repetition, but at a declining rate. If this hypothesis is plotted on a graph, it will have an S shape (see Exhibit 5-13). The first two repetitions are a threshold that audiences have to pass before advertisements become effective.

However, most researchers of advertising response curves have not found the S-shaped curve to occur very often. In fact, they have more often measured a different kind of curve, often called a convex curve (see Exhibit 5-14). Many

EXHIBIT 5-13

S-Shaped Response Curve

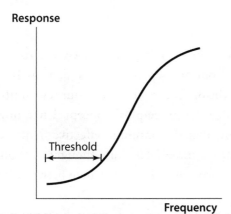

EXHIBIT 5-14

Convex Response Curve

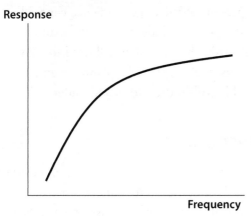

media planners who have adopted the concept of effective frequency believe that a convex curve represents a graphical picture of how repetition works in advertising. This curve is similar to the reach accumulation curve in Exhibits 5-6 and 5-12.

Effective-Frequency Numbers

Effective frequency is expressed as the number of exposures necessary to produce an effect. This number can vary from one repetition to as many as 10 or more. Some planners, at first, thought the optimum effective frequency number was always three or more. This was called the "three-plus" concept. Later, however, there was much greater agreement that the optimum effective frequency could be as low as one or as high as nine (or more). They also thought the number could actually be a range, such as a frequency level anywhere between two and seven.

To date, this question has not been resolved, and more research on response functions will be needed to settle the argument. In the meantime, planners must rely on their judgment to decide what the effective frequency level should be. This will be discussed in more detail in Chapter 6.

Effective Reach: The Other Side of the Coin

Once an effective-frequency level has been decided on, the planner needs to know *effective reach*—that is, the percent of the target audience exposed at the frequency level that is effective in the planner's judgment. If the planner thinks three exposures is enough to be effective, then the plan will need to show what percent of the target is exposed at this level. Typically, a planner wants to reach as many people at this level as possible within the authorized budget.

BRIEF HISTORY OF EFFECTIVE FREQUENCY

To this point, effective frequency has been discussed as a simple numerical concept. In fact, it relates to the far subtler question, How many times does a person need to see an ad before "getting" the message? The answer depends on the nature of the product, the creative message, the advertising objectives, the medium being used, and a wide variety of other marketing factors. But in the end, the answer requires a judgment, because it really depends on what happens in the mind of the target consumer. Over the years, numerous research studies have been conducted to help planners make this judgment. The two most important are Michael Naples's seminal work on effective frequency and the current Recency/Shelf Space Model of Media Planning.

Naples Study

Probably the greatest impetus to establishing the concept in the United States was the publication of *Effective Frequency: The Relationship Between Frequency and Advertising Awareness,* by Michael J. Naples.[2] Published by the Association of National Advertisers, this book became required reading for almost every U.S. planner. The concept spread throughout the media departments of U.S. advertising agencies and is still widely used.

After presenting many research studies that supported the idea of effective frequency, Naples arrived at some conclusions about the implications for media planners:

- One exposure of an advertisement to a target consumer group (within a purchase cycle) has little or no effect.
- Because one exposure is usually ineffective, the main thrust of media planning should be on emphasizing frequency rather than reach.
- Most of the research studies suggested that two exposures within a purchase cycle are an effective threshold level.
- Three exposures within a purchase cycle, however, are felt to be optimal.
- After three exposures within a purchasing cycle, advertising becomes more effective as frequency is increased, but at a decreasing rate. If this were drawn on a graph, it would appear as a convex curve rising from a zero point.
- Wear-out of an advertising campaign is not caused by too much frequency per se. It is caused by copy and content problems.

---

2. Michael J. Naples, *Effective Frequency* (New York: Association of National Advertisers Inc., 1979).

- Generally, small and less-known brands will benefit most from increased frequency. Larger, well-known brands might or might not be helped by increasing frequency, depending on how close they are to advertising saturation levels.
- Different dayparts on television are affected by different frequency levels. A similar idea applies to thin versus thick magazines, with the thinner ones having better response effects than the thicker ones.
- Frequency responses are affected by the amount of money an advertiser spends as a percentage of the product category total. Brands with the greatest proportion of exposures within their categories should also gain great effect when frequency is increased.
- The responses due to increased frequency are not affected by different media. What is true for one medium is true for others.
- Each brand might require a different level of frequency of exposure. One cannot generalize from a given brand's experiences to some other brand. Specialized research is required to find the unique frequency level for a brand.
- Two brands spending the same amount of money for advertising can have different responses to their frequencies.[3]

Questions Regarding Effective-Frequency Research

As time has passed, planners have challenged this effective-frequency research. These concerns are summarized and discussed in the following paragraphs.

Is There a Need for Product Category Differentiation?   One major problem of effective-frequency research was that most of it failed to show much difference between frequency effects for various product categories. This lack of differentiation tended to mislead planners into thinking that effective frequency is the same for all product categories. Now a growing number of planners are saying this idea cannot be correct. Frequency levels should vary from one product category to another.

---

3. Naples, *Effective Frequency,* 63–82.

Unfortunately, no measurements exist to show just which levels are needed for different kinds of products. Until this problem is resolved, media planners will have to make subjective decisions about how much frequency is enough. There is, however, some speculation that high-involvement products need less frequency and low-involvement products need more. The same idea applies to frequency levels of interesting and uninteresting products. The role of frequency, then, might be to help break through consumers' perceptual inertia for certain kinds of products.

Is There a Threshold?   Another problem with the concept is determining whether a threshold exists before consumers begin to respond to advertising messages. Most of the research on the subject has suggested there are relatively few responses to the first few impressions of an advertising campaign. Advertising in these studies began to work with the second or third impression. Those who believed in the three-plus frequency concept believed that advertising began to be effective with the third impression. But many direct-marketing practitioners objected, noting that in their business, the first impressions often drew tremendous responses. Gus Priemer, then director of advertising service and media at S. C. Johnson & Son, Inc., also noted that in his experience of new-product introductions, the first impression had been able to generate noteworthy responses.

Attendees to a "Symposium on Effective Frequency" held in April 1986 at Northwestern University also questioned whether a threshold was realistic. The consensus at that meeting was that most response curves are convex, not S-shaped. The S-shaped curve was the one that indicated there was a threshold. Nevertheless, many planners still believe in a threshold.

What Is the Relationship Between Good Advertising and Effective Frequency?   A great many questions have been asked about whether effective frequency could be influenced by the quality of advertising messages. Why, for example, should the ad message not play a more important role in determining how much frequency is effective? Dull, uninteresting copy could require a great deal more frequency than scintillating creative messages. But most of the research did not address that question. In fact, some planners believe that the role of media frequency in bringing about consumer response has been grossly overstated.

Does Advertising Wear Out When There Is Too Much Frequency?   Some of the research cited by Naples showed that negative responses occurred after using too much repetition. Some consumers will even forget an advertising message if frequency is too high. The research of Valentine Appel and L. Jacobovits (also reported in Naples's book) suggests that the shape of a wear-out curve looks like an inverted U. But among media planners, there seems to be no wide-ranging concern about this potential problem.

The effective-frequency concept for media planners relates most importantly to this point: How much media vehicle frequency is necessary to achieve the advertising exposure frequencies found in most of the research studies? Radio and television ratings and magazine audience exposures represent only exposures to vehicles. To go beyond vehicle frequency, we need research that either relates vehicle frequency to advertising frequency or directly shows the effects of vehicle exposure frequency to a given response. Some research studies have tried to do the latter, but more research is necessary.

Recency and the Shelf-Space Model of Media Planning

The most recent industry review of the subject came at an Effective Frequency Research Day, conducted by the Advertising Research Foundation in November 1994 and from which the following highlights were drawn.[4] Using Nielsen Household Panel data from the early 1990s, Professor John Philip Jones of Syracuse University challenged the conventional wisdom that 3+ exposures are necessary for an ad to be effective. He said, instead, "Effective frequency is provided by a single exposure . . . one exposure generates the highest proportion of sales."

Although Jones found differences from one campaign to another in the incremental effectiveness of the second, third, and subsequent exposures, in all cases the first exposure had the largest effect on sales. He concluded, "Additional

---

4. "Effective Frequency Research Day Proceedings," Advertising Research Foundation, November 2, 1994.

exposures add very little to the effect of the first." Media consultant Erwin Ephron expressed the concept more colloquially:

> If you tell a kid, "Remember to wash your hands before each meal" three times at 11 A.M., you are using frequency to teach. If you tell him once, right before dinner, you're using presence to remind. A reminder at the right time is a more effective way to influence behavior.
>
> Being there with a message for the consumer who is ready-to-buy, and being there continuously is what I call "presence." The media equivalent of "renting the shelf" . . . not being there with a message when the consumer is ready-to-buy is the advertising equivalent of being out of stock—which is why I call this the "shelf-space model of media planning."

Ephron relates this concept to media planning. Each week of the year, people are shopping and buying, and they should be exposed to a brand's message. Therefore, media plans should be evaluated in terms of weekly reach points delivered. The familiar convex curve of "diminishing returns" shows that reach builds rapidly at first, but beyond a certain point, additional GRPs yield mostly (wasted) frequency. Ephron compares two ways of scheduling 2,600 GRPs:

Plan 1
100 GRPs/week for 26 weeks
Weekly reach: 50 percent
Total reach points: $26 \times 50 = 1{,}300$

Plan 2
67 GRPs/week for 39 weeks
Weekly reach: 40 percent
Total reach points: $39 \times 40 = 1{,}560$

Both plans cost the same, and both deliver about 2,600 total GRPs, but Plan 2 delivers 20 percent more weekly reach points. Thus, according to Ephron, it is the most effective way to schedule weight—*if* we assume one hit is enough.

The recency model would suggest that consistent advertising is preferable to concentrating weight in flights. Taken to the extreme, the planner would simply divide the available budget by 52 weeks, then purchase as many GRPs per week as the budget permits. But this approach runs up against the long-standing threshold belief that a minimum number of GRPs per week is necessary to be effective. A study of media plans by Helen Johnston, vice president and director of media analysis at Grey Advertising, found minimum levels in the range of 70 to 100 GRPs per week:

> There was no relationship to budget. All planners felt there was a level below which advertising would be ineffective. Compromises were affected by limiting hiatus lengths. The average hiatus was 2.7 weeks, and there was an average of 7.6 hiatuses. As a result, only the richest brands attained true continuity or 52 weeks of advertising. . . .
>
> In summary, planners have a formidable task of weighing alternatives when they schedule media. Our task is not to persuade them of the importance of continuity. They fully appreciate that importance. However, they believe continuity to be an ideal that is beyond their brand's means.[5]

Summary

It should be clear by now that there is no simple answer to these "How much is enough?" questions of effective frequency, flighting versus continuity, minimum GRP levels, maximum hiatus weeks, response function shape, and the like. Research can provide guidance, but in the end, planners must use judgment to apply these general findings from the past to specific plans for the future.

---

5. Helen Johnston, "Research and Media Scheduling," *Journal of Advertising Research,* Nov./Dec. 1995: RC2–4.

CHAPTER SIX

Marketing Strategy and Media Planning

There are many ways to start the media-planning process, but the best way is by analyzing the situation of a brand in the marketplace. The reason for making such an analysis is to learn how successful a brand has been against its competition, with the objective of finding opportunity areas to exploit or problem areas to correct. Ultimately, the findings of a situation analysis should lead to the establishment of marketing objectives and strategies, which in turn lead to the establishment of media objectives and strategies.

Although the responsibility for conducting a marketing situation analysis seldom rests with a media planner, someone from the agency's media department, such as a media researcher, is often involved to some extent in the research activities. Media planners often are involved in the marketing situation analysis, particularly an examination of the consumer, the competitive weight, and geographic and seasonal sales.

WHAT A MEDIA PLANNER NEEDS TO KNOW

Every media plan is built around a brand's most important marketing problem. That's what marketing plans exist for: as a prelude to media-marketing planning. Other research about competitors and the market itself will be done later. However, recognizing the main problem is a problem in itself. Problems can come in all degrees of importance for a brand of product or service. If many interrelated problems are facing a planner, finding a solution could require a detailed situation analysis.

To help a brand achieve solutions, a planner must do a number of things. A good first step is to carry out a situation analysis. The following examples illustrate a few of the problems that could be critical for media planning:

117

- Sales are declining in the Southwest for Brand X.
- Consumers like Brand B better in the Southwest because they say it is lighter.
- The newest brand on the market has reduced its price below ours in the Southwest.
- The kinds of people who formerly used our brand have switched to Brand D.

Once the main problems have been identified, other details of the situation analysis should be decided on. Each can help the planner make significant decisions.

Along with the main problems, planners need to assess other elements of marketing, such as product quality, product uses, pricing, distribution methods, packaging, sales promotion use, personal selling activities, public relations, and advertising. From a practical standpoint, the planner does not need to know every detail, but only those items that are thought to contribute to product sales. These are elements of a situation analysis.

SITUATION ANALYSIS

A *situation analysis* is research prepared in document format to provide the background for a media planner to prepare a plan. It provides perspective on where a brand has been and where its potential lies in the future. Here are essential parts of a situation analysis:

- **History of the market.** This deals with sales of all brands in the market, including the brand for which planning is to be done. The analysis includes geographic sales distribution, market size in dollars and units, market shares, seasonal effects, and price effects. The goal is to find out where brands are now in terms of market share and how they got there. An important item, for example, might be pricing history. What happened to prices for various brands over the years, and how did these price manipulations affect sales? Another concern might be an analysis of cost history and profit related to sales, both for the brand under consideration and for competitors' brands, if known.

- **Distribution channels.** The objective here is to learn how a brand and its competitors distribute products. This includes the following information about each distribution channel: shelf-facings, inventories held, out-of-stock situations, methods of selling, display and advertising allowances, and how and why promotions are used. Problems of selling are sometimes caused by poor distribution, not advertising. Distribution information often affects media strategy because it can help the planner decide where to advertise.

- **Consumer of the product.** A profile of users of the generic product type includes personal demographics such as age, sex, income, and occupation, as well as geographic location. *Psychographics*—lifestyles and attitudes—also should be included. A consumer profile of those who buy a specific brand versus those who buy competing products is important as well. Buying habits also should be analyzed in terms of when products are purchased; in which kind of retail outlets; and which sizes, models, and colors are purchased most often. How and when consumers use these products also should be known. Finally, it would be helpful to know about the buyer, the user, and the persons who motivate buyers and users. All of this information helps the media planner select targets for media.

- **Product.** A history of the product and how it was developed is included in the product section of the analysis. When and why product changes were made and the effects of such changes on each competitive brand could be important. Consumer perceptions of the values of various brands also are important background information for the media planner.

- **Advertising and media analysis.** Probably the most important information for a media planner is an analysis of media expenditures for competing brands. This includes media classes used, names of individual vehicles, number of ads used, when advertising ran, and dollar and percentage allocation to each medium and market.

MARKETING STRATEGY PLAN

Once a situation analysis has been completed, identifying the problems of a brand in the marketplace, the next step is a search for selling opportunities. *Opportunities* are marketing facts that exist and, without much money or effort, sell the product naturally. Here are some examples of selling opportunities for Brand X:

- Brand X is outselling competitors by a wide range in key markets but spends less for advertising than the next three competitors. Is it possible that with a budget equal to or greater than any other single competitor in those markets, our sales and share can be considerably enhanced?
- Brands C and D are manufactured in smaller packages, which consumers tend to buy more often than Brand X's larger package. Can we produce our brand in smaller sizes without expending much money or effort?

In contrast to opportunities, *problems* demand some action to correct the situation. A problem area might be a situation in which a brand does not have a competitive advantage or one in which a brand has been steadily losing its share of market for any number of reasons. Finding the causes for the decline is a first step toward changing the situation. Most situation analyses turn up more problem areas than opportunities, but the delineation of each problem area is a necessary preliminary step to marketing and media planning.

Marketing strategy planning consists of planning marketing actions that will solve the major problems and take advantage of the opportunities. In effect, a marketing strategy and plan is a blueprint for action geared to selling the product, with the ultimate goal of gaining an advantage over a competitor.

Perhaps the weakest part of many advertising campaigns is the lack of a sound selling strategy. Arthur Tatham, formerly chairman of the board of Tatham-Laird & Kudner, once said, "Brilliant copy and art will never make a weak selling strategy succeed. But . . . once there is a sound selling strategy, then good copy and art will multiply its effectiveness." Tatham's statement also applies to media selection and use. Without a sound selling strategy, media planning represents wasted effort. Media planning does not exist as an activity unrelated to marketing; it is a service function of marketing and selling. The fact that media are often selected and used without being based on a sound selling strategy demonstrates poor logic and inefficient modes of operation. Selling strategy is the heart of a marketing strategy and plan.

In summary, the major goals in a strong marketing strategy and plan are as follows:

- Setting objectives that will help solve existing problems and take advantage of opportunities
- Deciding how the product should be sold
- Determining to whom the main selling effort (the selling strategy) should be directed
- Determining what role various elements of the marketing mix should play in the sale of a brand
- Determining what adjustments should be made in package shapes or sizes
- Determining how much should be spent

Most often, the marketing plan is written by someone other than the media planner. Yet even if the latter is not directly involved in drawing up the plan, there are a number of reasons why the marketing strategy plan is a significant document to media planners. The foremost reason is that the marketing plan serves as a unifying and organizing force for all activity within an agency on a given brand's marketing and advertising plans. This means that the market researchers, account executives, and creative people, as well as media planners, are all working from a single source of information. Thus, the plan serves to coordinate all efforts toward the same goals. Large advertising agencies often have so many persons working on so many different accounts that communication becomes difficult. The media planner, especially, needs to know that his or her decisions will be directed toward the same objectives as those of others on the agency team.

Once the plan has been written, it becomes easier to visualize the whole scheme of operations for a given brand. All proposed plans should be evaluated for their logic and completeness to avoid information gaps or contradictions. If a marketing plan exists only in someone's mind or in bits or scraps of memoranda, then errors are hard to locate, because no one has an overview of the entire operation.

Perhaps the key to the success of a marketing plan is the degree to which it spells out all tactics. Marketing consultant Herbert Zeltner long ago cautioned that many marketing plans are "either glossed over in the rush of hammering together a marketing program, or merely slapped together as a collection of ponderous clichés." In words still applicable today, he noted:

To be truly useful, the market strategy statement should not merely reflect some happy generalities about an increase in volume or share of market for the coming fiscal period.

But establishing the requirement that a specific percent volume increase is to be achieved—through the expenditure of a precise sensible sum of money—and that this increase can most realistically be expected through more aggressive development of certain stated territories or segments of the market . . . is the type of statement which gives a properly astute media planner the challenge he needs to create both a perspective and workable media recommendation.[1]

The media planner needs specific direction, explicitly stated, in order to begin making decisions. The media plan grows directly out of the marketing strategy whenever it requires that advertising be used. The various segments of the strategy statement, however, are not all equally significant to the media planner. Foremost in importance are the marketing objectives, the basic selling idea, sources of business, overall sales strategy, and spending strategy. Each of these will be discussed in more detail on the following pages. Exhibit 6-1 on pages 124–25 shows an outline of a basic strategy statement.

Marketing Objectives

The marketing goals that the company and agency agree upon should, if achieved, result in the solution of a marketing problem. Marketing goals are measurable in most cases and provide a means of determining whether the strategy employed has been effective. For the media planner, the objectives will undoubtedly affect the kinds of media selected and the ways media are used. In a sense, then, marketing objectives serve as controls for media planning.

Most marketing objectives relate directly to achieving share of market for a brand; others relate to communication objectives. Here is a sample of marketing objectives for different brands (taken from various strategy statements):

1. Herbert Zeltner, "Marketing Strategy Statement," *Mediad/Scope* (August 1964): 10.

- To increase share in an expanding segment of the X market
- To regain lost volume—increase sales a maximum of 5 percent and, in turn, shoot for a 14 percent share of market
- To acquire a 20 percent share of market the first year after national introduction, 25 percent the second year, and 30 percent the third year
- To introduce the product so that we have at least 5 percent share in each sales division
- To increase share of market and increase the morale of the sales force in the face of many competitive new-product introductions
- To find and persuade new customers for our product
- To maintain national coverage
- To provide regional and local impact where two-thirds of sales are made
- To increase the overall visibility of the product name against the potential customers and the trade across the country

Whenever marketing objectives require advertising in specific geographic areas, then the planner must select media that best reach those areas. Sometimes the objectives call for added promotional effort in a geographic region such as the West Coast. Or the objectives might call for a special advertising effort in a given market, such as Los Angeles or Portland. Such objectives will limit media choices, because few media vehicles are available in some areas. The marketing objectives give the planner direction in selecting media, but it is up to the planner to find media that best deliver the target audience specified.

When marketing objectives call for increases in share of market with special effort directed only at prospects, the media planner is called upon to increase the number of messages to known prospects. In such cases, media selection becomes secondary to methods of using media. One such method might be to increase the frequency of exposure of advertising messages to prospects.

Occasionally, objectives deal with some area other than market shares (e.g., to increase the image of authority among adults). In this situation, the planner might feel that adults, especially those aged 21–34, are good prospects, yet they are not buying the product. The marketing objective influences the selection of adult-appeal media, such as magazines and Sunday supplements, and perhaps

EXHIBIT 6-1

Outline for Basic Marketing Strategy Statement

I. Major Strategy
This should be the briefest possible statement of the major one or two strategies recommended for the planning period, with just enough statement of the problem to explain the strategy. If you can write this section in one or two sentences or paragraphs, do so. If it takes you more than a single-spaced page, it is probably too long.

II. Basic Objectives
A. Short term (next fiscal 12 months, unless otherwise stated):
   1. Increase share of total market
   2. Arrest decline in share
   3. Develop added volume
   4. Increase total market
   5. Achieve profit goal
   6. Reduce losses
   Translate objectives into approximate sales and/or profit goals.
B. Long term (any prescribed period beyond the next planning period):
   1. Increase share of total market
   2. Increase total market
   3. Increase profits
   4. Position goal, i.e., gain leadership
   5. Develop and establish a brand or corporate image
   6. Expand line of service or products
   Translate objectives into approximate sales and/or profit goals.

III. The Basic Selling Idea
A one- or two-sentence statement of the key selling idea. This is the base from which the creative strategy evolves.

IV. Presentation of the Basic Selling Idea
The creative strategy in its briefest form

V. Use or Uses for Which the Product Will Be Advertised
A. Major
B. Minor

VI. Sources of Business and Relative Importance of Each
A. Consumer sources—What are the characteristics of the people who are the best prospects?
   1. Regional factors
   2. City size
   3. County size
   4. Income groups
   5. Age of homemaker
   6. Occupation of head of household
   7. Family size
   8. Seasonal
   9. Sex—men, women, children
   10. Who is principal purchaser?

EXHIBIT 6-1 (*continued*)

Outline for Basic Marketing Strategy Statement

    B. Dealer sources—What is the relative importance of various types of outlets?

    C. Competitive sources—Important competitive brands or companies: national, regional, local

VII. Overall Sales Strategy

    A. Relative importance of price

        1. To the consumer

        2. To the trade

    B. Relative importance of personal selling

    C. Relative importance of dealers

    D. Relative importance of advertising

    E. Relative importance of promotion

    F. Relative importance of publicity

VIII. Product Strategy

    A. The need for product improvement—Analysis of product superiorities and weaknesses compared to competitive products

    B. The need for related products

    C. The need for adding new sizes or deleting unprofitable sizes

    D. The need for improving

        1. Packaging

        2. Package design

IX. Spending Strategy

    A. Is there a need for higher or lower margins? What effect will this have on price, quality, and quantity of the product?

    B. What is the proper amount to spend

        1. On introduction?

        2. On reintroduction?

        3. On an ongoing basis?

    C. Is an extended payout plan indicated, and if so, what is the optimum time?

X. Facts and Documentation

The pertinent facts needed to define the problems and to document the strategies outlined in the strategy sections the use of a well-known personality whose image is strong in the 21- to 34-year-old age group.

Marketing Mix and Strategy

The tools that marketers use for implementing strategy were discussed in Chapter 3. Recall that each element of the mix is a selling tool. A good product that meets consumers' wants and needs is one of the best selling tools. Price is a selling tool, as is distribution. If a grocery store does not carry a given brand of product, many customers will ask for some other brand instead. They usually will not go to some other store in search of the brand. Promotion in general—and sales promotion specifically—are each selling tools. Other forms of promotion are public relations (including event marketing), direct marketing, advertising copy and art, and media.

The idea of a marketing mix is that it takes a number of different marketing mix elements to sell a product. Selling bottled water requires a good product as well as price, distribution, advertising, and sales promotion. But selling automobiles requires a different mix: product, price, distribution, sales promotion, public relations, and advertising. In short, the idea of a mix is important in terms of finding the optimum elements for selling. The use of many marketing mix communication elements usually requires integration, because each element could convey a different message and thereby reduce the effectiveness of communication.

Budget

Once the marketing objectives have been stated, it is necessary to know how much money will be required to attain them. It is not realistic to make a grandiose marketing plan and then find that the advertiser is unwilling or unable to provide sufficient funds to make the plan successful. (Budgeting and allocations to markets and media will be discussed in Chapter 13.) At this point, the media planner can be called in to help estimate the costs of the media strategy, even before the main portion of the plan has been started. If enough money is not available to accomplish a given set of objectives, then the objectives must be reduced or revised.

Estimating the cost of a marketing plan usually involves two separate activities: estimating media costs and estimating production costs. Media costs are ascertained by checking published reference books that show media rates or by talking to professional broadcast buyers who know the latest costs and ultimately are responsible for buying the planned rating points within the specified budget. Production costs are estimated either by arbitrarily allocating a given percentage of the total budget for that purpose or, if the advertising is relatively simple, by obtaining estimates on specific kinds of production pieces that are needed, such as artwork, typography, videotape, or film. Generally, the media planner is responsible for estimating only the media cost portion of the marketing plan.

The main problem in estimating marketing costs is determining whether any given amount of money spent for advertising will attain a given set of objectives. Marketing and media planners most often rely on their experiences with other brands and products as a basis for making these estimates. But other factors also enter in. A new-product introduction could require heavy investments to get it off the ground. Competitors' advertising—where and how much—also influences the marketing budget. Brands that have to defend their market shares against the inroads of competitors, or those that aspire to increase market share, might have to spend heavily.

Determining the exact amount is by no means scientific. It is based mostly on experience, although some advertisers use mathematical models to estimate the effect of various spending levels. Experience might show, for example, that an advertiser increased its national share of market by three percentage points by spending $10 million. It could then be roughly estimated that it would cost $3.3 million to raise the share one percentage point. This linear relationship of spending and share of market, however, is seldom witnessed in the real world.

Sometimes the planner recommends spending an amount of money beyond the means of the advertiser. In such cases, either the objectives have to be changed, or the advertiser must realize that spending the available budget will not produce the results desired. Sometimes, no matter what sum is recommended, the advertiser has a preconceived notion of the maximum amount that can profitably be spent and will not entertain requests for larger amounts. It behooves the planner, therefore, to establish budget parameters before full media plans are devised.

Creative Strategy

A major part of the marketing strategy plan is an explanation of how the product will be sold or a statement of the basic selling idea. From that basic selling idea comes the creative strategy, possibly the single most important influence on the planner during the media selection process. The creative strategy often directs the planner to choose one medium over another or to select a combination of media.

A creative strategy in which color is an integral part requires magazines, direct mail, newspaper supplements, or television. Newspapers accepting freestanding inserts (FSIs) offer additional alternatives to the media planner. Where the creative strategy calls for the use of cartoon characters, then either comic strips or television will be most appropriate. Again, the creative strategy gives direction to the selection process.

Where a strategy calls for demonstration, one might first think of television. However, it is possible to demonstrate the use of a product in print advertisements with sequential panels showing the various steps in using the product. Radio also is capable of demonstration through the use of words, sound effects, and music, which play on the listener's imagination.

Sometimes the creative strategy calls for the use of an announcer or salesperson who can exude a feeling of warmth and sincerity. Either television or radio is required here, because each excels at conveying emotional impact.

If the creative strategy calls for music, media choices are limited to radio or television. An alternative is to record the music and advertising message on a CD and have it inserted into magazines. In this case, however, the creative strategy must give way to the budget, which might not accommodate the expense of recording and inserting the CD.

Occasionally, creative strategy calls for large illustrations. This suggests billboards to the media planner, although direct mail or a two-page spread in newspapers or magazines might be equally acceptable.

Some advertising messages seem to have more impact on consumers in one medium than they do in another. However, impact is a hazy concept. It is generally assumed to mean that advertising does something to audience members, such as make the message memorable, change attitudes toward the brand, impart significant bits of information, or perhaps serve as a motivating factor in buying. The assumption is not always valid, because there is often little proof that what is claimed to happen actually does. In any case, where creative strategies call for traditional media because of their perceived impact, the planner might find it difficult to break tradition.

Dealers and Distribution

A major factor in media decision making is distribution to dealers, as it makes sense to limit advertising to areas where the product is distributed. To do otherwise is to waste effort and money. There are, of course, exceptions, such as when a manufacturer will advertise in an area where the product is not distributed, in an effort to "force" distribution on the dealers in that area. Perhaps dealers have refused to handle a new brand because they feel they already have too many similar products on their shelves. Some grocery chains even practice a one-for-one policy, in which they refuse to take on a new brand unless the manufacturer removes an existing brand from the shelves. By advertising in an area where a product is not yet distributed, the manufacturer hopes that the advertising will create such a demand for the product that the dealers and distributors will be forced to carry the brand. This strategy, however, might sometimes backfire, because consumers who seek the brand and cannot find it might be alienated as future consumers of the brand.

For most products, however, advertising is limited to areas where the product is distributed and, even then, only to the markets that produce the most sales or have the greatest potential for sales.

Because dealers are important sources of business, the ability to select media that best communicate with dealers represents another aspect of that planner's job. Most frequently used is the trade press, but a planner could also choose to communicate with dealers through direct mail, trade shows and conventions, or even mass media.

Dealers also influence media decisions because they are so important in selling at the local level. They are on the firing line and often know which medium works best in their markets. At times they may communicate with the agency indirectly through distributors, wholesalers, or salespeople. Their influence can be very important for their own markets. Furthermore, they often dislike agency media choices, feeling that the media planner is too distant from the scene of action to know which local or national medium works best. In any case, the media planner must pay a great deal of attention to dealers and to the importance of distribution in the media plan.

Overall Sales Strategy

The media planner should examine each element of the marketing mix to determine how it might affect media selection and use. Foremost, of course, is the role to be played by advertising. Although one can conceive of a situation where sales promotion, for example, might be more important in attaining objectives, advertising usually plays a significant role in the marketing strategy, and its role should be defined. The more specific this definition is, the better the media planner can plan strategy. Generally, advertising is assigned a communication task that must be accomplished before a product can be sold effectively.

When pricing tactics are important in marketing strategy, a special media effort might be needed either to announce the price or keep the news in front of the consumers. Special prices to dealers may require special trade media selections and use.

Sales promotion, too, has special significance to media planners. Many promotions call for inserts, such as coupons, booklets, or sample CDs, in magazines or newspapers. All of these inserts require careful planning, especially in estimating their cost and timing. Marketing or creative plans might also require gatefolds, die cuts, or special inks, all of which require additional media considerations such as cost, production lead time, and availability. Furthermore, the media planner must often select media to announce and keep a special promotion in front of consumers. Contests, cents-off deals, and premiums can lose their impact if consumers do not notice them. To maintain the desired impact, the general media strategy is to buy media so as to get the largest reach possible.

For other promotions, it is necessary to tie in local store information with national advertising so the audience in any given market knows where to buy an advertised national brand. The names and addresses of stores carrying the product are usually listed at the end of commercials or next to or near newspaper or magazine ads.

Other parts of the marketing mix, such as personal selling, public relations, or packaging, are of less importance in media planning. But the planner should know as much as possible about the whole marketing strategy to maximize the effectiveness of media decisions.

Test Marketing

Whenever a marketing strategy plan calls for test marketing, there is likely to be media involvement. For example, a test-marketing situation might use three markets to test whether the following objectives can be attained:

- To gain a substantial share of each market's sales
- To determine whether the total market for the product can be expanded
- To determine how many repeat purchases will be made
- To accomplish the first three objectives within a reasonable length of time at a reasonable profit (this requires special media planning)

To carry out the test, the company would introduce the new brand in the three markets, using different marketing tactics in each test market. For example, in Market A, 50 percent of the households would be given a free sample. In Market B, 100 percent of the households would be given a free sample. And in Market C, local newspapers would carry a coupon redeemable for a free sample at local stores. Each test market requires local advertising to call attention to the offers, especially to the coupon offer. Sales in each market would then be measured and compared to see which performed best.

As another example, test marketing could affect media planning if media weight varied in each of the three test markets. Market A might receive 100 television GRPs per week; Market B, 150 per week; and Market C, 200 per week. Sales would then be measured to see how the different weights affected volume.

Still another way to test media weights in several markets would be to give each market a specified advertising weight for a limited time. Sales would be measured for that period, then a heavier weighting might be applied to each market equally or in different proportions, and sales would again be measured. (Test-marketing strategy affects media planning in ways ranging from simple dissemination of advertising to special testing situations within all or portions of the test markets. For more details on test marketing, see Chapter 14.)

In summary, the marketing strategy affects the media planner's operation in many ways. The media plan itself grows out of a marketing plan. It is inconceivable for the media planner to operate without first having some kind of marketing strategy as a basis on which to select and use media. The ideal situation occurs when the marketing strategy plan is written and available for all personnel who work on a product or brand within the agency. The plan then serves as a unifying force and directs action toward a common goal.

COMPETITIVE MEDIA EXPENDITURE ANALYSIS

Once the planner understands the marketing strategy to determine how media will be involved, it is time to consider the kinds of media and the way they are used by competition. Sometimes competition varies so much that the planner has to sort out local and regional competitors as well as those on the national level. The planner's first job is to know just who the competitors are; the second job is to know to what extent competitors affect sales.

There is little problem in finding such information if the advertiser or agency subscribes to syndicated research sources that provide this information (discussed later in this chapter). But when such research services are not purchased, there is quite a problem in discovering who competitors are. Some information can be obtained from news in the trade press about competitive media expenditures, but products produced and sold locally might not be identified very well, especially products that are not advertised much. Other sources of information are local media salespeople, media representatives, local media research departments, and the company's own sales staff.

In determining the effect of competitors' media plans and devising strategies to counter such effects, the key piece of information is the share of market held by each competitor as compared with the advertiser's brand. Brands that lead or are close behind the advertiser pose a threat. As far as media planning is concerned, the question is, Should we use the same media our competitors use or make special efforts to use different media? Another question is, How much advertising should we put into a market to counter competitors' advertising effects?

The answers to these and other questions about competitors depend greatly on an advertiser's marketing objectives and an evaluation of what effect competitors will have in preventing the attainment of such objectives. Each situation is different. Whether to use the same media that competitors use might not be as important as identifying which medium or combination of media most effectively reaches the kind of prospects who are likely to buy the advertiser's brand. These media might happen to be identical to the media used by competitors. But the media planner, although considering competitors, should not necessarily imitate them simply because they happen to have larger shares of markets.

Planners should try to assess weaknesses in competitors' media tactics. Perhaps a competitor is not using a medium properly, or has dissipated advertising money in too many media, or is missing an important segment of the market. These errors represent opportunities in media selection and use, and such opportunities should be exploited. Marketers do not analyze a competitor's activities and their effects on a brand in order to copy the competitor's tactics, but rather to assess its strengths and weaknesses in light of the marketing objectives. Plans for attaining objectives are based on problem as well as opportunity situations.

In essence, the planner must know at least the following information about competitors before making plans:

- How much money is being spent by the largest competitors and the industry in total?
- Which media are used?
- How much is spent in each medium?
- In which markets are media concentrated?
- How much weight is placed in each market? What TV dayparts?
- Which issues, broadcasts, and times of year are used? In other words, when do competitors use various media, and how are they used?

Principal Sources of Expenditure Data

Media spending information can be obtained by subscription to the two most widely used reporting services: CMR Taylor Nelson Sofres (CMR) and Nielsen's Monitor-Plus. For additional information, see www.cmr.com and www.nielsen media.com. These services do not provide a perfect picture of competitive media expenditures, however, because it is economically unfeasible to measure every dollar spent in every medium for every product. Expenditure analyses are therefore never quite complete. Furthermore, such analyses are not precise, because the expenditures reported do not incorporate negotiated discounts on the purchase of space or time. There may be large variations between what the syndicated services report and what buyers actually spend. Finally, reports often suffer from insufficient detail in the breakdown of spending allocations when more than three brands appear in a single ad. In other words, the entire cost of the ad may be credited to one of the brands, excluding the others. The best way to assess the accuracy of competitive media reports is to compare the findings of these reports to the actual media used for the product you have planned and placed in media.

These limitations simply mean that competitive media expenditure data are not to be interpreted literally. Nevertheless, coupled with other marketing and media information, such data provide a more complete picture of a competitor's spending activities.

CMR and Monitor-Plus both measure competitive media expenditure data for the following 11 major media, with some variations in source comprehensiveness between the two services:

1. Network TV
2. Spot TV
3. Cable TV networks
4. National syndication TV
5. Network radio
6. Spot radio (nationally placed)
7. Spot radio (locally placed)
8. Consumer magazines and Sunday supplements
9. Local newspapers
10. National newspapers
11. Outdoor

CMR also monitors business-to-business advertising via its *Business 1200 Report,* and Internet spending is monitored by CMRi's AdNetTrackUS and Nielsen's Nielsen//NetRatings. Both services provide separate information on competitive commercial executions and TV ratings data to one degree or another if the clients wish it reported to them.

Users should be aware that the data may sometimes be missing significant information simply because it isn't being picked up by the reporting services or their sources. Therefore, it may be necessary to alter the spending reported in order to incorporate the more accurate information.

CMR Monitored Media/Syndicated Reports

Now let's examine each of the 11 media reported by CMR. Although Monitor-Plus's data are similar, we use CMR as our exemplar because it is the oldest and most widely used reporting service.

In the past, CMR delivered the data in the form of monthly printed reports. The company has replaced these expensive and bulky documents with the CD-based Ad$pender system, which summarizes spending information by brand, by product category, and by medium. An online system, StrADegy, provides highly detailed spending and GRP information by market, station, program, daypart, and commercial length for network, cable, syndication, and spot TV. It also provides detailed information about print schedules that include the publication title, issue date, ad size, page number, and other information.

The following lists summarize the information currently available from CMR, but users should check the website for the latest enhancements.

Network TV
- 7 broadcast networks: ABC, CBS, FOX, NBC, UPN, WB, PAX
- 2 Hispanic broadcast networks: Telemundo, Univision
- 24-hour-per-day monitoring
- Local clearance available by market
- Monitored since 1958
- Occurrences available seven days after the end of the week; dollars six to eight weeks after the end of the month

Spot TV
- 100 monitored markets—approximately 82 percent of U.S. TV homes
- Monitored since 1953
- More than 472 monitored stations
- Occurrences and unadjusted dollars available 14 days after the end of the week; monthly occurrences with adjusted dollars available six to eight weeks after the end of the month

Cable TV Networks

- 37 networks representing more than 90 percent of total cable network dollars
- 24-hour-per-day monitoring
- Reports published weekly, monthly, and quarterly
- Monitored since 1982
- Occurrences available seven days after the end of the week; dollars six to eight weeks after the end of the month

National Syndication TV

- Approximately 200 satellite-fed programs per month, transmitted from four satellites and 12 satellite transponders
- Local clearance available by market
- Monitored since 1986
- Occurrences available seven days after the end of the week; dollars six to eight weeks after the end of the month

For all television media, CMR obtains information about programs and brands with its MediaWatch™ system of "pattern recognition technology." With this system, computers recognize a given commercial by its unique digitized electronic code. However, for syndication, CMR continues to videotape its satellite feeds and manually record commercial activity. The most significant benefit of MediaWatch™ is its ability to monitor 100 spot TV markets continuously, thus improving the accuracy of activity and cost estimates.

In addition, MediaWatch™ has a "Checking Service" that reports irregularities in commercial placement. This service watches for product conflicts, overcommercialization, multiple spotting, and other irregularities, then reports them to subscribing agencies.

To estimate brand spending, MediaWatch™ assigns a dollar value to each program and applies this rate to each monitored brand's television commercial. Network cost estimates are developed from information provided by the networks. Syndicated program rates are based on cost data supplied by advertisers and agencies. Spot TV rates are provided by a few agencies and buying services and are adjusted to agree with station revenue information compiled by the Television Bureau of Advertising. The entire reporting process is done manually.

Network Radio
- Service includes 12 radio sales networks
- Monitored since 1958
- Reports available three weeks after the end of the month

Spot Radio (Nationally Placed)
- Rep-placed national spot radio, representing approximately 98 percent of national spot and 20 percent of total spot radio, collected for 200 markets from 3,500 stations
- Reports published quarterly
- Measured since 1964
- Reports available 8 to 10 weeks after the end of the month

Spot Radio (Locally Placed)
- Directly placed spot radio available for 18 markets and approximately 200 radio stations
- Measured since 1989
- Reports published quarterly

Consumer Magazines and Sunday Supplements
- National measurement of 330 magazines that are members of the Publishers Information Bureau—provided by the CMR/PIB Magazine Service.
- Four national Sunday supplements—*New York Times Magazine, LA Times Magazine, Parade,* and *USA Weekend*—plus locally edited Sunday magazines distributed with more than 50 local Sunday newspapers
- Detailed analyses of regional, demographic, and split-run advertising by edition (available separately)
- Data available seven days after the end of the month
- Reports available dating back to 1926

Costs for magazine data are estimated by using the one-time rates for each insertion. Seasonal rates are used if an advertiser has earned all the usual frequency and volume discounts. Regional rates are supplied by the publishers. Advertisers that buy a great deal of magazine advertising may show overspending because they earned volume discounts that were not reported. Not all magazines are covered.

Local Newspapers
- 250 daily and Sunday newspapers in the top 52 DMAs
- Detail-level data available for 575 subcategories
- Reports available 8 to 10 weeks after the end of the month
- Newspaper service in place more than 65 years

Actual measured advertising is multiplied by the one-time rate (SAU open rate per column inch) of each newspaper measured. Costs also reflect rates for premium-space portions of a newspaper, such as group supplements, preprinted inserts, color comics, and rotogravure and color advertising.

National Newspapers
- *New York Times, Wall Street Journal,* and *USA Today,* including all regional editions
- Reports available eight weeks after the end of the month
- Measured since 1989

Outdoor   The Outdoor Advertising Association of America (OAAA) sponsors the collection of information from 200 participating plant operators for poster and paint billboard expenditures.
- Covers 253 measured outdoor market areas
- Measured since 1966
- Data available 8 to 10 weeks after the end of the quarter

The CMR Outdoor Advertising Service reports national and regional 8-sheet and 30-sheet posters, painted walls, painted bulletins, and transit/bus shelters in markets with a population of 100,000 or more. Data on brand market-by-market expenditures represent gross sales volume for the plant operators who participate. Also, CMR publishes the *Buyer's Guide to Outdoor Advertising.*

Expenditure Summary Reports   Although planners typically retrieve CMR data from the StrADegy online computer system or the Ad$pender CD-based system, CMR continues to produce two quarterly printed summary reports:

1. Ad Summary lists 11-media total spending by brand, including parent company and classification codes

2. Company/Brand lists expenditures by parent company, showing dollars spent for the year to date in each of the 11 measured media, as well as an 11-media total.

Gathering and Assembling the Data

Studying competitive expenditures involves two major tasks. The first of these tasks is to gather and assemble the data. The second is to analyze the data.

What kinds of data should the media planner seek? The most obvious answer is to determine the amount of money each competitor spends annually in each medium. Such data provide a bird's-eye view of the competitor's media activities. To make such data more meaningful, the planner should analyze expenditures for individual brands, rather than total expenditures for a company. Because each brand is competing with others for a share of total market sales, specific expenditures by brands are most meaningful.

In gathering expenditure data by brand, it is advisable to include the planner's brand as well as competitors' brands, so all are compared on the same research basis. Even though planners may know actual spending for their own brand, it should never be compared with the measured activity of their competitors. Always compare measured spending for one's own brands to that of the competitors.

Furthermore, in analyzing expenditure data, it is important not only to show dollars spent in each medium, but also the percentage that figure represents of each competitor's annual expenditures. Exhibit 6-2 shows a sample report.

The proportion of each competitor's total expenditures in each medium makes comparisons easier, but problems with comparing percentages can occur when the bases differ widely. For example, suppose that two different brands spend 10 percent of their total budget in newspapers. The 10 percent spending might not be equivalent if one percentage is based on a $3,000 budget and the other on a $3 million budget.

The study of annual expenditures is only one approach to analyzing competitors' marketing and media strategies. Another useful analysis is to compare expenditures of a brand with its competitors on a market-by-market basis. This technique suggests which markets are most important to competitors, and the analysis can serve as one basis for weighting media in a given market.

EXHIBIT 6-2

Sample Report from CMR Ad$pender

LNA/MEDIAWATCH MULTI-MEDIA SERVICE
PRODUCT VS MEDIA REPORT

	REPORT TOTAL	NETWORK TELEVISION	CABLE TV NETWORKS	SYNDICATED TELEVISION	SPOT TELEVISION	NETWORK RADIO	NATIONAL SPOT RADIO	MAGAZINES	SUNDAY MAGAZINES	NEWSPAPERS	NATIONAL NEWSPAPERS	OUTDOOR
BRAND (CLASS CODE) - [TIME PERIOD]												
[JAN-DEC 00]												
BUD LIGHT BEER (F612)												
$(000)	107,305.0	85,052.3	9,927.8	310.6	10,271.9	--	--	186.0	--	72.0	226.6	1,257.8
HORZ %	100.0	79.3	9.3	0.3	9.6	--	--	0.2	--	0.1	0.2	1.2
BUDWEISER BEER (F611)												
$(000)	146,106.4	113,208.9	11,256.4	650.3	9,918.1	--	--	6,990.4	--	962.1	200.7	2,919.5
HORZ %	100.0	77.5	7.7	0.4	6.8	--	--	4.8	--	0.7	0.1	2.0
COORS BEER (F611)												
$(000)	40,716.1	25,900.7	9,477.0	--	3,848.1	--	--	--	--	295.2	--	1,195.1
HORZ %	100.0	63.6	23.3	--	9.5	--	--	--	--	0.7	--	2.9
COORS LIGHT BEER (F612)												
$(000)	110,530.2	79,277.9	14,717.2	39.6	13,159.7	2.8	1,091.9	32.9	--	280.0	--	1,928.2
HORZ %	100.0	71.7	13.3	--	11.9	--	1.0	--	--	0.3	--	1.7
MILLER GENUINE DRAFT BEER (F611)												
$(000)	24,103.1	9,540.1	4,076.0	31.7	9,972.6	--	454.8	--	--	--	--	27.9
HORZ %	100.0	39.6	16.9	0.1	41.4	--	1.9	--	--	--	--	0.1
MILLER LITE BEER (F612)												
$(000)	89,991.6	51,074.5	20,924.6	1,099.1	10,219.9	--	1,376.8	4,722.0	--	82.2	103.0	389.5
HORZ %	100.0	56.8	23.3	1.2	11.4	--	1.5	5.2	--	0.1	0.1	0.4
TIME PERIOD TOTAL												
$(000)	518,752.4	364,054.4	70,379.0	2,131.3	57,390.3	2.8	2,923.5	11,931.3	--	1,691.5	530.3	7,718.0
HORZ %	100.0	70.2	13.6	0.4	11.1	--	0.6	2.3	--	0.3	0.1	1.5

Still another kind of analysis is to compare the dollars that a brand and its competitors spent in each medium, correlated with the audience delivered for the dollars spent. This technique permits a quick analysis of the relative delivery effectiveness of competitors' media expenditures. Plans for a brand's reach and frequency often come from such an analysis.

Finally, it is important to learn how much was spent in each medium during each month of the year. Most brands have peak selling seasons and vary the weight of their advertising accordingly. This kind of analysis helps to establish timing and scheduling plans for the media selected later in the planning process.

Analyzing the Data

One worthwhile use of media expenditure figures is to examine spending by advertisers who lead in share of market. Those with smaller shares might want to learn which media, markets, and audiences are most important to the leaders. Sometimes it is possible to find that leading competitors ignore one or two media entirely. In such a case, it is possible for advertisers with lesser shares to preempt a medium for themselves. For example, if all of the share leaders emphasize network television, then a planner can select radio as a medium in which a brand could be significant. The planner should keep in mind, however, that a competitor's avoidance of a medium might signal the possibility that the medium is not appropriate for the product's advertising.

There are, of course, problems in analyzing media expenditure data. Most such data are incomplete, do not show any discounts earned in a medium, and cover only large advertisers. An additional problem is the age of the data: It is rare that any data are less than one month old, so the nature of the data is historical rather than contemporary. The question arises whether such data have very much meaning, especially if a competitor is not currently using the same media in the same ways as in the past. Yet if a competitor uses media in a predictably consistent pattern, then additional data might be of little value.

Probably the greatest danger in analyzing expenditure data comes from simply copying the leaders blindly. If a leading share competitor places 10 percent of its budget in Market A, then other competitors often follow the leader. But the followers' products and market strategies might not lend themselves to such weight in Market A. Furthermore, the share leader might establish its weight proportions for reasons quite different from those that followers should use.

An expenditure analysis is helpful as a means of knowing what competitors have done but not necessarily as a means of knowing what to do as a result. These analyses might show, for example, that a competitor is test-marketing a product, calling for a revised market strategy to combat the situation.

The best use of an expenditure analysis is as part of an organized intelligence system including other kinds of marketing information to provide a clear picture of competitors' strategies. Although some advertising agencies tend to deprecate the use of expenditure analysis as not being worth the investment in money or time, most large agencies find it valuable if used properly as an indication of spending strategy. When used intelligently, expenditure data are well worth the time and money invested.

Using Competitive Media Expenditure Analyses

Following is a list of uses of a competitive media expenditure analysis devised by the staff of *Media Decisions*.[2] It reviews the most important uses and values to be obtained by completing such as analysis:

1. The expenditure figures can show you the regionality and seasonality and how these factors are changing for all competitive and potentially competitive brands.
2. The data can give you a fix on ad budget size and media mix, market by market.
3. You can use the data to spot new-product tests and to track new-brand rollouts.
4. You can infer from where the money is being spent how competitors view their target audiences, how they profile their brands, and where they seek to position themselves in your marketplace.
5. You can watch spending patterns of the opposition—TV flighting, radio station rotation, position practices in magazines, or day of week in newspapers.

---

2. "Do You Know Your Competitive Brand Data?" *Media Decisions* (August 1975): 60.

6. Once you have complete knowledge of what your enemies are up to, you can make better decisions about where to meet them head-on and when to outflank them.

7. In new-product and line-extension planning, expenditure data are essential to estimate how much it will cost to get into a market, who is already there, and which competitive product types are growing fastest in the new product's market segment.

SOURCES OF MARKETING DATA

Size and share of market for a brand and its competitors, and other information contained in a situation analysis, can be obtained from a number of syndicated research services. Other data can be obtained from periodicals, association reports, government, and media. The following paragraphs provide brief descriptions of the major syndicated services and other sources of data, including Internet addresses, when available. Many of these companies maintain websites that provide limited but often highly useful data in exchange for a no-charge registration.

Major Data Services

The most widely used syndicated research services are those of A. C. Nielsen Company, Information Resources, Inc., Audits and Surveys Inc., Mediamark Research Inc., and Simmons Market Research Bureau. Numerous other research companies provide specialized lifestyle and other marketing information.

A. C. Nielsen Company Nielsen (www.acnielsen.com) provides a national brand-tracking service, Nielsen National Marketing Survey, covering almost every product sold in food stores, drugstores, warehouse clubs, and other mass merchandisers. Each of these product categories is tracked in a national sample of retail stores every week. The service provides share-of-market data based on sales to consumers at the retail level, in addition to weighted average retail prices, inventory, out-of-stock, dealer support (displays, local advertising, and coupon redemption), and major media advertising. The sample data are then projected in order to obtain national and regional data and retailer/chain specific data. The figures are further broken down by county size, store type (chain and independent), brand, package size, product type, and product attribute. This information is typically sold only to advertisers, who then pass on relevant information to their ad agencies. (Note that the A. C. Nielsen Company has no direct connection with Nielsen Media Research, which provides TV audience data. They share a common heritage but are different companies today with very different products.)

Information Resources, Inc. (IRI)   The InfoScan Census offered by Information Resources, Inc. (www.infores.com) is a syndicated tracking service for grocery industry data at the national, local market, and chain store levels. It integrates scanner sales, feature ad, coupon, display, and price data from more than 19,000 supermarkets, drugstores, and mass merchandisers with scanner panel data from 55,000 households. The InfoScan Census database comprises weekly feedback on 3.2 million products from stores representing the total movement of some 70 percent of all commodity volume in the United States. Data are available for more than 190 retail chain/market geographies in addition to the Retail Trading Areas of participating accounts. For additional detail on IRI's test-market capabilities, see Chapter 14. Like A. C. Nielsen, IRI sells data only to advertisers.

Audits and Surveys Inc.   Audits and Surveys (www.asw.surveys.com) measures the national total market based on a sample of a client's product class distribution. The sample of stores to be audited is drawn only from the types of outlets in which the client has distribution. Audits and Surveys provides information on sales, inventory, distribution, out-of-stock, and the number of days stock is on hand. It projects the data to the total United States and the client's sales regions. Audits and Surveys telephones a flash report to the client at the close of the audit, followed by a formal report two weeks later.

Mediamark Research Inc. (MRI) and Simmons Market Research Bureau (SMRB)   Both Mediamark Research Inc. (www.mediamark.com) and Simmons Market Research Bureau (www.smrb.com) provide marketing as well as media data on a regular basis. Each company reports how often products and/or brands are used, so that a planner can identify heavy, medium, and light users demographically. In addition, each company reports how users were exposed to network television programs and national magazines. As a result, the planner can select media that have not only the largest audiences, but also the largest audiences of heavy users of a given product or brand. These organizations also conduct special studies on a custom basis. MRI provides audience information by age, gender, and household income for all measured magazines as well as cable networks and top websites in exchange for no-charge registration. Go to www.mriplus.com.

Zip Code Marketing   There are three major providers of zip code–based lifestyle data: PRIZM, SPECTRA, and ACORN. PRIZM, a product of the Claritas division of VNU at www.claritas.com, provides marketing data at every microgeographic level, including zip codes, census tracts, census block groups, compiled list cells, and postal carrier routes. The service uses 62 distinct homogenous, lifestyle clusters with descriptors such as "money and brains," "back country folks," and "young literati."

SPECTRA, a product of Spectra Marketing Systems, Inc., at www.spectra marketing.com, combines groups of PRIZM clusters that have similar lifestyles with head-of-household age and presence of children to create profiles of packaged-goods users.

ACORN, a product of CACI Marketing Systems at www.demographics.caci. com, provides a classification of residential neighborhoods. It divides all U.S. neighborhoods into 43 distinct, homogenous lifestyle types or market segments—for example: Wealthy Seaboard Suburbs, Active Senior Singles, Prairie Farmers, and Prosperous Baby Boomers.

Other Sources of Data

The sources of data just described provide specific and pertinent data for a situation analysis but are relatively expensive. The cost might be too high for many small manufacturers or agencies, so it becomes necessary to find substitute sources of data. There are a number of relatively inexpensive sources, although they do not provide the same amount of detail, especially about competitors' sales and distribution practices. When the information is incomplete, advertisers must make assumptions about the missing data. Astute observers can, however, check these assumptions by taking note of the marketing actions of their own company and competitors. The following paragraphs, meanwhile, identify major sources of data for the situation analysis.

Sales & Marketing Management Survey of Buying Power   Marketing and media planners often find the _Sales & Marketing Management_ Survey of Buying Power a convenient source of three kinds of data about markets:

1. Population and household data for all major geographic markets in the United States
2. Effective buying income and spending statistics about markets
3. Retail sales data by broad product classes: (a) food stores; (b) eating and drinking places; (c) general merchandise stores; (d) automotive dealers; (e) furniture, home furnishings, and appliances; (f) drugstores; (g) apparel and accessory stores; (h) gasoline service stations; (i) building materials and hardware stores

No individual brand sales are shown, and the only classifications of consumers are by population and income. However, the report is convenient in locating and evaluating geographic markets by state, by Metropolitan Statistical Area, by county, or by city. Furthermore, the three factors (population, income, and retail sales) have been combined into a multiple-factor index number for each market, which simplifies comparisons among markets.

Convenient tables ranking markets by sales potential also facilitate comparisons by each of the nine retail product categories. A user trying to find and evaluate markets for a drug product, for example, will find a table that ranks markets from best to poorest on the basis of sales of drugs. _Sales & Marketing Management_ publishes its Survey of Buying Power annually.

SRDS   SRDS (www.srds.com) publishes media rate books for all major media. In its local media books (newspaper, spot radio, and spot television) are market data sections similar to those in the Survey of Buying Power. SRDS also shows geographic markets by state, Metropolitan Statistical Area, county, and city, but not in as much detail as the Survey of Buying Power. Local media rate books are published monthly, and the market data are revised annually.

SRDS publishes a quarterly TV and cable source, which contains a market profile for each local TV market in the United States, including demographics, sales data, and local media data. It also provides a reference for information on TV station representatives, owners of multiple TV stations, network TV personnel, commercial TV stations, TV syndicators, national and local cable TV representatives, and TV trafficking specifications.

In addition to the hard-copy books, SRDS makes available some of its information on the Internet. Subscribers receive one password for each paid subscription. As of this writing, SRDS makes online reports available on the following topics: consumer magazines, Internet, business-to-business magazines, radio, direct marketing, newspapers, and out-of-home. In coming months, SRDS plans to add reports on television and print production.

Marketer's Guide to Media Every year ASM Communications, Inc., publishes a handy reference resource titled *Marketer's Guide to Media,* which includes current rates and audience estimates for the major media. This guide describes trends in total advertising expenditures, costs, and audiences for network, cable, syndication, and spot television; radio; out-of-home; magazines; newspapers; and online services. It can be bought online at www.adweek.com/adweek/news_stand/directories.jsp.

TV Dimensions Another annual, *TV Dimensions,* provides advertisers, ad agencies, and the media with a 500-page analytical and reference tool that covers all aspects of the television medium. Sections include a history of television; the growth of cable, VCR usage, and the Internet; program type appeals; reach/frequency; qualitative factors regarding viewer interest and attentiveness; commercial exposure and impact; and intermedia comparisons. There are similar publications for magazines, the Internet, and consumer products. They can be bought online at www.mediadynamicsinc.com.

Editor & Publisher Market Guide An annual publication from *Editor & Publisher* magazine (www.editorandpublisher.com), the *Editor & Publisher Market Guide* contains geographic data that ranks markets by population, total income, total retail sales, total food sales, and household income. In addition, the text provides individual descriptions of markets. The website provides an exceptionally complete listing of media links to associations, city guides, magazines, more than 4,000 domestic U.S. and international newspapers, news services and syndicates, and radio and television websites.

Census Data   The Census Bureau (www.census.gov) of the U.S. Department of Commerce publishes many census analyses that are helpful in marketing planning. Most useful have been the Census of Business and Census of Population. But other census data, too numerous to list here, are available for special industries. The *Statistical Abstract of the United States,* published once a year, has been considered helpful as a quick source of data for media market planning. It is available online at the Census website.

Media Studies of Special Markets   Often local and national media conduct special market studies that are helpful resources for learning about geographical as well as special markets. Although the purpose of these reports is to show a given medium in a favorable light, the researcher should not assume that all such studies are biased. Often a medium will sponsor a study that represents a significant contribution to the understanding of markets and media. Sometimes the only research available on a special market or medium is these studies.

Among the most widely used sources of market data—and among the few that show brand share of markets—are brand preference studies conducted by local newspapers and provided free of cost to agencies. Different newspapers use different names for these studies, but they are essentially home inventories of the many different product brands that survey respondents have recently purchased. Because there are many such studies, comparing data from a composite selection makes it possible to get some idea of the relative share of market for a brand in various parts of the country.

Unfortunately, most studies are conducted only once a year, and some newspapers do not repeat their studies each year. Furthermore, there may be differences in the degree of control exercised in the collection and reporting of such data, so that it is difficult to know how valid the data are. Then, too, because the data are collected only once a year, there is no measure of total volume purchased.

A number of publications offer market and media data on a regular basis. The most useful ones are *Advertising Age* (www.adage.com), *Adweek* (www.ad

week.com), *Mediaweek* (www.mediaweek.com), *Broadcasting & Cable* (www.broad castingandcable.com), and *Editor & Publisher* (www.editorandpublisher.com). Information can be obtained by using search tools in the publications' websites to locate studies published in their past issues, which can be purchased online.

Associations   Many trade associations report market data for their members. In some cases, these data show sales by brands, but others tend to be rather general. Because there are so many different trade associations, it is advisable to determine whether the associations in a particular industry can be of aid in compiling the situation analysis.

Miscellaneous Sources   Yet other sources of data are available at relatively low cost to the market/media planner. Federal, state, and local governments all produce various kinds of research that can be helpful. Federal data can be found by contacting the Government Printing Office in Washington, D.C. (www.ac cess.gpo.gov) or by inquiring at a government depository library.

Chambers of Commerce, both national and local, can be helpful in finding the right kinds of data needed for marketing situation analyses. Obviously, data from these sources will be rather general, but the information might be useful for preliminary portions of the analysis.

Finally, for analysis of products and product values, *Consumer Reports* (www .consumerreports.org), which is published by the Consumers Union of U.S. Inc., provides monthly and annual publications for a small cost. *Consumer's Digest,* published six times a year, is a similar source. The magazines also produce an annual buyer's guide. Both of these organizations put various brands of products through tests to determine quality and the best buy for the money. Not all brands or models are tested, but many of the most popular brands on the market are analyzed. Ordinarily, this kind of information is difficult to obtain except by special research services, so these two publications make the job of finding product values relatively easy.

Media-Planning Resources on the Internet

The explosive growth of the Internet has made available a variety of media-planning tools and information. Virtually every medium, research supplier, and advertising-related company is represented on the Internet. The following paragraphs describe the most commonly used websites for media planners. Although some sites limit information by password to their customers, a great deal of information is available at little or no charge. The sites contain detailed information about available services, research methodology, and top-line demographic and media data. In some cases, they offer fully functional media-planning tools that can be obtained at no charge in exchange for registering the user's name and E-mail address.

GENERAL MEDIA-PLANNING SITES

Advertising Media Internet Center (www.amic.com)   The Advertising Media Internet Center website serves as an excellent starting point for media planners. It provides links to the major media research sources, media terminology, advice from a "media guru," and a broad range of other planning services.

Mediapost (www.mediapost.com)   At Mediapost, media buyers and planners will find a broad range of resources, including a secure, Web-based media-planning system called MPlanner. MPlanner lets you select, budget, schedule, chart, and share your media plan. All for free on the Web.

MediaPlan WEBRF (www.webrf.com)   The MediaPlan website provides a fully functional system for determining the reach/frequency of a television plan. Users can customize inputs to reflect the target audience demographic, effective frequency levels, creative appeal, behavioral objectives, and competitive and promotional activity. Results can be displayed in flowcharts. Reach and frequency can also be evaluated against product category volume from the Nielsen Homescan panel.

Advertising Research Foundation (www.arfsite.org)   The Advertising Research Foundation (ARF) is a nonprofit organization whose mission is "to improve the practice of advertising, marketing, and media research in pursuit of more effective marketing and advertising communications." It publishes the bimonthly *Journal of Advertising Research* and conducts numerous conferences and workshops devoted to the advertising profession. Its annual Week of Workshops features the latest developments in the area of media research. The website allows visitors to search past issues of the *Journal* for topics of interest. A synopsis is displayed, and low-cost reprints can be ordered online.

World Advertising Research Center (www.warc.com)   The World Advertising Research Center (WARC) provides online information for the world's advertisers, advertising agencies, media buyers, media corporations, and market research organizations. A search engine allows users to locate studies in virtually any field of advertising or marketing communications that have been published anywhere in the world.

Kidon Media-Link (www.kidon.com/media-link)   Kidon Media-Link provides Internet links to the websites of more than two thousand U.S. and international media services. The listing is organized by region of the world (Europe, United States, Americas, Asia, Africa/Middle East, and Oceania) and shows the name, medium (TV, newspaper, magazine, radio, etc.), and language of the site. In addition to editorial content, most sites provide information on advertising and sales representatives.

AllNewspapers.com (www.allnewspapers.com)   AllNewspapers.com is another site that provides links to international media services. This listing is organized by region, country, and media type (despite its name, the service includes all media in each country).

IMS and Telmar Computer Services (www.imsusa.com *and* www.telmar.com) Although each research service has its own proprietary software, IMS and Telmar both provide access to these databases through a unified set of computer programs that offers the same look and feel for all applications. Products of these "third-party software providers" include cross tabulations, CPM rankers, reach/frequency analysis, geographic allocation, media mix analysis, optimization, and a variety of other tools. Users must first subscribe to the basic research service and then pay an additional fee for the convenience of these third-party tools.

Media Life (www.medialifemagazine.com)   This no-cost online service provides daily information about the media industry, organized by medium and by market, as well as numerous links to Internet media services. The "Medialands" tab provides detailed demographic and media information about the top 50 markets. The "Research" tab offers an exceptionally useful *Guide to Test Market Selection and Planning.*

Ephron on Media (www.ephrononmedia.com)   Erwin Ephron is a widely known and respected consultant to the advertising industry. His Ephron on Media website is a compendium of the essays he has written over the years.

SINGLE SOURCE MEDIA/MARKETING RESEARCH SITES

The following services provide demographics, media behavior, and product usage from a single research sample.

Mediamark Research Inc. (www.mediamark.com)   The website for Mediamark Research Inc. (MRI) describes the company's service and provides top-line audience information for magazines, cable networks, and Internet usage through its link to MRI+. It also provides reports of consumer behavior for more than 50 products and services.

Simmons Market Research Bureau (www.smrb.com)   The primary service of Simmons Market Research Bureau (SMRB) is its "National Consumer Survey" of product usage, demographics, and media behavior. It is similar to MRI.

SMRB specializes in special studies that focus on a single market segment, including kids, teens, Hispanics, and business leaders.

Scarborough Research (www.scarborough.com)   Scarborough surveys 75 markets to provide information similar to the national MRI and SMRB research. Categories include local market consumer shopping patterns, demographics, media usage, and lifestyle activities. Scarborough uses a mail questionnaire, allowing it to provide detailed information about each market surveyed.

Media Audit (www.themediaaudit.com)   Media Audit is a multimedia qualitative audience survey that covers 86 local markets. These qualitative data cover things such as socioeconomic characteristics, lifestyles, retail shopping habits, and other selected consumer characteristics important to local media and advertisers. Media Audit uses a telephone interview with a random sample of persons in the markets surveyed. Its website provides top-line information about each market in the "News Release" tab.

BROADCAST-PLANNING SITES

Nielsen Media Research (www.nielsenmedia.com)   Although most of Nielsen's data are protected, the Nielsen Media Research site offers an overview of the TV rating service, a description of how television audiences are measured, and occasional free reports on current topics.

Arbitron (www.arbitron.com)   The Arbitron service is the primary source of audience ratings for local radio stations and radio networks throughout the United States. The Arbitron website provides information about the company's reports, market populations, and the latest information about its rating service. The free "Radio Today" report offers an overview of the radio industry and listening habits.

SQAD (www.sqad.com)   SQAD (Service Quality Analytics Data) is the primary source of local market costs per rating point in all 210 DMAs. The SQAD website gives an overview of SQAD's methodology, tips on how to use the data, and the current household CPP by daypart for each market. Although almost all television buys are planned on demographic target GRPs, such as women aged 25–54, the free household CPPs available on the site can be used for general planning.

Cabletelevision Advertising Bureau (www.cabletvadbureau.com)   The Cabletelevision Advertising Bureau (CAB) is a trade association that exists to promote cable television as an advertising medium. Its website presents the strengths of cable TV in comparison to broadcast network and syndication. It also contains detailed audience information, program schedules, and other material on about 65 advertiser-supported cable television networks.

Television Bureau of Advertising (www.tvb.org)   The Television Bureau of Advertising (TVB) is the not-for-profit trade association of America's broadcast television industry. TVB provides a diverse variety of tools and resources, including this website, to support its members and help advertisers make the best use of local television. The website provides a broad range of information about the television industry, viewing trends, advertising expenditures in all media (not just TV), and useful facts about the television market. Because the TVB is supported by local stations, there is only limited information about cable and network television.

Direct Marketing Association (www.the-dma.org)   The Direct Marketing Association (DMA) is the oldest and largest trade association for users and suppliers in the direct, database, and interactive marketing fields. The website provides extensive information on DM advertising, including a library of white papers, research and statistics, demographics, and various free services that are available in exchange for online registration.

Radio Advertising Bureau (www.rab.com)   The Radio Advertising Bureau (RAB) is a trade association that exists to promote radio as an advertising medium. The website has extensive information on radio-listening habits and the strength of the medium compared to other broadcast and print alternatives. The "Radio Marketing Guide and Fact Book for Advertisers," which is available through the link to "Radio Facts," is especially valuable. Like the other media-specific websites, this one contrasts the strengths of radio to the weaknesses of other media.

National Association of Broadcasters (www.nab.org)   The National Association of Broadcasters (NAB) is the principal trade association of the television industry. Its work focuses mostly on the business of broadcasting and governmental relations. The website contains reports on current events in the industry, regulatory issues, and technical advances. Although there is only limited information about advertising, the site provides useful background information for media planners.

PRINT-PLANNING SITES

MRI+ (www.mriplus.com)   The website provides rates, circulation information, topline MRI audience information, editorial calendars, and promotional media kits for more than 5,500 consumer magazines and business publications. This information is provided free on the Internet as a service to planners by Mediamark Research Inc. and the publications.

Audit Bureau of Circulations (www.accessabc.com)   The Audit Bureau of Circulations (ABC) verifies the circulation statements made by major consumer magazines and newspapers. Although the audit data are password protected, the site contains information about how to use the various reports. A "Hot Links" button offers links to numerous media-related websites.

Business Press Audits (www.bpai.com)   The Business Press Audits (BPA) provides a service that is similar to the ABC but deals primarily with controlled circulation publications—magazines and newspapers that are subsidized entirely by advertising and offered at no cost to the reader. These tend to be trade or special-interest consumer publications whose readers request a subscription by filling out a questionnaire about their job titles, responsibilities, and product purchases. By using the BPA, advertisers can select the publications that most directly reach their particular marketing target. The website provides free access to all BPA reports and is a valuable resource for business-to-business advertisers.

Magazine Publishers of America (www.magazine.org)   The Magazine Publishers of America (MPA) exists to promote the value of magazines as an advertising medium. The MPA website provides a wealth of free information about the magazine industry and the way people read magazines. Because MPA is an industry group, however, the site has no data on individual titles that might be used to sell one versus another. The annual *Magazine Handbook* in the Research/ Resources section provides especially useful information about the medium.

MediaStart (www.mediastart.com)   MediaStart provides fast, free access to consumer magazine planning data. The site lists each publication's editorial category, rate card price at various frequency levels, circulation, and availability of special creative units (gatefolds, inserts, response cards, etc.). Results of a search can be downloaded to a spreadsheet. Unlike MRI+, MediaStart does not include any audience information.

Newspaper Association of America (www.naa.org)   The Newspaper Association of America (NAA) is a nonprofit organization that represents more than 1,800 newspapers in the United States and Canada. The website's Information Resource Center provides extensive free information about newspapers, readership, and advertising expenditures in the medium.

Verified Audit Circulation (www.verifiedaudit.com)   The Verified Audit Circulation (VAC) provides circulation audits for paid and free community newspapers; Total Market Coverage flyers; shopping guides; alternative newsweeklies; ethnic, special interest, and niche publications; business, parenting, and senior periodicals; trade and consumer magazines; and *Yellow Pages* directories.

OUTDOOR-PLANNING SITES

Outdoor Advertising Association of America (www.oaaa.org)   The Outdoor Advertising Association of America (OAAA) is the lead trade association representing the outdoor advertising industry. With nearly 1,100 member companies, the OAAA represents more than 90 percent of industry revenues. The association's website presents information about the medium and various creative units available. Links to outdoor companies can be used for gathering information about pricing and local market planning.

Lamar Advertising Company (www.lamar.com)   An out-of-home media agency that covers 37 U.S. states, Lamar Advertising also runs a useful website.

The site offers resources and information for media buyers and planners. It also contains rates and poster details for the areas served by Lamar.

Eller Media Company (www.ellermedia.com)   Eller Media is one of the largest outdoor companies in the United States. The company's website provides links to outdoor companies, a glossary of outdoor terms, rates for various outdoor media in the major markets, and other information to help plan out-of-home media.

INTERNET-PLANNING SITES

Internet Advertising Bureau (www.iab.net)   The Internet Advertising Bureau (IAB) presents itself as "the first global not-for-profit association devoted exclusively to maximizing the use and effectiveness of advertising on the Internet." The IAB website provides general information about Internet advertising, industry standard ad sizes, and an exceptionally complete listing (including hot links) to the many tools of the trade.

Jupiter Communications, Inc. (www.jup.com)   A leading Internet marketing research company, Jupiter Communications provides strategic analysis and insight about the commerce on the Internet. It tracks industry trends and forecasts future business activity. The Jupiter website offers summaries of the company's current presentations and top-line marketing information about the Internet in exchange for guest registration.

ClickZ Today (www.clickz.com)   The INT Media Group's ClickZ Today site offers the latest information, techniques, and advice on Internet advertising. In addition to providing material on the site itself, ClickZ offers direct links to both paid and free Internet newsletters with information on E-marketing, business-to-business marketing, Internet technology, advertising practices, and so on.

Internet Glossary (www.matisse.net/files/glossary.html)   This is an extensive glossary of Internet terms provided by Matisse Enzer, an Internet project manager who lives in San Francisco.

ADVERTISING PUBLICATION SITES

Advertising Age (www.adage.com)   *Advertising Age* is the oldest weekly trade publication of the advertising industry. Its website provides current information on all phases of advertising, media, creative, and Internet communication.

Adweek (www.adweek.com)   *Adweek* is a weekly trade publication that covers the advertising industry. Its website, *Adweek* Online, provides daily headlines and excerpts from the magazine.

ADVERTISING INDUSTRY SITES

American Association of Advertising Agencies (www.aaaa.org)   The American Association of Advertising Agencies (AAAA or the 4As) is the national trade organization that represents the advertising industry. It offers its members information regarding the operation of ad agencies; management; media, print, and broadcast production; secondary research on advertising and marketing; and international advertising. The website lists current activities of the association and provides a catalog of available publications. It offers useful background for media planners but relatively little information for nonmembers.

American Marketing Association (www.marketingpower.com)   The American Marketing Association (AMA) is the world's largest and most comprehensive professional society of marketers, consisting of over 40,000 worldwide members in 82 countries and 400 chapters throughout North America. The AMA is the only organization that provides direct benefits to marketing professionals in both business and education and serves all levels of marketing practitioners, educators, and students. Its website contains information about the organization and its members but has no media-planning resources.

American Advertising Federation (www.aaf.org)   The American Advertising Federation (AAF) describes itself as "The Unifying Voice for Advertising." The AAF says, "We are the only professional advertising association that binds the mutual interests of corporate advertisers, agencies, media companies, suppliers and academia." The federation's website provides information about the organization and its publications, but there are no media-planning resources.

CHAPTER SEVEN

Strategy Planning I

WHO, WHERE, AND WHEN

Once the advertiser has an overall marketing strategy, a media strategy can be developed. The first three parts of the strategy answer three questions:

1. *To whom* should we target our advertising?
2. *Where*, geographically, should we advertise?
3. *When* should we advertise?

The answers to these questions will drive other decisions made later in the development of a media strategy. For example, if it has been agreed that advertising should be directed primarily to women 18–34, then media alternatives such as sports magazines or TV programs directed primarily to men would not be appropriate. (Obviously, there are some exceptions—but not many.) Because they will affect every aspect of the media plan, decisions about the target market must be made early. The remaining parts of the media strategy—weighting, reach, frequency, and continuity—will be discussed in Chapter 8.

Sometimes the media planner makes these decisions alone, but more often the process includes input from creative, the account group, and marketing planners, as well as from the client. Most often, the decision making is a team process.

Answers to each of the three big questions rely most heavily on numerical analysis of marketing and media data, but they also involve judgment and subjective appraisal. Numbers that are evaluated literally are subject to error. One must know where the numbers came from—how they were obtained or calculated. The best planners know the value of research methodology as well as how to analyze the numbers. The search for objectivity in planning requires both abilities.

TARGET SELECTION

A media plan's *target audience* is the group of people whom the advertising is attempting to influence. Most typically, advertising is directed to current users of the product or service. Although targeting information is available for products that appeal to specialized markets such as upper-income households (Mendelsohn Media Research at www.mmrsurveys.com) and teens (Teenage Research Unlimited at www.teenageresearch.com), the most commonly used services are Simmons Market Research Bureau (SMRB at www.smrb.com) and Mediamark Research Inc. (MRI at www.mediamark.com). Both studies begin with a survey of product usage and media behavior from a random sample of homes in the 48 contiguous states. Exhibit 7-1 shows the MRI survey's question dealing with the use of bottled water and seltzer.

The results of the survey are made available to subscribers on a computer database that allows custom cross tabulation of the data. Exhibit 7-2 shows the format of these tabulations. Although this example is from MRI, it illustrates the universal concepts of horizontal (percent of the demographic that uses the product), vertical (percent of the product's users who fall into the demographic), and selectivity index. In the analysis of media vehicle audiences, "vertical" equates to coverage; "horizontal" equates to composition.

The goal is to identify the targets—those who are most likely to buy. Targets are identified on the basis of one or more demographic characteristics of consumers who have purchased the product or brand in the past. Purchasers are typically described in terms of age, income, occupation, education, and so forth. Custom-made research can provide this kind of information, but it is usually quite expensive and time-consuming.

One of the first media-planning action steps is to decide whether to concentrate on all users or a narrower product usage category. A great deal will depend on whom the advertiser wants to reach. This is a marketing as well as a creative and media decision. Most likely, the creative personnel and agency account representative will recommend the segments they believe can be convinced to buy the brand. Sometimes the goal is to convince consumers to switch brands; other times it will be to convince persons not using the product category to try it. But once the buying category has been decided, the targets will then be found by studying demographic and lifestyle data. Planners use indexes

EXHIBIT 7-1

MRI Survey on Bottled Water and Seltzer

BOTTLED WATER & SELTZER	You Personally:	
	Drank in last 6 months	Drinks or glasses/ last 7 days
134 **TOTAL:**	☐	_____ 00
TYPES:		
Flavored	☐	_____ 01
Non-Flavored	☐	_____ 02
KINDS:		
Sparkling	☐	_____ 03
Non-Sparkling	☐	_____ 04
FORMS:		
Sweetened	☐	_____ 05
Unsweetened	☐	_____ 06
BRANDS:		
Acquafina	☐	_____ 07
Arrowhead	☐	_____ 08
Calistoga	☐	_____ 09
Canada Dry Seltzer	☐	_____ 10
Clearly Canadian	☐	_____ 11
Crystal Geyser	☐	_____ 12
Crystal Springs	☐	_____ 13
Dannon Water	☐	_____ 14
Deer Park	☐	_____ 15
Evian	☐	_____ 16
Great Bear	☐	_____ 17
Hinckley & Schmitt	☐	_____ 18
Ice Mountain	☐	_____ 19
La Croix	☐	_____ 20
Mountain Valley	☐	_____ 21
Natural Mineral Water	☐	_____ 22
Naya	☐	_____ 23
New York Seltzer	☐	_____ 24
Ozarka	☐	_____ 25
Perrier	☐	_____ 26
Poland Springs	☐	_____ 27
Schweppes Seltzer	☐	_____ 28
Seagram Seltzer	☐	_____ 29
Sparkletts	☐	_____ 30
Utopia	☐	_____ 31
Vermont Pure	☐	_____ 32
Vintage Seltzer	☐	_____ 33
Zephyrhills	☐	_____ 34
_____	☐	_____ 999
OTHER (Write In)		

Do you receive home delivery of bottled water? Yes ☐ 1 No ☐ 2 135-0

SOURCE: Mediamark Research Inc., 2000.

EXHIBIT 7-2

Demographics of Medium/Heavy Bottled Water and Seltzer Users

BASE: ADULTS		TOTALS	MEDIUM/HEAVY* BOTTLED WATER AND SELTZER— LAST 7 DAYS
Totals	(000s)	198,450	52,856
	Vert%	100.0	100.0
	Horz%	100.0	26.6
	Index	100	100
Men	(000s)	95,259	23,423
	Vert%	48.0	44.3
	Horz%	100.0	24.6
	Index	100	92
Women	(000s)	103,191	29,433
	Vert%	52.0	55.7
	Horz%	100.0	28.5
	Index	100	107
Age 18–24	(000s)	25,250	7,555
	Vert%	12.7	14.3
	Horz%	100.0	29.9
	Index	100	112
Age 25–34	(000s)	39,610	11,640
	Vert%	20.0	22.0
	Horz%	100.0	29.4
	Index	100	110
Age 35–44	(000s)	44,592	13,189
	Vert%	22.5	25.0
	Horz%	100.0	29.6
	Index	100	111
Age 45–54	(000s)	34,236	10,627
	Vert%	17.3	20.1
	Horz%	100.0	31.0
	Index	100	117
Age 55–64	(000s)	22,430	5,196
	Vert%	11.3	9.8
	Horz%	100.0	23.2
	Index	100	87
Age 65+	(000s)	32,332	4,649
	Vert%	16.3	8.8
	Horz%	100.0	14.4
	Index	100	54

There are 198,450,000 adults in the United States.

There are 52,856,000 medium/heavy bottled-water users.

26.6% of adults are M/H bottled-water users (52,856/198,450).

There are 25,250,000 adults aged 18–24.

12.7% of all adults are aged 18–24 (25,250/198,450).

There are 7,555,000 M/H bottled-water users aged 18–24.

14.3% of M/H bottled-water users are aged 18–24 (7,555/52,856).

29.9% of 18- to 24-year-olds are M/H bottled-water users (7,555/25,250).

Adults 18–24 are 12% more likely to be M/H bottled-water users than the average adult (14.3/12.7).

Adults 55–64 are 13% less likely to be M/H bottled-water users than the average adult (9.8/11.3 − 1).

*Drink at least two glasses a day.

SOURCE: Mediamark Research Inc., Doublebase, 2000.

to show how the demographics of product users compare to the population as a whole.

Index Number Analysis

In analyzing numerical data, there are three commonly used bases: raw numbers, percentages, and index numbers. Raw numbers are used least often, because they are so large and because it is difficult to compare the raw numbers of one brand with those of another brand, each of which can have radically different bases. Percentages are a means of equalizing the bases of numbers from two or more companies, so they are usually preferred over raw numbers for making comparisons. Index numbers are the ratio of two percentages and are most preferred for comparisons.

An *index* is a number that shows a relationship between two percentages or between two raw numbers. Generally, index numbers are printed as whole numbers. The value of an index number is that it relates sales or product usage to population demographics, enabling one to have a convenient common method for comparison. If the population segment is considered to be "average," then an index number for sales tells how much above or below average sales are, in absolute terms. An index number of 100 is equal to the average; 125 is 25 percent above average, and 80 is 20 percent below average. Exhibits 7-3 and 7-4 provide an example of using index numbers.

Which demographic segments should be selected as target markets for media to reach? The usual answer is to select those demographic segments with the largest volume of sales or the largest number of users. In other words, advertise where the brand has a history of success. According to the traditional point of view, then, the 35–44 age group shown in Exhibit 7-2 might be the prime target because it accounts for the largest percent of total users (25 percent). But the 45–54 age group accounts for 20 percent of users, and the brand manager might think there is more potential in this group because these consumers are more likely than the younger age group to use bottled water. Obviously, income, occupation, education, and other demographic categories would also have to be checked before a final decision could be made.

There is also another way to look at the data in Exhibit 7-2, and that is to compare the percentage of usage in each age segment to the percentage of population in that segment. (One could compare the raw numbers of usage and pop-

EXHIBIT 7-3

Medium/Heavy Users of Bottled Water by Age Segment

AGE SEGMENT	NUMBER OF ADULTS IN U.S. (000)	PERCENT U.S. ADULTS	NUMBER OF M/H BOTTLED-WATER USERS	PERCENT OF ADULT USERS
18–24	25,250	12.7%	7,555	14.3%
25–34	39,610	20.0	11,640	22.0
35–44	44,592	22.5	13,189	25.0
45–54	34,236	17.3	10,627	20.1
55–64	22,430	11.3	5,196	9.8
65+	32,332	16.3	4,649	8.8
Total adults	198,450	100.0%	52,856	100.0%

SOURCE: Mediamark Research Inc., 2000.

EXHIBIT 7-4

Calculating Index Numbers (Based on Exhibit 7-3)

AGE SEGMENT	CALCULATION	INDEX
18–24	14.3 ÷ 12.7	112
25–34	22.0 ÷ 20.0	110
35–44	25.0 ÷ 22.5	111
45–54	20.1 ÷ 17.3	116
55–64	9.8 ÷ 11.3	87
65+	8.8 ÷ 16.3	54

SOURCE: Mediamark Research Inc., 2000.

ulation distribution in each segment, but such comparisons are more difficult than those made using percentages.) When the percentage of usage is compared with the percentage of population distribution in each segment, an index number can be calculated to make the comparisons easier to analyze. The formula for calculating such numbers is as follows:

$$\text{Index number} = \frac{\text{Percentage of users in a demographic segment}}{\text{Percentage of population in the same segment}} \times 100$$

Using the formula to calculate index numbers for the data in Exhibit 7-3 yields the index numbers in Exhibit 7-4. The index numbers in Exhibit 7-4 show how much the product is being used compared with the potential (or population proportion) in each segment. An index number below 100, as seen in the 55–64 and 65+ age groups, indicates lower than average usage. So, even though the groups together account for almost one-fifth of volume, they still consume less than would be expected, given the size of the 55+ population. Now one can clearly see that the younger age segments represent the best prospects—both because they account for the largest percent of users and because they are far more likely to use bottled water than the population as a whole. In this sense, index numbers more accurately indicate potential for usage or sales. One cannot easily see this kind of relationship, however, without first calculating the index numbers.

It is helpful to think of index numbers as measures of central tendency, just as averages or means are in the statistical world. An average does not describe any one person in a group, only the group as a whole. Likewise, an index number over 100 means that the usage of the product is proportionately greater in that segment than one that is average (100) or below average (any number below 100). Segments with index numbers over 100 do not necessarily have numerically more users in them than in other segments; they might only have proportionately more. Theoretically, the segment with the highest index number represents the best potential for usage. In analyzing marketing data, one should calculate index numbers for all demographic groups, such as age, sex, income, occupation, and education.

Although the technique of calculating index numbers shown in Exhibit 7-4 can be used, there is a simpler way to compute the numbers, shown in Exhibit 7-5. Briefly stated, the method starts with a measurement of the total number of users in a market. A percentage of the universe is then computed. This percentage indicates that, of the total population, *x* percent are users. The number of users is divided by the number of individuals in each population segment, and percentages are calculated. Finally, each of these segment percentages is divided by the total percentage of users to obtain an index number. Note that the index numbers obtained by this method are identical to those obtained in Exhibit 7-4.

Be careful not to be misled about index numbers: The demographic segment with the highest index number does *not* always represent the best poten-

EXHIBIT 7-5

Another Method of Calculating Index Numbers

Step One: Find the total number of users compared with the total population in the market:

    Total number of users in all segments (000): 52,856
    Total number of adults in the United States (000): 198,450
    Percentage of total adults who are users (users/adults): 26.6

Step Two: Divide to find the percent of users in each demographic segment (from Exhibit 7-3).

AGE SEGMENT	NUMBER OF USERS (000)	POPULATION SIZE	USERS/POPULATION
18–24	7,555	25,250	29.9%
25–34	11,640	39,610	29.4
35–44	13,189	44,592	29.6
45–54	10,627	34,236	31.0
55–64	5,196	22,430	23.2
65+	4,649	32,332	14.4
Total adults	52,856	198,450	26.6%

Step Three: Divide each of the percentages in Step Two by the percentage in Step One:

AGE SEGMENT	USERS/POPULATION	USERS/ADULTS	INDEX
18–24	29.9%	26.6%	112
25–34	29.4	26.6	110
35–44	29.6	26.6	111
45–54	31.0	26.6	116
55–64	23.2	26.6	87
65+	14.4	26.6	54
Total adults	26.6%	26.6%	

SOURCE: Mediamark Research Inc., 2000.

tial. Aside from the fact that one segment might have some other qualification that is of great marketing value, there is also the possibility that a segment with a high index number has a low degree of product usage or sales or a low population size for that segment. If so, the segment with the highest index number would not represent the best potential for continued usage.

To illustrate, Exhibit 7-6 shows marketing data for a fictitious brand. Although the 18–24 age segment has the highest index number (134), it also has

EXHIBIT 7-6

An Example of Misleading Index Numbers

AGE SEGMENT	POPULATION IN EACH SEGMENT	PRODUCT USAGE IN EACH SEGMENT	INDEX
18–24	11.1%	15.0%	134
25–34	19.3	17.8	92
35–49	30.2	29.2	97
50+	39.4	38.0	96
Total	100.0%	100.0%	

the lowest percentage of product usage and the lowest population percentage of any segment. It would not be very meaningful, therefore, to limit the selection of media to those reaching the 18–24 segment and ignore the other segments, especially because 85 percent of the usage is in the 25-and-older segment. First examine the volume of usage or sales in each demographic segment to determine whether the volume warrants inclusion as a media target. Only then will index numbers help locate good potential target segments.

It is also important to note that index numbers between 90 and 110 are generally insignificant. So, for instance, in Exhibit 7-4, the 25–34 age segment, which indexes 110, is significantly above average, but just barely so.

Lifestyle Analysis

Demographics paint a general picture of the target and are needed for buying broadcast media, but by themselves, they are dry statistics that mask the human side of product users. To add some personality, media planners also analyze product users' *lifestyles*—that is, how they spend time and money. Following are the most commonly used lifestyle analysis tools that give planners a more intuitive understanding of their target.

Storyfinder   The previous example of an MRI cross tabulation (or "crosstab" for short) showed demographics, but it is also possible to cross tabulate product usage with all of the answers in the survey. A Storyfinder ("Golddigger" in MRI software) is essentially a large crosstab. The column represents the product user

EXHIBIT 7-7

Storyfinder Analysis of Medium/Heavy Bottled-Water/ Seltzer Users

Base: Adults
Target: Medium/Heavy Bottled-Water & Seltzer Users
Population: 52,856 (000)

	VERT%	HORZ%	INDEX
Totals	100.0	26.6	100
Bought weight-lifting/training shoes past year	0.8	58.5	220
Heavy users of port, sherry, & dessert wines	1.1	55.6	209
Personally ordered by Internet other health/ medical supplies past 12 months	0.6	55.4	208
Heavy users of specialty wines & aperitifs	0.7	54.5	205
Heavy users of prepared mixed drinks without liquor	0.8	53.2	200
Heavy users of individual big block/thick bar candy	3.0	53.1	199
Heavy users of ready-to-drink iced cappuccino	1.0	52.8	198
Bought any lens filter(s) for camera in last 12 months	0.9	52.2	196
Personally ordered by Internet shoes past 12 months	0.6	50.9	191
Personally ordered by Internet vitamins past 12 months	0.7	50.7	190
Bought 35mm SLR (single lens reflex) camera last 12 months	0.5	50.6	190
Bought other high-ticket sport/recreation equipment past 12 months	0.5	50.6	190
Personally ordered by Internet sports equipment past 12 months	0.7	50.4	189
Heavy users of ale	0.5	50.1	188
Bought any other accessory lens(es) for camera in last 12 months	0.7	50.0	188
Personally ordered by Internet home furnishings past 12 months	0.5	49.3	185
Heavy users of imported dinner/table wines	1.9	49.0	184
Bought video still camera last 12 months	0.3*	48.6	182
Heavy users of malt liquor	1.2	48.5	182
Personally ordered by Internet pet products/supplies past 12 months	0.4*	48.1	181
Personally have personal loan for vacation only	0.6	47.8	179
Participated in surfing/windsurfing in past 12 months	1.2	47.6	179
Bought weight-lifting equipment past 12 months	2.3	46.9	176

EXHIBIT 7-7 (*continued*)

Storyfinder Analysis of Medium/Heavy Bottled-Water/ Seltzer Users

	VERT%	HORZ%	INDEX
Bought foreign-language instruction prerecorded tape/CD last 12 months	1.1	46.7	175
Heavy users of prepared mixed drinks with liquor	1.1	46.6	175
Bought Spanish/Latin prerecorded tape/CD last 12 months	3.9	46.3	174
Personally ordered by Internet cookware/kitchen accessories past 12 months	0.5	46.2	173
Personally ordered by Internet baby accessories past 12 months	0.4*	46.1	173
Bought other exercise equipment past 12 months	1.7	45.9	172
Heavy users of car rental (personal use)	4.1	45.6	171
Bought hiking/backpacking clothing past year	2.5	45.6	171
Bought cycling shoes past year	0.5	45.5	171

*Projection relatively unstable due to small base—use with caution.
SOURCE: Mediamark Research Inc., Doublebase, 2000.

that the planner is studying, and the rows (more than 2,800 of them) reflect every product and service that is measured. The planner then sorts the analysis by index in order to identify the most selective behaviors that might shed light on the user's lifestyle.

Exhibit 7-7 shows the results of a Storyfinder for adults who are medium/ heavy users of bottled water and seltzer. It is clear from these activities that the target users enjoy an active and energetic lifestyle, use the Internet, are concerned about their health, and have the financial resources to enjoy the finer things in life. These insights are not apparent from demographic analysis alone.

Note that some of the groups are so small the data are unstable and should be used with caution. The asterisk indicates that the sample consists of fewer than 50 respondents. This represents the practical limit to a planner's ability to fine-tune the target.

EXHIBIT 7-8

Selective Buying Styles of Medium/Heavy Bottled-Water/Seltzer Users

Base: Adults
Target: Medium/Heavy Bottled-Water & Seltzer Users
Population: 59,764 (000)

	"AGREE MOSTLY" WITH STATEMENTS		
	VERT%	HORZ%	INDEX
Totals	100.0	29.8	100
I prefer products that offer the latest in new technology.	15.0	39.8	134
I think shopping is a great way to relax.	14.5	38.3	128
I'd pay more for a product consistent with the image I want to convey.	9.9	38.1	128
I'm always one of the first to try new products or services.	6.6	37.5	126
I'm a spender rather than a saver.	16.9	36.8	123
People often come to me for advice before making a purchase.	7.5	36.7	123
I am influenced by what's hot and what's not.	7.3	36.5	123
If I really want something, I'll buy on credit rather than wait.	16.5	36.3	122
I tend to make impulse purchases.	9.8	35.8	120
I always check ingredients/nutrition content of food products before buying.	18.5	35.5	119
I buy brands that reflect my style.	23.5	35.4	119
My children have a significant impact on the brands I choose.	9.4	35.3	118
I buy the brands I grew up using.	11.7	33.9	114
I'm willing to pay more for products that are environmentally safe.	16.0	33.7	113
I buy based on quality, not price.	26.7	33.6	113
I often seek the advice of others before making a purchase.	7.9	33.6	113
I prefer stores that specialize in a specific type/style of product.	9.9	33.5	112
I'd rather receive sample of a product than price-off coupon.	27.0	33.2	112
A celebrity endorsement may influence me to consider/buy a product.	3.0	33.0	111
I will gladly switch brands to use a cents-off coupon.	6.7	33.0	111
My grocery store offers low prices on all products every day.	16.9	32.8	110

SOURCE: Mediamark Research Inc., 2000.

Buying Styles   MRI also asks respondents a series of questions about their attitudes toward buying various products. Exhibit 7-8 shows the top Buying Styles ("Agree Mostly") for medium/heavy users of bottled water or seltzer. This analysis tells planners that their target is technologically savvy, is willing to try new products, and wants to be perceived as a person who reflects the latest fashion.

Leisure Styles and Consumer Innovators   The Storyfinder is a simple cross-tab of every measured behavior although it fails to combine a number of behaviors that may, taken together, signal a lifestyle or consumer interest. MRI's Leisure Styles and Consumer Innovators codes were developed from a factor analysis of the MRI database. Like the Buying Styles, these groupings can offer insights into the consumer, but they are seldom used to select specific media vehicles.

Exhibit 7-9 shows the selectivity of these lifestyle groups for medium/heavy bottled-water users. They score significantly above average in the Leisure Style groups: Outdoor Energetics, General Actives, and Party People. And they are above average on all of the Innovator groups (55 percent more likely than average to be a "Super Innovator"), confirming the earlier observations of their active lifestyle seen in the Storyfinder.

Focus Groups   While not a statistical tool, media-oriented focus groups can provide insights into the target that are unavailable from questionnaire-based research. Using Foote, Cone & Belding's "Mind & Mood" process, media planners talk to target consumers in their natural surroundings (for example, men drinking beer in a bar). This relaxed, but carefully structured, meeting probes the target's daily life patterns—these consumers' interests, what they do for fun, what frustrations they experience, their social life, their goals for the future. Of special importance is a discussion about their involvement with and attitudes toward the media.

For example, a Mind & Mood session on behalf of a state tourism association revealed that respondents look forward to the weekends when they can get away from their busy and hectic weekdays. This observation led to a campaign that suggested weekend automobile trips to points of interest in the state. Media weight was concentrated on Thursday and Friday evenings when people were planning their weekend activities, as well as Sunday newspaper ads that contained specific travel directions.

EXHIBIT 7-9

Leisure Styles and Consumer Innovators of Medium/Heavy Bottled-Water/Seltzer Users

Target: Medium/Heavy Bottled-Water & Seltzer Users
Population: 52,856 (000)

	VERT%	HORZ%	INDEX
Totals	100.0	26.6	100
Leisure Styles			
Outdoor Energetics	5.7	33.1	124
Passives	31.4	20.7	78
General Actives	6.1	35.1	132
Party People	14.3	35.2	132
Hunters & Fishers	3.3	21.2	79
Collectors	3.3	26.1	98
Nesters	27.9	30.1	113
Golf	8.0	29.2	110
Consumer Innovators			
Leisure Innovators	18.1	37.7	141
Food	14.6	34.3	129
Electronics	21.3	35.4	133
Financial	11.4	32.9	123
Home Appliance	9.1	31.2	117
Super Innovators (3+ of above segments)	6.1	41.3	155

SOURCE: Mediamark Research Inc., Doublebase/Consumer Innovator & Leisure Styles, 2000.

The use of focus groups illustrates the value of understanding the marketing target's human side, as well as the cold statistical characteristics of these consumers.

WHERE TO ADVERTISE

The question of where to advertise has a number of answers. The simplest, of course, is to advertise wherever the brand is distributed. Obviously, advertising in a geographic market where the brand is not distributed is usually a waste of money. Occasionally, however, the objective might be to "force" distribution by creating a demand for a brand through advertising, even though the brand is not yet distributed in the market. When the planner has this objective, it makes sense to advertise before distribution is available.

Beyond the obvious answer, however, is the question of whether it is better to advertise in geographic markets where sales for a given brand have been good, or where sales have not been good. Some planners believe that to advertise where sales have been good is a solid defensive strategy. One should protect what one has and also try to build on it. Additionally, one should ask, Have sales in the good markets been fully exploited? If not, why not spend more money there, rather than going to some other market where the risks would be greater? After all, many customers like the brand well enough to buy it repeatedly, and their word-of-mouth influence could well prompt sales to people who have not purchased the brand in the past. Also, distribution and retail acceptance of the product have been established.

Choosing where to advertise is really a matter of risks. Despite the observation that "it is always good sense to fish where the fish are," is an advertiser missing productive new markets by placing most advertising in the best markets? Conversely, can the advertiser afford the risk of losing the best markets to sound out new, unknown markets? The "defensive strategy" minimizes risks and maximizes potential.

Advertising in markets where a brand's sales are low is called an "offensive strategy," because success will require heavier advertising expenditures than previously used. Again, the risks must be carefully weighed. If competitors have been selling well in these markets but the brand in question has not, the question is, why? Are the poor sales a result of poor distribution? Or have advertising expenditures in the market been insufficient? Are there other reasons? Can these problems be corrected?

A planner selecting a market with a low sales history should be able to answer the following question: Is there any evidence that increased advertising in this market will produce a corresponding increase in sales? This question is difficult, but necessary, to answer. Students in practice exercises often want to increase advertising because they believe "advertising sells." But they usually cannot find any other strong reason for doing so except that competitors are selling well in the market. One must understand, however, that once a competitor becomes entrenched in a market with a good brand that meets the needs of consumers, consumers might not see a reason to switch brands. In fact, getting them to switch brands might be impossible, unless the new brand has some superior attribute. The risks of trying to exploit such a market are great, and the likelihood of success is, at best, indeterminable.

Finally, the greatest risk is to select new markets where neither the designated brand nor competitive brands have been exploited through advertising. These markets might have great sales potential, but they could also be difficult places to sell a given product. It also might be assumed that if these markets really had great potential, competitors would have known about it, too, and would have made efforts to exploit that potential.

Aside from these basic guides for market selection, other factors should be considered, such as selecting one or perhaps more markets in each of the client's sales territories. Almost all companies with nationally distributed products divide the country into sales territories, and these in turn are usually subdivided into small groups. The names of such territories vary from company to company. Some use the terms *divisions* and *districts,* others use *regions* and *divisions,* or other designations. No matter what the territories are called, it might be necessary to include at least one market in each of these divisions, depending on the needs of the company. The weight (or amount of advertising used) in these areas will vary, however, so the better markets receive more dollars of advertising than the poorer markets.

Thus, to answer the question of where to advertise, planners study distribution, sales records, or brand and product usage. Simmons and MRI provide data on users, and Nielsen and similar companies provide data on sales.

Classification of Geographic Areas

Sales should be analyzed by different geographic patterns, from the largest—i.e., regions of the country—to the smallest neighborhoods possible. (In some situations, analysis by neighborhood is impossible because of the lack of research data.) The idea behind geographic analysis at all levels is to learn precisely where prospects live. This information guides media selection. The following geographic categories are the most commonly used:

- Regions
- States
- TV market delineations such as DMAs
- Metropolitan or nonmetropolitan areas
- Counties

In studying marketing and media research data, the analyst will find a number of different methods used to divide the country geographically. The U.S. Census Bureau divides the country into four regions and nine divisions. The Media Audience Research Committee of the American Association of Advertising Agencies recommends that the country be divided into four divisions. Nielsen Media Research uses a division consisting of six geographic territories, although it will divide the country in almost any way most suitable for a specific client. Exhibit 7-10 compares these divisions. Exhibit 7-11 maps the states in Nielsen's six territories.

What is a local market to a media planner? A *market* is a group of people living in a certain geographic area who are likely to buy a given product or brand. But that definition is unsatisfactory for planners when it comes to determining the nature of a local market, because definitions vary depending on the research company providing the data for a given area.

EXHIBIT 7-10

Comparison of Geographic Divisions

4As MEDIA AUDIENCE RESEARCH COMMITTEE DIVISIONS	TELEVISION INDEX NIELSEN'S TERRITORIES	CENSUS BUREAU'S NINE DIVISIONS	CENSUS BUREAU'S FOUR REGIONS
1. North East	1. Northeast	1. New England	1. Northeast
2. North Central	2. East Central	2. Middle Atlantic	2. Midwest
3. South	3. West Central	3. East N. Central	3. South
4. Pacific	4. Southeast	4. West N. Central	4. West
	5. Southwest	5. South Atlantic	
	6. Pacific	6. East S. Central	
		7. West S. Central	
		8. Mountain	
		9. Pacific	

EXHIBIT 7-11

Nielsen Television Index Territories and Time Zones

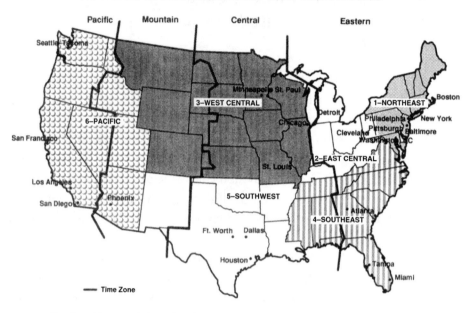

SOURCE: Reprinted by permission of Nielsen Media Research.

Different research companies define markets differently to meet the needs of their users. A local retailer advertising exclusively in newspapers in a given city might prefer to think of its market as a retail trading zone, which includes the central city and surrounding suburbs. But a national advertiser using all media might prefer that a market be defined in terms of the entire metropolitan area and would use the Census Bureau's Metropolitan Statistical Area definition. Another manufacturer using television almost exclusively might prefer to use Nielsen's DMA. Each of these local market definitions is somewhat different.

As a result, it becomes important for the planner to know the various definitions of what constitutes a local market when planning media. Which definition is most suitable? Some media planners have asked for standardizing definitions, but without much success. Until standardization becomes acceptable, the differences should be clearly understood. Following are explanations of the definitions used most often.

Designated Market Area (DMA)   The Designated Market Area (DMA), used by Nielsen Media Research for a television market, identifies an exclusive geographic area of counties in which the home market television stations hold a dominance of total hours viewed. There are 210 DMAs in the United States.

Metropolitan Statistical Area (MSA)   The Census Bureau developed the Metropolitan Statistical Area (MSA) as a replacement for the Standard Metropolitan Statistical Area definition used in the past. An MSA is a population area with a large nucleus at the center and adjacent areas that have a large degree of economic and social integration with the center. MSAs are classified on the basis of the following population levels:

Level A: Population of 1,000,000 or more
Level B: Population of 250,000 to 999,999
Level C: Population of 100,000 to 249,999
Level D: Population of less than 100,000

PMSA and CMSA   Within metropolitan areas of one million or more population, the Census Bureau defines separate components of an MSA if the parts meet certain criteria as follows:

- Principal Metropolitan Statistical Area (PMSA)—The MSA defined by counties
- Consolidated Metropolitan Statistical Area (CMSA)—Large metropolitan complexes that contain PMSAs

The following analysis is shown to better explain how these designations look for Chicago. The Chicago PMSA (MSA) consists of the following Illinois counties, according to the 2000 census:[1]

---

1. FAIR: www.fairus.org/html/msas/042ilchi.htm.

Cook	Kendall
De Kalb	Lake
Du Page	McHenry
Grundy	Will
Kane	

The Chicago-Gary-Kenosha Consolidated Metropolitan Statistical Area (CMSA) consists of the following PMSAs:

Chicago PMSA
Gary PMSA
Kenosha PMSA
Kankakee PMSA

City Zone and Retail Trading Zone   Newspapers define their markets in terms of city zones and retail trading zones. A *city zone* represents the corporate city limits plus heavily populated areas adjoining a city in which the newspaper is sold, as designated by an agreement between the publisher and the Audit Bureau of Circulations. A *retail trading zone* is an area beyond the city zone from which retailers draw sufficient customers to warrant spending advertising dollars to reach them. This area is also determined by an agreement between the publisher and the Audit Bureau of Circulations.

Newspaper Designated Market   Another newspaper classification, a *newspaper designated market* covers the geographic area in which the newspaper provides primary editorial and advertising services. Decisions about areas to include and the boundary lines are made by the Audit Bureau of Circulations in consultation with the publisher. Publishers who report their circulations by newspaper designated markets usually eliminate circulation data by city and retail trading zones.

Newspapers can also define markets by counties in which coverage percentages are computed. Data show where newspapers have at least 50 percent coverage, 20 percent coverage, and so forth.

To illustrate how market definitions vary, even within one geographic market, Exhibit 7-12 shows different definitions in the city of Chicago and outlying areas. The DMA includes 16 counties in Illinois and Indiana. The Chicago

EXHIBIT 7-12

DMA, MSA, and Newspaper Designated Markets of Chicago, by County

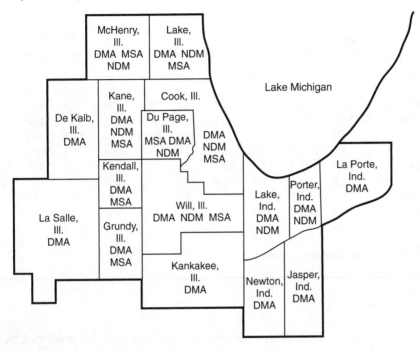

TV DMA—16 counties
MSA-PMSA—8 counties
Newspaper Designated Markets (NDM)—8 counties

MSA (which is the same area as the PMSA) covers 8 counties. And, for the *Chicago Tribune,* the newspaper designated markets include 8 counties in Illinois and Indiana.

Sales Analysis

Gathering data about the sales volume of a brand and its competitors makes it possible to start deciding where to advertise. One approach is to select geographic markets on the basis of sales or market share produced in the past. In this situation, the deciding factor is the volume of past sales, rather than the

EXHIBIT 7-13

Sales of Brand X and Competitors, by Region

	TOTAL INDUSTRY SALES			BRAND X		BRAND Y		BRAND Z	
REGION	U.S. HOUSE- HOLDS	SALES	INDEX	SALES	INDEX	SALES	INDEX	SALES	INDEX
New England	5.8%	3.4%	59	3.5%	103	3.5%	103	2.4%	71
New York	8.4	5.0	60	4.6	92	4.5	90	6.5	130
Middle Atlantic	11.4	10.8	94	11.0	102	10.1	94	12.9	119
East Central	15.8	17.6	111	19.5	111	16.8	95	18.3	104
West Central	14.0	16.0	115	17.5	109	16.2	101	16.4	103
Chicago	3.7	5.4	144	7.1	131	5.4	98	5.3	98
Southeast	15.7	13.3	85	13.1	98	12.1	91	14.0	105
Southwest	9.9	8.8	89	9.4	104	9.2	105	7.5	85
Los Angeles	5.1	7.0	138	4.7	67	9.1	130	5.8	83
Remaining Pacific	10.2	12.7	124	9.6	76	13.2	104	10.9	86
Total	100.0%	100.0%		100.0%		100.0%		100.0%	

SOURCE: Data provided by a major advertiser.

index of potential sales. Without a doubt, the volume of sales produced by a geographic market in the past must be the first consideration in making the selection. The question of whether to go to high-index potential markets depends to some extent on whether sales have been optimized in the existing high-volume markets. Perhaps an increase in advertising in current markets will result in an equivalent increase in sales.

Exhibit 7-13 shows the sales of a company and its competitors reported on the basis of seven regions plus three large metropolitan areas: New York, Chicago, and Los Angeles. The index numbers in this table were computed by comparing sales percentages for each brand with total industry sales by region.

Does Exhibit 7-13 tell the planner precisely where to advertise? No, but it tells where the brand is doing well relative to competitors: in New England, East Central, West Central, Chicago, and the Southwest. The planner needs to obtain and understand this kind of information before proceeding to more specific information that will help pinpoint markets in which to advertise.

EXHIBIT 7-14

Sales of Brand X and Competitors, by County Size

COUNTY SIZE	POPULATION DISTRIBUTION	TOTAL MARKET		POWDERED MARKET SEGMENT		LIQUID MARKET SEGMENT	
		SALES	INDEX	SALES	INDEX	SALES	INDEX
A	41.4%	42.3%	102	39.1%	94	45.4%	110
B	27.2	26.9	99	27.6	101	26.2	96
C	16.3	19.2	117	20.6	126	17.9	109
D	15.1	11.6	76	12.7	84	10.5	70
Total	100.0%	100.0%		100.0%		100.0%	

SOURCE: Data provided by a major advertiser.

Sales analysis by regions usually is followed by a county analysis, which provides another dimension for the media planner to consider in selecting media to reach markets. To deal with county sizes conveniently, Nielsen classifies them with an A, B, C, D system:

- A counties—All counties located within the 25 largest metropolitan areas
- B counties—All counties not included in A that have more than 150,000 population
- C counties—All counties not included in A and B that have more than 40,000 population
- D counties—All remaining counties

Exhibit 7-14 shows a sales breakdown by county size for liquid and powdered forms of a given product. For the total market, county size C has the best potential. For the liquid market segment, county size A shows the best potential, followed closely by C counties. For the powdered market segment, C counties have the best potential. Once again, note the potential for sales shown by index numbers and the actual sales volume shown for the total market and its segments. In all cases, county size A has the highest percentage of sales. The decision should weigh both volume and potential.

Heavy-User Data

Although a geographic analysis begins to answer the question of where to advertise, an examination of data about heavy users will provide additional insights. Often, a small percentage of heavy users account for the largest percentage of product usage. This is true for many product categories, but not for all.

Studying heavy users gives a different dimension of a market's location. If the marketing strategy calls for heavy users, then their whereabouts becomes important. Exhibit 7-15 shows that medium/heavy users of bottled water and seltzer tend strongly to live in metropolitan suburban areas. Stated more specifically, medium/heavy users of bottled water are 13 percent more likely to live in MSA suburban areas than is the average adult. The significant below-average index in the non-MSA (rural) areas is another indication of the young, active, upscale lifestyle of bottled-water users.

Buying Power Indices

Another method for determining where to advertise is to use buying power indices. These indices help a planner evaluate sales and product usage or general sales potential in certain geographic areas. Buying power indices include the brand development index (BDI) and category development index (CDI), as well as weighted BDIs and CDIs.

EXHIBIT 7-15

Total Versus Light and Medium/Heavy Users of Bottled Water by Type of Metropolitan Statistical Area (MSA)

	INDEX TO TOTAL ADULTS		
	TOTAL USERS	LIGHT USERS	MEDIUM/ HEAVY USERS
MSA—central city	99	98	99
MSA—suburban	111	106	113
Non-MSA	76	88	71

SOURCE: Mediamark Research Inc., Doublebase, 2000.

Brand Development Index (BDI)   One useful tool available for helping a media planner decide where to advertise is the *brand development index (BDI)*. This index measures the number of cases, units, or dollar volume of a brand sold per 1,000 population. It is calculated from data for each individual market in which the brand is sold, according to the following formula:

$$\text{BDI} = \frac{\text{Percentage of a brand's total U.S. sales in Market A}}{\text{Percentage of total U.S. population in Market A}} \times 100$$

Following is an example of how the BDI would be calculated for a brand in Seattle:

$$\frac{\text{Sales of the brand in Seattle (\% of U.S.)}}{\text{Population in Seattle (\% of U.S.)}} \times 100 = \frac{3.09}{1.58} \times 100 = 1.96 \times 100 = 196$$

The BDI is an index number representing sales potential. It conforms to the same basic characteristics of index numbers discussed earlier. The larger the sales in a market relative to population percentage, the higher the BDI in that market.

Category Development Index (CDI)   The *category development index (CDI)* is similar to the BDI, except that it is based on the percentage of sales of a product category, rather than a brand, in a given market. The method of calculating the CDI is as follows:

$$\text{CDI} = \frac{\text{Percentage of a product category's total U.S. sales in Market A}}{\text{Percentage of total U.S. population in Market A}} \times 100$$

An example of the CDI in Seattle would be set up as follows:

$$\frac{\text{Category sales in Seattle (\% of U.S.)}}{\text{Population in Seattle (\% of U.S.)}} \times 100 = \frac{2.71}{1.58} \times 100 = 1.72 \times 100 = 172$$

Both the BDI and CDI are useful in decision making. One tells the planner the relative strengths and weaknesses for the brand, and the other, the relative

EXHIBIT 7-16

BDI/CDI Relationships

	HIGH BDI	LOW BDI
High CDI	High share of market Good market potential	Low share of market Good market potential
Low CDI	High share of market Monitor for sales decline	Low share of market Poor market potential

strengths and weaknesses for the category. These indices should be calculated for any market where the brand is sold. As summarized in Exhibit 7-16, the following results are possible:

- **High BDI and high CDI**—This kind of market usually represents good sales potential for both the brand and the category.
- **High BDI and low CDI**—Here the category is not selling well, but the brand is. This is probably a good market in which to advertise, but surely one to watch to see whether the brand's sales decline in time.
- **Low BDI and high CDI**—This kind of market shows potential for the category but demands that someone study the reason why the brand is not doing well here. Is it because of poor distribution? Not enough advertising dollars, GRPs, or reach in the market? To advertise in this market without knowing the answer would be a risk.
- **Low BDI and low CDI**—This kind of market represents a risk for any brand. Here, too, a planner might want to know why the category does not sell well. Such a market would probably not be a good place to advertise under most circumstances.

In using BDI/CDI data for each market in decision making, the planner has a number of ways to proceed. One is to set arbitrary criteria for each market. For example, a planner could decide that for a market to be selected, it would have to meet at least one of the following requirements:

- A BDI of 125 or greater
- A BDI at least 10 points higher than the CDI
- A certain percentage sales increase over a previous year in that market, and/or a sales volume of x dollars in the market

Market selection on such a basis might seem arbitrary, but it could be based on the experience of a planner who, over a period of years, simply knows which market characteristics have been the most profitable.

Weighted BDIs and CDIs   Another method of selecting markets might be to weight the BDI and CDI to arrive at a single combined index. Before this weighting is done, however, a marketing strategy decision must be made to guide the media planner in the proper weighting of the two indices. A marketing strategy that calls for x dollars of advertising spending in direct proportion to sales (a basically defensive posture) requires that the BDI be used exclusively in allocating media expenditures to each market. At the other extreme, if a marketing strategy requires that brand advertising be allocated only on the basis of category development (a basically offensive posture, generally used for new brands without a sales pattern), the media planner would have to use only the CDI in deciding spending by market.

Any mixture of these two strategies requires a mixture of weights for the BDI and the CDI. For example, suppose the marketing strategy states that brand sales should be protected in all high-sales areas but that spending should be increased where category development is high and brand development is low. In that situation, the planner might elect to weight the BDI 75 percent and the CDI 25 percent (weights must add up to 100 percent). The following example illustrates how that calculation would be made in a typical market:

Weighted BDI = 165 × .75 = 124
Weighted CDI = 140 × .25 = 35
Weighted BDI + Weighted CDI = 159

All markets would be evaluated on the basis of a similar weighting, and only those that reach a certain level would be selected.

Weighting is risky, however, unless the planner knows exactly what each weighting signifies. A safer procedure would be to weight BDI and CDI 50 percent each and then combine them. Nevertheless, some kind of arbitrary decision would have to be made. The cutoff point might be set at 125—that is, any market indexed at over 125 would be selected and any under 125 rejected, at least until experience dictates otherwise.

Using Buying Power Indices   Sometimes an advertiser does not know a product's sales volume in each geographic market, possibly because the advertiser sells through distributors and wholesalers. Although many manufacturers in the food, drug, and appliance fields know, from their own records, how large their sales are to wholesalers or distributors, they often do not know how well sales are going at the retail level, or there is a long time lag between wholesale and retail sales. Furthermore, even if a manufacturer should eventually learn how consumer sales are going, this information might not be indicative of a brand's share of total sales compared to its competitors.

The best these advertisers can do is to examine the number of wholesale shipments into each market and prepare their media plans on such a basis. However, these data could be misleading because of shipments to regional distribution centers operated by large retail chains. As a result, the number of shipments by a manufacturer into a given market might not be equivalent to the sales potential of that market. Lack of sales volume and share, market by market, handicaps the media planner in deciding where to place advertising. Nevertheless, many small advertisers simply cannot afford to purchase sales volume and share data from the syndicated research services. They have to use shipments or sales potentials determined through other ways.

One source available to almost all advertisers and agencies is *Demographics USA* (www.tradedimensions.com), which can help determine the sales potential of geographic markets. This book is published annually and is available at a relatively low cost. The data are based on census measurements plus updated projections. The survey computes a multiple-factor index for every major U.S. metropolitan area. A factor is a market quality that affects sales. Therefore, it is possible to examine the general sales potential of every geographic market. Generally, the more people there are in a market, the greater the sales potential, so population is a factor. Another factor is effective buying income, based on total income after taxes (similar to disposable income). A third factor in the survey's index is total retail sales. The three factors are judgmentally weighted to indicate that some factors are more important than others in making sales. Population could be weighted double, total retail sales weighted three times, and effective buying income weighted five times. When added together, the result is a single number reflecting these judgments that can be used for market selection.

On one hand, the indices described help the planner determine the relative value of each market. These values in turn can be used to determine budgets or media weights. On the other hand, the indices might be too general for certain kinds of products. Some specialized products will need additional or more specific marketing data. However, the information in *Demographics USA* can be used with data from other sources to provide a better and more selective index. Taking the market for air conditioners as an example, the planner could combine survey data with information on average maximum annual temperature and average annual humidity to create a special index number for each market. Furthermore, factors would be weighted in any way necessary to get a better perspective of the relative value of each market. One can use the buying power indices for a quick evaluation of alternative geographic markets.

The question of where to advertise is based on an analysis of sales and product usage or general sales potential, plus consideration of the marketing objectives. The users of the buying power data will find that the index numbers are an easy way to compare a large number of categories. If raw numbers or percentages are needed, they are usually provided so that users need not make any further preliminary calculations.

Cutoff Points

In selecting markets for advertising, it is often difficult to judge at which point to drop markets at the bottom of the list. The place at which the list is divided is called the *cutoff point*. One way to establish a cutoff point is to select markets on the basis of some arbitrary number, usually in multiples of 10, 25, or 50. This is a widespread practice in the industry. Using this method, whatever markets are listed as number 51 or lower are eliminated. Yet most media planners would agree that there is not always much difference between the 50th market and the 51st market.

A more logical way to set the cutoff point is to determine how much weight (in terms of dollars) should be assigned to the best markets. Once these dollars have been allocated, then all remaining money is distributed to the poorer markets based on a weighting system. Usually such weighting would be based on spending a minimum amount of money in a market. If a market's potential does not justify such an expenditure, then advertising to that market might not be worthwhile. Weighting systems divide markets into groups titled A, B, C, and so on. An A market might receive a given number of dollars of advertising. The B markets receive somewhat less, and C markets receive much less.

At times, a system of gross rating points is used to determine how much money will be spent in a market. The money is allocated from the top of the list down, until it runs out, thereby automatically establishing the cutoff point. In many cases, media planners and client representatives have, through experience, developed a minimum number of markets that must be on any list. They add markets if any money is left after allocating money to the basic list.

One problem in establishing cutoff points is that often a few markets account for a large percentage of sales. For example, 25 markets might account for 75 percent of a brand's sales. The next 25 largest markets might account for only 8 percent additional sales. Usually media planners prefer to have fewer markets and spend enough money on each to fully exploit the selected markets.

Often, too, marketing objectives affect the length of a list. For example, if an objective is to protect the brand's share of market from inroads of competitors, then more money might be put into markets where competitors are trying to sell against the brand. Usually a brand has its best markets, so the list has to be reduced somewhat in order to allocate extra money at the top of the list.

The process of selecting markets and determining cutoff points is not the sole responsibility of the media planner. Usually, the account executive and a client representative share this responsibility. In such cases, decisions are made by compromise as well as by logic. In a personal conversation, one media planner once explained the situation this way:

> This give-and-take process between the account executive, the client, and myself is often logical, but sometimes ludicrous. For example, I'll have both Rochester and Albany on my market list. The account man may take Albany

off but leave Rochester in. But the client puts Albany back in and removes Rochester. Why? Well it could be that we can't afford both, or the client feels that he has to back a stronger sales force at Albany. But the whole process of selecting markets is an "editing" operation, in which we each edit the others' recommendations until a market list takes shape.

In summary, market lists and cutoff points are established on the basis of subjective factors as well as objective criteria. The most important criteria are the sales goals and the money needed to attain them in each market. Experience, compromise, and some arbitrary factors also influence the process at various times.

WHEN TO ADVERTISE

Decisions about when to advertise depend on a number of important considerations, including the following:

- Monthly sales patterns
- Budget constraints
- Competitive activities
- Specific goals for the brand
- Product availability
- Promotional requirements

Each of these points deserves individual discussion, but one point underlies them all: Advertise when people tend to buy the product in question. It is difficult if not impossible to make them buy at any other time. Studying sales by product category over a period of 20 or more years shows that buying takes place at fairly regular intervals and not capriciously. Therefore, it is important to learn when people tend to buy and to capitalize on these buying habits.

Monthly Sales Patterns

The most important consideration in deciding when to advertise is to know when sales peaks occur for the product category compared with when sales

EXHIBIT 7-17

Category and Brand Sales, by Month

MONTH	CATEGORY SALES	BRAND SALES	INDEX*
January	8.2%	6.8%	83
February	7.7	6.5	85
March	8.5	8.2	96
April	8.2	7.5	91
May	8.5	8.9	105
June	8.2	8.9	109
July	8.5	9.4	110
August	8.5	10.3	121
September	8.2	8.2	180
October	8.5	8.8	103
November	8.2	7.6	93
December	8.5	9.5	112

*Brand sales ÷ category sales × 100.

peaks occur for the brand. Exhibit 7-17 shows category sales indexed to brand sales by month. Sales for the category in question tend to be rather flat month by month, but the brand tends to have rather clear-cut highs and lows. Theoretically, the brand should advertise more heavily in months when its sales have been higher.

The answer is not always so clear-cut, however. Perhaps the category sells well in a particular month, but the brand does not. Thus the dilemma: Should the brand advertise more heavily in months when the category is selling well or in months when the brand is selling well? Usually, one would advertise more heavily in the months when the category is selling well. Although other considerations can require a change in this strategy, some planners use only category sales as their guide in planning.

Usually a monthly sales analysis for a product category will indicate a seasonal effect. Thus, in studying monthly sales records, a planner should keep in mind the effect of certain seasons on sales. Back-to-school or graduation months certainly influence the sales of certain kinds of products, as do Christmas or

Easter. January and August have become the "white sale" months to sell bed linens, towels, and tablecloths. If a brand belongs to a category that is affected by seasons, then monthly sales should be more carefully studied so as not to miss an opportunity.

Budget Constraints

Often the advertising budget is not large enough to permit year-round advertising. In such a situation, the planner will probably allocate the advertising dollars to the best selling months. Whether to maintain continuity (continuous advertising all year long) or flights (periodic advertising interspersed with no advertising) depends on the recency theory discussed in Chapter 5 as well as other considerations that will be discussed later.

Competitive Activities

In planning a media schedule, it is important to consider when competitors advertise. If their timing pattern is different from that of the overall category, then the planner will have to decide how important the difference is. Does it put the planner's own brand in a weaker position? If so, the planner will want to copy a competitor's timing. Most often, however, competitors tend to follow category sales patterns fairly closely.

Specific Goals for the Brand

At times, a marketing or media objective is to react aggressively to competitive strategies. Perhaps such a strategy will be necessary to attain a market share increase. In such a situation, one might time heavy advertising to begin before most competitors start. As a result, a brand can achieve greater and quicker visibility before the normal buying season starts. Another specific goal might be to outspend competitors in some particular month. This could require withdrawing money allocated to the year-long advertising effort for the concentrated attack. Other marketing/media goals also affect timing. New-product introductions, for example, require a timing pattern of heavy initial advertising (first quarter of sales year) and relatively lighter weights later on.

Product Availability

In certain marketing situations, marketing demand outstrips a manufacturer's ability to supply the product. Even if a company is building a new plant to keep up with demand, the added capacity will not be ready for some time. In such a case, the timing of advertising has to be related to production availability. Most often a problem with availability occurs when new products are introduced, but it occasionally happens when there is a surge in sales of existing products.

Promotional Requirements

If the advertiser plans an aggressive sales promotion campaign for a brand preceding or during the brand's regular advertising campaign, this will affect timing. A cents-off deal, for example, might require aggressive advertising when the campaign to announce the promotion starts.

CHAPTER EIGHT

Strategy Planning II

WEIGHTING, REACH, FREQUENCY, AND SCHEDULING

Chapter 7 discussed three major media-planning strategy decisions: to whom to advertise, where to advertise, and when to advertise. These decisions must be made early in the planning process, because they control other strategy decisions. The additional decisions, which are discussed in this chapter, include choices about geographic weighting, reach and frequency, and scheduling.

GEOGRAPHIC WEIGHTING

Geographic weighting is the practice of giving extra consideration to one or more markets that have more sales potential—because of location or demographics or other reasons—than other markets. A record of good sales and/or good potential for sales for the product category and the brand being advertised can make one market more important than others. If all geographic markets had an equal record of sales and/or sales potential, then there would be no need to add extra advertising weight. But markets are rarely equal in value, so weighting is necessary.

There is another reason for weighting markets. Advertisers who buy national media usually find that the gross impressions delivered by a media plan do not align with differences in local sales potential. Some markets might have good sales potential but receive relatively few impressions from national media, whereas others have weak sales potential but receive many more impressions than required.

Exhibit 8-1 illustrates the difference in gross rating points delivered by a nighttime network TV schedule in different markets. As the table shows, the delivery of GRPs by a national medium such as network television is generally

EXHIBIT 8-1

An Index of How Network Television Delivery of Gross Rating Points Varies by Market

	NETWORK PRIME-TIME HOUSEHOLD GRPs: INDEXED
National average	100
New York	109
Miami	91
Detroit	116
Chicago	115
Corpus Christi	78
Minneapolis–St. Paul	123
Huntsville	72

SOURCE: Nielsen Media Research, *Network Programs by DMA Report*, February 2000.

distributed unevenly among markets. If the delivery of these GRPs happened to closely match sales potential in each market, there would be no need for adjustment. Unfortunately, this rarely happens, so advertising weights must be adjusted.

The final determination of the need for weighting is the wide variance in media costs—again, not necessarily in relation to sales potential. On one hand, a planner who allocates dollars on a proportional basis might be unable to buy as much advertising as required in the best markets because costs are too high. On the other hand, the planner might be able to buy more impressions than needed in less expensive markets.

To illustrate the variation in media costs, Exhibit 8-2 analyzes cost per thousand (CPM) for several spot TV markets. Recall that CPM numbers can reflect the relationship between target audiences delivered and the costs of media in delivering those targets. Exhibit 8-2 shows that media CPMs for reaching women aged 25–54 in various markets are inversely proportional to the size of each market. Smaller markets (e.g., Wilmington, Albany, Utica, Palm Springs) often have a higher CPM than larger markets (e.g., New York, Chicago, San Francisco) to reach a given target audience.

EXHIBIT 8-2

Cost-per-Thousand Analysis

MARKET	% U.S. HOUSEHOLDS	SPOT TV CPM, WOMEN 25–54 (PRIME TIME)
New York	6.82	$ 49.84
Chicago	3.18	61.58
San Francisco	2.40	68.48
Wilmington, Del.	0.13	91.33
Albany, Ga.	0.13	119.71
Utica, N.Y.	0.08	132.61
Palm Springs, Calif.	0.10	164.13

SOURCE: Copyright SQAD Inc., December 1999, used with permission.

Forms of Weighting

Different weighting techniques will accomplish the same objectives. The simplest way, the *dollar allocation technique,* allocates proportionately more money to good markets. Therefore, if Market A accounts for 10 percent of total sales, it receives 10 percent of the advertising budget. This technique, however, does not consider varying media costs.

A second technique, *gross impression weighting,* does consider varying media costs. It allocates the budget on the basis of gross impressions desired: Good markets are budgeted to receive more impressions, and weaker markets, fewer.

Exhibit 8-3 illustrates the differences between the first and second weighting techniques. The table shows that when dollars are allocated proportionately, gross impressions vary. When gross impressions are allocated proportionately, dollars vary.

Why do these two techniques differ? Dollar allocation does not consider media gross impressions. Therefore, 10 percent of the available dollars buys more impressions in Market A than in Market B, because cost per thousand is lower in Market A. So the dollar allocation technique leaves Market B with fewer gross impressions per year than Market A, even though sales potential is equal. To equalize the number of gross impressions in A and B, the planner will tend to favor gross impression allocation.

EXHIBIT 8-3

Differences in Weighting Methods

		DOLLAR WEIGHTING		GROSS IMPRESSION WEIGHTING		
	TOTAL SALES	CPM	10% OF DOLLARS	NUMBER OF GROSS IMPRESSIONS 10% DOLLARS BUY	10% OF IMPRESSIONS	COST OF 10% OF IMPRESSIONS
Market A	10%	$2.50	$100,000	40 million	32 million	$ 80,000
Market B	10	3.75	100,000	26 million	32 million	120,000
Total			$200,000	66 million	64 million	$200,000

SOURCE: Ogilvy & Mather.

Nevertheless, each technique has different values. Dollar allocation tends to generate the following results:

- More impressions in cost-efficient markets—that is, markets where the cost per thousand is relatively low
- Fewer impressions in inefficient markets or high-CPM markets
- The opportunity for good markets to develop their potential because more gross impressions are received in these markets, presumably generating more sales
- A slightly unbalanced advertising weight-to-sales ratio

Gross impression allocation tends to generate the following results:

- Proportional communication pressure, regardless of cost
- Balanced reach and frequency based on sales potential, meaning good markets get proportionately more reach and frequency than poor markets
- The opportunity for good markets to develop their potential because more gross impressions are received in these markets, presumably generating more sales
- A slightly unbalanced advertising-to-sales ratio

In deciding which weighting techniques to use, the planner should consider which best meets the marketing objectives. In many instances, gross impression weighting is considered better because it is more directly related to communica-

EXHIBIT 8-4

How U.S. Dollar Allocation Matches Sales Distribution

| | | | DOLLAR ALLOCATION | | |
MARKET	SALES (%)	COST (THOUSANDS)	TOTAL COST (%)	GROSS IMPRESSIONS THAT CAN BE BOUGHT (MILLIONS)	TOTAL GROSS IMPRESSIONS (%)
A	45%	$ 675	45%	343	48%
B	30	450	30	214	30
C	15	225	15	93	13
D	10	150	10	64	9
Total U.S.	100%	$1,500	100%	714	100%

SOURCE: Ogilvy & Mather.

EXHIBIT 8-5

How Gross Impression Allocation Matches Sales Distribution

MARKET	SALES (%)	GROSS IMPRESSIONS PLANNED FOR (MILLIONS)	TOTAL GROSS IMPRESSIONS (%)	COST OF GROSS IMPRESSIONS PLANNED (THOUSANDS)	TOTAL COST (%)
A	45%	318	45%	$ 637	42%
B	30	212	30	444	30
C	15	106	15	251	17
D	10	71	10	168	11
Total	100%	707	100%	$1,500	100%

SOURCE: Ogilvy & Mather.

tion goals. One central goal of media strategy planning is to reach large numbers of target audiences with a certain amount of repetition. Within a given budget, gross impression weighting accomplishes this goal best because it considers media costs. In the dollar allocation technique, even if costs are directly proportional to sales, audiences still might not be reached often enough or in sufficiently large numbers.

Exhibits 8-4 and 8-5 provide another picture of the relationships of both processes. Exhibit 8-4 shows again that even when dollars are matched perfectly against sales percentage, gross impressions do not match (except in Market B). Exhibit 8-5 shows that when gross impressions are matched perfectly against sales percentages, dollar costs do not match (again, except in Market B).

Share of Voice (Message Weight Distribution)

A planning concept that is sometimes used in making media decisions is called *share of voice* or, more appropriately, *message weight distribution.* This concept requires a planner to determine how much advertising is being done for a brand relative to the amount being done for competitive brands. A share of voice is a percentage of total advertising weight for each brand.

The assumption underlying share of voice is that if a brand is not spending an amount equal to or exceeding the expenditures of competitors, then it might not be able to achieve its goals. This assumption is not necessarily valid, because many variables other than media spending affect the success of an advertising campaign. Success likely depends at least in part on the superiority of the brand, the uniqueness of the copy, the amount and quality of distribution, or the frequency and quality of promotions, to name a few variables. In fact, many planners do not use the share of voice concept at all, and others think of it as a general ideal that can help in determining allocations and/or budgets.

If, however, one is inclined to determine share of voice, it is important to do so on other bases than comparing the percentage of dollars spent. "Dollars spent" do not buy a constant number of gross impressions or target rating points. Thus, it would be better to begin by finding how many gross impressions or target rating points can be purchased for a given number of dollars, then convert this information into percentages. Comparisons can be made, for example, on the basis of the actual number of messages (or commercials) delivered.

Exhibit 8-6 shows the share of TV messages to women 18–39 for nine brands. It is important to note that the share of voice (TV messages) does not match share of TV dollars in the example shown. Exhibit 8-6 also analyzes nine competitors and their message weight deliveries. The table shows that Brand A has 35 percent of the market but spends only 25 percent of the total TV dollars and has a relatively lower percentage of message delivery than does Brand B.

The planner should ask a number of questions to determine why Brand A has such a high ratio of market share to message share. Is Brand A inherently superior in quality to B? Does Brand A have better distribution? Better copy?

EXHIBIT 8-6

Share of Voice (Message Weight Distribution) for Nine Competitors

BRAND	SHARE OF MARKET	SHARE OF TV DOLLARS	SHARE OF TV MESSAGE TO WOMEN 18–39
A	35%	25%	19%
B	26	25	28
C	17	16	16
D	8	8	12
E	7	4	6
F	4	3	6
G	3	2	4
H	N/A	14	8
I	N/A	3	1
Total	100%	100%	100%

SOURCE: Paul Roth, "How to Plan Media," *Media Decisions* (1976): 26.

Most other brands show a high degree of consistency between market share and message share. Additional message weight analysis should be made of individual markets to see how they, too, relate to market share.

Guidelines for Geographic Weighting

No one formula is used for determining advertising weights to apply in different geographic areas; instead, weighting decisions are usually a result of many factors. Using one or the other of the techniques described, a planner can weight advertising in geographic markets in a number of ways. The following guidelines are important considerations in weighting.

A general concept is to apply extra weight to markets where sales volume or market share is high. In a market-by-market analysis, a planner might look at the brand development index (BDI) and compare it with a category development index (CDI). At times, more weight is added to markets with high BDIs. More often, however, when a CDI is high and a BDI is low for a given market, additional weight is added to bring the market up to its potential (as shown in the CDI).

Market potential, as a basis for weighting, depends on any one, or perhaps all, of the following considerations:

- **History of each market's responsiveness to advertising**—If a local market has not responded well to advertising in the past, then additional weight might not help.
- **History of profitability**—Although additional weight in a local market can improve sales volume or market share, it might do so at an unprofitable level. There is a point of diminishing returns relative to profits as extra weight is added to a market.
- **Pipeline problems**—If distribution levels in a market are low or difficult to increase, or if there are other marketing channel problems, then these problems will influence the amount of extra weight to apply.
- **Sales force input**—Some companies use salespeople as sources of marketing intelligence at the local level. Their information can affect the manner in which weight is applied.
- **Local market idiosyncrasies**—Some local markets have problems in communication and/or selling that may not exist in other markets. For example, an advertiser might find that an equal number of GRPs applied to both large and small markets usually produces greater awareness in smaller markets, regardless of other factors. If such idiosyncrasies exist, then the weighting decision should account for them.
- **Competitive noise levels**—If competitors advertise heavily in a market, the net effect of the noise level will require heavier weight in that market.
- **Cost-efficiency of advertising in the market**—Additional weight could cost too much or result in cost-inefficiency.

After evaluating these considerations, the planner should decide on a course of action to influence the final weighting. Does the advertiser want to defend strengths in good markets? Improve weaknesses in problem markets? Develop opportunity markets? After making this decision and considering other factors, the planner can make weighting decisions for local geographic areas.

Case Studies 8-1, 8-2, and 8-3 are examples of how different advertisers have used weighting techniques. No single method is used to the exclusion of all others. Each technique meets the needs of individual advertisers.

CASE STUDY 8-1

Allocating Weights to Spot TV Markets on a Pro-Rata Basis

This example shows weights by the amount of money allocated to each spot TV market in a media plan. Only five markets are shown, but this technique could be used for more than 100 markets if necessary.

For purposes of illustration, assume that a manufacturer sells a product in five geographic areas (or markets). Exhibit A shows sales percentages for each of the five areas, along with a proportional allocation of the budget to each sales area. Also shown is the percentage of network television delivery in each sales area.

EXHIBIT A

A Budget Allocated Proportionately to Sales Made by Each Area

AREA	SALES MADE BY EACH AREA	BUDGET GOAL	NETWORK DELIVERY*
A	30%	$1,500,000	25%
B	15	750,000	15
C	10	500,000	20
D	10	500,000	10
E	35	1,750,000	30
Total	100%	$5,000,000	100%

*Delivery is based on a number of selected network programs that cover targets.
SOURCE: J. Walter Thompson Company, *Allocating Advertising Weight Geographically* (1973): 9.

The table shows that each area received a proportional amount of dollars equal to the percentage of sales made in the area. However, a close look at the relationship between sales and network delivery percentages shows some anomalies. For example, Area A delivered 30 percent of total sales but has only 25 percent of total network delivery. As a result, the advertiser might have to allocate some of the budget to local television.

The problem that arises is how to divide the television budget between network and spot so that each area receives an equitable portion of the budget. Ideally, a planner would like the percentage of network television delivery to match sales percentages in each market. Therefore, if a market provides 20 percent of total U.S. sales, then it should receive 20 percent of the budget. Unfortunately, when advertisers use network television, the delivery in some markets is more than is needed, and the delivery in other markets is less than is needed.

For example, if sales in Market A are 30 percent and the percentage of total U.S. network program delivery is 20 percent, then the advertiser needs some way to bring television delivery up to the 30 percent level. One way to do this would be to add a certain amount of dollars to local spot television. However, if a market accounts for 10 percent of sales and network television delivery is 20 percent of the U.S. total, one cannot easily cut network, market by market. So a technique has been created to take dollars from network television in certain markets and add them to spot television to bring each market up to a percentage equal to its sales. The following steps in this technique apply to Exhibit B.

EXHIBIT B

Allocation of Budget to Network and Spot TV

SALES AREA	SALES MADE BY EACH AREA	BUDGET GOAL	TOTAL NETWORK DELIVERY	INDEX: NETWORK TO SALES DELIVERY	NETWORK BUDGET	SPOT TV (LOCAL) BUDGET
A	30%	$1,500,000	25%	83	$ 625,000	$ 875,000
B	15	750,000	15	100	375,000	375,000
C	10	500,000	20	200	500,000	—
D	10	500,000	10	100	250,000	250,000
E	35	1,750,000	30	86	750,000	1,000,000
Total	100%	$5,000,000	100%		$2,500,000	$2,500,000

SOURCE: J. Walter Thompson Company, *Allocating Advertising Weight Geographically* (1973): 9.

1. A national advertiser buys a regional feed of network television advertising in five markets. (It is rare to buy so few markets with network TV, but it illustrates the solution that would work for all 210 markets.)

2. The planner starts by allocating a predetermined national budget of $5,000,000 for the five markets. The pro rata system would allot each market the same percentage as it accounted for in sales. Market A received $1,500,000 (that is, .30 × $5 million); B received $750,000 (.15 × $5 million), etc.

3. Now the marketer has to know how much network delivery went into each market. This can be obtained from Nielsen's *Network Programs by DMA Report*. All the impressions for all the markets are added, and a percentage of delivery is calculated. These percentages are the data in the column labeled "Total Network Delivery." Although this information is readily available for network TV, the delivery of cable and syndication must be estimated.

4. The planner now can see some anomalies. For example, Market A was underdelivered, because it developed 30 percent of sales but received only 25 percent of national television delivery. It should have received 30 percent. Market B was right on target with 15 percent sales and 15 percent network delivery. Theoretically, B does not need additional spot television. Market C is overdelivered. It had 10 percent sales but received 20 percent network delivery.

5. To clarify over- or underdelivery, an index is calculated for each market:

$$\text{Index of delivery} = \frac{\text{Percentage of network TV delivery in a market}}{\text{Percentage of sales in the same market}}$$

Here are indices of delivery: A = 83; B = 100; C = 200 (C is the most overdelivered market); D = 100; and E = 86.

6. At this point, the planner calculates the total for the five markets based on Market C's overdelivery (with only 10 percent of sales). The formula for this would be as follows:

$$x(.20) = \$500,000$$

Solving for x, the answer is $2,500,000, which becomes the network budget. Another $2,500,000 would be used for the spot TV budget. So $2,500,000 is the budget based on Market C's TV delivery.

7. To find the amount that would go into a new network allocation, multiply each market's pro-rata budget by delivery percentage. That number has been recorded in the column labeled "Network Budget" and was obtained as follows:

Market A: .25 × $2,500,000 = $625,000
Market B: .15 × $2,500,000 = $375,000
Market C: .20 × $2,500,000 = $500,000 (unchanged)

8. Each market's new network budget is subtracted from its pro-rata budget, and this amount is now a first estimate of how much money to allot to spot TV to enable each market to match sales percentages with delivery. Check the math for the spot TV budget. Note that Market C received no money for spot TV. Why?

CASE STUDY 8-2

Weighting Markets on the Basis of Minimum BDIs and CDIs

The previous chapter discussed how BDIs and CDIs are generally used in selecting target markets. These two evaluative statistics can also be used to weight markets on the basis of minimum standards. This method begins with setting sales goals for each individual market. Then 5 percent of the budget is cut from each market and reallocated to problem and/or opportunity markets. A problem market might be defined as follows:

- At least 1 percent of brand sales
- CDI and BDI less than 100
- An unfavorable sales trend

In contrast, an opportunity market would meet criteria such as the following:

- At least 1 percent of brand sales
- CDI over 100, but BDI lower than CDI

- Client's brand showing an unfavorable sales trend within a successful product category

In general, when CDI is over 100, the category is doing well. A BDI under 100 usually indicates a brand is not doing well.

The 5 percent that was cut from each market's budget is now distributed to both problem and opportunity markets. The idea underlying this practice is that problem markets are strengthened by additional dollars, but opportunity markets need extra dollars to optimize potential. At the same time, all markets were allocated some money based on potential.

In this example, all markets will receive some advertising weight through the use of network television or national magazines. The weights discussed in this case are added to national weights.

CASE STUDY 8-3

Weighting Markets by Combining Quantitative and Qualitative Values for Each Market

Advertisers can also use the technique of weighting by combining quantitative and qualitative values for the markets. An advertiser used this technique to purchase network TV to provide national coverage and spot TV to weight the best markets. The value of each market was determined as follows:

1. **Calculate the cost index.** The cost index is simply the CPM for each individual market divided by the average CPM for all spot TV markets in the country. If the average CPM for the country is $2.50 and the CPM for Market A is $3.50, then the cost index would be 140:

$$\text{Cost index} = \$3.50/\$2.50 = 140$$

2. **Calculate the CDI/CPM value for each market.** If Market A has a CDI of 120, then the CDI/CPM value for each market would be 86:

$$120/140 = 86$$

Market A now has less value than it had before, because the CDI/CPM value is so low.

3. **Determine each market's responsiveness to advertising.** This is primarily a qualitative judgment. If sales last year rose by more than 15 percent in a market, that market could be described as responsive. If sales rose between 3 percent and 15 percent, it might be described as somewhat responsive. If sales rose less than 3 percent, it might be described as not responsive. (An alternative method for making this decision is at the end of this section.)

4. **Judgmentally assign extra weight on the basis of the following criteria.** Group A markets receive 50 percent more weight than average because of these conditions:

- CDIs are high.
- CPMs are reasonable.
- Network delivery is low.
- Responsiveness to advertising was good in the past.

Group B markets receive 25 percent more weight than average because combinations of the considerations with Market A yield a lower number but show that the market is important. Group C markets receive no spending for spot TV.

Exhibit C shows three sample markets assigned extra weight as just described:

EXHIBIT C

Sample Markets Assigned Extra Weight

MARKETS	SHARE OF U.S. POPULATION	INDUSTRY SALES (MILLIONS)	NETWORK TV DELIVERY	CDI	CDI/ SPOT CPM	SALES TREND LAST YEAR	WEIGHTING USED
Chicago	4.0%	4.7	97	117	158	+19%	A—add 50%
Seattle	1.2	1.8	85	150	117	+6	B—add 25%
Indianapolis	1.1	1.2	109	101	83	−1	C—none

Responsiveness to advertising could be determined differently. For example, an advertising-to-sales ratio (or A/S index) could be calculated as follows: If sales in Market A were $1,450,000 and advertising in that market were $340,000, then the ratio of advertising to sales would be 340/1,450 = 0.235. Then an index of advertising to sales could be calculated, dividing the A/S index for Market A by the A/S index for the entire country (e.g., 0.235/0.405 = 0.58). These indices could be added to the CPM average for each market and the CDI for each market, resulting in a multiple-factor index, as shown in Exhibit D:

EXHIBIT D

Market A Multiple-Factor Index

	MARKET A
CDI/CPM index	86
CDI	120
A/S index	58
Total	264
Average for Market A (264 ÷ 3)	88

Population of Market A as % of total U.S. × Average index
= Percent of the total allocation for Market A

.05 × 88 = 4.4% of total allocation

This technique could be used to allocate spot dollars proportionately throughout the country.

REACH AND FREQUENCY

Recall that reach refers to the number of people exposed to a vehicle at least once, and frequency refers to how often the average person is reached in a given period (often four weeks). Almost all media plans cover the subjects of reach and frequency. But some plans emphasize reach more than frequency, and others do the opposite. This section describes the different types of situations for emphasizing each.

When to Emphasize Reach

As a general rule, emphasizing reach is appropriate whenever anything new is being planned in the marketplace. The meaning of "new" can be applied to announcing a new price, for example. Consumers usually will not respond to a message until something has been changed in the marketplace in a way that benefits them. A new price can be a benefit if it is lower than it was. Old marketing practices do not need to be changed if they are judged to be successful in selling. Like a reduced price, the following examples of new marketing factors that require a reach strategy can benefit some consumers to some degree:

- New distribution (stores that now carry the brand)
- New features of a product that meet consumers' needs
- New advertising copy (new words and/or pictures)
- New sales promotion incentives
- New packaging
- New models of the brand being introduced

- New media being used for the first time
- New positions in the store where the brand is to be found
- New servicing opportunities
- New home-delivery patterns
- New marketing and/or advertising objectives for the brand

One difficult decision facing a media planner is setting the level of reach needed for a media plan. It is difficult because there is little hard evidence from research or experimentation that provides the necessary direction. What is known about how much reach to use is the product of tradition, experience, common sense, and research done for particular brands in certain market situations. But there is little evidence to indicate that a given reach level is correct for a given marketing situation. Therefore, the guidance provided here—based as it is on widely held beliefs—has to be general. Even with all these qualifiers, some planners will disagree with this approach.

New-Product Introduction/Brand Awareness   It is generally held that high reach is necessary for introducing a new product, the rationale being that few people know the name of the brand or its value. As many people as possible must be informed, thus the need for high reach. But determining just how much reach is necessary is difficult.

The purpose of high reach is to generate awareness of the new brand. The reach level depends to some extent on the objectives for brand awareness level. Is the goal to make 65 percent of the targets aware of a brand name? Some people will need only one exposure to a vehicle to become aware of that brand. Others will need multiple exposures, so a certain level of frequency will be needed in addition to reach.

Some planners might opt for a reach level higher than the desired level of brand awareness, on the assumption that not everyone exposed to a vehicle will be exposed to the ad and the brand name. Others will want reach and frequency, which for planning purposes can be expressed in gross rating points. Within a given number of GRPs, the reach and frequency levels can be juggled to bring either one to a required level. Some available research has attempted to relate GRP levels to brand awareness levels. For example, one study conducted by a well-known advertising agency found that about 2,400 household GRPs had a 60 percent chance of producing about 70 percent brand awareness. Although the research failed to indicate the time period over which the weight was delivered, many consider this GRP level effective for a new-product introduction, and would schedule it over 13 weeks.

Advertising Support for Sales Promotion Activities   Sales promotion activities also need a high degree of reach because consumers must be made aware when certain deals or promotional options are available. In planning media to advertise a cents-off deal, a high level of awareness is a requirement. As before, the precise amount of reach needed cannot be expressed.

Competitors' Levels   One media-planning strategy might be to set a reach level equal to or surpassing that of competitors who are deemed to be vulnerable to attack. Presumably these competitors have products that are not as good as the brand in question, or perhaps they are not advertising enough or to the right targets. Setting a reach level equal to or higher than that of certain competitors offers a potential advantage to the planner, who may use it as one way to determine how much reach ought to be attained.

Budget   Another consideration in planning reach is the budget. No matter which media are chosen, a fixed budget size limits the amount of reach possible. To set a reach level, the planner simply calculates the amount of target reach that can be afforded within the available budget, plus the amount of continuity desired.

Another media strategy stretches media dollars and reach as well. This strategy is to cut ad unit sizes, so more money will be available to buy new reach. (The same strategy can be used to buy more frequency.) If the planned ad unit is 30-second commercials or full-page ads, the advertiser can stretch media dollars by running 10-second IDs or half-page ads. But there are two penalties for cutting unit sizes. First, the cost of smaller unit sizes usually is not exactly proportional to larger sizes. A 15-second spot on network TV costs half as much as a 30-second unit, but in spot TV, 15-second commercials cost from 65 to 75 percent as much. Likewise, a half-page ad costs 55 to 65 percent of a full-page ad. Second, the smaller ad unit may have less communication value.

Previous Levels   Probably the best level of reach is determined by looking at what levels were used previously. If a brand has successfully achieved certain marketing goals in the past with a given level of reach, this same level (or proportional adjustment) should probably be used again.

In essence, then, the amount of reach needed for a media plan is based more on judgment and experience than on research evidence. Because media plans almost always require a certain amount of frequency, the combination of reach and frequency can be calculated in terms of gross rating points. But research on GRPs and communication effects is inconclusive, and the GRP level is also a matter of judgment and experience.

When to Emphasize Frequency

Whenever repetition, not dispersion, is the key selling strategy, the planner should emphasize frequency. This has implications for reach, too, because reach and frequency are inversely related: At a given GRP level, as frequency is increased, reach will decrease. Consider the following examples of these relationships:

- High reach: 60 reach $\times$ 2.3 frequency = 140 GRPs a month
- High frequency: 9.3 reach $\times$ 15 frequency = 140 GRPs a month

As seen in the second example, it is possible to have very high frequencies and yet reach less than 10 percent of the market. Can a planner tolerate failing to expose 90 percent of the target even once, although the remaining 10 percent will see it an average of 15 times? Deciding how much frequency is enough to do the job and the related budgetary question of how many people can be exposed at this level (effective reach) are the most challenging issues facing media planners. Despite a great deal of thinking and research on this subject, there is still no simple answer beyond the cliché, "It all depends."

The bottom line is, frequency should be emphasized over reach whenever repetition of a message is necessary. Generally, high frequency is necessary to compete in a highly competitive market or when a product is sold frequently. Most planners find that there are practical reasons for needing more than minimum amounts of frequency.

The first reason for needing frequency is that not everyone hears or sees an ad the first time it appears. Why? So many ads bombard a person each day that it is impossible for anyone to pay attention to all of them. Even if an individual has seen an ad many times, the person might have absorbed little or none of the information. Therefore, one goal of frequency is to surpass the threshold of the first few exposures so the audience member will absorb the message. Research has shown that there are indeed threshold levels for some advertising, although it is not known precisely whether the threshold is one, two, three, or more exposures.

The second reason is that frequency of exposure to a media vehicle is not the same as frequency of exposure to the advertising it contains. In media planning, research services measure vehicle exposure. But not everyone exposed to a vehicle also sees the ads in that vehicle. Any frequency expressed as part of a media plan overstates the number of times a person is exposed to the ads in the vehicle chosen. Because there is no syndicated research measurement of ad exposure, a planner must allow for more frequency than seems necessary. This creates a cushion of loss of exposure to account for audience members who see the vehicles but don't see the ads of a given brand.

Determining the optimal frequency level is a challenge: Many media planners believe that for effective communication to take place, the target audience should receive at least three exposures. Other planners disagree, saying that the frequency level must vary depending on the situation. The following paragraphs describe conditions that can affect the amount of frequency needed.

Uniqueness of Message   The uniqueness of the advertising message, for example, can affect the necessary frequency. The more innovative and unusual the message is, the more likely consumers will notice it and pay attention to it. The converse is also true: A rather ordinary ad message might need many more than four exposures to be seen and remembered. (In all discussions on frequency levels, the planner must be aware that creative executions vary from brand to brand, and the creative element can argue for more or less frequency than the competition uses.)

Perceived Value of the Brand   Another consideration affecting the frequency level is the perceived value of a brand as compared with the values of competitors' brands. When a brand has an important and easily perceivable benefit not shared by competitors, then less frequency is called for. In other words, the brand has an easily exploited advantage over competitors. But when a brand is very much like all other brands in a product category, more frequency is necessary for the message to be noticed or remembered.

Noise Level   The noise level in a product category also plays a role in deciding how much frequency is needed. If many similar brands are being advertised simultaneously, consumers will find it difficult to recall the message for any one brand amid the confusion caused by the noise level of competitors. When few competitors advertise, less frequency is required.

Competitors' Levels   Some planners think a frequency level should be based on the level of that used by a brand's most serious competitive threat. A similar tactic is to single out the competitor who is the most vulnerable to a brand's promotional attack efforts. This view calls for a frequency level that equals or surpasses that competitor's level, with the objective of gaining an advantage.

Media Values   Media values can also be used in conjunction with gross-rating-point planning to determine frequency (as well as reach) levels. *Media value* is simply the judgment that a given medium has been found, through experience, to be more effective for a brand and its creative message, thus justifying more frequency in that medium. The chief problem, however, in combining media evaluations and frequency levels is that of making too subjective an evaluation of each medium. Is daytime television always less than 35 percent as effective as prime-time television? To say it is always less effective is an unreasonable assumption. For certain brands, in certain marketing situations, at certain times, the 35 percent differential is true, but generalizing is dangerous. The method is a good one, however, when research evidence can be used to back up a generalization about media values.

Frequency levels in media plans therefore range quite a bit. When planners base decisions on the threatening or vulnerable competitor technique, frequency levels average as many as 15 exposures a month. But these levels are not selected in a scientific manner in terms of a cause-and-effect relationship. Even when various frequency levels are tested in three or four local markets and one is found to be better than others, there is no guarantee this level can be projected nationally. Among many national advertisers who have used test marketing for setting frequency levels, the experience varies from a few who have had excellent results to many who have had costly failures.

EFFECTIVE FREQUENCY AND REACH

The question of how to set effective-frequency (and effective-reach) levels cannot be answered very well. Although the three-plus level has been used for a number of years, planners should not automatically assume this should be the goal for every media plan. The reason, as discussed in Chapter 5, is that it is oversimplified. The three-plus concept overlooks too many variables in planning.

One way to estimate the number of exposures needed for communication to take place is to begin by reviewing the different variables that can affect it. Then, starting with a frequency level needed to account for these variables, add them to what is already known about effective frequency. In other words, considering all the variables that affect normal frequency, one might arrive at a two-plus level. Adding that to the three-plus level arrived at by some research on effective frequency results in a five-plus level. However, a planner could end up with a one-plus plan just as well, depending on these variables.

Joseph Ostrow, in a talk at a 1982 Advertising Research Foundation conference, spelled out the variables that planners should first consider. Ostrow's ideas are presented in Case Study 8-4, along with some numbers that could be applied for every consideration that Ostrow recommends.

CASE STUDY 8-4

How to Set Effective-Frequency Levels

One problem facing media planners is deciding how much effective frequency a media plan should have. Although the research can be interpreted to suggest a three-plus level, there is great dispute about it.

One suggestion about how to set a frequency level was made by Joseph W. Ostrow, former executive vice president of the Foote, Cone & Belding agency, at the 1982 Effective

Frequency Conference sponsored by the Advertising Research Foundation.[1] Although this concept was presented 20 years ago, it is still used today and has found its way into the planning philosophies of numerous top advertising agencies.

Ostrow specified a number of conditions that should influence the decision, based on considerations about marketing, media, and creative strategy. He pointed out that "the right level of frequency for a media plan is the point at which effective communication takes place." These conditions might include, for example, "getting consumers to understand the message; helping consumers become more positive about a product (or service) or influencing the purchase decisions directly."

Some additional suggestions are provided here for Ostrow's model to help solve the problem of setting the correct frequency level. The planner should add a certain amount of frequency points to a base if the marketing, media, or creative condition meets his or her needs. (These additional frequency points are only suggestions.) The planner should use these additional points by starting with a base, such as a three-plus level, then adding or subtracting points as the situation dictates.

Here is an example of how to use these suggestions. Suppose a planner is faced with the following situations for a new-product introduction:

1. The introduction is in a highly competitive market.
2. The product has a short purchase cycle.
3. The brand will be among those that are less well known.
4. The product is not used daily.
5. The ad copy is somewhat complex.
6. The copy is more unusual than competitors'.
7. The copy will be in large ad units.
8. There is high ad clutter in category media.
9. The media environment is compatible with the product.
10. Advertising will be continuous.
11. Many media will be used.
12. There will be many opportunities for repetition.

The planner should consult Ostrow's considerations and note the suggested point levels to add for setting effective frequency levels, as shown in Exhibit E.

The next step is to determine how many additional points beyond three-plus should be added to arrive at an effective frequency level. Ostrow's criteria are the source of these considerations; we have used the criteria to suggest points. Note that not all of Ostrow's criteria apply to a given situation. However, it is conceivable that a planner's own criteria should be added to the list to make it more relevant.

---

1. Joseph W. Ostrow, "Setting Effective Frequency Levels," *Effective Frequency* (New York: Advertising Research Foundation, 1982): 89–102.

EXHIBIT E

Factors That Affect Effective Frequency

FACTOR	FREQUENCY NEEDED	COMMENTS
Marketing Factors		
Established brands	Lower	Repetition helps consumers learn a message.
New brands	Higher	New brands need to be learned.
High market share	Lower	High market share assumes that brand loyalty must be high, so less frequency needed.
Low market share	Higher	
Dominant brand in market	Lower	Large brands do not benefit from more repetition if the market is saturated.
Smaller, less well-known brands	Higher	Smaller brands can benefit from more frequency.
High brand loyalty	Lower	An inverse relationship usually exists between frequency and brand loyalty.
Low brand loyalty	Higher	
Long purchase cycle	Lower	Consumers think more about products with longer purchase cycles.
Short purchase cycle (High-volume segments)	Higher	
Product used daily	Higher	Products used daily, or more than once daily, probably need higher frequency.
Product used occasionally	Lower	
Needed to beat competition	Higher	In heavy-spending categories, more frequency is needed above the level that achieves effective communication.
Advertising to older consumers or children	Higher	Special targets need higher frequency levels.
Copy Factors		
Complex copy	Higher	Copy research augmenting good copy is needed to determine how copy is perceived.
Simple copy	Lower	

EXHIBIT E (*continued*)

Factors That Affect Effective Frequency

FACTOR	FREQUENCY NEEDED	COMMENTS
Copy Factors (*continued*)		
Copy less unusual than competition's	Higher	Copy uniqueness translates to less frequency.
Copy more unusual	Lower	
New copy campaign	Higher	Just as a new-product introduction needs higher frequency, so does new copy.
Continuing campaign	Lower	
Image type copy	Higher	Image campaigns are deemed more complex and subtle, needing more frequency.
Product sell copy	Lower	
More different kinds of messages	Higher	This covers the question of how much message variation there is, and is tied to the number of commercials in a pool of commercials.
Single kind of message	Lower	
To avoid wear-out:		
New messages	Higher	Has advertising worn out? Measurements will need to be made to learn the answer.
Older messages	Lower	
Small ad units	Higher	Advertising units, in either broadcast or print, will need more or less frequency.
Larger ad units	Lower	
Media Factors		
High ad clutter	Higher	This is an oddity, because high clutter requires more frequency, which adds to the clutter.
Lower ad clutter	Lower	
Compatible editorial environment	Lower	An example of compatible environment would be a dog food ad appearing in a television pet show.
Noncompatible environment	Higher	

Continued

EXHIBIT E (*continued*)

Factors That Affect Effective Frequency

FACTOR	FREQUENCY NEEDED	COMMENTS
Media Factors (*continued*)		
Attentiveness high	Lower	Some media vehicles have higher attentiveness levels than others.
Attentiveness low	Higher	
Continuous advertising	Lower	Interruptions in advertising, such as in pulsing or flighting, need more frequency.
Pulsed or flighted advertising	Higher	
Few media used	Lower	Each medium used requires a minimum level of frequency.
More media used	Higher	
Opportunities for media repetition	Lower	Certain media offer better and more opportunities for repetition, and these require less frequency.
Fewer opportunities for repetition	Higher	

Marketing Factors

FACTOR					COMMENTS
Established brands	−.2	−.1	+.1	⊕+.2	New brands
High market share	−.2	−.1	+.1	+.2	Low market share
Dominant brand in market	−.2	−.1	+.1	⊕+.2	Smaller, less well-known brands
High brand loyalty	−.2	−.1	+.1	+.2	Low brand loyalty
Long purchase cycle	−.2	−.1	+.1	⊕+.2	Short purchase cycle (high-volume segments)
Product used daily	−.2	⊖−.1	+.1	+.2	Product used occasionally
			+.1	⊕+.2	Needed to beat competition
			+.1	+.2	Advertising to older consumers or children

EXHIBIT E (*continued*)

Factors That Affect Effective Frequency

FACTOR	FREQUENCY NEEDED				COMMENTS
Copy Factors					
Simple copy	−.2	−.1	+.1	(+.2)	Complex copy
Copy more unusual than competition's	(−.2)	−.1	+.1	+.2	Copy less unusual than competition's
Continuing campaign	−.2	−.1	+.1	+.2	New copy campaign
Product sell copy	−.2	−.1	+.1	+.2	Image type copy
Single kind of message	−.2	−.1	+.1	+.2	More different kinds of messages
To avoid wear-out: New messages	−.2	−.1	+.1	+.2	Older messages
Larger ad units	−.2	(−.1)	+.1	+.2	Small ad units
Media Factors					
Lower ad clutter	−.2	−.1	+.1	(+.2)	High ad clutter
Compatible editorial environment	−.2	(−.1)	+.1	+.2	Noncompatible environment
Attentiveness high	−.2	−.1	+.1	+.2	Attentiveness low
Continuous advertising	(−.2)	−.1	+.1	+.2	Pulsed or flighted advertising
Few media used	−.2	−.1	+.1	(+.2)	Many media used
Opportunities for media repetition	(−.2)	−.1	+.1	+.2	Fewer opportunities

SOURCE: Joseph W. Ostrow, "Setting Effective Frequency Levels," *Effective Frequency* (New York: Advertising Research Foundation, 1982). Reprinted by permission.

As discussed in Chapter 5, setting the effective-frequency level is just the first step. Planners must also decide what percent of the target will be exposed at this level. For instance, the Ostrow method might suggest that a person must be exposed five times for effective communication to take place. But at this level, the budget may allow the planner to expose only 10 percent of the target. In this case, the planner will need to adjust other aspects of the plan in order to increase the number of people exposed at this effective reach level.

SCHEDULING

An important part of timing advertising is scheduling it so that it appears at the most propitious selling times. A major objective of scheduling is to control the pattern of times when advertising appears by plotting advertising timing on a yearly flowchart. There are three major methods of scheduling advertising, each

---

EXHIBIT 8-7

Advertising Time Patterns

Continuity Pattern

Flighting Pattern

Pulsing Pattern

---

with a somewhat different pattern: continuity, flighting, and pulsing. Exhibit 8-7 shows yearly time period graphs for each pattern.

The media planner must decide, as part of the strategy, which pattern to use. The first step in selecting a pattern is to examine purchasing patterns for the product category. Because most product categories have unique purchasing patterns, it is important to learn what they are before thinking about a scheduling pattern. An unusual example of a purchasing cycle is the market for Christmas trees. Trees are rarely purchased at any time of the year other than November or December. This would suggest the need for a seasonal flighting, or bursting, advertising pattern. In contrast, face soap is a product purchased throughout the year, though with heavier consumption in the summer. For such a product, the best scheduling plan might be pulsing (year-round advertising with "heavy-up," or extra weight, in the summer).

Continuity

As its name suggests, the *continuity* pattern (sometimes called *straight-through advertising*) is continuous, sometimes with short gaps at regular intervals when no advertising is done. One continuity pattern would be to run one ad every day for 365 days. Another continuity pattern would be one ad a week for 52 weeks. The time gaps show up in a pattern of dashes on a flowchart.

Continuity is necessary when an advertiser has a message that it does not want consumers to forget. Continuous advertising works as a reminder, keeping the message always before the consumer. That is a strong argument for continuity. Another advantage of continuity is that it covers the entire purchase cycle, because there will be no gaping holes in time. This assures the planner that most of the customers are reached at all times, both when they will be purchasing and during times when they might not be buying. The recency theory of advertising suggests this is the most effective strategy, and many service and packaged-goods advertisers use a continuity pattern.

Another reason for using continuity is that it permits the advertiser to take advantage of larger media discounts granted when so much advertising is purchased. Such discounts provide cost-efficiencies, because the cost per target reached will tend to be lower than in plans that do not contain such discounts. In addition, the advertiser will have an advantage in obtaining certain kinds of desirable positioning within media. Because the advertiser is buying a fairly large block of advertising, it is easier to find the broadcast programs or times that are most favorable. There can also be positioning advantages in print, where certain parts of the magazine or newspaper become more readily accessible to anyone who will buy a great deal of advertising over a long period.

Flighting

Flighting (sometimes called *bursting*) is an intermittent pattern with gaps of time when no advertising is done. Advertising done once a month might be called flighting. Most often, however, flighting patterns are more irregular, with heavy concentrations of advertising at certain times interspersed with no advertising for shorter lengths of time.

An advantage of flighting over continuity is that it allows the advertiser to meet competition better by placing advertising at the most favorable times relative to competition. Advertising can be concentrated in periods of high sales potential, either in broadcast time or print space. Advertising can be timed precisely to reach the best purchasing cycle periods with little waste when buying is slow.

Ostensibly, flighting is used when there are budgeting limitations or sharp sales fluctuations. The advertiser buys ads only when sales are growing and drops out when sales trends are declining. This tends to save money. Furthermore, flighting allows the planner to support advertising in one medium by using another medium simultaneously. If an advertiser plans to use television as the basic medium, then flighting allows concentration of radio and newspaper support at the same time.

Finally, flighting allows a series of commercials to appear as a unified campaign rather than as a series of unrelated ads. Concentrating them at certain times of the year causes the ads to appear to the consumer as part of a single communication entity. By concentrating advertising, an advertiser can sometimes catch competitors off guard and gain an advantage over them, especially if the competitors tend to use continuity rather than flighting in their strategy. The advantage is simply that the advertiser buys much heavier weight than competitors for a relatively short time.

But there are risks in flighting, too. The first is that so much advertising may be concentrated in one time period that the commercial's effectiveness wears out before the flight is over. Great amounts of flighting in concentrated periods tend to build high frequency.

A second drawback of flighting is that so much time may elapse during the hiatuses between flights that consumers might forget the essence of the advertising message. However, the effectiveness of advertising does not stop the moment advertising is stopped. There is some carryover.

Finally, competitors sometimes take advantage of the advertiser by placing heavy ad weights at precisely the time the advertiser is not advertising. During those times, competitors have an advantage over the advertiser.

Pulsing

Pulsing is a mixture of continuity and flighting, and represents the best of both techniques. With pulsing, all of the advantages of continuity and flighting are possible, with none of the disadvantages. Pulsing is the safest of the three because it covers different marketing situations. Not all advertisers, however, are advised to use pulsing. It best fits product categories that are sold year-round but have heavier concentrations of sales at intermittent periods.

Both continuity and flighting can develop the same reach and frequency over a long period (such as 16 weeks), as shown in Exhibit 8-8. However, there

---

EXHIBIT 8-8

GRPs in Continuity Versus Flighting

WEEK NO.		1	2	3	4	5	6	7	8	9	10	11	12	13	14	15	16	
Continuity pattern	GRPs	40	40	40	40	40	40	40	40	40	40	40	40	40	40	40	40	Total 640
Flighting pattern	GRPs	80	80	80	80	*				80	80	80	80	*				Total 640

*Higher four-week reaches due to higher GRPs.
SOURCE: Ogilvy & Mather.

EXHIBIT 8-9

Reach and Frequency of Continuity Versus Flighting

	CONTINUITY	FLIGHTING
Monthly GRPs	160	320
Reach	57	76
Frequency	2.8	4.2

FREQUENCY DISTRIBUTION: NUMBER OF TIMES REACHED	CUMULATIVE REACH	
	CONTINUITY	FLIGHTING
1	57.1	75.8
2	39.1	61.5
3	25.8	49.4
4 or more	15.7	39.0

SOURCE: Ogilvy & Mather.

will be considerable differences of reach and frequency over the short run, as shown in Exhibit 8-9. The table shows that, for a four-week period, the flighting pattern had a considerably larger reach than continuity had. The reason is the larger concentration of GRPs.

The question of flighting versus continuity is one of the age-old debates in advertising. In the end, the planner must resolve this dilemma by using judgment and experience with the advertised brand.

CHAPTER NINE

Selecting Media Classes
INTERMEDIA COMPARISONS

The preceding chapters covered broad, major strategy decisions comprising a part of the activities involved in media planning. This chapter and the next deal with the selection of media, including decisions that usually follow marketing strategy decisions, such as the selection of media classes—whether to use television, magazines, newspapers, the Internet, or some other medium. This chapter focuses on the selection of media classes, and the next chapter covers decisions about selecting specific vehicles within classes.

COMPARING MEDIA

To make decisions about media classes, a planner must make *intermedia comparisons*—that is, comparisons among different media. Comparisons among media vehicles in the same class—such as among Magazines A, B, and C—are called *intramedia comparisons*. Obviously, intermedia comparisons should precede intramedia comparisons.

The main question with intermedia comparisons is whether they can logically be made on a statistical basis. Although it is sometimes valid to compare media classes statistically, in most cases it is not. The numbers for one media class are visually not comparable to those of another class. Comparing readers, viewers, and listeners is like comparing apples, oranges, and peaches. The definition of a reader is so different from that of a television viewer or a radio listener that comparing these numbers is misleading. For example, would it be correct to compare the cost per thousand viewers of a television program with the cost per thousand readers of a magazine? Only partially. Audience numbers tell us if one vehicle delivers more audience at a better cost-efficiency than another in a different media class. But it is questionable whether a television commercial, which is measured in terms of the number of people who are watching during the average minute of a program, can be compared to the total number of people who have read or looked into a magazine during its 30-day publication period. Besides, there are obvious differences in creative impact between a television commercial, with its sight, sound, and motion, and the static appearance of a four-color print advertisement.

Yet such comparisons must be made whenever it is necessary to choose between two different media classes. Although the planner provides important input, the decision about which media to use is shared by all who work on a campaign: the agency account team, the creative group, the media planner, and most important, the advertiser who must give final approval before any work begins.

CONSUMER MEDIA CLASSES

Following is a brief review of reasons for and against using major measured consumer media—newspapers, magazines, newspaper supplements, television, cable TV, radio, Internet, direct response (including direct mail and telemarketing), outdoor, and transit. The pros and cons of each medium are summarized in Exhibit 9-1 on pages 226–27. The pros and cons of using a medium often grow out of a planner's perceptions and impressions rather than from objective evidence. Therefore, some media experts might take exception to the reasons and/or limitations stated here.

Newspapers—Reasons for Using

Sense of Immediacy   Readers tend to perceive newspapers as being the most immediate local medium in the market. Every day a newspaper contains something new, and with the news come new advertisements. Newspapers are considered to have a "now" quality at all times. This quality is important when advertisers want to communicate something immediately. When manufacturers introduce new products to the market, they usually include newspapers as part of the media mix.

Local Emphasis Almost all daily newspapers have a local quality that is important to advertisers. Even if advertisers use a national medium such as network television, they might also want to use a medium with local impact. All selling is local, and the newspaper helps emphasize that fact by advertising local merchants' names and addresses.

Flexibility Newspapers are geographically flexible—they can be used nationally, regionally, and locally in a media plan. Even when a manufacturer's markets are widely scattered, it is possible to reach them by using local newspapers.

Production flexibility allows copy to be changed easily and quickly. For example, some national advertisers want to have different prices for the same products in different markets. There are also special production techniques available. Perhaps an advertiser wants to include preprinted inserts in newspapers in certain geographic markets. Newspapers offer these and other production alternatives.

Preprinted Color Inserts Through the use of preprinted inserts, newspapers can compete favorably with magazines in given markets. Color printing gives the advertiser brilliant, lifelike colors similar to those that enhance the brand's advertisements in magazines. Furthermore, any printing technique can be used on any quality paper to provide high-fidelity color.

Mass Reach Because newspapers are read by so many individuals in each market, total reach per market can include many individuals in each family. When a product's target audience includes adults and children alike, then newspapers are an ideal medium.

Catalog Value A newspaper often serves as a catalog for consumers who are doing comparison shopping. Many consumers search their daily newspapers before they go shopping. The effect of such a search is that many consumers are presold before they walk into a store to buy the product. Some readers even cut out ads and bring them along as a reminder.

Ethnic Appeal Although newspapers are considered a mass medium, they have the power to reach selective ethnic classes as well. If the local newspaper

EXHIBIT 9-1

Pros and Cons of Consumer Media Classes

MEDIA CLASS	REASONS TO USE	LIMITATIONS
Newspapers	Sense of immediacy Local emphasis Flexibility	Lack of target audience selectivity High cost Higher national advertising rates Small pass-along audience Variation in ROP color quality
Magazines	Selectivity Reach of light TV viewers Fine color representation Long life Pass-along audience Controlled circulation	Early closing dates Lack of immediacy Slow building of reach
Newspaper supplements	Local market impact with magazine format Good color fidelity Depth of presentation Broadened coverage area Less competition on Sundays High readership Flexibility	Little pass-along or secondary readership No demographic selectivity High cost
Television	Sight and sound for dynamic selling Flexibility Reach of both selective and mass markets Cost-efficiency	High cost Low attention Short-lived messages High commercial loads (clutter) No catalog value
Cable TV	National audience Added reach and frequency Relatively low cost Precisely defined target audiences Broader spectrum of advertisers HH penetration now more than 80 percent Lifestyle and special-interest targeting	Fragmented audiences Less than full national coverage Spot cable not easy to buy
Radio	Reach of special kinds of target audiences High frequency Supporting medium	Many stations in one market No catalog value Low attentiveness for some formats

EXHIBIT 9-1 (*continued*)

Pros and Cons of Consumer Media Classes

MEDIA CLASS	REASONS TO USE	LIMITATIONS
Radio (*continued*)	Excellent for mobile populations High summer exposure Flexibility Local coverage availability	
Internet	Active medium Low-cost corporate legitimacy Supplemental information Easy documentation of effectiveness Low-cost marketing research	High cost Conflict between Internet sales and traditional sales channels Variable value Limited creative flexibility Limited penetration Extreme clutter High competitive clutter
Direct mail	Easy verification of response Personal quality Flexibility Long life for certain mailings Potential savings	High cost Inaccurate/incomplete lists Variance in delivery dates Clutter and consumer resistance
Telemarketing	Selectivity Easy verification of response Personal quality Geographic flexibility	Inaccurate/incomplete lists Time constraints Message space Legislation Technical impediments
Outdoor advertising	Wide coverage of local markets High frequency Largest size print ad available Geographic flexibility High summer visibility Around-the-clock exposure Simple copy theme/package identification	Limited to simple messages High reach does not necessarily mean high recall High cost Limited availability in upscale neighborhoods
Transit media	Mass coverage of metropolitan area High frequency Relative efficiency Flexibility Opportunity to position messages to consumers on the way to their points of purchase	Limited message space High competition from other media and personal activities Frequent inspection

does not reach these markets, however, then an ethnic newspaper might do the job.

Newspapers—Limitations

Lack of Target Audience Selectivity   Although individuals can be targeted through the use of various sections of the paper (investors in the business section, male tire buyers in the sports section), the advertiser must pay for all of the copies that are delivered to people who do not read these sections. This makes newspapers a relatively inefficient media buy for targeted campaigns. Newspapers are high-coverage but low-composition media vehicles.

High Cost   Although newspapers are indeed a flexible medium, the cost of buying national coverage is very high and is prohibitive for national advertisers with limited budgets. National coverage can be achieved with *The Wall Street Journal, USA Today,* and the *New York Times*; however these are upscale, targeted publications whose combined coverage is only about 3 percent.

Even achieving adequate coverage in major markets through newspapers can be expensive. The large-circulation daily newspapers seldom cover more than a third of major-market DMA households. Therefore, achieving 60 percent coverage requires placing an ad in numerous local papers that serve secondary communities, which raises costs and reduces media efficiency. For example, the *Seattle Times/Post-Intelligencer* combination covers 24 percent of the Seattle DMA (circulation ÷ DMA HH). To achieve 51.6 percent coverage, an advertiser must buy 14 other papers.[1]

Higher National Advertising Rates   Most daily newspapers charge more for national advertising than they do for merchants with a local address. Of course, an advertiser that must advertise in a particular local market will pay the premium rate without question.

Small Pass-Along Audience   Newspapers are rarely passed along to other readers as magazines are. Therefore, advertisements in yesterday's editions have

---

1. *SRDS Circulation 2001.*

a limited time value. Relatively few other persons will see the newspaper after family members have finished reading it.

Variation in ROP Color Quality   An advertiser buying advertisements printed in ROP (run of press or run of paper) color will find great variations in color fidelity from market to market. This variance means the message may be more effective in one market than in another, even though all markets have the same value.

Magazines—Reasons for Using

Selectivity   Magazines are very successful in reaching certain kinds of selected audiences. Every year, an increasing number of magazines is started to meet the interests of special groups such as tennis or chess players, cooking enthusiasts, hobby fans, or those wanting to know more about investing in the stock market. In addition, some magazines have demographic editions, such as a physicians' edition, a college students' edition, or one limited to chief executive officers. Finally, magazines often have geographic editions that enable the planner to reach broad or narrow markets. This versatility and flexibility enable the planner to use magazines in many different ways.

Access to Light Television Viewers   Advertisers often use magazines to provide additional media weight to upper-income, upper-education demographics that tend to be light television viewers.

Fine Color Reproduction   Many magazines are able to reproduce advertisements with excellent color fidelity. The necessity for fine color reproduction is obvious for certain kinds of product advertising such as ads for food, clothes, and cosmetics. Magazines also outdo newspapers in controlling color variations from copy to copy.

Long Life   Magazines usually have a long life—at least a week and sometimes a month or even years. The effect of long life is that the advertiser can continue to build reach long after the present campaign has formally ended. Even if the product featured in the ads has been discontinued, the effect on a person who reads an ad years after it originally ran is to build brand awareness for long periods. However, long-term exposure to the advertising will not help the planner attain short-range goals, so in some situations this advantage can be a disadvantage.

Pass-Along Audience   Magazines usually have pass-along audiences, which increase the reach to people in barbershops, waiting rooms, etc. The size of the pass-along audience varies from magazine to magazine.

Controlled Circulation   Because magazines are able to locate and meet the needs of special-interest groups, many of them can offer *controlled circulation*. In this arrangement, the publisher is able to identify a special group of targets, typically by profession or occupation, and then send each of these individuals the magazine free of charge. The publisher then informs advertisers that a circulation audience of a certain size can be guaranteed by the BPA (www.bpai.com). Most controlled-circulation magazines are in the business field.

Magazines—Limitations

Early Closing Dates   Some magazines require advertisers to have their artwork and type for four-color ads in the printing plant as much as two and a half months before the cover date. Consequently, the marketing, creative, and production work on the campaign must be completed so far ahead of publication date that the advertiser loses the advantage of timeliness. It is even possible for a marketing situation to have changed by the time an ad appears in print.

Lack of Immediacy   With the exception of weekly newsmagazines, most magazines lack a sense of urgency and immediacy. In other words, readers might not even look at the latest issue of a given magazine until some time after it has reached their homes. Not even newsmagazines have the sense of immediacy associated with newspapers, broadcast media, and the Internet.

Slow Building of Reach   Because some readers do not open their magazines quickly, reach tends to build slowly in this medium. Some readers read a small portion of a magazine immediately and then continue at later dates and times, whenever it is convenient. Active, busy people sometimes will scan through a number of issues at one time, to catch up with their reading. At other times, they just ignore a number of issues and read only the most current one.

Newspaper Supplements—Reasons for Using

Local Market Impact with a Magazine Format   Newspaper supplements such as *Parade* and *USA Weekend* offer the advertiser the advantage of being able to reach local markets with a format that closely resembles magazines. Therefore, many of the qualities of magazines are also qualities of supplements. Most important, however, is the ability of the planner to reach many local markets with a magazine format, although there are limitations on a planner's ability to buy supplements on a market-by-market basis.

Good Color Fidelity   Newspaper supplements are usually printed on gravure presses. This gives them high color fidelity.

Depth of Penetration   Whereas magazines usually have limited penetration in any given market because of their specialized natures, supplements have high penetration because they are distributed with Sunday newspapers. Thus, supplements reach large numbers of individuals for whom the editorial features are of general interest.

Broadened Coverage Area   One bonus of using supplements is the ability to reach some markets normally covered by daily newspapers that do not carry the supplement. This is possible because newspapers serving large metro areas often have extensive area coverage far beyond the MSA. Consumers in these bonus markets carrying the supplement usually read their local newspapers on weekdays but a large metro paper on Sunday.

Less Competition on Sundays   Supplements usually have less competition from other media on Sunday mornings when readers are relaxed and spend more time reading than on other days.

High Readership   Because supplements have large penetration in individual markets, it is not surprising that they are widely read, especially by women. Working women tend to have the time to read this format—because it is available on Sunday, it is part of a newspaper, and many features tend to cover women's interests.

Flexibility   Supplements allow the planner to place advertising locally, regionally, or even nationally. But supplements also allow production flexibility such as the option of running a full-page ad in some markets while running smaller ads simultaneously in other markets. This flexibility is limited to larger markets.

Newspaper Supplements—Limitations

Little Pass-Along or Secondary Readership   Because supplements come with weekend newspapers, they inherit some of the weaknesses of newspapers. One of these is that supplements rarely are passed along to others; instead, they usually are thrown away after the family has read them. In addition, one rarely finds supplements left in hair salons or doctors' or dentists' offices for secondary (pass-along) readers, as one finds magazines.

No Demographic Selectivity   Newspaper supplements have virtually no demographic selectivity. Ads targeting men can be placed in the sports section, but the cost reflects all readers—those the advertiser wants to reach as well as those it doesn't.

High Cost   Because of the supplement's high circulation and coverage, the cost of an ad is two to four times more than in mass-circulation women's magazines such as *Better Homes & Gardens* or *Good Housekeeping*. Advertisers can buy half the circulation for a little more than half the price, but that is still a sizable investment for a publication that is primarily a one-day read.

Television—Reasons for Using

Sight and Sound for Dynamic Selling   Audiovisual demonstrations are one of the best teaching methods known. The combination of sight, sound, and motion gives the advertiser the benefit of a technique that comes closest to personal selling. Television selling is very dynamic. It is also one of the best methods of demonstrating the uses or advantages of a given product.

Flexibility   Network, cable, and syndicated television offer broad national coverage, while spot television allows the planner to use markets in any number of combinations. Spot cable allows geographic targeting down to the neighborhood level.

Reach of Both Selective and Mass Markets   Television can be used to attract both selective and mass markets through program selection. When professional football games are being broadcast, the audience is largely male. Children's programming on Saturday mornings and daytime television tend to reach selected audiences. On the other hand, some programming such as movies, comedies, or special events will attract audiences consisting of many different kinds and ages of people.

Cost-Efficiency   Television can be cost-efficient at times. Daytime television, for example, usually has low costs per thousand, as does fringe time. Although the overall costs are high, the audiences are large.

Television—Limitations

High Cost   The cost of commercial time is beyond the means of some advertisers. The widespread use of 15-second, and even 10-second, commercials reflects advertisers' need for lower total cost. TV commercial production is also expensive compared to other media.

Low Attention   Only about 60 percent of the people who watch prime-time programs report paying full attention to the TV set. Attentiveness is even lower in other dayparts, especially early morning, when only about 25 percent of viewers pay full attention.[2]

---

2. Mediamark Research Inc., Spring 2001.

Short-Lived Messages   Although audiovisual messages have the potential for high recall, the nature of television commercials is such that viewers either pay attention or miss the message entirely. The commercial's life tends to be fleeting.

High Commercial Loads (Clutter)   Television networks average more than 16½ minutes of nonprogram material per hour in prime time and almost 21 minutes per hour in daytime.[3] Although there is limited research into the specific effects of clutter on commercial effectiveness, advertisers are becoming more and more concerned as commercialization increases.

No Catalog Value   It is evident that viewers do not search for commercials when they are in the market for a product. Although they pay greater attention to a commercial if they are in the market for the product advertised, they usually have little idea of the exact time such commercials will be broadcast.

Cable TV—Reasons for Using

Cable television has shown dramatic growth in the past 15 years and is now a national medium with a stature that complements network television. About 70 percent of U.S. households are wired for cable, and an additional 13 percent of homes have a satellite dish or other service that allows them to receive the national cable networks.[4] Because of this high penetration, the number of advertisers who have added cable to their media plans has grown enormously. Spending in cable has tripled since 1995, from $3.4 billion to $10.2 billion in 2000. At the same time, spending in broadcast network has increased 64 percent, from $12.4 billion to $20.3 billion.[5] Cable is now a readily accepted, and even expected, part of any national television plan.

National Audience   With a projected 83 percent penetration and the percentage growing each year, cable is truly a national medium, whether used alone or in combination with more traditional media.

---

3. Association of National Advertisers, Television Commercial Monitoring Report, 1999.
4. Nielsen Media Research, Cable + Alternate Delivery Services through July 2001.
5. CMR Taylor Nelson Sofres, 2000.

Added Reach and Frequency   Although advertisers can use cable in lieu of network TV, it can also be added to network TV and any other media chosen for a media plan. The effect of this strategy is to add more reach and frequency. When cable is used this way, some of the weight goes to increasing reach, while impressions in cable homes already reached by other media add frequency to the plan.

Relatively Low Cost   Although cable's rates are rising, it still costs less than advertising on the major television networks. Local cable is usually less expensive than local television. For example, a commercial on a Chicago television station can cost $5,000; the same commercial on cable might cost only $600. However, this is partly a reflection of cable's low ratings—generally less than 1 percent of DMA households.

Precisely Defined Target Audiences   Cable programmers have been better able than networks to define the kinds of audiences who watch their programs—whether for sports, music, or education. This enables advertisers to focus more accurately on targets they want to reach; however, planners face the familiar trade-off between high composition and low coverage from these highly selective cable channels.

Broader Spectrum of Advertisers   When competitors are advertising on certain cable networks, it is sometimes strategically important for other competitors to be in the same medium. As more advertisers use cable, it will draw other product category advertisers, and audiences can expect to find certain kinds of products there.

Reduced Total and Average Spending Costs   National cable television, costing less than network television, can help reduce total and average spending costs for advertisers who need effective media at a lower cost. Shifting even as little as 20 percent of an advertising budget to cable can reduce costs.

Growing Penetration in Major Markets   Not long ago, some major markets had low cable penetration. But that has changed, and the top 20 U.S. markets now have an average of 79 percent penetration of cable or satellite service, with a range of 67 to 86 percent.[6] This is especially important for spot advertising in markets where additional weight is needed.

Cable TV—Limitations

Fragmented Audiences   Cable today accounts for 42 percent of all prime-time viewing,[7] but with over 60 advertiser-supported channels, viewing is so fragmented that the average channel receives less than a 1.0 rating, and many receive less than 0.5. Achieving adequate GRP levels requires a large number of telecasts, increasing frequency, and possibly requiring more creative executions than would be needed with higher-rated broadcast networks.

Less than Full National Coverage   Although 83 percent of homes can receive cable channels, penetration varies by cable network. Some, such as ESPN, CNN, and USA, do reach all cable households. Newer channels may cover as little as 15 percent of the United States. This must be taken into account when placing ads on networks that appear to be selective to the marketing target but may offer only limited reach potential.

Difficulty Buying Spot Cable   Spot cable using different cable systems is presently difficult to buy because there are few organized means of selling. When marketers choose a selected list of markets they want to be in, the cable industry must service the customer in a manner much like that of broadcast television. Although firms that represent local cable systems, such as National Cable Communications (NCC at www.spotcable.com), have simplified the process, the multiplicity of cable operators serving each market makes buying spot cable more difficult than broadcast.

In addition, because of the small audiences (typically less than 1.0), the sample size is too small to provide accurate ratings in spot markets. Planners are forced to assume that a given cable channel will have the same rating in the local market as it gets nationally. This assumption may or may not be correct, but it is impossible to verify.

---

6. Nielsen Media Research, DMA Cable+ADS Universe Estimates, May 2001.
7. Nielsen Media Research, Total Viewing Sources, June 2001.

Radio—Reasons for Using

Reach of Special Kinds of Target Audiences　Radio is able to reach certain kinds of audiences very well. Through programming specialization, a radio station becomes known for its "sound" and attracts special kinds of audiences, such as men, women, teens, farmers, ethnic populations, or the elderly. Many ethnic groups have programs dedicated to their interests. Religious groups, too, have found radio to be an excellent communication medium.

High Frequency　Where a great deal of repetition is necessary, radio is the ideal medium. The total cost is relatively low, and there are usually many stations with time available to permit building a media plan with high frequency.

Supporting Medium　Because of the low cost and good reach of special target markets, radio is often used as a supporting medium. Often, when a plan uses print predominantly, radio can be added at low cost to bring sound into the plan.

Excellent for Mobile Populations　Because most Americans own and drive automobiles, radio becomes a means of reaching them while they are traveling. Many people drive long distances to and from work, and the distances are getting longer as suburbs develop farther from cities. Listening to the radio in what is known as "drive time" helps pass the long commuting time and is an excellent means of reaching commuters.

But commuters are not the only ones who travel every day. Homemakers often take their cars to shopping centers that are located far from their homes. They, too, will often turn on the radio to help pass the traveling time. In fact, radio is the last medium that homemakers are exposed to before they enter retail stores. Local retailers might very well carry on a campaign to communicate with these customers before they arrive at the stores.

High Summer Exposure　Because we are a mobile population and so many people travel during the summer months, radio is an excellent medium to reach them en route. Some experts dispute this, however, claiming that radio tune-in is no higher in the summer than it is at any other time. The time when listeners tune in, however, does change during the summer, especially among teenagers, who are not in school during the day.

Flexibility   Radio, like television, can be used locally, regionally, or nationally. Radio also offers a number of production advantages, because copy can be changed quickly and added to or eliminated from a program quickly. Despite these advantages, radio is not highly regarded for its great production flexibility.

Local Coverage Availability   Advertisers usually purchase local radio, because it reaches a given market well. But AM radio signals can be carried far from the originating market into other geographic areas, especially at night. For a national advertiser trying to build brand awareness in many different markets, this added feature is perceived as a bonus when a planner buys local radio.

Radio—Limitations

Many Stations in One Market   In many large metropolitan markets, so many radio stations are vying for attention that only a relative few are listened to by even 20 percent of a market's adult population. For example, the New York metropolitan area has 41 AM and 45 FM stations.[8] A planner who wants to build large reach via radio will have to buy more than one station—usually at least five stations.

Another consequence of the large number of stations available is the fragmentation of audiences caused by specialized programming. On the one hand, specialized programs do waste few exposures because the program structure is not attractive to everyone. On the other hand, they fragment the audience too much for an advertiser who wants a mass—not class—audience.

No Catalog Value   Like television, but even more so, radio messages are fleeting. Listeners miss many advertisements, and they forget others that they only partially hear.

---

8. *SRDS Radio Advertising Source,* August 2001.

Low Attentiveness for Some Formats   Listeners treat some radio formats as "background" music. They may give the messages on these stations less attention than messages on stations that feature all news or talk.

Internet—Reasons for Using

Active Medium   Unlike television or radio, which are relatively passive media used primarily for entertainment, the Internet requires active participation. The user enters the address of the website he or she wants to visit, and the Internet delivers the page to the user's computer. Nothing happens until the user again takes action by clicking on a link or entering a response. But once a request has been made to a website, it can search through virtually unlimited files to return data, pictures, audio, and video. This ability makes the Internet ideally suited to the transactional communications that are part of most businesses.

Low-Cost Corporate Legitimacy   Today, virtually every company has a website that introduces its product or service to potential customers, suppliers, employees, and anyone else wishing to do business with them. A website is the first place to go for information. Lack of an Internet presence sends a strong message that a company either doesn't exist, or is so far behind the times that any dealings with the company would be suspect.

Supplemental Information   The Internet is heavily used as a medium to publish information. Virtually all major consumer magazines, newspapers, and even television stations and cable networks have a website that supplements their traditional media product. In addition to reinforcing the medium's brand image, these sites bring in revenue from advertising placed by companies that want to deliver a message to the site's visitors. Although some sites have attempted to charge a subscription fee in exchange for a password that grants access, the great majority offer their editorial content for free. With advertising their only source of revenue, many of these sites went out of business when the economy slowed in 2001.

Websites also can be used to provide detailed information about a manufacturer's entire product line. Because there are no size constraints, sites can provide product information, technical specifications, operating instructions, dealer locations, answers to frequently asked questions (FAQs), and telephone numbers and addresses of company offices. Websites can also provide customers with an opportunity to feed back questions and comments. In this way, a website becomes a strong additional element in the advertiser's marketing plan.

Easy Documentation of Effectiveness   Because the Internet is a transactional medium, the advertiser knows exactly how many prospects were delivered by each website where an ad is placed. There are also reports showing the time of day when a site is visited, how much time a visitor spends, how deeply the visitor goes into the site, and many other characteristics of the visitor's contact.

Low-Cost Marketing Research Tool   The Internet is an inexpensive, fast-turnaround medium for conducting marketing research. For example, the Harris Poll Online (www.harrispollonline.com) maintains a list of more than seven million E-mail addresses and basic demographic information about panelists in two hundred countries, compiled when respondents signed up. Periodically, Harris sends these people an E-mail message that requests participation in a survey related to shopping habits, use of the Internet, and other topics. Responses from previous surveys are kept on file so that Harris is able to target individuals with certain behavioral habits for future surveys.

Internet—Limitations

High Cost   Having a website is similar to having a toll-free telephone number: It is open to anyone, but advertising is needed to create awareness that the site exists. This requires a possibly expensive conventional advertising campaign in traditional media, as well as Internet advertising in the form of buttons and banners that will lead prospects directly to the advertiser's website.

Conflict Between Internet Sales and Traditional Sales Channels   Advertisers must be careful not to undercut conventional sales from their own stores or distributors. Yet if the price offered online is the same as local retail, there is no incentive to buy from the Internet, especially when the company charges additional fees for shipping and handling.

Variable Value The Internet is most valuable for products that are information based—travel, financial services, hotel reservations, online auctions, and the like. When the dot-com bubble burst in late 2000, companies offering information-based products were more likely to survive than companies that merely took a retail sales model online.

Limited Creative Flexibility Although penetration of high-speed cable modems and DSL is growing, the majority of users still access the Internet via 56k dial-up connections that limit the advertiser's ability to use full-motion video advertising. The majority of Internet advertisers use the traditional 468 × 60 pixel banners and a range of smaller units. These units can be downloaded quickly, but click-through rates to the advertised website have declined to less than 1 percent of exposures.

Limited Penetration Although 70 percent of adults have access to the Internet at home or at work,[9] the remainder cannot be reached by this medium. Penetration is expected to grow, but there is resistance from older adults and those with lower income and education. Their lack of exposure is a drawback when they are prospects for the advertiser's products.

Extreme Clutter The widely used search engines such as Yahoo! and Google can identify thousands, if not millions of websites for virtually any topic, creating a challenge just to be noticed. Some of the most popular sites and search engines sell banners or buttons on their home page to help advertisers stand out. To create awareness most websites need exposure on related sites.

Direct Mail—Reasons for Using

Direct response is a marketing strategy that often uses direct mail and/or telemarketing. This discussion of direct mail and telemarketing refers only to *outbound advertising,* whereby the marketer contacts the consumer. A direct-response

---

9. Mediamark Research Inc., Fall 2001.

strategy may also include *inbound advertising,* in which the consumer seeks out the marketer (for example, calling the toll-free number on a package).

Direct mail can be the most selective of all media, provided that the advertiser knows the names and addresses of a target audience and has a list that is up to date and complete. When such a list is available, there is minimal waste, so the advertiser pays only for targets that are reached. Another list source can be a marketer's own database of names. Lists of names and addresses can also be purchased from brokers. *The SRDS Direct Mail Source* provides direct-mail lists for virtually any target.

Easy Verification of Response   It is relatively easy to learn whether a direct-mail piece was effective: One simply counts the number of responses to an offer. The number of inquiries from direct mail might or might not be related to sales, but inquiries from direct mailings do constitute one form of measurement. Often the advertiser sends alternative copy treatments by direct mail, and the most effective one is easily verified. It is relatively simple to measure response functions in direct mail compared to traditional media.

Personal Quality   Most advertising is impersonal because it is impossible to address anyone by name. Direct mail, using specific names and addresses, comes closest to overcoming this problem. Of course, not all recipients of direct-mail pieces appreciate advertisers calling them familiarly by name. But many people do appreciate seeing their names in print and often pay more attention to the offer as a result.

Flexibility   Direct mail is probably the easiest of all media to tailor precisely to the geographic marketing needs of an advertiser. The beauty of this flexibility is that direct mail can be adjusted to small markets (by block or even by household) and also can be adjusted to as large an area as needed.

The medium is also flexible in terms of production. Almost any size and kind of paper and any kind of ink or special printing technique is possible. Advertisers with special creative problems turn to direct mail because it is so versatile. Samples of a product can be mailed with ads; special die cuts can be made; special kinds of foldings and special kinds of packaging are available only in this medium.

Long Life for Certain Mailings   Consumers tend to keep direct-mail catalogs for a long time and share them with friends. If the advertising material has value, it will be kept. Some educational materials also share this quality. If the educational matter has value, such as a chart showing how to administer first aid or a booklet on how to eliminate stains on clothing, consumers might retain it for a long time.

Potential Savings   No special envelope, special addressing, or extra postage is necessary when direct-mail advertising is sent along with bills or other packages. The bills must be sent anyway, so the addition of a direct advertisement might not even cost extra postage. There are creative limitations, however, due to weight restrictions and size of the contents of an envelope and/or package. Printing costs must be borne, as well, but even when the total weight of advertising enclosed with a bill is greater than the bill alone, there will still be substantial savings because there are no extra costs for the envelope and addressing. The addition of the advertising usually increases the total cost only slightly.

Direct Mail—Limitations

High Cost   Unless it is being piggybacked with another mailing, direct mail can be expensive. The main factor is, of course, the cost of postage. Beyond this, there are at least two additional situations where direct mail can be more expensive than any other medium. The first is when a production technique requires the use of heavy embossed or other expensive papers, or some unusual method of engraving, artwork, or printing. The second is when large mailings are made that cannot take advantage of bulk mailing privileges. There is no reason to think that postage rates will decline in the future, and these high costs will continue to affect direct-mail usage.

Inaccurate and Incomplete Lists   Without an accurate and complete mailing list, direct mail cannot do its best. So many Americans move frequently that it is difficult and expensive to keep lists up to date or develop new ones. In the past, it was possible to buy large mass mailings at low cost and not be concerned about the accuracy of the list. But today's high postage and production costs require the use of accurate and complete lists.

Variance in Delivery Dates   Even if a large mailing is taken to the post office at one time, the pieces will be delivered at widely different times. If time is not essential to the marketing objectives, then the lag does not matter. But timing of an advertising message is often critical, and the direct-mail user cannot control it very well. Compared with other media, direct mail comes off second-best in respect to timing. When ads are placed in newspapers, they are printed on the day requested. When broadcast commercials are purchased, they are delivered not only on the day, but at the hour, requested. In comparison, direct-mail delivery dates are unpredictable.

Clutter and Consumer Resistance   With the increasing popularity of direct-mail advertising, special techniques and more costly packaging are needed to entice consumers to even open the envelope.

Telemarketing—Reasons for Using

Selectivity   Telemarketing is as selective as direct mail. In fact, the phone numbers and addresses of a target audience often are derived from the same lists.

Easy Verification of Response   Telemarketing allows immediate response and has a quicker turnaround time than any other medium. Often, operators test different scripts to determine the most effective one. Finding the most effective message is therefore easy.

Personal Quality   Telemarketing is the most personal medium, because it involves one-on-one verbal communication. It is also the most intrusive medium. To avoid turning people off, marketers should target these efforts to the proper audience.

Geographic Flexibility   With regard to geographic flexibility, telemarketing is just like direct mail. Advertisers can adjust lists to reach a large or a small area.

Telemarketing—Limitations

Inaccurate and Incomplete Lists   Typically, 15 percent of phone numbers called are inaccurate because of people moving from one place to another.

Time Constraints With telemarketing, there is a limit to the hours when calls can be made. For consumer programs, advertisers should avoid calls to individuals at home after 10:00 P.M. For business programs, calls cannot be made after 5:00 P.M., Monday through Friday.

Message Space There is less message space in a telemarketing call than in a direct-mail piece. Because time is money, only the most essential questions can be asked.

Legislation About half of U.S. states have enacted laws requiring licensing or registration of telemarketing firms, and at least 24 states have particular telemarketing acts known as "do-not-call" laws.[10] Because there are loopholes in many of these laws, their effectiveness has not been proven, but their popularity points to broad consumer sentiment against this form of advertising.

Technical Impediments Many consumers have inexpensive answering machines and telephone number identification systems. These conveniences make it difficult for telemarketers to complete their calls with sales prospects. Consumers often do not answer the phone if they do not recognize the name or number of the person calling.

Outdoor Advertising—Reasons for Using

Wide Coverage of Local Markets Outdoor advertising is able to build large local coverage of the mobile population in many markets in a 30-day period. However, this coverage does not represent reading of the messages, only potential exposure to them.

High Frequency Billboards also have high frequency in reaching the mobile population of a market. It is in this area that billboards are strongest. Although the differences in reach of a 100 versus a 50 showing are not great, the frequency levels are quite different.

---

10. National Conference of State Legislatures website (www.ncsl.org), August 2001.

Largest Print Ad Available   Size is a powerful attraction. Outdoor allows the advertiser to buy the largest print ad available. The use of attractive color printing plus dramatic lighting and, at times, moving portions, all offer the advertiser great attention-getting power.

Geographic Flexibility   Outdoor can be used locally, regionally, and nationally. Even within any given market, it is possible to add emphasis wherever desired. Movable billboards enable an advertiser to concentrate messages in many places or to increase the potential for exposure.

High Summer Visibility   Media plans often include billboards in the summer, because they increase the visibility of a brand name at a time when people are traveling. Warmer weather encourages people to take to their cars, and it is possible to reach them through billboards and other outdoor signs.

Around-the-Clock Exposure   Because many billboards on main thoroughfares are lighted, anyone passing at any time of day or night can see the message. As long as there is a mobile population, this is an opportunity for exposures.

Simple Copy Theme and Package Identification   When the message is relatively short and simple and the package is distinctive, outdoor can be an excellent way to attract attention and build frequency for the message. Building brand awareness is a strength of the medium.

Outdoor Advertising—Limitations

Simple Messages   The best use of outdoor is for a simple message; complex or long messages do not work well. This restriction means that the medium cannot be used in precisely the same manner as other print media.

No Guarantee of High Recall   Outdoor provides high reach and sometimes good recall of ad messages, but it is not necessarily true that high reach means high recall. The creativity of the message is an important criterion in assessing people's ability to remember the message. But because of the nature of this medium, people often look at billboards but are unable to recall what they saw.

High Cost   Although the CPM is low, outdoor is a high out-of-pocket cost medium when compared to some other media, according to the Institute of Outdoor Advertising. For a 100 showing nationally (top 50 markets), the cost is more than $6 million for a month.[11] Considering that outdoor is a medium often in the background, that it requires very short messages, and that drivers' interests are focused primarily on the road ahead, this cost is prohibitive for many advertisers.

Limited Availability of Best Locations   Prime outdoor-advertising locations on freeways or high-traffic roads often are held by long-term advertisers who are given the right of first refusal when their contracts expire. Key positions are available to occasional advertisers who allow their boards to rotate to a different location every month—some are excellent, some are not as good, but they eventually give the advertiser total market coverage. Also, zoning restrictions limit the availability of billboards in upscale neighborhoods.

Transit Media—Reasons for Using

Transit media involve interior and exterior displays on mass-transit vehicles and terminal and station platform displays.

Mass Coverage of a Metropolitan Area   When an advertiser wants to reach individuals in the heart of a market, then mass-transit advertising is desirable. It is primarily a vehicle for reaching adults either on their way to, or returning from, work. But its reach is extensive.

High Frequency   Transit media take advantage of normal travel patterns that are duplicated many days throughout the year. As a result, it presents an opportunity for a great deal of repetition of message delivery.

Relative Efficiency   Based on potential exposures, transit can deliver large numbers of individuals at low unit costs.

---

11. OAAA/SRDS Out-of-Home Advertising Source, reported in *2000 Marketer's Guide to Media.*

Flexibility   An advertiser can select transportation vehicles in which to place ads that reach certain kinds of demographically defined groups. The advertiser does not have to select all mass-transit systems, only those that are known to have large numbers of targets.

Opportunity to Position Messages to Consumers on the Way to Their Points of Purchase   Local advertisers can buy messages that reach consumers on their way to their retail stores. Therefore, it is possible that, for some consumers, the transit ads will be the last medium they are exposed to before making a purchase.

Transit Media—Limitations

Limited Message Space   Most often, large or complex messages cannot be disseminated in this medium. Transit advertisements rarely have enough space available to carry such messages.

Heavy Competition from Other Media and Personal Activities   Transit is not an intrusive medium. Instead, it largely competes for attention with other things such as the attractiveness of scenery, the nature of the transit vehicle, or other people. The person who travels to and from work on the same transportation vehicle is often tired, bored, reading, or listening to music. Exterior displays often require extra creative pulling power to attract attention.

Frequent Inspection   Because transit advertising is exposed to the natural elements as well as graffiti, care must be taken to replace posters that become dirty, defaced, or otherwise unacceptable. This requires frequent inspection, a cost that must be included in budgets for outdoor media.

NEW MEDIA CONCEPTS

New media give planners additional ways to reach target audiences that may be more selective and have even more impact than traditional media. Another quality of the new media is that they often provide a means for making media planning more creative. Some of these techniques are innovative and more interesting than the techniques available for traditional media. They can help make media more effective in delivering an advertiser's messages to a particular target.

This section explains details of some of the major new media. However, this text will not evaluate all such media in detail. The media options discussed here are some of the best known or most widely discussed.

Place-Based Media

A large number of new media are distinguished by the fact that they are located out-of-home in a particular place. Exhibit 9-2 lists a small sample of some of the best-known categories of place-based media and a brief explanation of each. A complete listing is available in *SRDS Out-of-Home Advertising Source* (www.SRDS.com).

Each of these specialized media has its own advantages and limitations, but the general advantage of place-based media is that advertising can be seen in areas relevant to the products or services offered. Therefore, these media have more meaning for audiences than ads seen out of context. Often consumers are already motivated to buy, but these ads provide added impetus.

In general, a disadvantage of place-based media is that they are not available whenever wanted, as traditional media are. Timeliness of the message suffers. Furthermore, when consumers are tired, the message is not always seen or heard as when audiences are rested. Also, sometimes the advertisements are seen as intrusions rather than as helpful product information. There are probably some consumers who simply do not want to see these media and ignore them whenever they can, no matter what kind of information and entertainment are offered.

Another problem with place-based media is nonstandard measurement. Because none of the established services measure ad exposure, the only audience information comes from the medium itself. Planners must assume the research has been structured to provide optimistic estimates that will support ad sales.

Database Media Planning

Database media planning (sometimes called *data mining*) is a technique of building a list of individuals who are known to be purchasers of a given brand. Each person on this list is known by name, address, phone number, and sales poten-

EXHIBIT 9-2

Categories of Place Media

Aerial	Banner-towing airplanes
Airport/airplane	Displays inside airports In-flight video programming Bar news network located in airport bars Video monitors located throughout airports and carrying entertainment and commercials Laser billboards (rear-screen projection billboards)
Convenience stores	Ads attached to waste containers in stores Convenience store media (from ceilings, above coolers, etc.)
Golf courses	Colored posters framed behind Plexiglas, featuring golf subjects in clubhouses Colored ads on redwood tee-markers Ads on front and side of golf carts
Grocery stores	Ads on grocery carts inside stores Checkout channel: commercials on TV sets mounted above checkout aisles Pop radio: commercials interspersed with music and information heard throughout store Aisle ads: posters in aisles or ads on shelf (shelf talkers)
Health clubs	Full-color ads displayed on wallboards in general traffic areas and/or locker rooms
Movie theaters	Colored ads displayed in lobbies of movie theaters On-screen slide show during intermission
Phone booths	Ads on/in phone booths
Physicians' waiting rooms	Integrated multimedia system consisting of TV, magazines, wallboards, and take-home booklets
Schools	Newspaper dispensers with ads on them Campus media boards: posters framed and displayed in cafeterias, residence halls, etc.
Shopping malls	TV advertising shown between feature clips in malls and stores
Stadia/arenas	Use of giant, color TV–quality matrix with instant replay of sports plays and commercials
Advertising in motion	Full-color decals and signs applied to sides and rear of trucks Mobile ad units

tial, as a minimum. Then the data are placed in a computer to form the data-base. In essence, advertisers can theoretically eliminate waste in advertising because they know who the targets are and how to reach them.

Cross-Media (or Multimedia Integration)

Cross-media (also called *multimedia integration*) partnerships have received a great deal of coverage in the trade press. The basic idea of cross-media planning is the assembly of a select number of different media for the purpose of reaching specific target audiences for clients. The media are put together as a package that can include network television, cable, magazines, the Internet, and other media, tailored to meet diverse target audience needs.

The package, therefore, is an alternative to the present technique of dealing exclusively with one medium, like network television, or a group of media that tend not to be selective. The goal is to do a better job of communicating with hard-to-reach audiences and to take advantage of multimedia opportunities to combine promotions with advertising. But there are other appeals, too. For example, cross-media is a way to implement the principle of integrated marketing communications, plus value added and synergy.

Value added is closely aligned with cross-media planning. These terms are used to describe any element of a cross-media deal beyond the actual media buy, including special events. These special events are offered at a discount rate or no charge at all. Examples include premium positioning and bleed ads at no extra cost; tie-ins with other media such as direct mail and cable; in-store promotions or product sampling; bonus pages, custom publishing, and most recently, free exposure on the vehicle's website. Media, for example, will often add to a cross-media deal by printing booklets or providing trips to tennis or golf tournaments. Clients have come to expect value-added programs, and media companies are quite willing to give them.

Costing out cross-media deals is considered tricky. The reason is that cross-media deals are supposed to have synergy beyond values offered by traditional media. In other words, the totality of media values is supposed to be greater than the sum of each medium's contribution alone. But as some experts have commented on the synergy problem, nobody yet knows how to calculate how much greater.

Cross-media deals tend to be open-ended arrangements that require constant stewardship and fine-tuning. They are typically offered by large multimedia companies that hope to bring more revenue to the entire corporation than would be possible by negotiating one medium at a time. However, since these packages often mix very attractive properties with other venues that are struggling for business or may even be off target, planners generally avoid considering them. On rare occasions, large advertisers will attempt to negotiate cross-media deals that can be beneficial to both parties.

For example, in July 2001 Procter & Gamble, the country's third-largest advertiser, with over $1.5 billion in spending, inked a $300 million multimedia deal with entertainment giant Viacom. This marked a 50 percent increase in P&G's spending with Viacom, representing about 20 percent of its entire advertising budget and about 30 percent of its television spending. The deal includes Viacom's broadcast networks, CBS and UPN; eight cable networks, including MTV and BET; its syndicated television properties; and nonmedia, like promotions and sponsorships. Over time the deal may include radio, outdoor, and even deals with Blockbuster movie rentals.[12]

Advantages of Cross-Media   In a survey, 31 percent of respondents cited lower CPMs on cross-media deals as the primary advantage, and 27 percent cited the ability to deliver a single message in a variety of media as a secondary advantage. Low CPMs represent media cost-efficiency. In effect, those who choose cross-media for efficiency are looking for better media buys for the money.

MediaVest Worldwide, the buying service that put together the P&G deal, projects that up to 40 percent of media buys will be cross-platform in the next few years. However, other media professionals are skeptical. A problem may be that media companies are willing to offer the value-added programs during a recession, but not when the economy picks up. Nevertheless, agencies and their clients could insist on their continuing the practice.

Disadvantages of Cross-Media   The jury is still out on cross-media value. In other words, it is difficult to prove that this technique is better than buying tra-

---

12. Media Life, June 5, 2001 (www.medialifemagazine.com).

ditional media one at a time. However, cross-media plans certainly are more interesting communication vehicles to both consumers and advertisers. The problem in evaluating these deals is that it is difficult to know whether the deals will remain in the arsenal of planners for a long time, or whether they will tend to be used only in specific situations. Unless the deal is designed for a particular client's needs, it might be difficult to sell broadly.

INTERMEDIA COMPARISONS FOR NONMEASURED MEDIA

Almost every medium in existence has some qualities that are useful for one or another advertiser. As such, there are times when nonmeasured media are useful. A *nonmeasured medium* is one that lacks a periodic, predictable measure of who is exposed to it. Such media include car cards, telephone book advertising pages, theater or concert program advertising pages, and others. A planner who wants to use such media must rely on subjective judgments about audience sizes and/or demographics, especially when comparing nonmeasured to measured media.

Sometimes nonmeasured media will conduct research to help the media planner make intermedia comparisons. Unfortunately, most research is suspected of being biased in favor of the company that pays for it, because the company has a vested interest in the outcome. As a result, it is difficult to make intermedia comparisons even on a subjective basis for nonmeasured media except in simple, obvious areas.

One way to approach the dilemma of noncomparable measuring techniques for intermedia comparisons is to use response to advertising as a criterion of effectiveness. If it could be shown that an ad in one medium generates more recall than an ad in another medium, then a planner might assume that the medium with the higher recall is better. However, the ad or ads used for comparative purposes cannot be indiscriminately chosen. Nor can recall of one medium versus another be measured as the average recall of many ads, because some products or brands are inherently more interesting than others and therefore generate higher recall scores.

To prevent such bias, researchers usually measure the same ad in two different media. As a result, researchers hope, any variation in the recall scores is the effect of the medium rather than the ad. Although this procedure attempts to solve the problem, dual measurement is still questionable as a valid means of intermedia comparison.

For example, if a cola product is being tested on television and a similar ad is tested in a print medium, it would be difficult, if not impossible, to keep the copy and creative elements constant. A commercial for a cola drink usually features an announcer's voice, whether on or off camera. Most of the time the message features action and music rather than still scenes. Then, too, the audience sees the message on many different-sized television screens, some in black and white, but most in color.

If a similar cola ad were placed in print, the size of the ad would probably be constant from magazine to magazine, and there would be no sound of a well-known personality's voice and no music. Furthermore, if the print ad were placed in a magazine, there would be competition for attention from other ads, whereas the television program in which the commercial was placed would have no competition for attention at the same time (unless the viewer zapped a commercial while recording the program on a VCR).

Therefore, any results of recall measurements could not be considered unbiased. Any one of the variables exclusive to the ad in a given medium could account for the greater or lesser recall scores. Although such techniques are helpful for other purposes, they are not entirely valid for use in intermedia comparisons. In addition, by the time the ad agency has gone to the expense of developing creative executions, it is a foregone conclusion that the medium will be used. Since planners would ignore any research that suggests a medium is ineffective, it is doubtful that such a study would be conducted in the first place.

Often a medium in one class, such as magazines, will spend a great deal of money to prove that it is better than a medium in another class. Although the results are interesting, they cannot be considered valid for intermedia comparisons because of the problem of vested interests.

Finally, the overall subject of recall scores is controversial within the research community. The question is whether a high recall score indicates that product sales will increase. Does high recall necessarily relate to changing the consumer's attitude in a positive way toward the product? Does recall relate to persuasion? Many research professionals believe that recall does not relate to sales effectiveness.

MEDIA MIX

In planning strategy, the planner must decide whether to use a single medium or a number of media. When more than one medium is used, the result is called a *media mix,* meaning that the plan mixes a number of media classes to reach certain target audiences.

Generally, a planner uses a media mix because a single medium, such as television, cannot reach the target market in sufficient numbers or with sufficient impact to attain a media objective. When a planner does not define the target market narrowly, the targets represent such a broad spectrum of consumers that the only way to reach them is through multiple vehicles. Most planners narrow the definition of targets to reach only those with the best potential. Another situation that might call for a media mix strategy occurs when a planner has segmented targets into two key groups, each of which is about equal in importance.

During the process of deciding whether to use a media mix, a media planner ought to ask, "What part of the market cannot be reached with a single medium?" Generally, vehicles within one media class can reach a substantial part of a market, perhaps 90 percent. The percentage of the market not covered might not be worth the extra cost of employing an additional medium. If 20 percent of the population accounts for 80 percent of product consumption, and this 20 percent is within the reach of a single medium, it is inefficient to try to reach more with additional, but different, media. Inefficiency means that the additional media have substantially higher CPMs than the original medium.

Estimating Media Mix Reach and Frequency

Until recently there has been virtually no research into duplication patterns between different media, leading planners to assume that duplication is random. In this case, multimedia reach can be calculated with the following standard equation (sometimes called the Sainsbury method):

$$\text{Reach} = a + b - (ab)$$

where a = reach of the first medium (expressed as a decimal)
b = reach of the second medium (expressed as a decimal)
Reach = decimal percent of the target exposed to either of the two media

As an example, suppose a potential media plan has an estimated TV reach of 70 percent and a magazine reach of 40 percent. What percent of the target saw either of the two media?

Random duplication assumes that if 70 percent of everyone saw the TV ad, then 70 percent of the people who saw the magazine ad would also see the TV ad. The equation adds the TV reach plus the magazine reach (70 percent + 40 percent), then subtracts 70 percent *of* 40 percent (that is, the product of those percentages) to get the unduplicated audience:

$$\text{Reach} = a + b - (ab)$$
$$= .70 + .40 - (.70 \times .40)$$
$$= 1.10 - .28$$
$$= .82 = 82\%$$

To calculate the average frequency, add the GRPs from both media and divide by the calculated two-media reach. For three or more media, calculate the reach of the two highest-reach media. Then repeat the process, using this calculated reach and the third-highest medium, and so on.

Beginning in 1999, SRI conducted the first large-scale study of duplication among five key media: television, radio, the Internet, newspapers, and magazines. The MultiMedia Mentor™ researchers (www.statisticalresearch.com) measured time spent with each medium by age/sex, socioeconomic status, and product usage. Since all media were measured on a common base, the service can estimate the reach/frequency of multimedia combinations. An analysis by the authors found that duplication was slightly greater than random, but it varied by reach level, medium, and demographic.

When to Use a Media Mix

The following objectives are some important reasons for using a media mix:

- To extend the reach of a media plan (adding prospects not exposed by using a single medium)
- To flatten the distribution of frequency so there is a more even distribution of those who are exposed to a medium varying numbers of times

- To add gross impressions, assuming, of course, that the second or third medium is cost-efficient
- To reinforce the message or help audience members remember it by using different kinds of stimuli (a process called "creative synergy")
- To reach different kinds of audiences, perhaps differentiated by lifestyle as well as demographics
- To provide unique advantages in stressing different benefits based on the different characteristics of each medium
- To allow different creative executions to be implemented

Criteria for Media Selection Beyond the Numbers

Media usually are selected on the basis of quantified data showing the abilities of alternative media to reach select target audiences.[13] In many cases, however, media planners make comparisons on an objective and subjective basis, covering materials cited in this chapter. The latter two criteria deal with the strengths of media to do certain things better than others. Unfortunately, these latter criteria are subject to debate and sometimes are simply the idiosyncratic perceptions of either a planner or the client.

DDB Needham Worldwide presents the criteria in Exhibit 9-3 as a means of promoting the message and the medium in making selection decisions. If a planner disagrees with these decisions, at least the chart will encourage more thought about just what makes one medium more useful than another for achieving a client's objectives.

---

13. This section is adapted from DDB Needham Worldwide, "Which Media Do It Best?" (promotional brochure).

EXHIBIT 9-3

An Evaluation of Traditional Media for Different Uses*

KIND OF USE	LEAST VALUE	LITTLE VALUE	SOME VALUE	MORE VALUE	BEST VALUE
Authority	Outdoor	Radio	TV	Newspapers	Magazines
Beauty	Radio	Newspapers	Outdoor	TV	Magazines
Bigger than life	Radio	Magazines	Newspapers	TV	Outdoor
Demonstration	Outdoor	Radio	Newspapers	Magazines	TV
Elegance	Newspapers	Radio	TV/outdoor	TV/outdoor	Magazines
Entertainment	Outdoor	Magazines	Newspapers	Radio	TV
Events	Outdoor	Magazines	Radio	Newspapers	TV
Excitement	Newspapers	Outdoor	Radio	Magazines	TV
Features	Radio	Newspapers	TV	Magazines	Outdoor
Humor	Outdoor	Magazines	Newspapers	Radio	TV
Imagination	Outdoor	Newspapers	Magazines	TV	Radio
Information	Outdoor	Radio	TV	Magazines	Newspapers
Intimacy	Newspapers	Outdoor	TV	Magazines	Radio
Intrusion	Radio	Newspapers	Magazines	Outdoor	TV
Leadership	Newspapers	Outdoor	Radio	Magazines	TV
News	Outdoor	Magazines	Radio	TV	Newspapers
One-on-one	Outdoor	Newspapers	Magazines	Radio	TV
Package identi- fication	Radio	Newspapers	TV	Magazines	Outdoor
Personal	Outdoor	Newspapers	TV	Magazines	Radio
Prestige	Outdoor	Radio	TV	Newspapers	Magazines
Price	Outdoor	Magazines	TV	Radio	Newspapers
Product in use	Radio	Outdoor	Newspapers	Magazines	TV
Quality	Newspapers	Radio	Outdoor	TV	Magazines
Recipes	Outdoor	Radio	TV	Newspapers	Magazines
Sex appeal	Newspapers	Radio	Outdoor	TV	Magazines
Snob appeal	Outdoor	Radio	TV	Newspapers	Magazines
Tradition	Outdoor	Newspapers	TV	Radio	Magazines

*Evaluations are subjective.
SOURCE: DDB Needham Worldwide, "Which Media Do It Best?" (promotional brochure).

CHAPTER TEN

Principles of Planning Media Strategy

This chapter explains important principles that affect the creation and implementation of media plans. Some advertising practitioners consider media planning to be a few notes on the back of an envelope. Our approach is to have enough detail in the plan to implement the marketing strategy, so that the advertiser has as complete control as possible of a desirable outcome. In fact, our goal is to have the media plan implemented so that media and marketing objectives are fulfilled as planned. If this takes place, part of a desirable solution to the problem should be attained. The other part is control of the advertising message.

MEDIA STRATEGY CONCEPTS

Earlier, this book defined *media strategy* as a series of actions that planners take to attain media objectives. In addition, media strategies should achieve an advantage over competitors. If media objectives are achieved, it is because optimum strategies were employed. Thus, it is necessary to first state the objectives and follow with correct media strategies.

Will media strategies that have advantages over competitors always succeed? Not necessarily. Other factors—lower prices, good distribution, or better quality—also play a role in determining success. However, media strategies that have higher reaches and/or higher frequencies, spend more money, and have better creative messages are examples of gaining an advantage over competitors. This idea assumes that most other factors in the media plan are equal between competitors and the advertiser. It is hard to see how a plan with less reach, less frequency, and so on can make much difference in a competitive battle. Several prevailing media strategies are discussed in the following paragraphs.

Dominant Brand Presence in Media

A common practice in planning is to buy small amounts of media, presumably to save money. The result is that audiences do not notice the advertisements. In other words, small bits of media rarely accomplish much. It is better to combine media units into a few large media units to achieve presence.

Usually, being "big" in media is better. However, being dominant, or spending more money than a competitor, does not always guarantee success. The idea is to be visible and have a noticeable presence. This gives advertising a chance to be seen.

Advertise When People Are Buying

The uninitiated think advertising can make people buy a given product or brand. This belief is not supported by experienced advertisers. For seasonal products like tire chains, lawn mowers, or Christmas trees, it is almost impossible to sell out of season. Occasionally, fur coats are sold in the summer when drastic price reductions are made. However, when large numbers of consumers are buying the competition's brand at a certain time of the year, that is usually a good time for you to sell your brand.

Most advertisers have track records of sales by month, and these will show the optimum times for advertising. The strategy is to find these times and "heavy up" (increase) media weight to take advantage of the natural selling opportunity. On the other hand, for the many products that are sold at a steady rate throughout the year, the recency theory would suggest continuous media scheduling, without heavy-ups.

Creative Strategy's Impact on Media Strategy

Creative strategy is a significant consideration in planning strategy. In fact, it is often the starting place for all media planning. "Creative" indicates that some media are much more appropriate to the message than others. For example, when full color is needed, then print media are best because there is little variation in an ad's appearance from one carrier to another. (In contrast, consider the differences in color from one television set to another.) Sometimes creative can

EXHIBIT 10-1

Alternative Media Strategies

National coverage (buying all stations in a network television lineup)
Large national reach
Buying different dayparts to reach women at home and women who work out of the home
Buying national magazines or national newspapers
Buying local advertising in top 100 markets
Buying network radio
Buying national cable (e.g., ESPN)

be written so that it will be effective in all media. At other times, creative is restricted to a small market segment or is designed to be run in nontraditional media.

Alternative Media Strategies

Media planners should always assume that when they are choosing a suitable strategy, there is usually more than one available. Some alternative courses of action are equally viable, and a few are usually better than others. Exhibit 10-1 lists alternative media strategies that might be used to achieve a given media objective.

One problem with planning strategies, however, is finding the best from among the alternatives. Sometimes it is necessary to justify that the best one was chosen by writing a rationale in the media plan that explains why one was chosen over others. If it is not written, someone in the client's organization might ask for an oral explanation of the choice.

WHAT MEDIA PLANNERS SHOULD KNOW BEFORE STARTING TO PLAN

Although planners might want to start writing a media strategy from the moment they are assigned to a product and brand, they should first fully understand the other elements of the overall marketing strategy. These other considerations are discussed in the following paragraphs.

Marketing Problems

Almost all marketers have one or more marketing problems that require relatively quick solutions. These problems could be national, regional, or local in scope and might deal with many different aspects of business, such as advertising, sales, manufacturing, and sales promotion. However, marketing or advertising problems usually include the advertising message (or creative), sales volume, market share, and profits.

The marketer is responsible for devising solutions to these problems. Solutions are usually marketing mix elements (product, price, place, and promotion, which includes advertising, sales promotion, public relations, and direct marketing). When a solution calls for advertising, then media automatically become an important ingredient in the solution.

A careful and complete analysis of the problem often helps make a proposed solution obvious. On the other hand, a loose or careless definition provides a bare minimum of direction. The media planner should know precisely what the marketing problem is, including a history of the brand that is relevant to the present problem and the solutions that have been proposed.

Once the marketing problem is understood and the role of advertising has been identified, planners can determine the role of media in solving the problem. The next step is the development of media objectives and the strategies that will be used to achieve them.

Recommended Actions

The marketer who uses advertising recommends courses of action (strategies) to solve the problems. Shown in Exhibit 10-2 are alternative solutions to a marketing problem of declining sales. Each solution requires a different media strategy. If, for example, one solution is reducing prices, then the media planner could recommend large target reach and high frequency as two strategies. Reach will provide broad dissemination of advertising messages—the marketing strategy cannot work well if few consumers know that prices are lower. With greater reach, more consumers are more likely to take advantage of the offer. Furthermore, high frequency is necessary to help the message overcome the clutter of commercials that appear on television and radio.

EXHIBIT 10-2

Declining Sales: Possible Marketing Solutions

Reduce prices
Get wider and/or larger or better product distribution
Reduce price and use advertising to publicize
Use advertising to announce
Use innovative advertising messages to attract attention and communicate offer
Use sales promotion incentives
Use integrated marketing communications
Improve product quality
Use more attractive packaging
Choose new target segments (with different demographics and/or lifestyles)

Complexities of a Strategy

Strategy decisions are rarely simple, and their effects occur in many different ways. Neither of the two media strategies previously mentioned would always be feasible. The planner would need a different strategy if these require more money than the client is willing to spend, for instance. In that case, the planner must create a strategy to fit the budget. One way to do this is to limit the high reach and frequency to the three or four months when sales responses for the product have traditionally been high. Beer advertising, for example, could require a strategy that limits advertising to summer months or that uses a flighting strategy.

If the situation is more complex (e.g., consumers who regularly bought a certain brand have switched brands), the solution would require an explanation of just how these consumers are supposed to respond to advertising communication. In this example, the marketer should try to motivate the consumer to switch back to the original brand.

Marketing situations requiring the use of different media for public relations, sales promotion, and advertising have a unique problem: All of the communications objectives must appear seamless to consumers. The media strategist should remind creative personnel that multiple communications objectives can be confusing to consumers, because each was produced with a different communication technique. The goal should be to help the advertising speak with one voice in its use of various media.

How the Product Will Be Sold

A media planner should know how the product will be sold and which marketing mix elements will be used. The term *how* refers to the creative department's perception of the proposed advertising: Will it communicate with consumers? Generally, this is part of creative strategy. Specifically, it applies consumer behavior principles and research to explain how consumers might react to advertising.

How Advertising Sells a Product to One Customer

Gus Priemer, former marketing and media manager of S. C. Johnson & Son, Inc., urged media planners to first understand how to sell a product to *one customer* before planning large-scale media. Priemer also noted that planners should be able to describe how advertising communication is expected to work to influence the consumers' behavior toward a brand. The failure to do both is often the cause of unsuccessful strategies, because no one is sure how the consumers will respond to marketing efforts. If a planner cannot perceive how one person buys, how can he or she know what will happen when the advertiser is dealing with millions of consumers?

When a product's price is reduced, three elements can affect the consumer: price, communication method, and media choice. Simply telling consumers that a product's price is reduced often has little or no effect. Sometimes this is because the price is obtuse, such as when advertising features only the percentage discounts given. This type of information makes the consumer work to figure out the dollar value of the discount and can create doubt that the offer is genuine. Sometimes the price reduction is so insignificant that it has no motivational impact on the consumer.

The second factor in determining the success of the communication is the way the offer is announced. If the ad is dull, unnoticeable among more interesting ads, or lacks audience appeal, then the communication will fail. Even the personality of a presenter can make a difference in getting communication through.

The third element of a successful communication is media choice. Television probably has the best chance of getting a message to consumers, because it provides emotional and factual presentation techniques to help it sell. Media work best when combined with a motivating force—like price reduction—and an attractive message placed in a strong medium.

Sometimes the solutions are so obvious that no written rationale is needed. If, for example, the selling technique is to lower prices, the consumer motivation will be that because prices are lower (perhaps lower than all competitors' prices), the consumer will buy the product to save money and get a good or superior product value at the same time. In this case, the motivation does not really require that someone write every strategy statement about selling.

How to Neutralize the Competition's Strategy

Media strategies take place in a dynamic marketing environment in which competitors try to outsell each other and gain a larger market share. Planners of a media strategy cannot ignore these competing approaches, especially when any one of them is directly attacking their brand. How can a media planner neutralize the competition's strategy? In the area of media planning, certain successful strategies can be devised. Here are some examples:

- Reach more members of a target market than competitors do
- Reach a different demographic target market
- Use higher average frequency
- Reach targets in new and different media formats
- Run a special promotion in conjunction with a medium
- Use media creatively

Cost of Strategies

Once general strategies have been determined, the planner will provide a rough estimate of the cost to implement them and compare that to the amount of money in the media budget. If the advertiser has already given the planner a number that represents the most the client will spend, then the planner has to devise the solution with strategies that do not go above the budgeted amount.

At times, a planner might devise two different strategies. One strategy will cost about the amount the client wanted. Another strategy, called an *investment spending strategy,* will cost more, because the planner believes more money will return more in sales than the smaller budget.

OTHER ELEMENTS OF MEDIA STRATEGY

The media strategy section must reveal the decisions about the way the objectives will be accomplished. These decisions reflect the demographic characteristics of the people the advertising is supposed to reach (target audience), the way the choice of media complements the creative strategy, the balance between reach and frequency, the need for continuity, and the need to implement the plan within the budget.

Media Targets

To whom will advertisements be directed—users, persons who influence users, or both? The typical plan states the target in two ways: as a planning target and as a buying target.

The *planning target* is usually stated in terms of users or purchasers of the product as reported in MRI or other research. Here are some examples:

- Female homemakers in households that use frozen pizza
- Regular golfers who play at least once a month
- Working women
- Heavy users of low-calorie domestic beer

The planning target can be used to select print vehicles because MRI will tell the planner how many "regular golfers," for example, read various magazines. But broadcast media are only bought on the basis of age and sex demographics. Therefore a *buying target*—that is, a target categorized by age/sex demographics—must also be defined. Exhibit 10-3 shows suitable broadcast buying targets to match the planning targets in the previous list.

The more specifically a planner identifies targets by demographic or other means, the easier it will be to find media that will reach those targets. Occasion-

EXHIBIT 10-3

Broadcast Buying Targets That Match Planning Targets

PLANNING TARGET	BROADCAST BUYING TARGET
Principal shoppers in households that use frozen pizza	Women 25–54
Regular golfers who play at least once a month	Men 35–64
Working women	Women 25–49
Heavy users of low-calorie domestic beer	Men 21–34

ally, planners use some other descriptor, such as psychographics. The goal, however, is to be as specific as possible. Too broad a target, such as adults 18–64, means the plan will waste exposures on individuals who never buy a given product or brand under any circumstances.

Once the media target has been specified, all subsequent decisions are based on how well the media being considered reach this target. Media objectives often include a statement indicating where targets are located geographically, when that is a strategic consideration. Sometimes this information is stated in the strategy portion, rather than the objectives portion, of the plan.

Creative Strategy

The creative strategy and creative executions are the heart of an advertising campaign, whether one is planning a national campaign for an automobile manufacturer or a local campaign for a retail store. The reason should be obvious: Copy and art are the communication that drives advertising. They sell! Media might or might not sell, depending on the marketing situation, but unless the copy has been well planned and written, the product is unlikely to sell. Copy (including words, pictures, sound, color, white space) is a motivating force; it is what gets into the minds of consumers and affects sales in many ways.

Because of creative's importance, planners should not proceed until they know what the creative is and which media the creative people think would best suit the message. In fact, creative personnel should discuss their strategies before planning begins with media personnel. If they do not, then it is up to media planners to seek out creatives and learn which media are preferred. In fact, media planners can have worthwhile suggestions for creatives.

The creative strategy affects the choice of media classes and individual media. It also affects the degree of creative media planning that can result (discussed later in this chapter). It is inconceivable that a planner would ignore the creative plan.

Reach and Frequency

When planners select media they are, in effect, choosing those that will deliver a given number of target audience impressions. Delivery, however, is nothing more than exposures. Because all research data represent measurements taken in the past, the data therefore represent only estimates of exposures. The future will be somewhat different. But the number of estimated exposures contracted for in a media plan can be patterned in such a way as to maximize either reach or frequency, or to attain a given level of effective reach and frequency.

More explicitly, media objectives should state the frequency goal and the percent of the target that will be reached this number of times. Here, too, an explanation is needed to justify, logically, why any given level is desired.

Continuity

It should be apparent that media objectives will affect the kinds of strategies that later evolve. One important goal that will affect the timing of advertising during weeks and months of a year is continuity—the consistency of advertising placement. Like reach and frequency, continuity results in many contradictory patterns of placement if not controlled.

One placement pattern, for example, consists of advertising that appears every day of the year; another is limited to placing ads once a week. Which is better? The answer depends on a number of factors. What are the brand's marketing goals and strategy? Do they require a given pattern? Does the creative strategy require a different pattern? For example, if the creative strategy includes a very complex message in television commercials, will audiences be able to grasp the meaning if the commercials are shown once a week, or will a pattern of frequent showings be required? If the latter, then the media goals will have to be based, to some extent, on flighting and exposure concentration.

Budget Constraints

Even though the relationship of marketing objectives to media objectives is clear, a number of constraints often temper the planner's decision. The size of the budget, if known ahead of time, is one such constraint. Many times, the marketing budget is set before any media planning takes place. In such a situation, the media objectives will have to be written with the budget in mind.

If no budget is available, then media objectives can guide the setting of a budget, at least as far as the cost of time or space is concerned. Once planners have a general idea of their goals, they are in a position to estimate what it will cost to achieve them. Sometimes a budget cannot be set at the stage of developing media objectives, but must wait until the strategy has been worked out.

In such cases, media objectives will have to be rewritten later to accommodate the size of the budget. A series of marketing/media priorities should be set so that the planner achieves the most pressing goals, while secondary goals wait for another day. The client might reduce the size of a budget recommended by a media planner after examining marketing/media objectives and strategy.

CREATIVE MEDIA STRATEGY

In Chapter 1, we discussed the creative media plan as a problem to be solved. In this chapter, we will suggest ways to implement a creative media strategy that will help solve this problem to a great extent. First, the media planner should understand what is meant by the term *creative media strategy*. There is no universally agreed-upon definition of this term, but, in general, such a strategy is innovative enough to secure for an advertised brand some advantage over competitors' brands. The strategy might accomplish this by helping the advertising stand out against competitors' advertising, giving the messages a better chance of being absorbed.

Guidelines for a Creative Media Strategy

Many advertised brands in a product category tend to use similar media strategies. If all brands in a category are also similar, then consumers will have difficulty distinguishing one brand from another. Perhaps a creative media strategy will help solve the problem. More specifically, we offer four guidelines for implementing a creative media strategy.

Make Your Media Strategy Different from and More Innovative than Competitors'   A creative strategy is easily distinguished from competitors' strategies. However, simply being different is not enough. There is no evidence that a plan that is different from competitors' plans will accomplish anything. But media and marketing planners will testify that truly innovative plans can accomplish key goals and attain competitive advantages. The key elements of innovation are ideas that make a brand's advertising stand out from the competitors' advertising. The most effective plans are based on insights into the day-to-day lives of consumers as people, and the ways they relate to the product being advertised. This assumes advertising messages have something to say that is meaningful to consumers. This also means the creative media dollars should return more than a typical brand's media strategy.

The Ability to Be Creative Does Not Depend on Additional Dollars   Innovative strategies that cost more than what is considered normal are not valuable unless there is evidence that the increased spending will result in superior returns. Fortunately, it is possible to be creative without spending more.

Media Strategy Should Start with Quantitative Proof . . . Then Go Beyond Numbers   A creative media strategy is not a substitute for quantitative proof that the best media have been selected and used. Without measures of reach, frequency, effective frequency, and other kinds of useful numerical data, a planner would have to rely on instinct. It is difficult to convince clients who are spending large amounts of money for media to rely on instincts as proof. A solid media plan is built on good quantitative proof *and* a good creative strategy.

Creative Media Strategy Should Be Relevant to the Problems of the Brand   Being creative is sometimes interpreted as being "offbeat" or "new." It is important to make a creative media plan relevant to the marketing situation, not just "different." A media planner should contribute to the overall marketing plan with creative media strategies. Planners typically are thought of as "number crunchers," or people with only quantitative skills. Both stereotypes ought to be dismissed. When given an opportunity to be creative, a media planner should be able to think of innovative ways to solve problems.

Examples of Creative Media Strategies

The following examples summarize creative strategies that various advertisers used to achieve special attention for their messages.

Problem: Kodak's headquarters is in Rochester, New York. Its competitor in the copier field, Xerox, was about to sponsor the U.S. Open golf tournament in Rochester. The planner's challenge was to offset this competitive (and embarrassing) local Xerox exposure.

Solution: On the first day of the tournament, Kodak's agency published an ad in *USA Today* that looked just like the newspaper's real front page, except that all the stories were about Kodak's copiers. The single-page ad appeared in a special section on the U.S. Open and wrapped around the front page so that the first thing readers saw was the Kodak copier line; the real front page was underneath. The Kodak page appeared only in the Rochester area but was circulated at the tournament site, airports, and hotels. Kodak's planners were creative because they saw an opportunity that had not been apparent before.

Problem: Kodak needed a big media event without taxing the advertising budget.

Solution: Kodak's advertising agency suggested it buy and be the sole sponsor of a special issue of *Time* magazine. The issue had a theme that fit with the client and the medium: "150 years of photojournalism." This special issue went to subscribers free, as a bonus. It was also supported with a special ad campaign that appeared in key markets—a traveling photo exhibit that worked as a public relations event and received extra publicity from the local press.

Problem: An advertising agency had difficulty finding enough money to communicate with consumers in 10 of the client's key markets. The budget was only $250,000. Among those markets were Cincinnati, Cleveland, and Detroit.

Solution: The agency found an hour-long TV program on art in ancient China, produced by a station in Seattle. It bought the rights to that program and scheduled it in the 10 key markets. The agency localized the program to fit each market separately. It then got most stations in the markets to broadcast the show for free, arguing that it had a strong cultural-affairs type of appeal.

Media Strategy Is Not Science

In practice, planners have to remember that media strategy is not a science in the same manner as physics or medicine. Its outcomes cannot always be predicted with great accuracy. One significant reason for this is that the marketplace is constantly changing as competitors use many different tactics to gain an advantage over each other. In addition, the original marketing problem might not be solved after strategies have been implemented.

The outcomes of some media strategies, such as reaching 70 percent of a target market by placing ads in a certain group of vehicles, can be achieved quite well. However, it would be incorrect to assume that everyone reached saw an advertisement in the selected medium, or that all those who saw an ad will respond as intended. Therefore, planning strategy includes knowing precisely what each strategy means and implies.

For the most part, planners learn what each individual strategy will accomplish from personal experience. When planners have worked with a given product category or a brand for many years, they learn what a strategy will accomplish under certain marketing conditions. As time goes by, they modify their findings to develop a body of knowledge that enables them to make better predictions of the results. Exhibit 10-4 lists questions that cover basic media strategies. They should be included in a typical media plan. For complex strategies, they should be accompanied by a rationale.

Relationships Among Reach, Frequency, Continuity, Number of Markets, and Ad Size

In planning strategy, there are usually four elements that are closely related: reach, frequency, continuity, and the number of markets to be used. Though not media-related per se, ad size is a fifth element. Because of their close relationship, a person cannot plan for one of these elements without simultaneously considering the others. The relationship grows out of a fixed budget size, which

EXHIBIT 10-4

Questions for Planning Media Strategies

Marketing

1. What are the marketing problems that require media?
2. What marketing objectives and strategies have been planned?

Media

1. What are the creative strategy and recommendations for best use of creative?
2. What are the media objectives?

Strategy

1. Who should targets be? (demographic, product usage, and lifestyle description of prospects)
2. Which media classes are recommended? What percentage of the budget should go to each media class? (e.g., 60% network TV; 20% spot TV; 10% cable; and 10% magazines)
3. How much reach and frequency do we need? Effective reach and/or frequency? Why? How much reach, frequency, and GRPs are needed per quarter?
4. How large is the media budget? What percentage spending per month and quarter is required? Why?
5. What is the best timing and scheduling for this year?
   a. What pattern of continuity is recommended?
   b. Is there an introductory period? For how many weeks? Why?
   c. How heavy should introductory weight be compared to sustaining parts of the plan?
   d. Is there a heavy-up period? When? Why?
6. Geographic concentration:
   a. In which media should it occur? Why?
   b. What are the criteria for selecting markets?
   c. What is the importance of BDIs and CDIs?
   d. How many markets should we be in?
   e. What are the names of individual markets?
   f. How much weight should we plan for in each market?
   g. What are the seasonal variations in weighting?
7. Which daypart should be selected for broadcast media?
8. Media units:
   a. Sizes needed? 30 seconds or 15 seconds? Page or partial page units?
   b. Use of special color or treatments (gatefold, etc.)?

means, in effect, that the planner must balance trade-offs: When one of these elements is emphasized, the others will, of necessity, suffer.

Each of these elements costs a considerable amount of money to maximize. Emphasizing reach, for example, usually requires dispersing advertising messages widely so that many different persons in the target audience will have an opportunity to see the messages. Generally, one single media vehicle, such as one television program or one magazine, will not deliver a high reach. This emphasis requires multiple vehicles, greater message dispersion, and additional media weight. As the cost for reach goes up, the amount of money available for the other three elements becomes more limited.

The same holds true for continuity. If an advertiser wants to plan continuous advertising over 52 weeks, the cost will be high, leaving minimal amounts of money for the other three elements. Often as much as six or more months of advertising must be sacrificed in order for the reach to attain a high enough level in the remaining six months.

Likewise, the number and size of individual markets in a plan, where national media are used in conjunction with local media, clearly affect overall costs. Even if only local media are used, the same concept prevails. The more markets used, the higher the cost, and the less money available for the other elements.

Exhibit 10-5 shows to some extent what happens when a planner manipulates the four elements within the constraints of a fixed budget. The figure shows some ways to vary the weights of reach, frequency, continuity, and number of markets. Other possibilities, not shown, also exist. One part of a planner's job is to weigh each of the four alternatives and decide which needs more emphasis (usually at the expense of the others). Of course, if the budget size can be increased (unfortunately, it usually cannot), then different emphases can be achieved. As a consequence of this dilemma, the planner needs some criteria for weighing the alternatives.

Although not specifically a media consideration, the size of the ad also affects media planning and could be considered a fifth trade-off. A 15-second commercial on network or cable TV is typically half the cost of a 30-second commercial while in spot TV a 15-second commercial is about two-thirds the cost. So, although the shorter commercials would have less impact, if the goal of a campaign was simple brand awareness, a mixture of :15s and :30s would allow longer flights, more markets, and more reach and frequency.

EXHIBIT 10-5

Alternative Strategies Within a Fixed Budget

Reach	Frequency
Continuity	Number of Markets

You cannot plan for equal strategies on a fixed budget.

Reach	Number of Markets
Fre-quency	Continuity

To buy heavy amounts of continuity or markets, you must sacrifice reach and frequency.

Reach	Fre-quency
Number of Markets	Con-tinuity

Other combination strategies must sacrifice one or another of the goals.

Reach	Frequency
Continuity	Number of Markets

Most media plans do not have enough money to reach all goals.

Weighing Alternatives

The two most important elements of a media plan are reach and frequency. Because they occupy such an important position in a plan, they are usually considered before continuity or number of markets. When a media budget is larger, it is possible to achieve both high reach and high frequency levels. But most often, the cost is too high to do both.

If high reach is planned, it will probably cause the frequency level to decline somewhat, because reach and frequency are inversely related. If, however, reach is very high (90 percent), then frequency can be increased by extra dollar expenditures, because most of the money will go into building frequency and a very small increment will go to building reach. This is the natural consequence of trying to reach new persons who have not already been reached by some other mass vehicle.

Higher reach will be necessary when the media objectives call for anything new. Reach is also needed for building brand awareness. If a brand awareness level is now at 25 percent and an objective is to raise it to 75 percent, then higher reach will be required and frequency will be sacrificed. Another objective calling for higher reach is the announcement of various kinds of promotions, such as cents-off deals, special coupon promotions, or refund offers. Such promotions must build a great deal of awareness so that consumers will take advantage of the offer. Still another high-reach situation occurs when changes in the brand or changes in the creative strategy are important. Finally, more reach is needed when it becomes necessary to meet or exceed competitive reach levels. One goal could be to steal customers from a competitor by showing them that the advertised brand better meets their needs, in which case enough reach is needed to equal or better the competitor's reach.

More frequency is needed, at the expense of reach, when the brand awareness levels are already high due to the cumulative effect of past advertising. At that point, more frequency is needed to meet or surpass frequency levels of competitors. When the advertising noise level of all competitors is already high, then more frequency is needed to meet or surpass frequency levels of competitors. There are certain marketing situations in which a minimum frequency threshold must be passed before consumers start paying attention to the message. The effectiveness of the media plan is then directly related to high frequency, but the planner must also consider what percent of the target will be exposed at that level for a given budget.

Even if brand awareness is a campaign or creative objective, the campaign might require advertising in a pattern that matches the purchasing cycle of a product class. Some products are not sold to any great extent at certain times of the year. Computers, for example, require heavy media usage in spring, early fall, and at Christmastime. Reach levels also will probably be high at those times. In contrast, beer is sold all through the year, with summer peaks. For this product, reach levels might have to be sacrificed at some times of the year in order to have enough money to cover the year and, at the same time, spend heavily during the summer. When high reach is necessary, it is sometimes necessary to sacrifice continuity. In some situations, advertisers drop out of advertising for as long as six months, allowing the product to keep selling at lower volume levels, in order to have sufficient money to advertise at high levels during peak-volume seasons.

The final variable affecting the budget allocation is the number of markets to be used. Planners arrive at a number by using either of two methods. The older method consisted of creating national media plans in which the number of markets would not be considered until after other strategies were decided. Another technique starts with a market-by-market analysis and sets strategies for each market. To simplify planning, markets are then grouped into tiers that reflect different reach/frequency goals. For example, Group A markets would receive high-level support, Group B markets would get intermediate-level weight, and Group C markets would receive minimum-level sustaining support.

Ad size directly affects the media plan, because the larger the unit, the more it costs. In national television, a 30-second commercial costs twice as much as a :15. By shifting weight to the shorter unit, a planner can buy twice as many rating points or twice as many weeks of advertising, but with less impact. This is a critical decision that requires the agreement of the account team, the creative department, and the advertiser, because it directly affects the campaign's ability to meet the advertising objectives.

Setting Priorities

An important step in weighing the five elements is that of setting priorities. A planner should do this early so that it will be easier to decide which of the elements is most or least important. Priorities come from media objectives, and some objectives are obviously more important than others. If there is any doubt, then a planner must not only state the priorities but also explain why one objective is more important than another, and how much more important. Once the priorities are clear, the allocation of a budget to the five variables should be relatively clear.

CHOOSING MEDIA STRATEGIES

The discussion in this chapter to this point has been on elements that affect the planning of media strategies. Now the question arises, Which strategy from among the alternatives is the most appropriate? Many strategies could be used in one media plan, so planners need guidelines for studying alternatives. This section discusses a select group of strategies that media planners often confront.

Prevailing Wisdom

Remember that media strategy is not a science. There is little evidence one can refer to in trying to make the best decision. Many of what are called "best strategies" have not been proven to be best objectively, but are judged to be best by a planner based on the facts available. Many times, however, strategists speak with so much conviction that it is assumed they must be correct. On the other hand, many strategists have learned by experience what works best, and they use this learning in future decision making. In these cases, they are using their experience as a different form of research.

One must realize that the effects of some strategies cannot be measured. As an example, it is almost impossible for most marketing and media planners to prove how many sales were actually delivered as a result of a media strategy's contribution, because the strategy cannot be parsed out separately. What seems to be working might instead be the product of other variables that are difficult to measure. Furthermore, media responses are mostly affected by advertising's creative efforts.

Media's effectiveness is probably the most difficult of all advertising variables to measure. Ads are responded to, but mostly as a result of creative efforts. We can find out how many magazines were subscribed to, how many were sold on newsstands, how many readers there were, and even whether audiences saw a given ad in certain magazines. But how many sales did the magazine produce? That is not known, and it is probable that we will never know precisely this kind of information. The exception to this is direct-response advertising. With the use of toll-free and 900 telephone numbers, or business reply cards, it is possible to directly attribute sales to a distinct media vehicle. The effect of Internet advertising can also be precisely measured in terms of click-through from the banner to the advertiser's website, and from there to product inquiry or actual online sales.

Research into Effective Media Strategies

In 1991 Information Resources, Inc. published a major study that identified the common media and creative elements of 389 successful advertising and media weight tests conducted between 1982 and 1988. *Successful* was defined as an increase in sales that IRI was 80 percent sure did not occur by chance. The results of this and a follow-on study, referred to in the industry as AdWorks 1 and AdWorks 2, respectively, have led to guidelines that can help media planners. Here are the key findings from AdWorks 1:[1]

- There is no simple relationship between the size of the weight increase and the increase in sales.
- Additional weight was more likely to increase sales when there was a change in brand or copy strategy.
- Successful media plans tended to expand the audience or shift the target emphasis. Also, they used less daytime.
- Growing and frequently purchased product categories were more likely to benefit from increased weight.
- Successful tests continued to increase volume for up to two years after resumption of traditional spending levels.
- Advertising works by getting current users to buy more of a product, rather than expanding penetration to new users.
- Heavy trade promotion (price reductions) hinders the effect of advertising; consumer promotion (coupons, sweepstakes, etc.) enhances it.
- New brands and line extensions tend to be more responsive to media weight tests than are established products.
- For new products, the more prime time that was used, the greater the increase in sales. Front-loaded heavy-up plans also were more likely to increase sales.

---

1. Information Resources, Inc. 1991; summary from *FCB/Chicago Media Matters*, February 1992.

AdWorks 2, conducted from 1995 to 1996 by IRI and Media Marketing Assessment (MMA/Carat), expanded on AdWorks 1 to study more than 800 packaged-goods brands representing more than 200 product categories. Key findings from AdWorks 2 are as follows:[2]

- All the brands showed incremental sales over base equity in response to television advertising. In general, the more GRPs a brand received, the higher the percentage of total incremental sales volume due to television advertising.
- Continuity counts. Television advertising effectiveness increased as the average annual number of consecutive weeks on air increased.
- Consistent with several recall studies that indicate that :30 spots are more effective than :15s, as the percentage of :30 commercial units in a plan increased (compared to :15s), television advertising effectiveness also increased.
- Plans using multiple network dayparts and other television venues are more effective than those concentrated in one daypart or venue.

Typical Media Strategies and Alternatives

The following discussion covers selected marketing or media problem situations and the prevailing strategy opinions about them. We will examine some of the major strategies that planners have to deal with and show how and why they are used. Alternatives will also be discussed.

Scheduling   When the market for a brand seems flat during the entire year (sales are approximately even during all 12 months), the scheduling strategy and the recency theory suggest that advertising should be done every month. This implies that because consumers buy a product category evenly, the scheduling should reflect this evenness. This kind of scheduling therefore would call for even continuity during all 12 months.

---

2. Media Marketing Assessment (MMA at www.mma.com; link to "Products & Services"); "Publicly Released Highlights of AdWorks 2," October 5, 1999.

What is missing from a high-continuity strategy is the effects of all competitors' advertising. *Even continuity* means that spending is approximately the same during each month. But this strategy ignores the competition, unless the competition is also supporting its brand throughout the year. The net effect of even spending is to have lower reaches and frequencies (communication opportunities) each month unless a huge amount of money is spent. On the other hand, the strategy is certain to deliver advertising to buyers who would be missed during hiatuses if media weight was flighted.

Flighting   If the competition concentrates its advertising support during certain times of the year, a better scheduling strategy can be to sacrifice even continuity to concentrate money at certain periods during the year. The advertiser would choose periods when its own brand can be prominent compared to competitors' brands. This strategy is called *flighting* and is based on the assumption that advertising will be more effective with additional frequency over a short period of time. A schedule might concentrate advertising into bursts of four to six weeks at a time, with a two- to three-week hiatus between each burst. The effect of this strategy is that (assuming the budget is a fixed amount) more money is available to be spent during the bursts. The planner assumes that the accompanying positive effect on sales from greater reach and frequency when the bursts occur will exceed the loss of sales during hiatus periods.

Heavy Introductory Effort   If a brand is just being introduced, it has the problem of breaking through consumers' mental sets that have endured without this new brand. Competitive brands might have a strong hold on the market, making it difficult for the new brand to establish a foothold. A strategy here would require heavy spending at the beginning of a campaign, sacrificing advertising during the latter part of the year to ensure that enough money is available to properly launch the brand. The introductory period could run from one to three months.

The Information Resources, Inc. research mentioned earlier confirmed that "the concentration of higher TV weight into fewer weeks is related to an increase in sales."[3] The study concentrated only on television advertising, but the

---

3. Ibid.

same concepts would apply for other advertising media, with the exception that television is more dynamic.

In most new-product introductions, the client is willing to spend more money to get the product launched in the marketplace. But this additional money might not be enough. Beginning media planners are often surprised to learn that as much as 70 percent of an advertising budget is recommended to be spent in this introductory period. You might ask, What happens to advertising during the rest of the year, when so little money is left? The experienced planner will usually respond by saying, "If we cannot make it up front, the rest will be wasted anyway." One of the principles of strategy planning is to make advertising appear as large as possible, for maximum effect. So the up-front strategy for a new-product introduction is the best alternative.

Heavy-Up Scheduling   Most planners spend more on advertising when consumer buying is heaviest and spend less at other times. This is known as *heavy-up scheduling*. Many brands have two to four months a year of heavy buying activity. The opportunity to get competitors' customers to switch brands during these heavy buying seasons is greater at this time if advertisements say something worthwhile.

Advertising should show a brand's superiority over others. These heavy buying seasons are usually the best times to advertise because consumers are more responsive to advertising for the product category than at other times. It cannot be assumed that heavying up for two or three months will automatically cause sales to increase proportionately. Most consumers are looking for good values to meet their needs and wants.

However, a planner can have an advantage over competitors who also recognize that the buying season is the time to advertise. If all competitors are spending more at the same time, they might nullify each other. This could require a strategy for one competitor to start a month or two before all the others start heavy spending, and thereby get a jump on the market.

Geographic Market Weighting   *Geographic market weighting* means adding either dollars, GRPs, or a larger number of advertisements in a geographic market because that market has greater sales potential than others. Each of these dollars, GRPs, or ads represents the same idea to some extent. When any of them is added, it is assumed, advertising has a better chance of being more effective than the same market with lesser weights.

The need for extra weighting in certain markets is based on market potential, which is usually uneven nationally. A brand might be selling well in some markets and poorly in others. The assumption is that adding weight to low-volume sales markets represents a bigger risk than adding weight to markets that have already been producing good sales.

One principle of weighting, then, is to add extra weight to a market equal to its relative sales contribution. This is called *pro-rata budgeting,* which suggests that a market that produces 6 percent of a company's sales should receive at least 6 percent of the advertising budget. Under this principle, the weighting of markets can be based on the relative sales volume each market has already produced. Pro-rata budgeting has established a positive track record that serves as a guideline for weighting.

When some markets have done poorly and there is reason to believe that one of the reasons for the poor sales is the lack of advertising weight, then the pro-rata technique might not be adequate. A planner could experiment with added weight to see what will happen. Without evidence that sales would increase with more advertising weight, the pro-rata technique is a low-risk alternative.

Combining Media and/or Vehicles   Another strategy deals with how many different vehicles or media are optimum for achieving a media goal. In answering this question, the nature of the goal is a consideration. However, if the goal is building reach (e.g., 70 percent of a target market), then the media and dayparts or vehicles should be selected with consideration for the diversified audiences they reach. There are many ways to achieve the desired 70 percent reach, both within an individual medium and across media. For example, the use of multiple media means that there is less duplication within each individual medium. This is one way to build reach.

Planners also use multiple media to build concentrated reach of a demographically defined target market. Each medium will bring new audience members to a plan. But, as each additional vehicle is added to a list, more weight goes into building frequency than reach, because the target audiences of the latest-added medium have already been reached by the media selected first.

Conversely, if the media goal is to build frequency, then it is appropriate to concentrate weight on a small number of vehicles. As weight is added to the same vehicles, frequency increases as the same people see the ad over and over again.

One consequence of the inverse relationship between reach and frequency is that it is possible to buy high frequency and have reaches that are so small as to be of questionable value. A media mix that produces an average frequency of 20 might have a reach of only 12 percent. The value of high frequency would be lost on such a small market reach. This is something a planner has to avoid.

Share of Voice   In developing a competitive media strategy, the most common, if most simplistic, measure is *share of voice (SOV)*, expressed as percent of dollars spent. Knowing that our brand spent $30 million last year out of total category spending of $150 million (SOV = 20 percent) tells us a great deal about the brand's relative position in the marketplace and in the minds of our consumers. Our brand accounts for only 20 percent of total category advertising. Put another way, the consumer sees four competing commercials for every one of ours.

Dollars are a crude measure because they do not tell us how they affect the many important marketing variables. It would be more precise to describe share of voice in terms of national gross rating points. But that hides geographic differences in media weight, as well as possible creative differences in the commercial message. Yet a market-by-market competitive analysis by commercial length will hide possible differences in impact across different dayparts and program venues.

From this it should be clear that as the competitive analysis becomes more detailed, the planner runs the risk of getting lost in the numbers. These factors should be examined when they are directly relevant to the media strategy of our brand. Otherwise, the more general share-of-voice statistic is going to give the truest picture of the forces that drive the marketing situation.

The strategies discussed here are just a sampling of those that arise in a media plan. But they give an idea of the thinking that goes into planning and show the importance of exploring alternative strategies. Case Study 10-1 illustrates how a cross-media strategy would be planned for an artificial sweetener using Time-Warner facilities. The recommendations were made by Louis

Schultz, currently chairman and chief executive officer of Initiative Media Worldwide.

CASE STUDY 10-1
Planning a Cross-Media Strategy

Here's how it would work. If I had an artificial sweetener, it would make a lot of sense to start with a magazine, *Cooking Light*. Why wouldn't I start by running four spreads in *Cooking Light*? Now I also want to create, with your editors, a book on cooking light that's sponsored by my artificial sweetener.

I will use that as a premium giveaway—for a purchase—and I will mail that as a fulfillment. By the way, if you happen to have a production house, you will write it and produce it, because you can print all this stuff [inside your company]. While we're at it, since my consumers are interested in health, why don't I create a 30-second vignette, "How to cook better, sponsored by *Cooking Light*," and the artificial sweetener will be the other 30-second partner.

Now I've got the vignette; where do I run it? Why don't I go to your cable properties, and I'll buy your local cable interconnects, or I'll buy cable television, of which you'll get a part. Or, why don't I run a promotion or a sweepstakes on HBO and Cinemax, and I will partner up with somebody like an automotive company with a car.

We'll have a *Cooking Light* take-care-of-yourself sweepstakes and promotion tied in with HBO to bring in more subscribers. And you get an opportunity to win a week or two at a spa, cars, and such.

Why don't I also create an on-pack premium—knowing these people who are very active—with videotapes that I will offer from the Warner stable. They can write for them and can make it a self-liquidating item at a discount.

Why don't I take the vignette series I have and tie it in with Warner Brothers releases, and run this commercial on the front of that and create that whole program?

And continue on: You can build a whole marketing program within an organization like Warner. And by the by, when I do my vignette series, I'll have it produced by Sunset Fliks or Warner. I will look at their syndication properties, like "Jenny Jones." Maybe I can cut a deal with them as part of it. Maybe I'll have my commercial shot at their production facilities, rather than using somebody else's, all of which can be discounted. All of which is additional money that the parent group would not have gotten.

SOURCE: John McManus, "Lou's Laws of Multimedia," *Mediaweek* (July 8, 1991): 12–14.

CHAPTER ELEVEN

Evaluating and Selecting Media Vehicles

After devising strategies, the next step in media planning is to evaluate and select media vehicles. In this step, media buyers come into the planning picture. The planner provides criteria for buying, and the buyers follow the criteria as closely as possible. This kind of activity helps keep a number of different people working on the account closely orchestrated toward common goals and efforts.

With the exception of print, vehicle selection is determined primarily by professional buyers. Although the primary factor is cost, there are other considerations, which vary depending on the medium. For television, for example, the media plan specifies which dayparts are to be used, but buyers select stations and programs within those dayparts on the basis of rating size (coverage) and audience composition for the age/sex target audience. For radio, buyers choose stations on the basis of format, average quarter-hour rating, and cumulative audience. The buyer's goal for both TV and radio is to purchase a schedule of vehicles (programs, stations, time periods, etc.) that deliver the planned GRPs within the authorized budget. Newspapers are selected primarily according to their geographic coverage of the market under consideration. Outdoor billboard locations are selected on the basis of visibility, traffic flow, and market coverage.

Unlike broadcast and outdoor, magazine vehicles are usually selected by the planner on the basis of a variety of considerations in addition to media cost-efficiency. These considerations will be discussed in detail in the following section.

DETERMINING MEDIA VALUES FOR MAGAZINES

An elementary principle for selecting media is to select vehicles that reach a large number of targets at a cost-efficient price. Although this principle seems to suggest that this is all there is to the selection process, nothing could be further from the truth. A more advanced principle is to determine each vehicle's value in terms of the desired criteria and then select those that best meet these criteria. Some of them can be measured quantitatively, and the numerical values of various criteria can be combined into a single number. Others are qualitative, and it is more difficult to assign numerical weights to these. But the selection should consider both. Exhibit 11-1 lists the most important objective and subjective criteria usually considered in magazine selection.

EXHIBIT 11-1

Criteria for Determining Media Values of Magazines

Primary Objective Criteria

1. Composition and coverage
2. Delivery of demographic targets
3. Cost-efficiency of delivered targets
4. Delivery of product-class user targets
5. Delivery of strategic targets
6. Delivery of psychographic targets

Secondary Objective Criteria

1. Primary versus pass-along readers
2. Editorial features or other content related to brand's image
3. Special editions/issues/sections in print
4. Media imperatives
5. Color reproduction
6. Circulation trends in print vehicles
7. Geographic flexibility
8. Production flexibility
9. Positioning opportunities within print vehicles

Subjective (or Qualitative) Criteria

1. Writing tone
2. Reader respect
3. Leadership in media class
4. Believability

TARGET REACH, COMPOSITION, AND COST-EFFICIENCY

The most important criterion in determining media values is a combination of three principles: (1) finding vehicles that reach a large number of targets with (2) a high enough composition to avoid waste and (3) at a low cost per thousand. The logic of using these three principles in combination should be obvious. Advertising and marketing today are directed to certain demographic targets. Assuming these targets can be identified precisely, it follows that media vehicles should be selected to reach the largest number of targets efficiently with minimum waste.

Magazine Planning Process

How do magazines get selected for a media plan? Most planners follow a six-step process that leads to the final magazine schedule. Note that several of these steps require the use of proprietary computer systems that are available only by subscription from the data suppliers or third-party software vendors such as IMS or Telmar. Their use is shown here in order to illustrate these "real-world" processes.

1. **Determine the list of candidate magazines.** This is the time to cast a broad net to include any magazine that might be appropriate for the plan. Candidates can be identified by looking at the advertiser's experience in prior years, magazines used by competitors, and industry sources such as SRDS. Media planners also become aware of candidates through their frequent contacts with sales representatives from magazines that might be appropriate. Planners see sales presentations that give reasons why a particular magazine should be considered. As part of their efforts to maintain goodwill, sales representatives treat planners to luncheons, after-work parties, and other social events that are designed to make them aware of the sponsoring magazines and encourage planners to include them in the preliminary analyses. Through these contacts, planners learn of magazines that should be included on the candidate list.

2. **Identify the most efficient magazines with the CPM ranker.** In this step, the planner ranks all candidate magazines according to their CPM efficiency against the target audience. Typically, costs are based on the open rate of

a four-color bleed ad without any consideration for negotiation. This puts all of the candidates on an equal footing at this early stage in the process.

Exhibit 11-2 shows a sample CPM ranker for a magazine plan directed to female homemakers in households that are heavy users of frozen pizza. Recall that *composition* is the percent of the magazine's total audience who are heavy users of frozen pizza. *Coverage* is the percent of heavy users who read the magazine. The key to this ranker is the CPM. Magazines are ranked from most to

EXHIBIT 11-2

CPM Analysis of Female Homemakers Who Are Heavy Users of Frozen Pizza

Base: Female homemakers
Pop (000): 89,702

| | HEAVY USERS OF FROZEN PIZZA: 4+ PACKAGES/LAST 30 DAYS | | | | | |
	AUDIENCE (000)	COMP	COVERAGE	INDEX	4-COLOR BLEED COST	4-COLOR BLEED CPM
Total heavy users of frozen pizza	13,053	14.55	100.00	100	—	—
Magazines Included in Optimizer						
Woman's World	1,370	21.32	10.49	146	$ 47,390	$34.60
TV Guide	3,004	18.06	23.02	124	149,100	49.63
Reader's Digest	3,396	14.61	26.02	100	194,800	57.36
People	2,864	14.20	21.94	98	165,600	57.83
Redbook	1,490	18.99	11.41	130	88,000	59.06
Better Homes & Gardens	4,137	17.49	31.69	120	249,600	60.33
Woman's Day	2,711	15.98	20.77	110	165,315	60.99
Cooking Light	826	15.69	6.33	108	51,400	62.25
Family Circle	3,076	16.96	23.56	117	191,880	62.39
Good Housekeeping	3,000	15.89	22.99	109	192,260	64.08
Magazines Excluded from Optimizer						
School Parent & Child	785	23.49	6.01	161	51,750	65.92
Sesame Street Parent	808	23.04	6.19	158	55,400	68.61
Parenting	1,244	20.39	9.53	140	86,070	69.20

SOURCE: Mediamark Research Inc., Fall 1999.

least efficient, but be aware that differences of a few pennies are generally not significant.

Although a computer is needed to get the product user readership and CPM, total adult CPM can be calculated from information that is available on the Internet at www.mriplus.com. Magazine planning systems are also available at www.mediastart.com.

3. **Create a plan that delivers the most reach for the given budget.** All proprietary planning software has an optimizer function. Planners enter the budget, the target audience, and the list of candidate publications (with costs). The optimizer looks at thousands of alternatives and arrives at the plan that offers the most reach for the budget. Be aware that this is only a numerical solution; it doesn't account for any qualitative measures, negotiated pricing, special positioning, or a variety of other factors that need to be considered. But it does establish a benchmark that shows how much reach can be achieved.

Exhibit 11-3 shows the results of an optimization run—the theoretical highest-reaching plan for a $2 million budget. Notice that the planner drew the cutoff line at *Good Housekeeping*. All the magazines above that line are included in the optimization, while those below the line are out of consideration for this campaign. This plan costs $1,991,120. It will reach 78.4 percent of target female homemakers and deliver target women at an average $53.16 CPM impressions.

4. **Refine the optimal schedule to reflect marketing judgment.** The planner now adjusts the optimal plan to reflect any marketing factors that would suggest emphasizing one magazine over another. For instance, one might decide that it is important to have at least one of the "store" magazines (i.e., *Family Circle* or *Woman's Day*). The latter is chosen because it is slightly more efficient and has a lower out-of-pocket cost than *Family Circle*. With this in mind, the planner drops the insertion in *Good Housekeeping* and replaces it with *Woman's Day*. The planner might also be concerned that four insertions in *Woman's World* builds too much frequency in a plan that has a reach objective. By dropping two insertions in *Woman's World,* the planner saves almost $100,000, which, together with the saving from *Good Housekeeping,* could go to buying another insertion in *TV Guide*.

The planner makes these changes and reflects them as Schedule #2 (Exhibit 11-4). Notice that the reach has gone down only slightly, from 78.42 percent to 78.05 percent—a barely perceptible difference. It turns out that the revised plan

EXHIBIT 11-3

Magazine Optimization Model

Target: Female Homemakers/Frozen Pizza: Heavy Users (4+ Packages/Last 30 Days)
Pop (000): 13,053

MEDIA	SCHEDULE 1
Woman's World	4
TV Guide	1
People	3
Reader's Digest	2
Redbook	1
Better Homes & Gardens	2
Woman's Day	—
Cooking Light	1
Family Circle	—
Good Housekeeping	1
Total insertions	15
Total cost	$1,991,120
Gross impressions	37,457
Gross rating points	287
CPM gross impressions	$53.16
Reach percent	78.42
Average frequency	3.66
Net reach	10,236
CPM net reach	$194.51

Weighted by population (000).
SOURCE: Mediamark Research Inc., MEMRI2, Fall 1999.

is slightly over the $2 million budget, but this is based on open rates. Better rates often can be achieved through negotiations with magazines' representatives.

5. **Negotiate position, cost, and merchandising with the magazine sales representative.** Media planners are responsible for recommendations that involve millions of their clients' advertising dollars. But their decisions also represent success or failure to the representatives of the magazines whose job it is to sell advertising pages. In step 4, the decision to drop the insertion in *Good Housekeeping* represents the loss of a $192,260 order for that magazine's sales representative and an additional $149,100 order for the representative from *TV*

EXHIBIT 11-4

Magazine Optimization with Marketing Adjustments

Target: Female Homemakers/Frozen Pizza: Heavy Users (4+ Packages/Last 30 Days)
Pop (000): 13,053

MEDIA	SCHEDULE 1	SCHEDULE 2
Woman's World	4	2
TV Guide	1	2
People	3	3
Reader's Digest	2	2
Redbook	1	1
Better Homes & Gardens	2	2
Woman's Day	—	1
Cooking Light	1	1
Family Circle	—	—
Good Housekeeping	1	—
Total insertions	15	14
Total cost	$1,991,120	$2,018,495
Gross impressions	37,457	37,432
Gross rating points	287	287
CPM gross impressions	$53.16	$53.92
Reach percent	78.42	78.05
Average frequency	3.66	3.67
Net reach	10,236	10,188
CPM net reach	$194.51	$198.12

Weighted by population (000).
SOURCE: Mediamark Research Inc., MEMRI2, Fall 1999.

Guide. The planner uses these competitive forces to obtain the best media placement and lowest cost for the advertiser.

Note that for broadcast media, planners develop the goals in terms of GRPs, reach, frequency, scheduling, and market selection. But decisions regarding particular programs, TV stations, and broadcast networks are handled by professional buyers/negotiators who often live in another city. For magazines, on the other hand, the planner and buyer are typically the same person.

Starting with the revised "optimal" schedule, the planner now talks to the sales reps to see which magazine will give the best price. Although advertisers who buy only a few pages typically pay the open rate, steep discounts are offered for heavy, continuing schedules.

The other area open to negotiation is position. Traditionally, advertisers want their ads to appear "far forward, right-hand page." There is little research to indicate that ads in the front of the book are more likely to be remembered than those in the middle or back, but those words have become a standard by which magazine negotiations are measured. There will be more about position effects later in this chapter. Magazines also compete for the business by offering merchandising such as contests, proprietary research, new-product sampling opportunities, tickets to sports events, luncheons with key reporters, and other inducements.

6. **Present the recommended schedule to the client and adjust as necessary.** Although magazine sales representatives deal primarily with the media planner, they also make sales calls on the advertiser. Most clients accept the planner's recommendation as presented, but it is not uncommon for the planner to be told to add an insertion in a different magazine because the advertiser has made a side deal with the representative. This is no reflection on the ability of the planner; it just serves as a reminder that, in the end, it is the advertiser's money, and advertisers are free to spend their money as they see fit.

OTHER MEDIA VALUES

Many other factors besides CPM should be considered when evaluating and selecting media vehicles, especially at steps 3 and 4 in the process. Some of these factors are discussed in the following paragraphs.

Secondary Audiences

The total audience reported by research services such as MRI includes two kinds of readers. Primary readers are those who purchased the magazine themselves or who live in households where somebody subscribes. Secondary, or pass-along, readers come upon the magazine in a public place such as their doctor's office, or they read a friend's copy. Early studies reported less ad recall among secondary readers, suggesting that they are less valuable to the advertiser. A few planners reflect this in their analysis by scaling down (discounting) the secondary

EXHIBIT 11-5

Two Bases for Analyzing the Audiences of Magazine A

FULL-VALUE BASIS	NUMBER (MILLIONS)	OUT-OF-HOME AUDIENCE, DISCOUNTED 50% BASIS	NUMBER (MILLIONS)
Primary audience	27.75	Primary audience	27.75
Out-of-home audience	9.25	Out-of-home audience	4.63
Total audience	37.00	Total audience	32.38

readership. If secondary audiences are deemed less valuable, then it seems reasonable to discount them in some way. But few media planners ignore them entirely.

One method for discounting the pass-along or secondary audience is simply to cut their numbers in half. For example, suppose Medium A has a total audience of 37 million, of which 75 percent is primary and 25 percent is secondary (out-of-home) readers. The latter group (25 percent of 37 million) is discounted 50 percent.

Exhibit 11-5 shows an example that first treats the secondary audience at full value and then at a 50 percent discounted value. The example is based on the total audience. Typically, media planners discount only the demographic group that comprises the target audience, such as men aged 18–34 or women who graduated from college.

Not everyone agrees that the secondary audience should be discounted. In a classic paper on the subject, Seymour Marshak, formerly manager of advertising and distribution research of the Ford Motor Company, said it would be better to determine the value of a secondary reader on the basis of how important that individual was in the target audience and then determine what opportunities he or she had to see a given advertisement in a given medium.[1] For example, secondary readers might be even more important than primary readers when they receive only one or two exposure opportunities compared to primary readers

---

1. Seymour Marshak, "Forum Question: Generally Speaking, What Value Do You Place on the Secondary or Pass-Along Reader?" *Media/Scope* (February 1970): 26.

who might receive more than 20 opportunities. This assumes that high frequencies (or many exposure opportunities) are not automatically good media strategy. Each marketing/media situation is different. Foremost in this kind of evaluation is the assumption that secondary readers are the most important target audiences and have to be reached if the advertising message is to have the proper effect. In conclusion, although there are good reasons for and against discounting the secondary audience, most advertisers give them full value. The decision should be based on logic and clearly identified marketing reasons, rather than subjective judgment alone.

Editorial Environment

Occasionally vehicles that reach targets efficiently are not suited to an advertiser's message because the editorial environments of the vehicles under consideration are incompatible with the ad message. This concept is related to the need for psychographic data to fit demographic data. Two college graduates of the same age and in the same income class could lead radically different lives. Similarly, two media vehicles can reach the same demographic targets with about the same cost-efficiency, but each will feature editorial material of interest to different kinds of readers. This difference is important in determining a media vehicle's advertising value.

For example, suppose an advertiser for salad dressing is considering eight potential vehicles, each of which reaches the demographic targets fairly well. But the editorial environments differ widely, as Exhibit 11-6 shows. The editorial environment criteria in the table are number of food pages printed in four colors, number of food photographs, number of recipes, and number of editorial lines dealing with salads. The planner selected these criteria arbitrarily, so others could be substituted or added to provide a composite evaluation of the media alternatives. Based on the criteria shown, *Better Homes & Gardens* was found to be the best vehicle.

A magazine's editorial environment can be evaluated in detail with Hall's Magazine Reports (www.hallsreports.com). This service analyzes the editorial content of more than 120 magazines in terms of total lines, pages, and percent of pages according to eighteen major classifications such as Family, Travel, Automotive, Children, and Health. These are further divided into more than 200

EXHIBIT 11-6

Index of Editorial Environments for Salad Dressings

MAGAZINE	4-COLOR FOOD PAGES	FOOD PHOTOGRAPHS	NUMBER OF RECIPES	EDITORIAL LINES DEALING WITH SALADS	AVERAGE OF FOUR SCORES
Better Homes & Gardens	127	255	107	135	156
Good Housekeeping	138	56	89	192	119
Woman's Day	84	29	212	108	108
Sunset	12	165	102	121	100
Family Circle	136	83	105	59	96
Ladies' Home Journal	115	85	81	51	83
McCall's	104	70	57	53	71
American Home	86	56	48	81	68

SOURCE: Ronald B. Kaatz, *Dr. (un)Strangeperson, or, How I Learned to Stop Worrying (About Some Numbers) and Love My Magazine Plans!,* paper presented to the American Academy of Advertising Convention, April 1975, Knoxville, Tennessee.

subclassifications such as General Health, Personal Health and Safety, Adult/ Other Health, Children's Health, and Alternative Medicine.

By including these qualitative measures in the analysis, the planner is able to account for more subtle influences on advertising effectiveness than just the relatively simplistic measures of reach and cost-efficiency.

Special Opportunities in Magazines

Media planners who want to reach special or limited markets will find that magazines can be adapted to meet their needs. This is because some media have devised special demographic or geographic editions for just that purpose. Exhibit 11-7 lists some of the demographic breaks that are available in major consumer and business magazines.

In addition to offering special demographic and geographic breakouts, most of the larger-circulation magazines offer two-way (and in some cases even four-way) copy splits. *Reader's Digest,* for example, can distribute special copy to one out of every four subscribers across the nation through the use of zip coding

EXHIBIT 11-7

Some Demographic Editions of Magazines

PUBLICATION	NAME OF EDITION	TARGET
Better Homes & Gardens	Better by Design	Upper-income homes
Newsweek	Woman	Working women
Time	Business	Business executives
Time	Top Management	Top management
Time	Gold	Upper-income adults
Sports Illustrated	Homeowners	Homeowners
U.S. News & World Report	Blue Chip	Upper-income homes
Prevention	Masters	Adults over age 55
Reader's Digest	Family Plus	Adults under age 55 with children

and block coding. Other magazines use sophisticated printing and binding techniques that allow advertisers (for an extra charge) to print directly on the bound-in page the name and address of neighborhood stores where a product can be purchased.

Media Imperatives

Although some vehicles reach target audiences very well, the data on reach sometimes hide important facts. For example, a planner may find that television best reaches a given target audience, but those reached are light television viewers and heavy magazine readers. In other words, reach figures do not indicate the degree of exposure to a given medium. *Media imperatives* is the name given to an analysis by SMRB that provides information on the degree of exposure to television and magazines. MRI offers the same analysis under the name *media comparatives*.

Television imperatives show the percent of the target and selectivity index for people who are heavy television viewers and light magazine readers. *Magazine imperatives* show the same statistics for persons who are heavy magazine readers and light television viewers. Media imperatives can also show *dual audiences* (individuals heavily exposed to both media and individuals lightly exposed to both media).

EXHIBIT 11-8

Media Comparatives for Female Homemakers Who Are Heavy Users of Frozen Pizza

Frozen Pizza: Heavy Users: 4+ Packages/Last 30 Days

	POPULATION	(000)	HORZ%	VERT%	INDEX
Female homemakers	89,702	13,053	14.55	100.00	100
Media comparatives: heavy magazines—heavy TV	23,748	4,040	17.01	30.95	117
Media comparatives: heavy magazines—light TV	20,954	3,073	14.67	23.54	101
Media comparatives: light magazines—heavy TV	21,191	2,601	12.28	19.93	84
Media comparatives: light magazines—light TV	23,809	3,339	14.03	25.58	96
Total	89,702	13,053	58.00	100.00	100

SOURCE: Mediamark Research Inc., Fall 1999.

Thus, media imperatives are a means of comparing magazines and television based on the degree of exposure to each medium. They also show how many users of various product categories are accounted for by the four groups measured. Exhibit 11-8 provides an MRI media comparative analysis for heavy users of frozen pizza. This analysis shows that heavy users are 17 percent more likely to be heavy consumers of both magazines and television than the average female homemaker. It suggests that a media plan directed to this target group should utilize both media, rather than concentrating all weight in one or the other. The data do not answer all questions, but rather add another quantitative dimension to help solve the selection problem, as well as the problem of allocating money.

Position Alternatives

During negotiation, some print vehicles offer advertisers selected positions such as front-of-book or next to compatible editorial material, which, if accepted, can help the advertiser reach the target with more impact. Sometimes the vehicle charges premium rates for a preferred position, but the buyer's goal should be to get it without paying extra. The planner should consider the availability of favored positions as a factor in weighing one vehicle against another. Vehicles that offer selected positions can be a better buy than those that do not. The value of certain positions will be discussed later in this chapter.

Advertising Clutter and Product Protection

In both television and print media, it is possible to measure the amount of clutter that occurs. Presumably, the medium that reaches the maximum number of targets at the best cost-efficiency and with the least clutter would be the most desirable. There are, however, exceptions to this assumption. For example, in certain magazine classes (e.g., fashion and shelter), readers buy the magazine specifically to shop through the advertising.

But if all competitors are in the same magazine and many other ads are also in the magazine, it is questionable whether that vehicle is the most desirable for a specific advertiser. Brands with a clear-cut competitive advantage over other brands should prosper when placed near competitors. Other brands, perceived as less desirable, suffer from such competition. Generally, clutter is undesirable, and product protection is something to seek. This means keeping competitive ads within the vehicle at a reasonable distance from the advertised brand.

In evaluating clutter in a print medium, one should consider the Starch studies, which show that the readership of the average advertisement in a magazine declines as the number of ads in the vehicle increases. In television and radio, product protection, although desirable, is usually available only to advertisers who buy enough minutes in a program to qualify as a sponsor.

Circulation Trends

An objective measurement of a medium's value is the circulation trend over a period of at least a year or two. Because advertising is sometimes planned more than a year ahead of time, media planners might want to study the latest Audit Bureau of Circulations (ABC) circulation figures for the last five years to see what has been happening. If a magazine under consideration has shown a decline, it may be dropped from the list. On the other hand, magazines with increasing circulation trends are considered more valuable, although they can be expected to charge more in anticipation of increased readership.

Advertising Copy Checking and Product Restrictions

Some media have a reputation for examining the veracity of all advertising copy and claims and annually reject many pages of advertising. They publicize this fact regularly. The assumption here is that readers, knowing of this practice, will prefer to read ads in such a vehicle in preference to others that do not have this policy. *Good Housekeeping,* many newspapers, and network television organizations are among those that check copy carefully.

As part of their effort to maintain a quality reputation, some magazines refuse all advertising from potentially controversial product categories such as tobacco, alcohol, and direct-mail personal products. These policies are spelled out in the magazine's sales material and in SRDS. Planners working for these types of products must be aware of these policies and avoid recommending magazines that will ultimately refuse to carry the ads.

Response to Coupons, Information, or Recipes

Measurements of the number of readers who ask for information or clipped recipes is available in MRI and can provide a planner with the type of qualitative data that help him or her to differentiate one magazine from another. On the other hand, reader response to a particular advertiser's coupons is not public and can be difficult, if not impossible, to obtain. Some advertisers will share the general direction of coupon response, but they typically hold detailed response rates by magazine confidential, even from their own advertising agency and media planners.

Available Discounts

Sometimes the value of a medium is directly affected by the nature of the discounts that it offers. If a number of ads are planned for a calendar year in several vehicles that are otherwise about equal, the best value is the vehicle offering a substantial discount. Although target coverage and composition are important criteria, if all else is equal, the magazine with the greatest discount (hence the lowest CPM) will get the order.

Even before the recent economic slowdown, the pressure of cost negotiations has caused most magazines to provide unpublished discounts to high-volume advertisers. Those buying only one or two pages can expect to pay rate card, but for larger schedules, the published prices are just the starting point for negotiations. Large companies will use their clout by adding up the pages from all of their divisions in order to negotiate a single, extremely favorable (and highly confidential) corporate rate that will be used by all planners working on the account. The advertiser assigns a print "agency of record" the task of keeping track of all corporate pages, conducting these rate negotiations, and keeping planners informed of the negotiated price of each magazine.

Flexibility

Two kinds of flexibility can affect media value. The first is the degree to which a medium can be used to precisely reach geographically superior markets, while at the same time avoiding relatively weak markets. Generally, local media such as newspapers, spot radio, spot television, and outdoor are considered flexible media in the geographic sense. Magazines have some flexibility with their regional and local market issues, but often there is no local edition for a market that the planner deems necessary or no regional edition that covers an advertiser's sales divisions with much precision. A media vehicle that has the potential for geographic flexibility is more valuable than one that is not flexible.

A second kind of flexibility concerns the ability of the medium to make quick changes in copy—that is, production flexibility. There could be many reasons why an advertiser might need to change an advertising message quickly. In some media, this is relatively easy; in others, it is not. Black-and-white ads in print media can usually be changed quite easily and quickly in many vehicles. When a print ad is to be run in four colors, however, making changes is more difficult because it requires the printer to remake four-color printing plates. In broadcast, live or videotaped commercials are easier to change than filmed commercials. So production flexibility is a consideration in determining media value if changes in the advertising message are contemplated.

Color Quality

In print media, color quality can be important in determining media values, especially for food and cosmetic advertisers. The problem of color quality is twofold. First, there is the problem of achieving the color quality of the original artwork planned for an advertisement. Some publications find it difficult to attain this quality because of the kinds of ink and paper they use. A second problem concerns the maintenance of consistent color quality during the entire press run.

In high-speed offset presses, paper dust can deteriorate the printing plate and the blanket that transfers the ink to the paper. As a result, certain colors will print heavier or lighter than required. The planner should know the printing abilities of the publishing organization. Magazines that carry advertising for cosmetics are typically held to the highest print production standards.

QUALITATIVE VALUES OF MEDIA

As stated earlier, media selection is based mostly on the ability of specific media vehicles to reach precise target audiences with high cost-efficiency and little waste. Other considerations in planning include the total cost of the medium plus the reach and frequency to be generated. Before making a final decision for or against any medium, however, the planner should also consider the qualitative values of each medium and decide how important these values are for the plan.

A *qualitative value* is some characteristic of a medium that enhances the chances that an advertising message carried within it will be effective. Comparing the qualitative merits of one medium versus another (e.g., TV versus magazines) is a highly subjective exercise. The relative characteristics are obvious, but the decision that one is more appropriate than the other for a given campaign is the kind of judgment planners avoid, since it cannot be supported with research. Furthermore, the choice of which media to use has such far-reaching consequences that it is typically a joint decision of the account group, the creative team, the client, and the media planner.

Qualitative distinctions are based on the assumption that media are not simply passive carriers of advertisements; they also play an active role. These distinctions assume that a magazine offers a unique environment, with a personality that can rub off on its advertisements and make them more effective in communicating their messages.

The problem with studies of magazine environment is deciding what to do with the results. Knowing that one magazine has a different and presumably better image than another does not tell the planner anything about the magazine's advertising effectiveness—if its image is even related to effectiveness. In addition, qualitative studies conducted by one magazine seldom mention its competition, making side-by-side comparisons impossible. Therefore image studies, though a form of determining a qualitative value, have little importance in media planning.

Types of Qualitative Values

Notwithstanding early research on general qualitative values, there is still little consensus about the matter. When planners do use such values, they are apt to prepare the following kind of statement for their plans: "We feel that Magazine A reflects greater authority and prestige than other magazines, so we recommend purchasing *x* number of ads in it." Other terms that are used in the same manner as *authority* and *prestige* are *impact, mood, believability, atmosphere, excitement,* and *leadership.*

The words *we feel . . .* and the absence of numerical support are the tip-off that a planner has no data or solid research to back up the statement. However, qualitative measures still have a place in media planning. MRI and other research companies ask their respondents several questions that can suggest qualitative differences among magazines. These are discussed in the following paragraphs.

Reading Days   How many days, totally, are alternative magazines read? If a magazine is opened at any time on a given day, this constitutes a reading day. If, for example, there is evidence that Magazine A is read more total days than Magazines B, C, D, and E (all under consideration), then the planner has one more qualitative reason to select A. More reading days represent more opportunities to see ads.

Time Spent Reading   In a similar manner, it is possible to measure the total or average number of hours spent reading magazines. These measurements indicate that the magazine with the largest number of reading hours is more attractive than others. This conclusion assumes that audience members have more opportunities to see ads if they spend more time reading. However, some researchers question whether the survey's respondents can accurately report how much time they spend with a magazine. Once again, we are faced with practical limitations that restrict our ability to act on the information provided.

Page Openings   It is possible to measure the number of pages opened in alternative magazines. Researchers can use a technique in which a tiny spot of glue is applied to pages containing ads. Respondents are given specially glued magazines on a given day. A day or two later, the interviewer returns and picks up the special copies. The researchers count the number of pages pulled open.

A variation of page-opening measurements is simply to count page traffic on all ad pages. Using a recognition measuring technique, researchers count the number of pages where any ads on the page were noted by audience members who comprise a sample. Page traffic data is a measure of the net potential audience size of a magazine and plays a role in the final selection. But both of these are custom, one-time-only studies of a limited number of magazines and so are of little value to media planners.

Subjective Qualitative Values

Planners and magazine sales representatives sometimes use subjective (generally unquantifiable) qualitative terms to characterize the value of a media vehicle. Probably the most misused of all media qualitative value terms is *impact*. Print media executives often claim that their magazine has more impact than other magazines. If they mean that an ad in their magazine will sell more of the product than an ad in any other magazine, this cannot be proved and is, therefore, conjecture on the part of the executives. It is generally impossible to determine the effect of a media vehicle and an advertisement on sales.

Conceivably, a careful testing program could be conducted for one advertiser, with strict controls, to prove that more people recalled a given ad in one magazine than in any other. But recall and sales are quite different. How can one prove that what sold the product was not the price, the packaging, the distribution, or the sales promotion? Some vehicles are better than others, but not on the basis of impact, which is too vague a concept to be used in media planning. Only when a clear-cut cause-and-effect relationship can be established for the brand and the vehicle on sales can the concept of impact be used.

The *core reader* is another measure that is sometimes used, although researchers disagree on exactly what is meant by the term. According to one definition, a core reader is anyone who says he or she read at least three out of four issues. This seems logical enough until we realize that the definition helps magazines that derive a large percent of their circulation from subscriptions, as compared to those that are distributed primarily through newsstand sales.

Using Qualitative Values

Qualitative rationales for selecting media have a place in planning procedures. But users of such measures should keep in mind some reasonable guidelines:

- Qualitative, or subjective, rationales should never totally replace quantitative CPM and reach substantiation.
- Qualitative consideration should be used after quantitative analysis has been made to modify numerical relationships.
- If possible, more than one person should contribute to making the subjective analysis, to reduce the possibility of individual bias.
- Planners should be suspicious of media-sponsored research concerning qualitative values such as high impact, "liked most," and so forth. Much of this kind of research is highly promotional, rather than objective. It is very difficult to transfer the findings from one medium to another or one media vehicle to another.

In conclusion, qualitative values of media do exist, but they cannot be used as the main criteria in media planning. They are simply not objective enough to be used alone for decision making. Perhaps ways will be found to prove that one medium indeed has more impact than others, but at present it cannot be proved. Experts can only agree that media are not passive carriers of ads. They do have qualitative values, and some can be used for planning.

AD POSITIONS WITHIN MEDIA

Assuming that media vehicles have been selected, the budget allocated, and a schedule worked out, media planning could, in theory, end at this point. In practice, however, planners and others interested in media still have questions: Is there nothing else that can be done to help in the advertising communication process? Are reach, frequency, and cost-efficiency all there is? The problem is to find ways for the media planner to go beyond delivery and not only get vehicles exposed, but also get ads within those vehicles exposed and, finally, get the ads read.

To a great extent, this last responsibility belongs to the creative people—account planners, writers, and art directors who have special talents for getting advertising communication through to the reader. The copy people, for example, can write scintillating headlines and meaningful words. The art director can devise fascinating layouts. The creative people can ask for four-color ads, bleed pages, reverse printing, gatefold-size ads, two-page spreads. They can print ads on unusual stock such as acetate or aluminum foil. They can use unusual inks such as Day-Glo or perfumed inks. These are but a few of the many options open to the creative personnel in getting ads noticed and read.

What, then, can media planners do to help the situation? As part of the buying negotiations, they can ask for certain positions within media that are thought to be better than other positions. This, however, leaves them open to questions about positioning research and strategy.

Problems of Positioning Research

A number of media positions are thought to be better than others. For example, the fourth cover (the outside back cover) of a magazine is generally conceded to be the best place in a magazine for an ad. In fact, research confirms that the fourth cover is indeed one of the best positions. But since the back cover is sold for a premium price, there is a question whether the additional impact is worth the additional cost. And some researchers question just how much additional impact is provided. Nonetheless, there is some logic, even without research, to suggest that a fourth-cover position is valuable. There is not much agreement among experts about other media positions. The research tends to be inconclusive.

Perhaps the foremost problem of position research is that it is difficult to separate measurements of position from copy effects. Most research techniques used to establish the effects of position are really a mixture of copy and position. In some research studies, another dimension, that of size, is added. Then, too, averaging data for position effects that contain widely varying degrees of copy effectiveness do not truly represent the effects of position. Averaging tends to be unduly affected by extreme copy-effect scores. Some media experts question whether there is any totally valid copy-measuring device. Even assuming that most are valid, there is still no way, through present-day measurements, to know the effect of position alone.

A solution would be to design experiments involving ad copy that is held constant with the only variable being position. Because the same ads would be measured in different positions in different media vehicles, the effects of position alone could be found. However, there still is dissatisfaction with much research devised to measure position, because it is not carefully controlled to eliminate bias. Research designs are often poor or nonexistent. Samples are often nonrandom and selected haphazardly. Questionnaire design and interviewing controls are not always the best. As a result, much position research is suspect.

A major consideration in deciding whether to use a special position in a vehicle is the premium cost. Some positions are not worth the extra cost. And even if a position seems to be worth the cost, the questionable nature of the existing research can make it difficult to support a decision one way or the other.

Some Position Effects

Following is a brief summary of position effects that some media planners accept. The reader is cautioned about accepting them as valid evidence. They are presented to show a sample of the kinds of positions that could affect the communication power of advertisements placed in vehicles.

Position in Magazines   Using Starch Adnorm data as a guide, fourth-cover positions are usually considered better than any inside positions. Early studies suggest that second-cover and page-one positions are about equal and are the next best after fourth-cover positions. Front-of-the-magazine positions (from page 3 to about page 20) are the next best positions, and right-hand pages are somewhat better than left-hand pages, with some exceptions. These studies conflict with some planners' belief that ads are more effective if they appear near compatible editorial (e.g., a food ad placed near a recipe) that is usually farther back in the magazine. More detailed information on the effects of position and ad size are available on the website of the Magazine Publishers of America (MPA) at www.magazine.org.

Although there is virtually no research to substantiate the value of these positions for a given campaign, advertisers have come to expect that their agencies will have sufficient "clout" with the magazines that *they* will be given the choice spots. Because, obviously, only one advertiser can run on the back cover or page one or opposite the table of contents, planners compete fiercely to secure those premier positions—if not page one, then at least somewhere near the front. Planners keep track of the positions they are given by each magazine, and they use this information in subsequent negotiations. At a minimum, planners should expect an even rotation of their ads throughout the magazine.

Position in Newspapers   Ads near the front of newspapers are considered better than those near the back, but the differences are small. There is no significant difference between right-hand and left-hand pages. Inside a newspaper section is better than the last page of the section. There is little difference between ads above or below the fold. Editorial environment affects the readership of ads—ads for male products do better on sports pages, and ads for female products do better on women's pages.

Position in Television   Attention to TV programs is greatest during prime time and late fringe and poorest in early morning when the family is getting ready for work and school.[2] Daytime is about 50 percent to 80 percent as high

---

2. Mediamark Research Inc., "Percent of Viewers Paying Full Attention," Spring 2001.

as nighttime recall. Research suggests that a 30-second commercial has about 60–75 percent the recall of a 60-second commercial, and a 15-second commercial has about 60–75 percent as much recall as a 30-second commercial.

In the past, it was thought that people paid more attention to high-rated than to low-rated programs, and more attention to commercials that were inside the show, compared to those in breaks between shows. Recent studies have cast doubt on these generalizations regarding position effects. It is not known whether this is because the earlier research was flawed, or because the television environment has changed.

INTERNET MEDIA VEHICLES

Many of the processes and considerations discussed in this chapter are germane to evaluating, selecting, and buying Internet media. However, the processes are different enough to bear separate consideration.

Evaluating and Selecting Internet Media

The task of finding appropriate sites for Internet advertising is directly comparable to the task of vehicle selection in traditional media. The planner must answer the question, Where on the Internet can I find people who would be interested in my client's product?

As with any media plan, the first step is to identify the target audience and campaign objectives as they relate to the Internet. These can include maximizing direct-response sales and return on investment, building brand awareness, referring visitors to the advertiser's website, obtaining research from online questionnaires, or giving visitors additional sales information.

A key element in this process is determining the "metrics of success." That is, how will the effectiveness of the Internet campaign be measured? Some options include dollar volume of sales from the advertiser's website, sales profitability, number of visitors clicking through to the site, and change in brand awareness or attitude toward the advertiser before and after the campaign. There must be agreement on this point before the campaign begins. This agreement avoids the all-too-common situation where the advertiser starts with one objective, perhaps to build brand awareness, but then considers the campaign a failure if sales are below expectations despite strong awareness growth.

Once there is agreement on the target audience, campaign objectives, and success metrics, the next step is to identify websites that are selective to the target. This is done with survey-based research very similar to MRI. The most widely used service is @plan Advertising, a product of the Diameter research division of DoubleClick Inc.[3] @plan Advertising maintains a representative U.S. sample of 40,000 respondents who have used the Internet in the past 30 days for reasons other than E-mail. Respondents fill out an online questionnaire that first screens for visits to general categories of sites (search engines, financial, travel, auto, leisure, etc.). Then respondents are presented a list of sites and are asked to identify the ones they have visited in the last 30 days. The result is a database that advertisers can use to identify the sites that have the highest coverage and composition for their marketing target.

Exhibit 11-9 lists the most selective websites for an Internet target that might be appropriate for the golf club example in Chapter 2: men 25–54 who bought sports equipment online in the last 30 days. Note that the site's audience is expressed with the same composition and reach (coverage) concepts that were used for magazines.

Another way to identify possible sites associated with the product is to use search engines such as Yahoo!, Google, and Alta Vista. For example, a planner working for a golf club manufacturer would find a range of potential sites by entering the keyword *golf.*

Competitive reporting services such as Nielsen//NetRatings (www.nielsennet ratings.com), Jupiter Media Metrix AdRelevance (www.jmm.com), and CMRi's AdNetTrackUS (www.adnettrackus.com) also can provide useful leads. These services show which sites are used by an advertiser's competitors. Note that all of these services are password controlled and require a paid subscription for access.

After identifying candidate sites, planners should visit and evaluate each. In addition to their qualitative judgment, planners can use Nielsen//NetRatings to evaluate each site's coverage and composition against conventional demograph-

---

3. For more information, see www.webplan.net.

EXHIBIT 11-9

@Plan Advertising Listing of Most Selective Websites for Men 25–54 Who Bought Sporting Goods Online in the Last Six Months

All sites custom optimization—804 results
30-day audience comparison
Results: 1–804 in % Comp. Order
Target audience: 25–54, Male, Sporting Goods (purchased online in last 6 months)
Online market size: 1.8%, 2,381,765

ALL SITES	% COMP.	ONLINE INDEX	% REACH	REACH ONLINE
Mountain Bike	13.6	770	4.3	101,318
Field & Stream and Outdoor Life Online	12.2	689	6.8	160,847
GORP.com	10.6	598	4.6	110,741
CART.com	10.3	580	2.7	64,326
Family PC Magazine	9.7	546	2.5	58,887
InformationWeek.com	9.5	539	3.4	81,937
Iwon Sports	8.7	493	6.7	160,373
CNET Tech Jobs	8.3	472	3.1	72,701
Silicon Investor	8.3	470	1.8	43,533
Golf Online	8.3	467	3.2	75,228
Byte.com	8.2	464	2.1	51,067

SOURCE: *@plan Advertising Planning Report,* Spring 2000 Release.

ics. Nielsen has recruited a panel of Internet users who agree to put tracking software on their computer. Each time panel members sit down at the computer, they log in and identify themselves. Then the software records every keystroke, allowing the researchers to know when the visits occurred, what sites were visited, how long the person stayed at the site, what pages within the site were explored, how long the person stayed on each page ("stickiness"), and a variety of other data that are useful to planners.

Because the service gathers data automatically, it is able to report on almost 6,000 websites and provide far more detailed information than @plan Advertising, which is limited to the respondent's memory of exposure to about 800 sites. On the other hand, it reports only conventional demographics, while @plan Advertising also shows both demographics and product usage. To get the complete picture, planners should consult both services.

Exhibits 11-10 and 11-11 list the top 10 websites visited by women 25–54 years of age, according to Nielsen//NetRatings. The sites are sorted by both coverage and composition. Note, as we have seen before, that the most demographically selective sites have the least coverage, while the larger sites, such as www.yahoo.com, give much greater coverage but also have much more waste. A good media plan will place ads on both types of sites.

Buying Internet Media

After selecting a number of appropriate sites, the planner sends each a request for proposal. This request identifies the advertiser; campaign objectives and strategies; the planner's name, address, phone number, and E-mail address; the dates of the campaign; ad unit size; target audience; and the expected budget. The website's advertising department confirms the site's ability to accept the advertising and gives the number of impressions that can be bought for this budget. From this the planner can calculate the site's CPM and compare it with other submissions.

The website's server computer makes a record each time a banner or other ad unit is sent to a visitor's browser. This documented exposure is the natural unit of value that allows Internet advertising to be priced in terms of CPM impressions. After negotiation, a planner might say, "I agree to buy 100,000 impressions at $20.00 CPM, for a total cost of $2,000." The contract is signed, creative materials and rotation instructions are provided, and the website begins sending the advertiser's banners, pop-up ads, or other creative messages to the designated target visitors. Each impression is counted. When the ordered 100,000 impressions have been delivered, the campaign ends, and the advertiser is billed.

In addition to CPM impressions, advertisers may agree to pay only for site visitors who click through the banner and are then redirected to the advertiser's site. Because the click-through rate is typically less than 1 percent of the people exposed, the CPM click-throughs will be much higher than CPM banner impressions. On the other hand, these people are far more valuable because they have demonstrated interest in the advertiser's product.

Advertisers can also buy site sponsorships, ad placement only in selected cities or zip codes, or placement on selected pages of a larger website (similar to

EXHIBIT 11-10

Top 10 Internet Sites Ranked by Coverage

Target: Female Aged 25–54, In-Home Usage

SITE	UNIQUE AUDIENCE	COMPOSITION %	COVERAGE %	INDEX
yahoo.com	10,766,516	29.3	46.7	97
aol.com	10,519,821	31.0	45.7	103
msn.com	7,726,726	28.5	33.5	95
bluemountain.com	5,624,459	38.8	24.4	129
geocities.com	5,283,213	28.3	22.9	94
go.com	4,552,312	29.3	19.8	97
netscape.com	4,543,156	30.0	19.7	100
microsoft.com	4,214,586	28.3	18.3	94
passport.com	3,782,122	26.5	16.4	88
lycos.com	3,638,375	27.5	15.8	91

SOURCE: Nielsen//Net Ratings, February 2000.

EXHIBIT 11-11

Top 10 Websites Ranked by Composition

Target: Female Aged 25–54, In-Home Usage

SITE	UNIQUE AUDIENCE	COMPOSITION %	COVERAGE %	INDEX
chadwicks.com	143,888	84.2	0.6	280
ltdcommodities.com	220,196	74.3	1.0	247
weightwatchers.com*	88,127	73.6	0.4	245
toysmart.com*	87,891	73.4	0.4	244
education-world.com*	111,299	72.3	0.5	240
stretcher.com*	81,209	71.3	0.4	237
avon.com	128,827	70.6	0.6	235
physique.com*	84,423	70.5	0.4	234
newport-news.com	114,497	70.5	0.5	234
allherb.com*	83,825	70.0	0.4	233

*Low sample size; use for directional purposes only.
SOURCE: Nielsen//Net Ratings, February 2000.

placing an ad in a particular section of a newspaper). Some sites allow planners to deliver impressions only when the local temperature or pollen count or rainfall meets some criterion. For example, a soft-drink company might want to deliver impressions only when the local temperature exceeds 90 degrees. The possibilities for customized pricing models and modes of advertising exposure are virtually unlimited.

Many websites keep track of visitors by placing a small record, called a *cookie,* on the hard disk of the visitor's computer. This enables the site to identify repeat visits. One creative execution will be served at the first visit; then on subsequent visits, the existence of a cookie will alert the server to send a different ad. This keeps the creative fresh and improves the chances that the visitor will click through to the advertiser's website.

Some companies use cookies to develop a profile of the visitor's browsing behavior. Through arrangements with hundreds of websites, a record is made whenever a given computer (identified by the cookie on the hard disk) appears at any one of them. This allows the profiling company to identify a person who, for instance, visits a sports website, a financial site, a golf pro site, an auto racing site, and a business news site. When that person (cookie) shows up again, the profiler knows to serve a banner for a financial service advertiser, for instance. Another user, whose cookie indicates an interest in child-oriented sites, would be served a banner for products targeting parents.

Internet websites and ad serving companies see profiling as an aid to advertisers who wish to target their messages better; some consumer groups, however, have objected to the practice as an invasion of privacy. It remains to be seen how this debate will be resolved.

Internet Still in Its Infancy

Although advertising volume is down substantially from its peak in 1998–2000, the general principles of selecting and buying Internet media still apply. As technology advances, new ways of measuring the Internet audience will be developed, along with ways of delivering and pricing advertising impressions. Planners must stay informed about these rapidly occurring changes so they can help their clients take advantage of the many opportunities that will arise.

CHAPTER TWELVE

Media Costs and Buying Problems

Every media alternative considered for the media strategy has a different cost. The final media plan emerging from the marketing strategy should effectively maximize the delivery of the designated marketing target in the most cost-efficient manner. Therefore, the media planner must be familiar with market definition and be fully versed in how people utilize various media. In some instances, as is the case with television time, the cost of media varies with supply and demand. Other media, such as magazines and newspapers, remain fairly constant in cost, thereby providing a high degree of predictability as planners develop costs for the media plan.

The costs that go into the final media plan are always in a state of flux. Estimating such costs is as much an art as a science; it depends heavily on the experience and professionalism of the media planner and the media buyer. If a plan is based on costs that are out of line with marketplace realities, it can result in delivery of a faulty media plan. For example, if a planner estimates that 100 gross rating points of prime-time television can be purchased for $200,000, and the actual cost of that time is $300,000, the deliverability of the plan is seriously impaired. The client can then justifiably question the value of that media plan, as well as the competence of the planner.

Estimating media costs is a complex task. In addition, different media have different problems connected with the buying process. This chapter will identify the importance of the planner's involvement in the media-buying process and explain why this involvement requires familiarity with both the cost of media and the problems associated with purchasing different media types.

SOME CONSIDERATIONS IN PLANNING AND BUYING MEDIA

The value of a media plan is related to how well it delivers the designated marketing targets at the lowest cost with the least amount of waste. The criteria for determining how well the plan accomplishes its mission are related to such concepts as reach, frequency, and target market impressions delivered. The gross number of target market impressions, coupled with the reach and frequency associated with those impressions within the designated budget, form the nucleus of an effective media plan. The media planner must go through a calculated process of matching the cost of various media alternatives with the delivery of the plan to arrive at the optimal relationship between cost and delivery.

For example, assume the cost per rating point of women 18 years of age and over for daytime network television is $5,869 (:30 basis), and cost per rating point for the same audience segment in nighttime network is $21,091. A set budget placing all dollars in daytime network will deliver almost four times more GRPs to women 18+ than will nighttime network based on these costs. For a $10 million budget over a one-year period allocated to 30-second commercials, it is estimated that the average four-week reach and frequency for nighttime would be lower (29 percent) than the same budget in daytime (33 percent), as illustrated in Exhibit 12-1. However, the reach of nighttime will be considerably higher than the daytime reach over the total 52-week period. Conversely, the frequency in daytime will be higher than the frequency in nighttime over the total year.

From this discussion, it is clear that a key part of the broadcast planner's work is determining the best daypart mixture—that is, deciding how many rat-

EXHIBIT 12-1

Women 18+ TV Delivery by Daypart for $10 Million Budget

	NIGHT NETWORK	DAY NETWORK
Commercial unit	:30	:30
Cost per rating point (CPP)	$21,091	$5,869
Total affordable GRPs ($10 MM/CPP)	474	1,704
Total 52-week reach/frequency	82%/5.8	54%/31.8
Average four-week GRPs (total GRPs/52 × 4)	36	131
Average four-week reach/frequency	29%/1.2	33%/3.9

SOURCE: Nielsen Media Research: *CPM Report,* March 2000; True North Communications, Reach-2000.

ing points should be placed in each daypart. In the past, this was only possible as a trial-and-error process with a computerized reach/frequency analysis system. (A generic version is available on the Internet at www.mediaplan.com/WebRF/.)

In recent years, sophisticated broadcast optimizers have become available that will estimate the reach of thousands of combinations and then report the plan that offers the most reach for a given budget. Although the daypart optimizer caused great excitement in the industry when first released, it has since taken its place as one of many tools available for planners and buyers.

Planners have also become aware of the optimizer's limitations. First, the results are largely determined by the cost per rating point given for each daypart. But since these are only estimates of future prices, the resulting "optimal" plan may not reflect market conditions when the buy is made. Second, and equally important, optimizers can work only with past audience data, but their results must apply to the next season's programs, which may not even exist at the time of the analysis. These two "garbage in, garbage out" factors limit the usefulness of optimizers and reinforce the need for judgment in developing a broadcast plan.

Although broadcast is planned with CPP, comparisons among media are usually based on costs per thousand gross impressions or on net reach. Whichever method is used, the cost-efficiency of media delivery is important. The medium with the largest reach may not necessarily be the best buy, because it might provide less cost-efficiency. Exhibit 12-2 shows a rough comparison of alternative media deliveries and cost-efficiencies.

An examination of the table shows that different coverage levels are achieved by different media vehicles, with certain implications for CPP. The media planner's task is to combine familiarity with media costs and delivery dynamics with the goals of the marketing plan to reach designated audiences. The planner must be careful to employ correct media cost assumptions in the development of the plan.

Exhibit 12-2 also shows that if inappropriate cost assumptions are used in estimating the costs of daytime network versus women's service magazines, it would be possible to include one media type in the plan to the exclusion of the other. There are several ways media planners can help to ensure correct and current media cost estimates. Although we refer to media planners here, it is

EXHIBIT 12-2

Alternative Media: Cost and Delivery

	ADVERTISING UNIT	NATIONAL EQUIVALENT COST ($000)	WOMEN 18+ NUMBER (000)	WOMEN 18+ CPM	MEN 18+ NUMBER (000)	MEN 18+ CPM
Network TV—prime time (6 net—reg)	:30	$ 81.9	4,000	$20.48	2,777	$29.49
Network TV—daytime (5 net)	:30	11.4	2,001	5.70	653	17.46
Network TV—weekend sports (reg)	:30	6.3	855	7.37	1,423	4.43
Network TV—early news (M–F 3 nets)	:30	49.2	5,474	8.99	3,856	12.76
Network TV—late night (M–F)	:30	24.6	1,569	15.68	1,121	21.94
General magazine (5-mag avg)	Pg 4/C Bl	129.4	13,670	9.46	10,172	12.72
Women's magazines (5-mag avg)	Pg 4/C Bl	168.9	17,287	9.77	2,383	70.86
Newspapers (top 100 markets)	Full P B/W	4,337.6	56,900	76.23	55,300	78.44
Network radio (:60) (avg 21 networks)	:60	4.6	1,031	4.46	1,157	3.98
Outdoor (top 100 markets)	50 showing	3,127.0	2,662,740	1.17	2,447,160	1.28

SOURCE: Nielsen *CPM Report*; SRDS; MRI; Fall 1999; *Marketer's Guide to Media*, 2000; RADAR; Outdoor Services, Inc.

common for media buyers, professionals trained in purchasing, to make these decisions.

First, the planner must maintain close contact with cost mechanisms in the media marketplace. For example, despite the additional inventory coming on the market from cable TV and syndication, network television costs have risen steadily each year since 1993. The cost-efficiency of other media has grown at a more modest rate, but still well ahead of inflation, as shown in Exhibit 12-3.

Today, both the broadcast media and magazines are influenced not so much by the cost of the product as by the law of supply and demand. The media planner assesses supply and demand in these media by maintaining constant contact with suppliers—that is, the media representatives. These contacts give the planner a feel for what is transpiring in the market and thus enable the forecasting of changes (upward or downward) in pricing.

Second, intelligent media planners will include media buyers in the development of media cost estimates. Many agencies and advertisers employ media-buying specialists whose sole responsibility is the purchase of media. Such media buyers are in regular contact with the media suppliers with whom they do business on behalf of the agency and client. During the course of the numerous media buyer–seller transactions, the buyer acquires a familiarity with what is occurring in the marketplace. Such familiarity can assist the media planner in forecasting media price changes. Media buyers are expected to maintain good relations with media suppliers to facilitate this flow of information. Media planners should make it a point to maintain close communications with the media buyers so as to tap this source of media cost information.

Third, agencies develop expertise in estimating media cost changes based on the agency's total experience. Over a period of time, the agency can compile media cost information in various markets, or nationally, by generalizing from various specific buying experiences. It is not necessary to breach security within an agency in order to develop this information. Generalized experience is one reason why many agencies organized their buyers as market specialists who purchase media in their assigned market for every brand that the agency handles. The specialists become intimately acquainted with their markets and can usually negotiate more favorable rates than buyers who are only active in a market from time to time.

EXHIBIT 12-3

Media Cost per Thousand Percent Increase/Decrease over Prior Year

	1992 (OVER 1991)	1993 (OVER 1992)	1994 (OVER 1993)	1995 (OVER 1994)	1996 (OVER 1995)	1997 (OVER 1996)	1998 (OVER 1997)	1999 (OVER 1998)	2000 (OVER 1999)	2001 (OVER 2000)
Consumer Price Index	3.0	3.0	2.6	2.8	3.0	2.7	1.6	2.2	3.4	2.7
Network TV*	−0.5	4.5	4.5	11.0	10.4	8.1	9.5	7.0	14.5	2.0
Spot TV	6.0	3.5	7.0	5.0	10.8	6.5	7.6	5.0	12.0	1.0
Cable TV	7.5	7.0	2.0	3.5	11.1	7.4	6.3	11.9	11.5	5.0
Network radio	−10.0	6.0	−1.0	6.5	6.1	4.0	7.4	7.0	14.0	5.0
Spot radio	−2.5	6.5	6.0	3.5	4.6	9.0	8.4	7.5	12.0	2.0
Magazines	3.0	3.5	5.0	3.5	7.7	3.6	6.0	5.0	4.0	3.5
Newspapers	1.5	1.5	3.5	5.0	4.7	3.6	5.0	4.5	4.0	3.5

*Olympics premium removed from years 1996, 1998, 2000.
Estimates prepared before September 11, 2001.
SOURCE: American Association of Advertising Agencies, *Media Matters*, October 3, 2001; Commerce Dept.

Once the media plan has been implemented and the schedules completed, the media planner should examine how closely the media cost estimates match actual costs. This is called *postbuy analysis.* By conducting a postbuy analysis, the planner can sharpen the capability to forecast costs by reviewing what went into the original estimates. Such trial-and-error devices assist the media professional in developing the personal art of media cost forecasting. Major variations between cost estimates and actual plan delivery cost might reflect flaws in understanding or thinking or might be the consequence of significant cost changes in the media marketplace that could not have been anticipated. In any event, the media planner, in checking back over the implemented plan, should consider the exercise an important learning experience.

MEDIA COSTS

As shown in Exhibit 12-4, national advertisers spent almost $100 billion in major consumer media in 2000. The bulk of spending was in television, news-

EXHIBIT 12-4

National Advertiser Media Expenditures (Jan.–Dec. 2000)

MEDIA	DOLLARS SPENT	
	MILLIONS	PERCENT
Network television	$20,276	21%
Cable TV networks	10,206	10
Syndicated television	3,188	3
Spot television	17,378	18
Consumer magazines	17,690	18
Sunday magazines	1,189	1
Local newspapers	18,913	19
National newspapers	3,805	4
National spot radio	953	1
Network radio	2,719	3
Outdoor	2,398	2
Total	$98,715	100%

SOURCE: CMR Taylor Nelson Sofres and Publishers Information Bureau.

papers, and consumer magazines. Note that this figure does not include well over $100 billion in additional spending by local advertisers such as retail stores, automobile dealers, and local services. The magnitude and complexity of planning and buying these media require close attention to cost implications.

Within these broad media types are numerous alternatives with which the media planner must be acquainted. In addition to understanding general media cost relationships between television and magazines, for example, the professional planner must be familiar with costs of network versus spot and the different availabilities within the general broadcast medium, as well as the changes over time. This assignment is complex and difficult, but necessary.

Television

Combined television expenditures, the first four categories in Exhibit 12-4, accounted for 52 percent of total advertising dollars spent in 2000. Most of the television investment was for consumer goods and services. However, there has been a growing use of the medium by industrial and business-related advertisers. In view of the magnitude of the investment in television, a media-planning professional must be fully conversant with all phases of the medium.

The major characteristic of television, insofar as media costs are concerned, relates to the "perishability" of the inventory. Generally speaking, there is a fixed amount of television time available for sale (called *inventory*). Unlike a magazine or newspaper, which can expand or contract the number of advertising pages available for sale in any given issue, a commercial minute that is unsold can never be recovered. The sellers of television time must contend with this perishability concept in selling the medium.

Although marketplace pricing conditions prevail at any given time, these prices are subject to change as advertisers' demand for that time increases or decreases. The stronger the demand and the earlier the sale in relationship to the program air date, the more likely that pricing will be higher. Less advertising demand close to air date can create lower pricing, assuming inventory availability. These interrelated conditions of perishability, demand, and inventory create a dynamic marketplace.

Because these market conditions are constantly changing, broadcast planners must ensure that they have the most recent costs before they begin the planning process. These costs are expressed in terms of cost per rating point and are obtained either from the buyer who is responsible for executing the plan or (with the buyer's approval) from published sources such as SQAD. This contact with the buyer is critical because the planner is, in essence, saying, "I want you to buy this many GRPs, and I'm giving you that much money to do it." If planners give the buyers more money than they need, the returned excess becomes an embarrassment because it could have been spent in other places. Conversely, if the buyers are given too little money, then they will be unable to buy as many GRPs as the plan calls for—an equally embarrassing situation. Buyers typically have 5–10 percent leeway, but anything more than that will require a letter to the client explaining what happened.

Buyers need *all* of the following information in order to provide planning costs:

- Geographic area (total United States or list of markets)
- Buying target audience (women 25–54)
- Commercial length (30-second)
- Dayparts to be used in the plan (daytime, prime, news, late fringe, kid)
- Schedule dates (typically a different CPP for each quarter)
- Special buying instructions, such as the need to purchase high-rated (high-cost) programs, sports sponsorships, promotional requirements, etc.

Based on this information, buyers will estimate the planning CPPs to be used. These costs are based on the buyers' recent experience in the market, contacts with station sales representatives, and their sense of future market demand. Typically, one group of people is responsible for buying national broadcast (network, cable, and syndication), while another group buys local market spot TV and radio.

Large companies that employ the services of several advertising agencies maximize their buying clout by giving all buying responsibility to a single organization (ad agency, buying service, or media specialty company). This *agency of record* is responsible for providing cost-per-point estimates to all planners who work on the business.

Planning costs are highly confidential because they are the basis for price negotiation. Obviously, if a station finds out that the buyer expects to spend

$500 per point, there is little incentive to offer a package that comes in at $450.

Under the broad heading of television, there are basically four subcategories: national network, local spot, syndication, and cable. Let's start this section with a short discussion of a television-wide concept, dayparts.

Dayparts   For both planning and buying purposes, the day is broken into a series of time periods that reflect different program types and audiences, called dayparts. Typical dayparts and time periods are listed in Exhibit 12-5.

These dayparts are the basis for planning television campaigns. The planner's task is to determine how many GRPs should be purchased in each daypart in order to achieve the plan's media objectives. Dayparts will be discussed in more detail in the following section.

Network TV   Certain parts of the broadcast day are programmed by the national networks: the American Broadcasting Company (ABC), the Columbia Broadcasting System (CBS), the National Broadcasting Company (NBC), the Fox network (FOX), Warner Brothers (WB), and Paramount (UPN). Exhibit 12-6 illustrates the dayparts when network programming is usually made avail-

EXHIBIT 12-5

Television Dayparts

DAYPART	DAY/TIME	KEY DEMOGRAPHICS
Early morning (EM)	M–Su/7–9 A.M.	Business/professional
Morning kids (EM)	M–Su/7–9 A.M.	Kids
Daytime (DAY)	M–F/9 A.M.–4 P.M.	Women; adults 50+
Early fringe (spot only) (EF)	M–F/4–6 P.M.	Women; kids
Early news (EN)	M–Sa/6–7:30 P.M.	Adults 50+
Prime access (spot only) (PA)	M–Sa/7:30–8 P.M.	Total persons
Prime time (PR)	M–Sa/8–11 P.M., Su/7–11 P.M.	Total persons
Late news (spot only) (LN)	M–Su/11–11:30 P.M.	Adults 25–54
Late fringe (LF)	M–F/11:30 P.M.–1 A.M.	Adults 25–54
Weekend sports (WS)	Sa–Su/10 A.M.–6 P.M.	Men 18+; professional
Saturday late fringe (LF)	Sa/11:30 P.M.–1 A.M.	Teens; adults 18–34

able to affiliates (the individual stations that constitute a network lineup). The number of stations serviced by a given network can vary from 150 to 210, depending on the strength of the network programming available. The networks sell time to advertisers who run commercials within specific programs. These programs can appear throughout various parts of the day (e.g., daytime network, prime-time network, or late night).

Prime time (8:00 P.M. to 11:00 P.M. EST) generally provides the highest ratings because of the high number of homes using television (HUT). This time period tends to deliver a family audience with high reach levels of most viewing segments. Prime time also reaches the most light viewers, although this group makes up only a small proportion of the audience at any one time. Media costs for prime time are generally the highest of all network time segments available for sale. The cost for 30 seconds in prime time, as indicated in Exhibit 12-2, averages $81,900. Individual program costs will vary, depending on rating level (substantially more for the higher-rated shows) and the amount of inventory available for sale. As discussed earlier, the less inventory, generally, the higher the cost.

Daytime network (10:00 A.M. to 4:00 P.M. EST) is normally the least costly of the network dayparts. An average cost for 30 seconds will be somewhere in the vicinity of $11,400, with an average household rating of approximately 2.6. This results in an extremely efficient cost-per-thousand delivery of homes and homemakers, although the audience composition tends to skew to older adults.

Late-night network programming (11:30 P.M. to conclusion EST) varies from network to network and over time. This time period is generally pro-

EXHIBIT 12-6

Daypart Programming Available for Network Use

6	7	8	9	10	11	12	1	2	3	4	5	6	7	8	9	10	11	12	1	2
A.M.						P.M.												A.M.		

| LOCAL | Network | LOCAL | Network daytime programs | LOCAL | NETWORK | LOCAL | LOCAL ACCESS | Network prime-time programs | LOCAL | LOCAL NEWS | Network late-night programs | LOCAL |

grammed with talk or news programs such as the "Tonight Show with Jay Leno," "The Late Show with David Letterman," and "ABC Nightline" during the week, and variety entertainment shows such as "Saturday Night Live" on the weekend. Because fewer sets are in use than during prime time, pricing for the weeknight shows tends to be about $24,600 for 30 seconds, with an average household rating of 2.4. Although the rating levels for late night are comparable to daytime, late night includes a dual audience (both men and women) that is not generally the case in daytime. Thus, pricing for that dual audience tends to be somewhat higher than daytime.

Most network programming on weekends is in the sports and children's areas. Sports programming, for the most part, is the domain of the male-oriented advertiser. Such products as beer, male grooming aids, investment counseling, and automobiles are heavily represented on weekend sports programming. In general, there is a limited amount of broad-scale sports programming compared with other network program time. Therefore, pricing tends to be comparable to prime time on a CPP basis. However, many advertisers believe the value of identifying with a major high-interest sports event rubs off on brands associated with such programming.

Children's programs, often referred to as "kid TV," are the primary fare on Saturday mornings. Nearly all of this programming is cartoons, but there are some live-action shows, especially in the action/adventure and sports areas. The predominant audience is children, and the advertising, therefore, is highly child oriented. Advertisers of cereal, toys and games, fast food, and candy concentrate a significant portion of their advertising budget in kid TV. The growth of cable networks such as Nickelodeon and the Cartoon Network have made kid programming available throughout the day and have reduced advertisers' dependence on Saturday morning as the sole national kids' daypart.

The diversity of programming provided by the networks ranges from the all-family interest generated in prime time to highly selective shows of interest to relatively few households. Such diversity provides the media planner with rich opportunities for reaching broad national markets with programming aimed specifically to the interests of target markets. Costs for such programming will change as marketplace demand changes, so the media planner must be ever alert to the buying implications of the programming selected for inclusion in the media plan.

Local Stations Announcements can be purchased on local television stations, which are either affiliated with a network or independent. Affiliated stations carry network programming at certain times of the day. Independent stations do not have any network affiliation and so must program the entire day on their own. They can choose to produce programs in their own studios (such as local news), or they can purchase syndicated programs.

Costs for local announcements vary from market to market based on the size, the audience delivered, and advertiser demand for the available commercial time. Generally, the costs for scheduling announcements in markets like New York, Los Angeles, and Chicago are higher than those for smaller markets because of the large number of people reached by the big-city stations.

Time is made available for sale, whether the station is network-affiliated or independent, across almost the entire day. Even within dayparts programmed by the networks, such as in prime time, certain segments of time are set aside for local sale. This means that it is possible for a local advertiser to purchase a 30-second announcement (if available) in a network-originated program or between programs at the station break.

Because independent stations program for the entire day, they have far more inventory available for local sale, allowing advertisers to select specific dayparts and programming to reach the target audience. In addition to availabilities adjacent to, and on occasion, within network programming, commercial time can be selected in what is termed *fringe time*. In general, the fringe dayparts and the programming contained therein might look something like Exhibit 12-7.

Pricing for dayparts and specific programs within dayparts varies based on audience delivery and availability of commercial time. Costs are provided by the buyers who will be purchasing the time. Their estimates are based on their experience with the market, but if this is a new market for them, or one that has not had recent activity, both planners and buyers will use SQAD, the most commonly accepted source of spot television costs. This service offers low/average/high planning cost-per-point estimates for all 210 DMAs and a variety of commonly used demographics. Exhibit 12-8 shows an example of the SQAD computer report of costs for four major markets. Note the difference in costs by daypart.

Costs are updated monthly and are accessed through SQAD's proprietary computer software. More general household data are available through the

EXHIBIT 12-7

Sample Fringe Schedule

STATION	LOCAL TIME (EST)	PROGRAM
A (network affiliate)	6:00 P.M.–6:30 P.M.	Local news
	6:30 P.M.–7:00 P.M.	Network news
	7:00 P.M.–7:30 P.M.	"Hollywood Squares"
	7:30 P.M.–8:00 P.M.	"Entertainment Tonight"
	11:00 P.M.–11:30 P.M.	Local news
	11:30 P.M.–conclusion	"The Tonight Show"
B (independent)	5:00 P.M.–5:30 P.M.	"Wayans Bros."*
	5:30 P.M.–6:00 P.M.	"Fresh Prince"*
	6:00 P.M.–6:30 P.M.	"Friends"*
	6:30 P.M.–7:00 P.M.	"Drew Carey"*
	9:00 P.M.–10:00 P.M.	Local news
	10:00 P.M.–10:30 P.M.	"Seinfeld"*
	10:30 P.M.–11:00 P.M.	"Mad About You"*
	11:00 P.M.–conclusion	Late movie

*Syndicated reruns of programs formerly on the networks.

Marketer's Guide to Media. For more information about SQAD, see their website at www.sqad.com.

Estimating the cost of a television campaign is simply a matter of multiplying the cost per point by the number of GRPs to be bought. In Exhibit 12-8, the average cost to buy one woman 25–54 rating point in the listed markets in fourth quarter 1999 totaled $6,371 for prime time and $1,769 in early morning. So, for example, it would cost $1,274,200 to buy 200 GRPs of prime time in each of the four markets (200 × $6,371). The same weight in early morning would cost $353,800 (200 × $1,769).

Syndication   *Syndication* is the development or packaging of programming that is sold directly to the advertiser and/or cleared on a market-by-market basis by the syndicator. Clearances for a syndicated property can range from a program run one time in a few markets to weekly series clearing in 70–90 percent of the United States for extended periods. Each station makes its own decision

EXHIBIT 12-8

Sample SQAD Cost-per-Point Report

SQAD for Windows—Version 2.22—QuickView Report

Source: *NSI TV* Issue: December, '99 Level: Average Pop Base: DMA (CPP)
Qtr Weights: 4Q '99 (1.0000)
Target: Women 25–54

MARKET	RANK	POPULATION	EARLY MORNING	DAY	EARLY FRINGE	EARLY NEWS	PRIME ACCESS	PRIME	LATE NEWS	LATE FRINGE
New York	1	4,436,005	603	497	581	869	1,233	2,211	1,193	825
Los Angeles	2	3,580,286	586	574	591	769	1,002	1,811	1,053	695
Chicago	3	2,025,154	288	302	388	585	653	1,247	855	368
Philadelphia	4	1,604,024	292	308	376	477	607	1,102	688	408
Total		11,645,469	1,769	1,681	1,936	2,700	3,495	6,371	3,789	2,296

SOURCE: SQAD Inc., December 1999.

EXHIBIT 12-9

Top 10 Syndicated Properties, February 2000

RANK	PROGRAM	U.S. HOUSE-HOLD RATING	NO. OF MKTS	% U.S. COVG	M–F DAY		E. FRINGE		ACCESS		PRIME		L. FRINGE		WEEKEND DAY		WEEKEND FRINGE	
					# MKTS	% U.S.	# MKTS	% U.S.	# MKTS	% U.S.	# MKTS	% U.S.	# MKTS	% U.S.	# MKTS	% U.S.	# MKTS	% U.S.
1	"World Wrestling Federation"	16.3	94	73	—	—	—	—	—	—	12	11	74	60	30	23	7	2
2	"Wheel of Fortune," M–F	12.1	201	99	—	—	77	42	121	62	5	8	1	2	—	—	—	—
3	"Judge Judy"	11.1	199	99	49	20	152	84	21	13	13	12	14	9	1	2	4	—
4	"Jeopardy"	10.0	195	99	9	2	113	61	70	34	4	2	1	2	—	—	1	—
5	"WCW Wrestling"	7.9	122	84	—	—	—	—	—	—	14	11	47	32	67	51	15	8
6	"Friends"—Syn	7.8	161	92	1	—	113	71	51	37	77	27	50	49	2	1	99	55
7	"Entertainment Tonight"	7.8	158	95	1	1	53	38	83	49	6	2	26	11	—	—	—	—
8	"Oprah Winfrey Show"	7.3	201	99	2	8	199	91	—	—	3	3	2	4	—	—	—	—
9	"Frasier"—Syn	6.5	180	97	4	1	55	32	62	26	33	25	70	45	4	3	9	9
10	"Seinfeld"—Syn	6.3	199	99	4	—	54	27	79	50	16	7	56	21	2	1	1	—

SOURCE: *Nielsen Television Index: Nielsen Report on Syndicated Programs.*

about which syndicated programs to buy and when to put them on the air. The stations in a market compete intensely for the best programs. Although it happens rarely, stations have been known to buy a program and then not put it on the air, just to keep it away from a competitor. Syndicated properties include first-run talk shows, specials, sports events, entertainment, information, and game shows, as well as off-network reruns of sitcoms and serials. Exhibit 12-9 lists the top 10 syndicated properties in February 2000. Nationalized ratings, percentage coverage, and time period clearances also are listed.

Syndicators and local TV stations make four types of deals: straight barter, part barter/part cash, all cash, and scatter. In *straight-barter syndication* the local station receives the program and a percentage of the commercial time within the program for local sale in return for airing the show. *Part-barter/part-cash syndication* requires the local station to pay a license fee to broadcast the program. This arrangement gives the local station control of most of the commercial time, with the syndicator selling a smaller percentage of the commercial minutes to national advertisers. In an *all-cash syndication* deal, the local station pays cash for the syndicated property and can sell all the commercial time to both local and national advertisers. *Scatter syndication* is a unique situation in which the stations are obligated to run national commercial spots for a specific syndicator. The local station can drop or retain the syndicated show, but if the station elects to run the show, it must run the program in a predetermined time. The time period restriction gives the syndicator the means to guarantee national coverage by daypart for its national advertisers.

The costs and efficiencies of the top-rated syndicated properties are comparable to network program costs and efficiencies. However, overall syndicated cost-efficiencies generally run up to 25 percent better than network cost-efficiencies.

Cable TV

Cable TV can be purchased on either a national or spot basis. Although each cable network schedules programming differently, general dayparts mimic traditional network TV: early morning, daytime, prime time, and late night.

Today, most major advertisers and their agencies consider cable TV to be a necessary media option. However, until recently, cable was considered a new medium, one that played only a minor role, if any, in most media plans. Today, cable plus "Alternate Delivery Services" (ADS) such as direct broadcast satellite can reach 82.8 percent of U.S. TV households.[1] With 56 measured networks currently on the air, cable TV has become a routinely accepted part of most media plans.

Including cable TV in a media plan delivers three main benefits. First, each cable network targets selective audience groups. For example, Arts & Entertainment targets upscale, educated individuals; ESPN primarily reaches men; and Nickelodeon attracts children aged 2–17. This type of selectivity, referred to as *narrowcasting*, allows advertisers to be extremely focused in their targeting efforts although planners must keep in mind the coverage/composition trade-off seen in other media. Second, cable tends to be more cost-efficient than other TV options. By including cable in its plan, an advertiser can add lower-cost exposures to a national network TV plan. Finally, homes wired for cable in the United States tend to watch less network television than the 18 percent of U.S. homes without cable because of the numerous cable choices available to them. Therefore, advertisers' national broadcast network schedules might underdeliver their planned GRPs to these cable households. Placing a portion of the media budget in cable can make up the network underdelivery in cable homes in a relatively efficient and inexpensive way.

Magazines

The two major print advertising categories are magazines and newspapers. Pricing for print space tends to be slightly more stable than for broadcast media, because magazines and newspapers can adjust up or down the number of pages they print on an issue-to-issue basis. Thus, the cost of printing is somewhat variable, in contrast to the fixed commitment of television and its resultant perishability of commercial time.

Newspapers and magazines generally issue *rate cards* that cover future costs, although published magazine rates are no longer reliable, due to negotiated rates and package deals. A media planner constructing a plan for a year in advance must be careful in projecting magazine rate increases during the course of the

---

1. Nielsen Media Research, July 2001.

year, particularly if the magazines the buyer plans to use are among those nego-tiating their rates. In those cases, the buyer must make judgment calls about the rates to be used in the future media plan.

There is considerable diversity within the broad category of magazines. Some of the categories include general-interest, women's service, and home magazines.

General-Interest (Dual-Audience) Magazines   Such publications as *Reader's Digest, TV Guide,* and to some degree *People, Time,* and *Newsweek* are viewed as general-interest magazines in view of the diverse audiences they reach. Their editorial content by nature does not exclude any potential reading group. Along with the large circulation delivered by these publications goes a commensu-rately high cost per page. As such, the costs per page for these dual-audience magazines take into account the audience they reach, although their circula-tions vary. Exhibit 12-10 shows sample costs and circulation numbers for these magazines.

Women's Service Magazines   More editorially selective publications, such as *Ladies' Home Journal, Good Housekeeping, Family Circle, Woman's Day,* and *Red-book,* gear their interest primarily to women. The editorial content of these pub-lications is designed to be informative and entertaining. Male readership, as a

---

EXHIBIT 12-10

General-Interest Magazines: Sample Costs and Circulation

MAGAZINE	COST PG 4/C	CIRCULATION (000)	TOTAL ADULT READERS, AGE 18+ (000)
Reader's Digest	$194,800	12,556	44,264
TV Guide	149,100	11,116	32,692
Time	183,000	4,123	21,663
Newsweek	184,118	3,147	19,130
People	165,600	3,544	34,469

SOURCE: Mediamark Research Inc. (www.mriplus.com), June 2000.

EXHIBIT 12-11

Women's Service Magazines: Sample Costs and Circulation

MAGAZINE	COST PG 4/C	CIRCULATION (000)	TOTAL ADULT READERS, AGE 18+ (000)
Ladies' Home Journal	$147,900	4,525	14,507
Good Housekeeping	192,260	4,550	23,312
Family Circle	191,880	5,003	21,086
Woman's Day	165,315	4,281	19,781
Redbook	88,000	2,250	9,797

SOURCE: Mediamark Research Inc. (www.mriplus.com), June 2000.

percentage of total readership, is not very high compared with general-interest magazines. Exhibit 12-11 shows sample costs for these selected magazines.

Home (Shelter) Magazines   Other magazines segment their editorial target in a different way, namely by environmental considerations such as sports, children, or the home. Magazines such as *Better Homes & Gardens,* for example, speak to the interests and concerns of homeowners. By their editorial nature, these magazines tend to be adult and dual-audience oriented. Here again, selectivity of editorial content as well as audience gives the advertiser an opportunity to position a commercial message in a highly compatible environment. The costs for some of these magazines are listed in Exhibit 12-12.

Categorization of these magazines is somewhat arbitrary. One could argue, for example, that *Better Homes & Gardens* is really a general-interest publication based on the duality of the readership. In the final analysis, categorization is not nearly as important as the quantity and quality of the readership, compatibility of editorial with the sales message, and the cost of running the insertion—all of which must be taken into account by the media planner. A cost delivery relationship, however, is a good starting point in categorizing magazines from which to select those to qualify based on editorial content.

"Twenty-Something" Adult Magazines   In recent years a new category of magazines has appeared that caters to young-adult readers. These include *De-*

EXHIBIT 12-12

Home Magazines: Sample Costs and Circulation

MAGAZINE	COST PG 4/C	CIRCULATION (000)	TOTAL ADULT READERS, AGED 18+ (000)
Better Homes & Gardens	$249,600	7,611	33,591
Martha Stewart Living	107,935	2,364	10,491
House Beautiful	88,987	876	6,351
Traditional Home	72,157	832	2,869
Sunset	70,510	1,448	4,402
Southern Living	99,850	2,536	12,621

SOURCE: Mediamark Research Inc. (www.mriplus.com), June 2000.

tails, ESPN the Magazine, FHM, Maxim, Spin, Vibe, Stuff, and *Jane.* Because many of these magazines are still too new to be measured, planners must estimate their audience. But their edgy, irreverent tone and modern graphics make it clear to whom these publications appeal.

Newspapers

In 1999, there were 1,483 dailies and 905 Sunday newspapers in the United States,[2] in addition to thousands more nondaily newspapers (weekly, biweekly, and so on). Newspapers provide the distinct benefits of flexibility in adjusting efforts from market to market, quick closing dates, strong local market coverage, and individual market identification. As with other media, newspapers are also highly diverse in the ways they can be bought and the advertising units available for sale. The major categories include run of paper, supplements, and custom inserts.

Run of Paper   Run of paper (ROP) advertising can be purchased in virtually any size, from a full page down to just a few inches, in both black and white and

---

2. Newspaper Association of America (www.naa.org), "Number of U.S. Daily Newspapers," reprint of *Editor & Publisher* estimate.

color. If one color is added to black and white, the premium runs about 10–15 percent. Where available, four-color cost premiums run 20–40 percent. However, it is possible to package certain groups of newspapers to reduce the cost premium or to eliminate it entirely. ROP space is sold by the column inch for a set of Standard Advertising Units (SAU) that ranges from a few inches to a full page. In recent years, specific dimensions have varied by paper.

Supplements   Preprinted newspaper-distributed supplements can be purchased either on a syndicated basis (*Parade, USA Weekend*) or on an independent basis (*New York Times Magazine, Chicago Tribune Magazine*). Preprinted supplements provide all the benefits of newspapers in today's market coverage with four-color, magazine-type reproduction when desirable. Costs for independent supplements vary from market to market. Costs and circulation levels for the national syndicated supplements are shown in Exhibit 12-13.

Custom Inserts   In addition to ROP and magazine supplements, newspapers can carry advertising inserts that are printed by outside firms and stuffed into the paper along with the other sections. These inserts can be used in many different forms. They can be printed on fine-quality or inexpensive papers, in many different sizes, used as single sheets or booklets, and printed in many different ways. All of these alternative production techniques allow advertisers to create unique advertising that will communicate whatever they want and can afford. Costs for custom-tailored inserts vary, depending on how elegant they are. Each newspaper charges a different price for stuffing and carrying the in-

EXHIBIT 12-13

Syndicated Supplements: Sample Costs and Circulation

MAGAZINE	COST PG 4/C	CIRCULATION (000)	TOTAL ADULT READERS, AGED 18+ (000)
Parade	$724,200	37,050	79,858
USA Weekend	443,040	20,376	44,966

SOURCE: Mediamark Research Inc. (www.mriplus.com), June 2000.

serts. Note that inserts are normally bought by the advertiser as part of its consumer promotion plan, rather than by the ad agency's media planner.

Radio

Radio is offered on a national network basis and on an individual local market spot basis.

Network Radio   Network radio programming available for advertiser sale includes news, music, sports, and drama. Costs for network radio announcements are comparatively low. Network radio costs range from $2,000 to $9,000 for a 30-second announcement and deliver an average rating of 1.2 to men and 1.0 to women.

Spot Radio   Formats of local radio stations vary widely from market to market. In major markets, such as New York, Los Angeles, and Chicago, numerous radio formats appeal to a wide variety of listener interests. Programming ranges from talk shows to various kinds of music formats to total news. In smaller markets, stations concentrate on local news, country music, and music with more general appeal.

As is the case with spot television, the diversity of the medium makes it extremely difficult to generalize about costs. In overall terms, however, spot radio selectively purchased against designated target audiences can be an exceptionally cost-efficient medium for reaching these audiences. Spot radio costs are available from SQAD Radio, using the same computer system that delivers television costs.

Internet

Internet advertising prices are stated as the cost per thousand impressions delivered to the user's browser. As with all media, the price varies substantially, depending on the size of the ad.

Banners   By far the most commonly used and least expensive creative unit is the banner ad. Banners are measured in terms of *pixels*—the small, discrete elements that together constitute an image. Exhibit 12-14 shows the most com-

EXHIBIT 12-14

Commonly Used Internet Advertising Units and Sample Costs

AD DESCRIPTION	SIZE (PIXELS)	BASE RATE CPM
Full banner (most common)	468 × 60	$60
Half banner	234 × 60	50
Square button	125 × 125	55
Button	120 × 60	45
Micro banner	430 × 30	55
Micro bar	88 × 31	40
Vertical banner	120 × 240	65
Wide banner	600 × 60	70
Skyscraper	120 × 600	85

Targeting Selection (Cost in Addition to Base Rate)

Zip code	$10
No. annual business trips	15
No. annual leisure trips	15
First offer to new users	50

SOURCE: SRDS *Interactive Advertising Source,* August 2001.

monly used ad sizes and the rate-card cost per thousand impressions charged by a large travel-oriented website. Using this card, the cost of 500,000 "run of site" impressions of a full banner ad would cost $30,000 ($60/thousand × 500 thousand impressions). Note that, like some other media, the rate card published by SRDS is just a starting point for cost negotiations. According to Jupiter Media Metrix, the CPM for a full banner ranges from $3.50 for community sites to $100 for telecommunications. The average CPM is $30.52, with discounts averaging 33 percent.[3]

For an additional charge, advertisers can take advantage of a variety of targeting options to deliver banners customized to the person visiting the site. For example, visitors in a given zip code could be shown ads for travel to featured

3. Jupiter Media Metrix website, www.jmm.com/intelligence/special_rate.pdf.

vacation spots. Business travelers (more precisely, visitors whose cookie indicates that this computer was used to book airline tickets for business) could be shown a banner with promotional rates to business centers. The high cost ($50 CPM) indicates the extra value placed on new visitors to the site.

Rich Media   With the maturing of the Internet, the effectiveness of banners has fallen off sharply. Typically, less than 1 percent of people exposed to a banner will click through to the advertiser's website. As indicated in the sample rate card, websites are offering larger and more creative units (wide banners, sky-scrapers, wrap-arounds, and others) in hopes of improving response. But the most effective technique employs sound, motion, and intrusiveness to get the user's attention. These so-called *rich media* employ a variety of visual elements:

- Animated banners, moving cartoons, flashing words, alternating colors, and other effects
- Streaming banners that display a continuous stream of text such as a news wire or video
- Streaming audio banners that play a commercial or audio track when the banner is presented
- Pop-up ads that appear when a page is requested but before it has completely loaded (sometimes called *interstitial ads* because they are delivered between the pages of requested content)

Rich media ads experience higher click-through rates than banners. However, they are considerably more expensive, and they are not accepted by all websites (including the site used in this example). Furthermore, as the use of rich media increases, there is the possibility of user backlash against interruptions to Internet browsing.

Other Internet Advertising   There are many other ways of using the Internet. These include site sponsorships and targeted E-mail. To address concerns about user backlash, some advertisers use "opt-in" advertising, delivered only if the user requests to see certain kinds of advertising. Another option is to use direct links to the advertiser's website from words in the site's content or from a logo display.

Out-of-Home Media

Out-of-home media come in a wide range of availabilities that differ dramatically in size and location. Out-of-home media are the most local of all media forms, inasmuch as one advertising unit can be purchased in one very specific location geographically. The most popular varieties of out-of-home media are poster panels, painted bulletins, and transit advertising.

Poster Panels   A *poster panel* is an outdoor advertising structure on which a preprinted advertisement is displayed. The most widely used poster sizes are standard, junior, and three-sheet. The standard poster, or 30-sheet poster, measures approximately 12 feet high by 25 feet long. The junior panel, or 8-sheet poster, is about one-fourth the size of a standard poster. The 3-sheet poster is used extensively at transit or train stops. It is 60 inches by 46 inches.

Poster panels are generally sold in packages of daily gross rating points, called *showings*. For example, a 50-GRP package, or "50 showing," will deliver in one day exposure opportunities equal to 50 percent of the population of the market. The cost for posters varies tremendously from one market to another, and often from one location to another in a given market. The cost to purchase a 50 showing for one month in standard 30-sheet posters in the top 10 markets of the United States is approximately $1.5 million. The same purchase encompassing the top 50 markets is about $3.8 million.[4]

Painted Bulletins   A *painted bulletin* is an outdoor advertising structure that is painted with the advertising copy. "Paints" are generally larger than posters and measure, on average, 14 feet high by 48 feet wide. Paints are sold both individually and in packages. The cost for one painted bulletin can range from as low as $3,000 in smaller markets to more than $20,000 in high-traffic areas of larger markets for an average month.

There are basically two types of paint availabilities: permanent and rotary. In the case of a permanent paint, the advertiser buys the specific location for one or more years, and the units vary in size. Permanent paints are usually in the most desirable locations, along the most heavily traveled highways, and are

---

4. BPI Communications, *Marketer's Guide to Media*, 2001.

priced accordingly. Because existing advertisers have the right of first refusal when their contracts come up for renewal, the best locations are rarely available to new advertisers. The rotary bulletin is moved from location to location within a market on a set schedule (30-, 60-, or 90-day cycles, depending on the market). Rotary locations are typically in high-traffic areas along expressways and major arteries, giving advertisers broad exposure to the market over the purchased cycle. They are sold individually or in packages.

Transit Advertising   Transit advertising is available on buses, taxi cabs, trains, and in carrier terminals (train stations, airline terminals, etc.) in selected cities. Numerous sizes and shapes can be purchased, including spectaculars that cover the entire bus. Advertising costs vary depending on the market, the medium, the size of the advertisement, the length of the purchase, and the scope of the purchase.

MEDIA-BUYING PROBLEMS

The media planner works with dayparts, GRPs, reach, frequency, scheduling, and geographic weight in order to accomplish the brand's marketing objectives. But the plan only says that *this* many GRPs will be purchased for *that* much money. It is the job of the professional buyer to decide which programs will carry the advertising. The buyer is responsible for placing the commercials on programs that will deliver the desired GRPs within the allotted budget. Knowledge of how media sell their product is vital both for the development of the plan and for its ultimate implementation. This section discusses some of the timing and buying implications associated with various media. Here again, as in the case of cost estimating, the major distinction rests between broadcast and print.

Network TV

Network television is a negotiated medium; it is bought and sold somewhat like a commodity on the commodities exchange. The market for network television is a supply-and-demand market whose goods are highly perishable. A minute not sold is a minute wasted, resulting in lost revenue for the network. Consequently, the first problem the network television buyer must consider is timing. Other factors include packaging and costs.

Timing   Incorrect timing and mistakes in assessing when to buy can lead to severe implementation problems. For example, if the network buyer waits too long before committing the designated budget, all of the availabilities could be exhausted, thus leaving nothing to buy. Generally, the earlier the network buy is initiated, the more likely the buyer will obtain desired programming in terms of audience delivery and stability. The longer the buyer waits before committing to a buy for a specified period, the less likely it is that the most desirable programming will be available. Waiting does, however, increase the possibility of lower pricing for the inventory that remains if demand is low.

The ideal time to buy is when sellers are anxious to sell, just before others enter the market. In general, in a seller's year, an advertiser should buy early, before prices rise and quality inventory is gone. In a buyer's year, an advertiser should buy as late as inventory is available and prices are likely to be favorable.

Packaging   Network television time can be purchased in packages of shows or by the individual program. Scatter packages—multiple programs with a few commercials per program during the course of the advertising schedule—provide maximum programming dispersion. Therefore, they tend to generate broader reach for the available budget. In addition, scatter packages reduce the risk of not delivering the specified weight levels, because the outcome of the buy is not based on one or two programs achieving their audience levels. In preparing packages, networks typically include a mixture of high-rated prestige programs and new, unproven shows that reduce the overall CPM while still delivering the target audience.

Most network time is purchased as scatter packages, but networks also make individual programs available for sale on a continuity basis. Commercials regularly appearing on one or two shows can be highly effective when the planner can identify the specific audience values in those shows that achieve the objectives of the media plan.

Cost Considerations   Determining network costs depends on three factors: (1) demand by advertisers, (2) estimates by both buyer and seller of audience delivery and cost per thousand, and (3) network overhead and expenses in doing business. By far, advertiser demand is the most important determinant of network costs. Seasonal demand and the strength of the network and its programming best illustrate the effect of supply and demand on the network television marketplace. During the time of the year when an advertiser's sales are expected to be greatest, advertising time is in great demand, so network prices are high.

For example, for toy makers, the pre-Christmas season, the fourth quarter of the year, is a time of great seasonal demand. In addition, advertisers generally prefer high-rated, popular programming in any given daypart. Such programming enables them to reach a large audience in a good commercial environment. This preference increases the price for that particular programming. In many cases, it increases pricing for an entire daypart on a network if that particular program dominates the daypart. To deliver the planned rating points within the budget, buyers will accept units in lower-rated, less desirable programs that lack the marquee value but deliver the target audience efficiently.

Another set of key determinants of network pricing consists of the buyer's and seller's estimates of audience delivery and the resulting cost per thousand. In most major agencies, network TV buyers estimate delivery for all network programming before negotiations begin. They base their estimates on consistent tracking of audience shares from week to week to determine audience trends. Network buyers are also aware of any network scheduling changes, new programs, and program cancellations. In addition, the networks project audience delivery. Network projections are usually higher than agency projections.

For example, assume a buy in fall prime time when 60 percent of homes are using television (HUT). The dialog between the network salesperson and the agency buyer might run something like this:

> NETWORK SALESPERSON: This is a great action program by the same people who developed "Survivor." It's sure to do at least a 20 share and a 12 rating.
> AGENCY BUYER: Oh, give me a break. Everybody and his brother is doing a reality knockoff. It'll be lucky to do a 15 share and a 9 rating.

Keep in mind that the average cost per point of network prime time is about $21,000. When the network salesperson says the show will do a 12 rating, he is saying that a :30 spot will cost $252,000 (12 × $21,000). The buyer thinks it is worth only $189,000.

When a substantial long-term network buy is made using mutually agreed-upon audience projections, the network normally guarantees delivery. If the network does not meet its guaranteed projections, it must offer compensatory units.

Finally, the network's expenses also affect network pricing. The network will try to cover the cost of programming and business overhead. An expensive production is priced at a premium to offset its costs. In addition, there are mechanical charges for national and regional advertisers. In the past, networks charged an "integration" fee to splice the commercial into its proper place in the tape containing the program. Modern computerized traffic systems have eliminated this manual operation, but networks continue to impose the charge. Additional fees are also charged to regional advertisers for the labor of setting up regional feeds, program cut-ins, and regional blackouts.

Buying Network TV

Advertisers purchase network television in three primary ways: up-front (or long-term), scatter (or short-term), and opportunistic (or last-minute) buys.

Up-Front (Long-Term) Buys   An *up-front,* or *long-term, buy* is the purchase of inventory for all four quarters of the coming broadcast year. Advertisers' dollars are committed up front in the spring or summer for the following television season, which begins in September. Up-front buying usually involves a guaranteed audience delivery, expressed as a guaranteed cost-efficiency and consisting of premium inventory. If the purchased programs fail to deliver the expected rating points, the networks will honor the contract by offering additional "audience deficiency" commercial units at no charge. Committing dollars in the up-front market gives the advertiser insurance against sellouts but little flexibility with regard to possible cancellation. At best, networks will generally grant cancellation options on a portion of the last half of a long-term buy.

Scatter (Short-Term) Buys   A *scatter,* or *short-term, buy* is the purchase of inventory within a specific quarter, made before the start of that quarter. Scatter buys are negotiated on a quarterly basis and give the buyer a better fix on the marketplace. That is, the buyer knows pricing from the up-front market as well as pricing from the previous quarter. Scatter buys offer the advertiser more financial flexibility, with dollar commitment required only one to two months before the air date. Buying scatter does, however, involve inventory and efficiency risks, because the best inventory might already be sold. Also, scatter has historically tended to be less efficient (priced higher) than the up-front market. Finally, networks rarely guarantee scatter buys.

Opportunistic Buys   *Opportunistic buys* involve the purchase of inventory on a last-minute basis if the networks have any remaining inventory to sell. Opportunistic buys have a high risk of sellout. On the positive side, these buys can sometimes be very efficient, because the networks are trying to get rid of last-minute inventory just prior to air date.

Other Types of Network Buys   Occasionally, advertisers purchase network television programs on a full or partial *sponsorship* basis. A full sponsorship involves purchase of all of the commercial time available in one or more telecasts of a program. Partial sponsorship requires purchase of at least three or four 30-second units of commercial time in one or more telecasts of a program.

In the early days of television, sponsorship was common. Today, although very few hours of network television are fully sponsored, partial sponsorship is common. Sponsorships have several advantages. Audiences identify the sponsor with the program. The advertiser gains additional exposure in the form of opening and closing billboards. Sponsors may use cast members in commercials. Sponsorship also can enable participation in high-quality programming. Sponsorship is especially valuable for advertisers with multiple divisions and product lines where brands with minimal advertising budgets can get high-visibility exposure.

However, sponsorships are generally expensive. Also, the advertiser takes a chance that the program will not do well. An additional drawback is that audience reach is limited with a single program, compared to spreading the buy over a variety of programs.

Special-event network programming can be purchased unit by unit or as program sponsorship. Specials such as holiday parades, election night coverage, and award presentations provide a good environment for new-product introductions and for seasonal advertisers because they frequently have mass audience appeal and high visibility. In general, special-event programming carries a premium price.

Finally, *network regional time* also is available. In a regional network buy, an advertiser buys only a portion of the country, and another advertiser or advertisers buy the rest. Regional network availabilities can benefit advertisers who seek certain types of programming identification, have products with less than national distribution, or are introducing new products to specific regions. Regional network time purchases are generally difficult to execute and involve considerable planning and discussions with the network sales departments. An alternative for national advertisers is to purchase a unit that covers the entire country, then use regional feed patterns to deliver different commercial messages to different parts of the country.

Spot TV

The United States has 210 spot television markets (DMAs) with more than 1,200 commercial television stations. The number of stations per market, which directly influences spot inventory, ranges from a high of 11 in Los Angeles to 3 or 4 stations in many small markets.

Major markets with multiple stations offer a considerable spot inventory from which to select. The multiplicity of spot commercial availabilities in such markets allows the buyer to be somewhat selective about programming and timing. Spot schedules are generally purchased two weeks to two months in advance of the start date of the schedule. Spot time can be bought for specified flight periods or on a continuing basis until canceled. Most station contracts call for cancellation notice to be given four weeks before the end of a schedule.

Syndicated TV

Syndication is bought much like network television—the advertiser makes one national buy. However, unlike buys for network television, syndication buys can include either packages of time on several shows or time purchased on one program. Here again, the percentage of national coverage varies by syndicated property, and pricing varies according to coverage, projected performance, and demand. Audience delivery guarantees are often available.

Cable TV

Cable TV is negotiated the same way as network TV—the buy is negotiated on a cost-per-thousand efficiency basis with a guaranteed audience delivery. Like network TV, the cable networks are pitted against each other during negotiations to provide the best possible pricing. The cable marketplace is unique because it has limited mass appeal. Except for the cable networks that program like network TV (e.g., USA), most target specific demographic groups. Nevertheless, it is possible to pit these niche networks against each other in negotiations, as long as the buyer is not particular about program environment.

Cable can also be purchased market by market in the same manner as spot TV, but the process is far more complicated. Orders must be placed, one at a time, on each cable system that serves an area. Although this allows very precise geographic targeting, managing the price negotiation, purchase, stewardship, and payment for potentially thousands of low-cost commercial units is highly inefficient. In addition, because the ratings are generally less than 1.0, and because of the small Nielsen sample in spot markets, no local ratings are available for most cable networks. This makes local cable a valuable medium for retail advertisers, which can measure its effectiveness by store traffic. Local cable is less useful for national advertisers that do not need spot cable's geographic targeting capabilities.

Magazines

Although magazines publish a rate card in SRDS, the medium has become extremely negotiable, especially for high-volume advertisers. Most national publications accept space reservations guaranteeing that advertising space will be available in the desired issues. Space reservations can be made almost any time in advance of the issue. The final date for contracting to appear in a given issue is called the closing date. This date varies by publication. Closing dates for monthly magazines will generally be 60 to 90 days in advance of issue. Closing dates for weekly publications normally fall about three to seven weeks prior to issue.

National magazines provide regional and test-market circulation breakouts for achieving coverage in specified geographic areas. The regional availability can include multiple states or just a limited area, such as New York City. The rest of the circulation carries either another advertiser or editorial material. Magazines also make available test-market circulation breakouts that conform closely to television market coverage patterns, thus permitting test translations of national plans into local test areas. Normally, advertisers must secure costs and availabilities of such special breakouts from the magazines before placing an order because the numbers are subject to change.

Many magazines also make available what are called *A and B copy splits.* This means two different blocks of copy can appear in alternate copies of the magazine in the same issue. These copy splits provide opportunities to test alternative copy approaches, or different brands can use splits when national coverage is desired and half of the circulation is considered adequate for each brand. Some magazines also make available demographic breakouts. Such demographic editions allow advertisers to place ads only in copies going to physicians, or businesspeople, or some other breakout provided by the publication.

As media planners continue their education, they should keep abreast of the flexibilities provided by the ever-changing publishing industry.

Newspapers

Unlike magazines, newspapers are not generally considered a negotiable medium for national advertisers. The rate card sets the price, and that is what advertisers pay. Large local advertisers (supermarket chains, major retail stores, shopping centers, and others with a specific local street address) will negotiate prices at the (unpublished) local rate. Those prices are significantly below what is paid by national advertisers. This can lead to intricate negotiations when national advertisers such as fast-food chains buy newspaper space on behalf of their local franchisees.

Space closing for ROP space is only a few days before the actual issue. If a special unit is desired, such as a two- or four-color half-page, then additional time in ordering such space is generally required. However, the advance notice to the newspapers is still relatively short, compared with the longer closing dates of national magazines.

Newspapers have been very aggressive in developing special sections geared to various audiences and issues. For example, many food advertisers look for what is called the "Best Food Day." Best Food Day in most markets is Wednesday or Thursday, the days that major food chains schedule their advertising. The advertiser is positioned adjacent to the special editorial sections that the consumer is likely to read before going to market. Positions within these sections are generally available at no extra cost.

Other sections that can be advantageous in reaching selected audiences include sports, business, and special features on fashion, grooming, and home care. In addition to such regular opportunities for positioning, newspapers offer availabilities for special preprints, such as card stock inserts. In most cases, the advertiser provides the particular preprint to the newspaper. Such advertising units have to be ordered well in advance to ensure space availability.

Radio

Network radio programming tends to offer relatively few format types, such as news and sports and some special events. Network radio is purchased in the same way as network television; that is, with a contractual obligation for a specified number of commercials over a designated period.

Spot radio provides different buying opportunities in view of the tremendous selectivity and diversity of programming and stations in many major markets. Arbitron rating information is available in most markets but does not provide the total picture in buying radio. The number of men, women, and teenagers listening at various times to specific radio stations can be identified. However, the format—whether contemporary music, country-western, stock market reports, music/weather, or sports—can be an important factor influencing station selection. The planner must rely heavily on the buyer's experience in executing a local-market radio buy and ensuring a close match among the commercial copy, audience, and station format.

Internet

An Internet ad campaign can involve dozens of websites and potentially millions of ad impressions rotated among numerous creative executions to multiple target audiences. This daunting task has led to the emergence of *third-party ad servers* such as DoubleClick Inc. (www.doubleclick.com), Bluestreak (www.blue

streak.com), and Fastclick (www.fastclick.com). These services automate the execution of online advertising programs. For an additional 40–50 cents per thousand, they assist in planning, budgeting, insertion order generation, creative trafficking, and postbuy analysis. Planners tell the ad server which sites they have bought, the number of impressions to be delivered on each, the creative executions and rotation instructions, and the target audience. Then when called on, the server delivers an ad to the user's Web browser. When the contracted number of impressions have been delivered, the server bills the advertiser.

Because the Internet is still in its infancy, the medium has numerous issues and shortcomings. One relates to the simple act of counting impressions. The ad server maintains a count of the ads that it delivers, and the website maintains its own count. The two invariably disagree because there is no standard way of counting exposures. For example, one may count ads when they are sent out (even if the user clicks away while it is still downloading), while the other counts an ad only when it has been successfully displayed. The magnitude of the discrepancy can range from just a few hundred impressions up to a significant proportion of the campaign. Because these counts tie directly to billing, they must be resolved.

The practices of "window-shopping" and "abandoned shopping carts" also have become a serious problem for companies that sell goods directly over the Internet. The *Industry Standard* reports,

> Of the millions of people surfing through the more than 10,000 e-tailing sites (of which 1,000 have annual sales of $500,000 or more), 97 percent leave before buying. And of those who start to fill up a cart, 65 percent abandon it before going through the checkout process, according to a Shop.org study by Boston Consulting Group.[5]

The reasons range from confusing forms and checkout procedures to problems with credit card acceptance and unanswered questions about the product. Whatever the reasons, the problem of consumers not initiating or completing purchases represents the loss of billions of dollars in sales to online retailers.

---

5. Gary Andrew Poole, "The Riddle of the Abandoned Shopping Cart," *Industry Standard,* November 10, 2000.

CHAPTER THIRTEEN

Setting and Allocating the Budget

Despite the time and thought that have been given to it, one of the most difficult tasks facing advertising and agency planners is that of determining the optimum amount of money to spend for advertising. The main difficulty in determining the budget size is that no one knows precisely how a given amount of money spent for advertising will affect sales or other marketing goals. In a timeless explanation, media expert Herbert D. Maneloveg summarized the problem as follows:

> Our major problem, I believe, is that we really don't know how much advertising is enough. And we haven't done much about trying to find out. Not until lately. When someone asks about the amount of advertising pressure needed to make a potential consumer aware of the merits of a brand, we fumble and grope. When asked to justify an increase or decrease in advertising budget, we are lost because of an inability to articulate what would happen with the increase or decrease: if sales go up, we credit advertising; if sales go down, we blame pricing, distribution, and competition.[1]

In other words, there is no simple cause-and-effect relationship between the amount of money spent and the sales results that are supposed to occur because of the expenditure. Some manufacturers have learned from experience how much money they should spend to obtain a desired share or sales volume at a given time. But even these manufacturers do not assume the relationship will remain constant at all times. At some time or other, they and most other advertisers are in the same quandary about how much to spend on advertising.

---

1. Herbert D. Maneloveg, "How Much Advertising Is Enough?" *Advertising Age* (June 6, 1966): 30.

What further complicates the matter is that each brand usually has a number of competitors whose changing activities make it difficult to anticipate correctly what they will do. The dynamic marketplace situation makes the task of budget setting—including having to estimate probable competitors' activities and allow a portion of money for contingencies—difficult for most advertisers.

Finally, advertising is not the only factor that contributes to the sale of a product. Other elements of the marketing mix, such as pricing, sales promotion, personal selling, and packaging, also play a role. But who can separate the precise contribution of advertising from the effects of the other marketing mix elements?

Despite these problems, advertising budgets must be established, and the task is performed based on as much knowledge as is available at the moment. This chapter outlines some of the major methods and problems of setting budgets, along with their advantages and disadvantages.

SETTING THE BUDGET

Before they begin, planners must be absolutely clear about what the advertising budget is expected to cover. Many marketing executives consider promotional brochures, sales meetings, coupon redemption, and even coffee cups or T-shirts to be part of advertising. This is in addition to the obvious advertising-related expenses of commercial production, talent charges, print production, and so on. Regardless of how the budget is determined, in the end planners need to know how much money is available for "working media," that is, the cost of advertising time and space. They must also know if this figure is "gross" (that is, it includes agency commission) or "net," meaning the planner must first deduct the 15 percent agency commission offered by most media (published rate multiplied by 0.85).

Planners also need to know the dates of the advertiser's budget or "fiscal" year. For some, this is a standard calendar year beginning on January 1, but for others, the year may begin on July 1, or on September 1 with the start of the school year, or it may be tied to governmental years, which begin on October 1. Whatever the dates, the media plan and flowchart must reflect these budgeting realities. In this section we will discuss the various methods of determining budget size—both traditional and nontraditional—as well as several of the factors that must be considered in the budgeting process.

Traditional Methods of Budget Setting

A number of methods are widely used to determine the budget: percent of sales, competitive spending, objective and task, expenditure per unit, and the subjective judgment of what is affordable. Those used most often tend to be simple to understand and quick and easy to compute. In the ideal situation, these different methods will yield roughly similar budget levels.

Exhibit 13-1 reports on an international study of budgeting methods used by the top 100 advertisers in Canada, the United Kingdom, and the United States. About half of these advertisers used several methods, but the most commonly used was objective and task, either on its own or in combination with other methods (most often the affordable and percent-of-sales methods). These will be discussed in detail below.

Percent of Sales   To arrive at budget amounts, the *percent-of-sales method* multiplies projected sales revenue for the year by a given percentage to be spent on advertising. The amount of money available for advertising purposes, there-

EXHIBIT 13-1

Methods Used by Top 100 Advertisers to Set Advertising Budgets

BUDGETING METHOD	NUMBER OF COMPANIES USING METHOD*	PERCENT OF TOTAL USAGE
Objective and task	61	32%
Affordable	41	21
Percent of anticipated sales	32	17
Percent of last year's sales	10	5
Unit sales	9	5
Competitive relative	25	13
Competitive absolute	13	7
Total usage	191	100%

Sample base: 100 completed questionnaires (Canada, 36; United States, 36; United Kingdom, 28).
*Amounts add to more than 100 because 52 companies gave multiple responses.
SOURCE: C. L. Hung and Douglas C. West, "Advertising Budgeting Methods in Canada, the UK, and the USA," *International Journal of Advertising,* vol. 10, no. 3 (1991).

fore, is based directly on the sales achievement of the brand. As sales increase, so does the advertising budget. If sales decline, the budget also declines.

The heart of this method is the *multiplier,* the percentage by which the sales base is multiplied. In determining which percentage to use, one must consider the cost of goods and the pricing policy of each industry. If a brand costs 15 cents to manufacture and distribute and sells for $1.25, a considerable margin is available for advertising, promotion, and profit.

The first step in setting a budget based on percent of sales is to determine the expenses incurred in manufacturing and distribution. The difference between this cost and the selling price helps determine the margin available for advertising, promotion, and profit. (There are, of course, other costs to be factored in, such as overhead.) Smaller margins mean a smaller percentage available for advertising.

The key to this method of setting budgets is finding the best multiplier. This multiplier is often set arbitrarily. At other times, industry standards are used as a base.

The percent-of-sales method of budgeting might appear to be totally inflexible. This is not true. Often the percent of sales is only the starting point. After the percentage is multiplied by gross sales, the total can be adjusted to compensate for special marketing situations. When there are special marketing needs, extra dollars are added. Some companies, instead of adding to the total, will raise the multiplier when they are introducing a new product or when they are faced with very heavy competition. In some instances, however, the percentage multiplier remains constant year after year, no matter how much sales vary. When this happens, the multiplier tends to become a historical figure that is rarely questioned.

The multiplier is also affected by product pricing. Sales of low-ticket products such as drugs or supermarket items depend heavily on advertising, while high-ticket items such as appliances, cars, and home furnishings are less dependent on advertising. A guideline for determining whether the multiplier should be large or small is that the more advertising is used as a substitute for personal selling, the higher the multiplier (or the higher the margin to advertising).

The percent-of-sales budgeting method is easy to manage and understand. It is self-correcting as sales volume changes, and it can maintain a consistent profit margin. It also is suitable for both financial and marketing group needs.

However, there are many criticisms of the percent-of-sales method. For one, it seems illogical, because advertising is based on sales, rather than the other way around. When sales decline, the company will spend less for advertising, when perhaps it should spend more. Also, unless the advertising-to-sales ratios are analyzed by area, better sales areas will tend to get better and weaker sales areas will get little relief. This technique also assumes there is a direct linear relationship between advertising and sales, which is not always true.

Another criticism of this method is that it does not encourage companies to provide the research money needed to find the relationship between advertising and sales. The advice offered by marketing expert Alfred A. Kuehn holds true:

> Perhaps the best of these rules [methods of setting budgets] for an established brand is "budget a percentage of expected sales equal to the industry average." This rule is of particular interest since it is self-adjusting over time, and appears to be a low-risk policy for a firm which does not have a better understanding of the effects of advertising than do its competitors.[2]

On the other hand, if all competitive brands used this method and employed about the same multiplier, advertising budget sizes would be approximately proportional to market share, thus limiting investment spending for advertising warfare among competitors.

Competitive Spending   The *competitive spending method* depends on setting the budget in relation to the amount of spending by competing brands. The amount to be spent need not be precisely the same as that of competitors, though at times it is. Sometimes, a brand that has a smaller market share than its competitor receives a budget that is equal to or greater than the competitor, as a means of improving its share position.

A major criticism of this approach is that it assumes competitors know what they are doing or competitors' goals are the same as one's own. It also assumes, incorrectly, that a simple increase in advertising expenditures will automatically increase sales and/or market share. The products of competitors might be differ-

---

2. Alfred A. Kuehn, "A Model for Budgeting Advertising," *Mathematical Models and Methods in Marketing* (Homewood, IL: Richard D. Irwin, 1961): 315–316.

ent, or at least consumers perceive them as different, so a company's advertising must work much harder to make sales than competitors' advertising. Certainly, the marketing goals of one company are not the same as another, and the ability of advertising to create sales also is not the same.

Another competitive approach relates a brand's share of spending to its share of market. Because a given brand always loses some customers to competitors, this technique would suggest spending at a level that puts its share of spending a few points above its share of market. For new products, or to meet a goal of aggressive growth, the target share of spending could be as much as double the expected share of market. This method hinges on the advertiser's ability to predict the brand's future market share and its competitors' spending levels. It also depends, to some extent, on how the competitive set is defined.

Objective and Task   The *objective-and-task method* starts with someone setting specific marketing and/or advertising objectives. These are costed out, and the total cost represents the budget. Objectives can be sales, share volume levels, revenues expected, income, or profit.

There are two main criticisms of this method. First, this method finesses the core problem: Marketers usually do not know how much money it takes to attain any given objective. Second, the method does not consider the value of each objective and the relationship to the cost of obtaining it. Will the brand still be profitable after spending the money judged necessary to achieve any given objective?

Expenditure per Unit (Case Rate)   The *expenditure-per-unit (case rate) method* is a variant of the percent-of-sales method. In this method, the budget is generated as a result of sales, but the base is units sold, not dollar sales. Many of the advantages and disadvantages of the percent-of-sales method apply also to this method. However, there are two additional disadvantages:

First, unless the method is properly handled, the company might lose control of profits. This is particularly true if the product or brand has a wide range of sizes or prices. Shell Oil Company, for example, has four types of gasoline, ranging from Super Regular (premium price) to Regular (lowest price). Profitability varies for each. Spending on a cents-per-gallon basis must take into consideration the mix of the line.

The second disadvantage is that working with units and fixed rates of expenditures will not take inflation into account. To overcome this, the case rate must be adjusted from year to year.

Subjective Budgeting   *Subjective budgeting* systems involve making decisions on the basis of experience and judgment. The person setting the budget will also consider some objective factors, such as the minimum job that advertising will be required to do or available profit margins. But after such consideration, the final figure is decided on rather subjectively.

One subjective budgeting method is known as "all we can afford." Although at first glance this approach seems illogical or crude, it can be quite realistic if the subjective decision is accurate. This method generally starts by setting a profit percentage or dollar figure, then systematically analyzing the costs of doing business. The remaining figure, after all other costs are accounted for, is spent in marketing, a portion of which is advertising. A budget made on such a basis is difficult to defend, especially when there is reason to believe that if more money had been appropriated, the result would have been higher sales and higher profits.

Experimental Methods of Budget Setting

Some marketing and advertising professionals believe that the best way to determine the size of an advertising budget is by testing various levels of expenditures to see which will produce the most sales at the lowest total cost. The experimental designs for this purpose range from a simple before-and-after test in one market to elaborate designs in which many markets are tested and compared with control markets. Although the details of such experiments are usually kept secret, occasionally some are publicized.[3]

---

3. Malcolm A. McNiven, "Choosing the Most Profitable Level of Advertising" (case study), in *How Much to Spend for Advertising* (New York: Association of National Advertisers Inc., 1969); Thomas M. Newell, "What Is the Right Amount to Spend for Advertising?" in *Papers from the 1968 American Association of Advertising Agencies Regional Convention,* Palm Springs, Calif., October 6–9, 1968.

Essentially, experimental tests involve trying different advertising expenditure levels in different markets. In some experimental situations, advertisers discover that they can reduce advertising expenditures without any effect on sales. In other situations, increases in advertising produce varying degrees of sales increases.

In one example, Anheuser-Busch used three sets of markets (each set consisting of nine individual markets) to test alternative expenditure levels and measure the sales effects. In one set of markets, advertising expenditures were reduced from 50 percent to 100 percent below the level that ordinarily would have been used in those markets. In another group of markets, the budget was increased at rates ranging from 50 percent to as much as 300 percent. A third group was control markets, meaning there was no increase or decrease in normal advertising expenditures.

If the experimental method is indeed as effective as some individuals assume it to be, why is it not used more often to determine budget size? There are a number of reasons. George H. Brown, former director of the U.S. Census Bureau and a marketing expert, cited two problems involved with this method. The first is the relatively high cost of conducting the experiment, which involves finding and measuring a fairly large sample. The second problem is the long time span required, perhaps a year or more. By the time the experiment is completed, the marketing situation might have changed, making the final figures irrelevant. Brown also pointed out that, although the cost might not be considered too high if the payoff is accurate and valuable, the payoff might not be worth the cost.

At present, not many companies use the experimental method, although some that have used it are quite content with it. Unfortunately, most of these companies have not revealed the details of their methods, so no outside evaluation is possible.

Factors in Determining the Size of an Advertising Budget

Although it is not possible to determine a budget size scientifically, it is advisable to approach the task by weighting a number of factors that might affect the budget size. Setting a budget in this manner can be called *atomistic* in that one could think about each factor separately then assemble these factors into a final budget figure.

In weighting each factor, planners will find some are more important than others, suggesting that priorities for marketing the brand must be determined first. Furthermore, each factor must be judged on the basis of whether one should spend more than, the same as, or less than the previous year. Again, this is a subjective decision, but it might help the executive arrive at a final figure more easily. A brief discussion of these factors follows.

Assessing the Task of Advertising   Before deciding on any figure, it is reasonable to determine what role advertising is to play. Must it do the selling job alone, or will it be added to other marketing mix elements such as reduced prices and sales promotion? If advertising must do the selling job alone, the size of the budget will have to be substantial. If it works with other marketing mix elements, the size of the budget will be less.

Important in this consideration is an understanding of the power of advertising to sell the brand. Some brands simply are not sensitive to advertising. They may be too much like other brands on the market or may lack a unique selling proposition. Or perhaps it is difficult to be creative in presenting the message through print or broadcast media.

Long- and Short-Term Goals   To some extent, long- and short-term goals are set for advertising. However, when the objective is to build an image, then the budget should be treated as an investment, rather than an expense (as one would treat the budget for short-term goals). If both goals are required at the same time, then more money is required, because the advertising has a dual function. The advertising copy for immediate sales differs markedly from the copy whose goal is to build an image.

In a sense, however, the concept of dividing an advertising budget into an expense for immediate sales and an investment for long-term image building is invalid. Image-building advertising might not consist of special ads that are designed for that purpose. If the brand image is thought of as a "long-term investment in the reputation of a brand," then every ad that is run, no matter whether it opts for immediate sales or future image, contributes to that long-range goal.

The goals of the company and advertising's relationship with them, then, affect to some degree the amount of money to be spent. Companies perceive this relationship somewhat differently, so no general principle can be extracted.

Profit Margins　People in the industry assume that where there are larger profit margins, there will be larger advertising budgets. The converse is also assumed to be true. Profit margins are a limiting factor in setting marketing and advertising goals: What one would like to do cannot be done, simply because there is not enough money available to do it. It is ironic that when profit margins must be increased, advertising expenditures also should be increased, but there is little or no money available to do the job.

Degree of Product Usage　Products that are used nationally require more money for advertising than those whose usage is limited to a relatively small geographic area. However, some local and regional advertisers find it necessary to invest heavily in their marketing area to keep up with heavy competitive spending. This is often the case for fast-food firms and automobile dealers.

Difficulty in Reaching Target Markets　Some markets are unique, so no single medium reaches them well. The market for yachts is a good example. Reaching these consumers requires a number of different media, requiring more money. Likewise, targets may be so spread out geographically that mass media must be purchased, resulting in enormous message waste. When this occurs, more money is needed to do a reasonable job.

Frequency of Purchase　Most planners assume that brands or products purchased frequently will require more money for advertising than those that are purchased infrequently. An exception occurs when the advertising goals of infrequently purchased brands call for spending more money for reasons other than frequency of purchase.

Effect of Increased Sales Volume on Production Costs　If there is a danger of demand exceeding supply because of advertising's power, the consequence could be that the advertiser will have to build a new plant. In that situation, the amount of money spent for advertising should be limited until the factory is built or another decision is made. The advertiser might want to reduce advertising expenditures until it is possible to supply the demand.

New-Product Introductions　It is widely held that new-product introductions take a great deal of additional money to break into the market. How much more depends on the size of the market, the degree of competition, and the desirable qualities of the new brand. A guideline is that introducing a new brand takes at least one and a half times as much as is spent on established brands. Another guideline suggests that the share of spending behind a new product should be about twice the anticipated share of market.

Competitive Activity   In markets where competitors are active in advertising and sales promotion, it is necessary to match, or even exceed, their expenditures, depending on the marketing goals of the brand in question. While the preceding factors do not indicate exactly how much to spend on advertising, they do serve as decision-making guidelines.

ALLOCATING THE ADVERTISING BUDGET

Once the size of the advertising budget has been determined, then it must be allocated, or apportioned, in some reasonable way. When relating advertising to source of sales, advertising budgets are allocated to geographic areas. Many advertisers, however, particularly on a national level, allocate their budgets on the basis of national media selection, with relatively little concern for geographic business skews.

Geographic Allocations

Perhaps the most often used budget allocation technique is to allot at least equal portions to the amount of sales produced by a geographic area. The reasoning behind this method is that one takes a minimal risk in allocating the most dollars to areas where sales are known to have been good. If previous budgets succeeded in producing or at least contributing to sales, why would not more money (or an equal amount relative to sales) be equally effective? The concept is used not only to keep the risk low, but also to optimize whatever monies are available.

If a geographic area contributed 15 percent of total sales, then this technique assumes that it would get 15 percent of the budget. Of course, there could be a problem here: It is possible that much more than 15 percent of the previous year's allocation was necessary to produce 15 percent sales. In such a case, the budget could be based on a different method of allocation, one based on the amount of profit produced by the area in proportion to total profit nationwide. Allocating on the basis of profit is simply another method of distributing effort.

Other methods could be based on the market share contributed by each area or the anticipated sales produced by each area. The numbers could also be composites of a number of marketing variables, such as population, income, retail sales of the product class, and other related variables.

In practice, formula methods of allocating budgets tend to be only the starting point, rather than the endpoint, of the allocation procedure. The numbers usually must be adjusted to take into consideration special marketing problems. One such problem could be that the media in a particular area cost much more, proportionally, than in any other part of the country. More money would have to be added to the initial allocation figure to compensate for this problem. Another problem could be that competitors have started to promote more heavily in areas that have been most profitable for the brand in question. This situation, too, requires special adjustments to the original allocation.

To illustrate how a computer formula can solve the problem of allocating an advertising media budget among 210 geographic markets, Exhibit 13-2 on pages 366–67 shows the geographic allocation model of Interactive Marketing Systems (IMS). It is called the PAL system. In this example, a national advertiser wants to allocate a budget of $650,000 to both network and spot television in 210 markets. The total budget was determined by one of the alternatives discussed at the beginning of this chapter.

Is this the end of the allocation process? No. Adjustments now have to be made again, perhaps on a subjective basis such as whether each local market receives an adequate amount of dollars for spot advertising. (See Chapter 8 for a further discussion of weighting techniques.)

Payout Planning

Another kind of budgeting operation that media planners use is called payout planning. A *payout plan* is a budget used in new-product introductions requiring more money than usual to launch a brand. The extra dollars come not only from sales of the brand, but also from allocating the brand's profits for advertising for a limited time.

The following data provide background to the sample payout plan. A new brand could have the following costs and pricing:

	PER CASE
Selling price of brand by factory	$12.00
Costs of manufacturing, overhead, and selling the brand	− 7.00
Amount available for promotion and profit	$ 5.00
Normal amount available for promotion	$ 2.50
Normal amount available for profit	2.50
Full amount available for introducing the new brand: promotion + profit	$ 5.00

So, in new-product introductions, the manufacturer might be willing to forgo profits for a limited time and invest them in advertising, in addition to the usual advertising investment. This practice of investing both promotion and profit funds is called *full available*. In the first months, the brand does not earn enough to pay for its heavy advertising. Therefore, the company, in a sense, invests in the brand during the early periods of selling. But as the brand begins to sell more, it begins to be in a position to start paying back the investment that the company made. Finally, if everything goes well, the brand will be selling enough of the product to pay back the entire investment and stand on its own as a profit center. When that happens, the full available is divided so that part goes for profits and a portion for advertising.

Following is an explanation of the payout plan shown in Exhibit 13-3 on page 368. Each paragraph is keyed to the number at the beginning of each row on the plan. Although payout plans are not generally calculated by media-planning personnel, the media planner should be aware of the mechanics insofar as they bear on the final advertising budget.

1. **Time Periods.** Although the payout plan shows three periods, more or fewer could have been used. Furthermore, these periods could have varied from one to three years in length, or they could have been one to three six-month periods. The timing is a matter of judgment and experience on the part of the planner, who must estimate how long it will take to pay back the money necessary to get the brand launched in the marketplace.

2. **Size of Total Market.** A market can be described in any way suitable to the advertiser. Some advertisers prefer to use cases. Others use pounds of the

EXHIBIT 13-2

Television Allocation Analysis: The PAL System

Over four weeks

RANK	MARKET	(1) TV HOMES (%)	(2) BDI	(3) IDEAL DOLLARS (000)	(4) NETWORK DOLLARS (000)	(5) SPOT DOLLARS (UNADJ.)	(6) SPOT DOLLARS (000)	(7) TOTAL DOLLARS (NETWK + SPOT) (000)
1	New York	8.44%	80	$ 43.9	$ 46.4	$ −2.5	$ 0.0	$ 46.4
2	Los Angeles	5.34	107	37.2	29.4	7.8	5.9	35.3
3	Chicago	3.76	105	25.7	20.7	5.0	3.8	24.5
4	Philadelphia	3.17	126	25.9	17.4	8.5	6.5	23.9
5	San Francisco	2.49	106	17.1	13.7	3.5	2.6	16.3
6	Boston	2.38	118	18.3	13.1	5.2	3.9	17.0
7	Detroit	2.11	103	14.1	11.6	2.5	1.9	13.5
8	Washington, D.C.	1.84	113	13.5	10.1	3.4	2.6	12.7
9	Cleveland	1.78	125	14.5	9.8	4.7	3.5	13.3
10	Dallas–Ft. Worth	1.55	100	10.1	8.5	1.6	1.2	9.7
	10-market total	32.87%	103	$220.3	$180.8	$ 39.5	$ 32.0	$212.7
	210-market total	100 %	100	$650.0	$550.0	$100.0	$100.0	$650.0

Ranked on: Homes (000)   Cost pro rata: TVHH

Column 1. The basis for allocating dollars is the number of households in the market. Presumably, the product being advertised has adult/family appeal. The number of TV households in each market is recorded in this column as a percentage of the total United States.

Column 2. The BDIs of each market come from the client's own records.

Column 3. "Ideal dollars" represents the following formula:

Number of TV households × BDI × Total U.S. budget
.0844 × .80 × $650,000 = $43,900 for the New York market

Column 4. The cost of network programs in each market is derived by adding the gross impressions of all TV programs that a client intends to buy for each market and converting the sum into a percentage. For the New York market, the network dollars would be $46,400. The sum for the top 10 markets is shown as $180,800; for the entire United States, it is $550,000.

Column 5. In the New York market, the amount of network dollars is greater than the ideal dollars, so the amount is shown as a negative number (−2.5). But in Los Angeles, the differences between network and ideal dollars is positive and is the amount (unadjusted) to spend for spot TV in that market.

EXHIBIT 13-2 (*continued*)

Television Allocation Analysis: The PAL System

Column 6. Only the New York market has no dollars to spend for spot television among the top 10 (because of the negative dollars). (Data for the remaining 209 markets are not shown.) The sum of all negative numbers—like those of New York—is 31.3. (Other negative numbers in markets beyond the first 10 are not shown.) This represents overspending and must be deducted proportionately from all other markets. The formula used to adjust for the 31.3 is the following:

$$\frac{\text{Total spot dollars}}{\text{Total spot overspending}} = \frac{100}{131.3} = 76.2\%$$

Therefore, each unadjusted spot dollar is multiplied by .762 to arrive at the final amount of dollars to be allocated in each market. In Los Angeles, 7.8 unadjusted spot dollars $\times$ .762 = 5.9 dollars. This multiplication is done for every market until the 31.3 overspending is totally reduced. Some markets like New York received only network advertising messages, while most others received both network and spot.

SOURCE: Reprinted with permission of Interactive Marketing Systems (IMS).

---

product, packages, or dollars. The data for the number of cases that will be sold is an estimate, based on trend analysis, modified by the judgment and experience of the advertising executive. If these estimates are wrong, then the payout plan will have to be adjusted accordingly.

3. **Average Share for the Brand.** As a new product is introduced and begins to be purchased by wholesalers, retailers, and consumers, the share of market could vary considerably from month to month. So this percentage represents the average for the year, rather than the total. Either could have been used, but the more modest percentage is probably safer. Again, this is a crucial estimate. If it is incorrect, the plan has to be adjusted immediately.

4. **Year-End Total Share for the Brand.** This figure is shown only as a guide to what the executive hopes to achieve at year-end. It is not used in the calculations, though it could be substituted for average share, as previously mentioned.

5. **Cases Purchased by Pipeline.** The first factory sales could be to pipeline companies such as wholesalers and distributors (depending on how the product is distributed). This group of companies represents a portion of total sales. The

EXHIBIT 13-3

A Three-Period Payout Plan

(1) Time periods	PERIOD 1	PERIOD 2	PERIOD 3	TOTAL
(2) Size of total market in millions of cases	10	11	12	
(3) Average share for the brand	12%	18%	25%	
(4) Year-end total share for the brand	15%	25%	25%	
(5) Cases (millions) purchased by pipeline	0.4	0.2	0.1	
(6) Cases (millions) purchased at consumer level	1.2	2.0	3.0	
(7) Total shipments from factory (millions of cases)	1.6	2.2	3.1	
(8) Factory income @ $12 a case*	$19.2	$26.4	$37.2	
(9) Less cost @ $7 a case	$11.2	$15.4	$21.7	
(10) Budget (dollars available for promotion and profit)	$ 8.0	$11.0	$15.5	$34.5
(11) Reallocation of budget to place heavier weight in first period	$14.9	$11.7	$ 7.9	$34.5
(12) Percentage of reallocated budget	43%	34%	23%	100%
(13) Allocation of budget to advertising and sales promotion				
To advertising (85%)	$12.7	$ 9.9	$ 6.7	$29.3
To sales promotion (15%)	$ 2.2	$ 1.8	$ 1.2	$ 5.2
Total	$14.9	$11.7	$ 7.9	$34.5
(14) Profit (or loss)	($ 6.9)	($ 0.7)	$ 7.6	—
(15) Cumulative investment	($ 6.9)	($ 7.6)	0	—

*All dollar figures are in millions. Thus, 19.2 = $19,200,000.

amount in the pipeline at any time can be estimated from experience with similar types of products.

6. **Cases Purchased at Consumer Level.** This figure is calculated as the product of the average share expected times the number of cases expected to be sold in the total market: 10,000,000 × 12% = 1,200,000 cases.

7. **Total Shipments from Factory.** Pipeline and consumer purchases are added to find total shipments: 400,000 + 1,200,000 = 1,600,000 cases for period 1.

8. **Factory Income @ $12 a Case.** The decision was to price a case at $12. To find factory income for each period, this figure is multiplied by the number of cases expected to be sold for the period: 1,600,000 cases × $12 per case = $19,200,000.

9. **Less Cost @ $7 a Case.** To find the total cost, the manufacturing cost per case (set at $7) was multiplied by the estimated number of cases that will be sold: 1,600,000 × $7 = $11,200,000.

10. **The Budget.** Because the budget is composed of dollars allocated both for promotion and for profit (or full available), the amount of money available for promotion is simply the factory income minus the cost of cases sold per period: $19,200,000 − $11,200,000 = $8,000,000. The term *promotion* as used here does not mean sales promotion, but, more broadly, advertising and sales promotion. As a result of the subtraction in each period, a given amount of money is available in each. These amounts, when added together, equal $34,500,000.

11. **Reallocation of Budget.** Although $34,500,000 would be available for advertising and sales promotion, the budget as it is shown in row 10 is allocated in a strict mathematical fashion, rather than with an understanding of advertising investment needs. The budget is largest in the third period, but most of the money is needed in the first period, where extra expenditures usually are needed to launch a brand.

12. **Percentage Budget.** The executive has reallocated the budget total ($34,500,000) in the manner believed necessary. As a result, the executive allocated 43 percent of the $34,500,000 to the first period instead of the 23.2 percent that would have been available if the budget were accepted as shown in row 10: $8,000,000 ÷ $34,500,000 = 23.2%.

13. **Allocation of the Budget to Advertising and Sales Promotion.** The allocation is arbitrary, based on what the executive thinks is needed for each. Other executives with a different marketing situation and product might think the proportions should be different. Note that the $29,300,000 for advertising must be further split between commercial production and working media.

14. **Profit (or Loss).** At this point, the company must make an investment in the brand. Since the amount of money available for promotion in period 1 is only $8,000,000 (row 10) and dollars needed for the same period are

$14,900,000 (row 11), the company will have to invest an additional $6,900,000. That amount represents a loss for the brand for period 1. The brand now owes the company $6,900,000 for period 1.

In period 2, the reallocated budget is again more than the brand would earn for that period, $11,700,000 versus $11,000,000. Again the brand loses money, but not as much. If this amount is added to the amount already owed to the company from period 1, the cumulative total for period 2 is now $7,600,000. This means that the company has to give the brand $7,600,000 for the extra amount needed above sales dollars up to the end of period 2.

However, in period 3, the brand earns enough money ($7,600,000) to pay back the amount the company has given to it. At this point, it has made a profit, paid back the money given to it by the company, and presumably will make a profit to keep it going in period 4. When the brand makes a profit, it pays out money to the company.

Not shown in this example, but what obviously should be included in real situations, is the inflation factor. Money "loaned" to a brand in year 1 is worth more than its face value will be in succeeding years.

CHAPTER FOURTEEN

Testing, Experimenting, and Media Planning

This final chapter addresses custom-designed research that can help a media planner find answers that are not in syndicated research volumes such as IRI, MRI, or A. C. Nielsen. Essentially, a media planner needs answers to questions such as these:

- In which geographic markets should we place extra money to achieve our marketing objectives?
- Will extra media weight generate enough additional sales to justify the cost?
- Which advertising timing schedule is best for this brand?
- How much money is optimum to achieve the brand's goals?

TESTS AND EXPERIMENTS

Most of the research used to evaluate alternative media strategies falls under the general heading of tests and experiments. Briefly defined, a test is a simple field study of some advertising variable. An experiment is a carefully designed study in which the researcher controls and manipulates conditions to see how an experimental variable affects audience behavior.

Why Test or Experiment?

Testing or experimenting is necessary for a number of reasons. The most important reason was stated earlier: to help the planner make decisions. Often the planner is faced with alternatives that are seemingly equal, but there might be

371

differences of opinion between the planner and others (such as account executives or clients) about whether to use a given alternative. A way to resolve these differences is through custom-made research.

Another reason for testing or experimenting is to avoid making costly errors. The rising cost of media time and space and the proliferation of new media alternatives make this more necessary than ever. Furthermore, clients want more and better proof that they are getting their money's worth in media and that optimum media strategies are being used.

Finally, although media planners use numerical data in making decisions, they often modify the data with their own judgment, based on personal experience. But often such personal experience is not broad enough, or the current situation is vastly different from what it was in the past. Planners need research to support their judgment and answer the question of which strategy will work best.

How They Differ

Because both tests and experiments usually involve field studies, they seem to be alike. But tests are quite different from experiments. In advertising or marketing, a *test* is a simple piece of research in which one measures a variable (or treatment) introduced into the market to see what effect it has. Although advertising can be tested in one market, most often it is tested in at least two; each market is given a different treatment. For example, in one market $500,000 could be spent for advertising, while in the other $1 million could be spent, using the same medium in both markets. Results could be measured on the basis of which amount of advertising produced the greatest sales.

At the end of the test, the $1 million might have produced 10 percent more sales than did the smaller figure. Which treatment was better? The answer depends on the decision maker, who, on the basis of experience, judgment, or a payout calculation, says one expenditure is better than another. In this example, twice as much money yielded only 10 percent more sales, suggesting that the incremental spending was not justified.

The most important characteristic of the test is its simplicity and its minimal controls. Although some attempts are made to see that the two test markets are alike, the nature of testing is simplicity. Not too much trouble is exerted to control extraneous factors that could affect the test's outcome. Testing provides guidelines for decision making, rather than yielding definitive and projectable results.

An *experiment* resembles a test in that similar markets are selected for treatments, but great care is exerted to make sure that the markets are equivalent. Usually the same treatments are assigned to two or more test markets, and usually two or more treatments are used. Finally, the treatments must be assigned at random by using a table of random numbers or, in simple cases, by tossing a coin. Furthermore, for measuring the results of the different treatments, a random sample must be drawn from each test-marketing unit, and two or more replications are made of each advertising treatment.

Using the random sample drawn from each of the test markets, the samples are measured through normal survey techniques to determine the effects of the various treatments. Results from experiments are analyzed much differently from test results. In tests, the percentage of change from one market to the other is probably the most sophisticated analysis. In experiments, data are cast in the form of analysis of variance or some other statistical technique that helps tell the experimenter whether there is a cause-and-effect relationship between the treatment and the result.

Which Is Better?

Testing and experimenting each have advantages and limitations. The experiment provides the highest degree of objectivity. It is better controlled, it excludes the effects of extraneous variables, and it allows statistical inference that is usually more valid than personal judgment.

On the other hand, a test is less expensive than an experiment. Many companies that cannot afford the cost of an experiment still can find answers to their problems by conducting tests. Furthermore, tests usually take less time to conduct than experiments. Often there simply is not enough time for an experiment, but something needs to be learned. A test could provide this information. Then, too, although the test design promises less than an experiment, often what it promises is enough. For example, a planner might simply want some clues, rather than a complete rationale for a decision. Finally, a test is analyzed on the basis of relatively simple logic and reasoning that everyone can understand. Those who use experiments often err by substituting the elegance of their statistics for good, commonsense reasoning. The formulas of statistics are means to an end—not the end. For these reasons, advertisers use tests almost exclusively to obtain guidance and support for their marketing decisions.

Market Mix Modeling

In the late 1990s, with the advent of powerful desktop computers and the availability of detailed grocery store scanner data, some large packaged-goods advertisers began using *market mix modeling*. This technique uses regression analysis to model the effect of a broad range of marketing variables on sales (the dependent variable). Manufacturers assemble vast amounts of information about their products, city by city, and give it to outside consultants such as Media Marketing Assessment (MMA), which conduct the actual analysis. The data elements (independent variables) include the following measures:

- Weekly GRPs by daypart by commercial length
- Product distribution
- Number of grocery store facings
- Price of their own and competitors' products
- Weekly GRPs of the primary competitors
- Dates and values of consumer promotions (coupons, contests, etc.)
- Weather (average weekly temperature) where relevant
- Seasonal influences

With this information, the modeler can generalize from the past to predict what will happen to sales when media weight is increased or decreased. This analysis avoids the need to conduct lengthy and expensive test marketing.

Market mix modeling is expensive, both in fees to the modeler and in the time necessary to assemble the required information. Furthermore, the results are affected by errors or misinterpretation of the input data. Nevertheless, because of the technique's speed and ability to provide definitive answers to the age-old questions, market mix modeling has become an attractive alternative to test markets for some advertisers. Additional information is available from the MMA website at www.mma.com.

TEST MARKETING

Test marketing is the use of controlled tests or experiments (depending on how they are done) in one or more geographic areas to gather certain kinds of information or to gain experience in marketing a brand. Although any product or service can be test-marketed, marketers most often apply the process to *consumer packaged goods (CPG)*—products that consumers buy in grocery stores, discount warehouses, drugstores, and mass merchandisers.

In practice, test marketing means different things to different people. For some research-oriented people, test marketing means a precise method for gaining information or experience. At the other extreme, to some entrepreneurs, test marketing means "trying something out in the marketplace." Between these two extremes exist many other possibilities.

Test marketing is most common for new brands in existing product categories or for extensions of a product line. Even in new-product testing, the media portion of the test is usually not the first consideration, because the brand first has to be developed, packaged, and priced; selling strategies must be determined; and starting dates must be chosen. In a sense, then, media planning assumes the same relationship in test marketing that it does in an existing brand strategy: Marketing considerations must be decided first.

It is important for a media planner to have a good basic understanding of test marketing, because the planner is often involved in it when translating national media plans to a local level. Although it is beyond the scope of this book to provide all the details of test marketing, the following discussion covers the essential facts for planners.

Purposes of Test Marketing

Test marketing has two major purposes: (1) to examine the viability and potential profitability of new products, and (2) to test alternative media, creative, and marketing strategies for existing brands.

New Products   Before a company spends any money on a new product, managers want to know the likelihood of success for the product's concept and proposed marketing plan. Most packaged-goods companies hire outside research firms to make this assessment. One of the most widely used is A. C. Nielsen's BASES, which estimates how many cases of a new product will be sold as determined by three measures:

- Product distribution as a percent of *all commodity volume (ACV)*—the percent of grocery stores where the product is sold, weighted by store size (i.e., larger stores "count more")
- The estimated awareness of the new brand, based on the proposed media plan
- A survey of consumers' intent to buy after seeing a description of the product's concept

From this volume estimate, marketers can predict whether the brand will have enough sales to be profitable. BASES claims that in 970 validations worldwide, its average estimates are within 9 percent of actual sales, with 9 out of 10 estimates falling within 20 percent of actual sales.[1]

Once a new product's concept and proposed marketing plan appear promising, the next step is to determine whether real shoppers, in a real market situation, will try the product when it is introduced. More important, marketers need to know whether consumers will make the repeat purchases that are necessary for a brand's long-term success. A wrong decision in introducing a new product is costly, and despite all these efforts, many new products fail each year. Essentially, test marketing is conducted to reduce the risk of failure by providing top management with knowledge gained from advertising in a limited geographic area. Management then can project test findings to a large geographic area. The major objectives of test marketing are to estimate the brand's market share and volume that are likely once the brand is introduced nationally and to evaluate alternative marketing and advertising strategies that also might be effective on a national basis.

Specifically, the purpose of new-product test marketing is to help planners work out the mechanics of a market introduction while learning the local market share and effects of various strategies. If problems exist, then it is better to

---

1. A. C. Nielsen's BASES website (www.bases.com), *Global Validations*, October 3, 2001.

learn about them ahead of time and solve them before national introduction. Spending a relatively small amount of money in a local market is less risky than a national introduction. Once top management learns the local brand shares, it will try to project those findings to the national market. At that point, if there is not enough profit in the brand, management will decide not to go ahead. In such a case, the investment in the failed product is considerably less than it would have been had the brand been introduced nationally without test marketing.

Existing Brands   Although marketers can structure their own test markets for new products, most large packaged-goods companies use either A. C. Nielsen or Information Resources, Inc. (IRI). Both services have extensive experience in conducting tests and interpreting the results.

Nielsen's Scantrack Service provides detailed product movement and merchandising information for food stores and food/drug combinations. The service obtains its information weekly from the checkout scanners in a sample of more than 4,800 stores representing more than 800 retailers in 50 major markets.[2] This product sales information is supplemented by Nielsen's Homescan panel, which reports demographic and other information about the people who made the purchase. Panelists use a special "wand" device to scan the UPC (bar code) of all products that come into the home, so Nielsen can track sales in all types of stores. Nielsen specialists analyze the data and provide periodic reports to their clients. These reports provide the basis for evaluating the success of test-marketing efforts for new and existing products.

The other widely used service providing packaged-goods marketing data is Information Resources, Inc. (IRI). Its InfoScan service obtains checkout scanner data from a sample of more than 19,000 supermarkets, drugstores, and mass merchandiser outlets.[3] This service, supplemented by a wand-based household panel, provides data similar to Nielsen's and, like the Nielsen service, helps marketers measure the success of new products, as well as sales of existing brands.

---

2. A. C. Nielsen website: http://acnielsen.com/products/reports/scantrack/.
3. Information Resources, Inc., website: www.infores.com/public/us/prodserv/factsheet/us_fact_syndi catestore.htm.

BehaviorScan Test Market Service   Although Scantrack and InfoScan can be used to measure the effects of alternative marketing strategies for existing brands, many advertisers use the BehaviorScan service of IRI (popularly referred to as B-Scan). B-Scan provides marketers and their agencies with a measurable method for evaluating the impact of different marketing strategies on consumer sales for both new and established brands. Currently, B-Scan operates five test markets, four with targetable TV capability. These four markets are Pittsfield, Massachusetts; Eau Claire, Wisconsin; Midland, Texas; and Cedar Rapids, Iowa. The market without TV testing is Grand Junction, Colorado. IRI selected these markets to ensure geographic dispersion throughout the United States, as well as typical consumer demographics and retail conditions.

Television media influences are measured and controlled through local network affiliates, independent stations, and cable TV services. In addition, B-Scan tracks circulation and coupon redemption from local newspapers and women's service magazines. The service also measures competitive activity, providing a clear picture of pricing, displays, and features. Coupon redemptions are also collected from every panelist.

A panel of more than 3,000 households is maintained in each of the BehaviorScan markets. Panel members shop with an ID card presented to the checkout counter in scanner-equipped grocery stores and drugstores, allowing the tracking of specific consumer purchase behavior, item by item, over a continuous period of time.

B-Scan's targetable TV capability exists through a special device attached to the panelist's TV set that allows the marketer to broadcast alternative commercials to households in demographically balanced cells. In this way, the test can expose one group of homes to a test commercial or media plan while another group in the same market serves as a control.

BehaviorScan can test consumer promotions such as coupons, sampling, or refund offers through its balanced panel subsamples. This arrangement provides a laboratory environment for tests. Through direct mail or split newspaper-route targeting, a different treatment is delivered to each group. The sales and profits from each group can then be analyzed.

In addition to the household panel data, B-Scan continuously collects sales data from all the grocery, drug, and mass-merchandise stores in each market. Sales data from other outlets, such as convenience stores or hardware stores, can also be collected on a custom basis to ensure coverage of all appropriate outlets for testing.

Despite IRI's expertise, biases of many kinds can creep into test-marketing operations. For example, test markets may experience higher distribution levels than could be expected on a national scale. Or the local markets enjoy extra sales efforts that could not be expected nationally. Sometimes the expenditure of dollars for advertising is excessive at the local level and could not be duplicated nationally. Because residents of the BehaviorScan markets have historically been exposed to so many marketing tests, they may not react in the same way as people in other parts of the United States. Finally, markets change, people's attitudes change, and the economy changes. Therefore, by the end of a test-marketing operation, the national universe, as well as the local universe, might be far different from what they were during the initial test.

Advertiser-Run Market Tests

Although B-Scan and Nielsen tests are widely used, they are expensive compared to a test conducted by the advertiser using in-house resources. Following are some of the considerations and decisions that are necessary to ensure a successful test-marketing program.

Number of Markets to Use   No simple rules exist for deciding on a number of markets, but necessary considerations include cost and degree of accuracy. Using fewer than three markets could be considered inadequate for predicting national share, but some kinds of information can be learned from two markets or even one market. Although most marketing experts would agree that test marketing should use three or more markets, many tests use fewer than that because the cost is prohibitive. Even if managers think that using more markets will considerably enhance the results of an experiment, they still feel great reluctance to spend the extra money.

Kinds of Markets to Include   A number of criteria are used in selecting test markets. The primary factor is that a market should be representative of the universe. The markets selected are really samples from the universe. Therefore, the more they are like the larger area, the better. This would mean that the markets selected should have the same demographic distribution of population as the country (if the universe is the entire country).

As shown in Exhibit 14-1, Peoria, Illinois, has a population distribution that closely matches the population distribution of the total United States. Because of this similarity, marketers often use Peoria as a single test market. At times, it is used in combination with others. Yet despite the demographic similarity, researchers should question whether the lifestyle of Peoria inhabitants is comparable to lifestyles in other areas of the country.

Market Sizes   There is a difference of opinion about the optimum market size for test markets. One expert believes that the range should be a population of 100,000–1,000,000. Another expert employs a rule that the size should be about

EXHIBIT 14-1

Peoria Compared with the National Population (1999)

DEMOGRAPHIC	PEORIA DMA	TOTAL U.S.	INDEX
Men 18+	47.8%	47.8%	100
Persons 18–49/household	1.15	1.26	91
Persons 50+/household	0.73	0.71	103
Children 2–11/household	0.38	0.40	95
Effective buying income/household	$44,146	$43,459	102
Education (% DMA)			
Non–high school graduates	21%	25%	84
High school graduates	36	30	120
Attended college	25	25	100
College graduates	18	20	90
Total	100%	100%	100
Occupation (% DMA)			
Professional	56%	58%	96
Blue collar	26	26	100
Service workers	15	14	112
Farmers	3	2	133
Total	100%	100%	100

SOURCE: Nielsen Media Research, *Test Market Guide,* 1999.

2–3 percent of the national population. Yet another believes that the total population involved in test marketing should not be less than 20 percent of the United States, because anything less would cause too much statistical sampling variance. Probably the size of each market is less important than the kinds or numbers of markets used. However, size is an important consideration for controlling the cost of the test. In large markets, marketers could expect to pay relatively higher media costs.

What to Test   In addition to sales volume or share at a profitable level, a number of marketing variables can be tested. These include tests of advertising media weights, price levels, store promotion plans, trial and repeat buying rates, creative approaches, package sizes and assortments, brand names, brand awareness and/or attitude changes, and alternative media strategies.

When to Read the Test   Before any test starts, there needs to be general agreement about when it is appropriate to examine the results and determine success or failure. Experienced marketers suggest running a test for at least six months, but there is often pressure to make the decision sooner, sometimes after only three months or even before that. But early results can be highly misleading. Strong initial sales can indicate a successful launch with many people trying the product, but if these early buyers do not make repeat purchases, the brand cannot survive. Conversely, brands with a long purchase cycle may need many months for consumers to run out of their current product and be in the market for a replacement. Product seasonality also can influence the timing for reading a test.

Research Designs Used in Test Marketing

Research design refers to a plan of actions to be taken in the testing. This plan, or design, is carefully worked out to obtain certain kinds of information. Most often research design refers to experimental situations where the test data will be statistically manipulated. Research design can be very simple—for example, observing a market, introducing an experimental variable, and then observing it again to learn what effects the variable had on the market. Or the design can be simple to the extent that two or more markets, presumably similar in demographic characteristics, are tested at the same time, with each one getting a different treatment.

Control Markets   Before conducting test marketing, the planner must design the test in such a way as to guarantee its validity. *Validity* means that the test measures what it is supposed to measure. For example, if advertising is introduced into a test market as an experimental treatment, the planner will want to know the extent to which advertising had any effect on the outcome.

One method of assuring the internal validity of the test is to use a control market along with a test market. A *control market* is one that does not receive any special treatment. The control market, therefore, must be selected carefully so that it shares all the demographic and economic characteristics of the test market. If the research objective is to measure advertising's effect on sales, then advertising will be used in the test market only. Sales then are measured in both kinds of markets. If sales rise higher in the test market than in the control market, one can conclude that advertising had a significant effect on sales. But if sales rise to about the same degree in both markets, then advertising had little or no effect.

The design of a test and control market for a new brand is shown in Exhibit 14-2. This kind of test can involve more than a single variable. For example, different spending levels can be tested in different test markets and compared with the control group. In addition, market shares of all groups can be tested simultaneously for the total of all test groups and compared with the control group.

Randomized Block Designs   A *randomized block design* is one in which subjects to be measured are first grouped together into blocks. Each subject is carefully chosen so that he or she will be much like every other subject in that block. The selection process, however, is done on a random basis so that every person with the same characteristic has an equal chance of being chosen. Randomized blocks are designed to prevent situations in which the outcome results from differences with the sample, rather than differences in the treatments.

The matching or grouping of subjects can be on the basis of age (for example, people aged 18–34) or income (annual income of $75,000 or more) or store volume (grocery stores with less than $500,000 income). Once subjects

EXHIBIT 14-2

How Test and Control Markets Are Used

	TIME PERIOD 1 ➤	TIME PERIOD 2 ➤	TIME PERIOD 3 ➤	
Test market	Sales of new brand measured (no advertising)	Advertising introduced	Sales of new brand measured	Sales of markets compared on basis of percentage of change
Control market	Sales of new brand measured (no advertising)	No advertising	Sales of new brand measured (no advertising)	

are placed into blocks, the experimenter can compare the results of treatments among the blocks. If subjects are not combined into blocks, then the experimenter might not be able to find significant results, because the differences might be too small to be measured. The experiment can overcome this problem by using a very large number of subjects, but randomized blocks aid the experimenter in reducing the number of subjects to be used in an experiment.

Latin Square Designs A *Latin square* is a block divided into a number of cells containing coded letters and so arranged that a letter appears only once in each row and column. This design technique is more precise than the randomized block because it helps control the problem of two rather than one source of variation within markets that could not be controlled by careful selection. Exhibit 14-3 shows an example of a Latin square used in a marketing experiment. This experiment controls two variables (geographic variation and competitive expenditures) and applies three different treatments. This design assumes that each control or treatment is independent of the others and therefore will not affect the others in any way.

The problem illustrated in Exhibit 14-3 is this: If Brand X spends three varying amounts of money for advertising, which would produce the most sales,

EXHIBIT 14-3

A Latin Square Design Applied to a Test-Marketing Situation

	REGIONS OF THE UNITED STATES		
DEGREE OF COMPETITIVE SPENDING	EAST	CENTRAL	WEST
Low spending levels	A	C	B
Medium spending levels	C	B	A
High spending levels	B	A	C

Treatments: A = high spending level for Brand X; B = medium spending level for Brand X; C = low spending level for Brand X.
SOURCE: Benjamin Lipstein, "The Design of Test Market Experiments," *Journal of Advertising Research* (December 1965): 6.

or brand awareness, or other marketing variable? To make the experiment projectable to the entire country, the experiment tries different expenditure levels in different parts of the country and also in areas where different competitive spending levels took place. By controlling for both variables, the experiment eliminated them as possible reasons for variations in sales that were found through the experiment.

The method of eliminating the effects of both variables is to add the rows and average out the effect of regions. By adding the columns, it is possible to average out the effects of competitive spending levels. By adding the expenditure levels for Brand X (or treatments), it is possible to average out the effects of both regions and competitive activity to determine which Brand X spending level was best.

Factorial Design   With a *factorial design,* based on a factor as an independent variable, it is possible to measure the effects of different kinds of treatments. An added advantage of this design is the ability to determine whether the factors interact or are independent. In conceptual terms, this design can create experiments to determine the influence of two or more independent variables on a dependent variable. Independent variables are those that the experimenter controls, manipulates, or varies. Dependent variables are the yield, or the effect variables; they vary depending on the independent variable.

An example of differing treatments in an experiment could be the effects of old versus new packaging, or an old package price versus a new price. The goal is to determine whether price and package changes are related to each other or are independent.

Other Designs   Alvin Achenbaum suggested a *checkerboard design* as a valid means of obtaining data in test marketing. He described this design as requiring three basic elements:[4]

1. Divide a universe into groups of markets. These markets should be randomly selected and about equal in size (e.g., three television market groups from each of Nielsen's 10 geographic areas).

2. Use alternative strategies in groups of three. Perhaps one group would receive 80 percent of a current spending level, the second group 100 percent, and the third group 120 percent. Achenbaum would also use local media such as newspapers, spot television, and local magazines as the testing media. Three complete media plans at each spending level would then be produced.

3. Through syndicated retail auditing services, measure results over a year. The key to the success of this plan is representativeness, good control, and ease of measurement (because it uses Nielsen areas).

MEDIA TESTING

Media play an important role in most test-marketing operations. Although the objective of a market test is to learn whether certain marketing actions will result in a given level of sales or profits, usually other parts of a test are directly related to the selection and use of media. These other parts have different objectives, such as learning which spending levels or which media mixes to use.

Types of Media Testing

A media planner's initial responsibility in test marketing is to create a national media plan, then reduce the size of this plan to fit the individual markets to be

---

4. Alvin A. Achenbaum, "Market Testing: Using the Marketplace as a Laboratory," in *Handbook of Marketing Research*, ed. Robert Ferber (New York: McGraw-Hill, 1974): 4, 47, 48.

tested. (The reduction process is called *media translation* and will be explained in detail later.) The planner might have a number of different objectives to test, but any given test should be limited to a single objective, to avoid confounding the results. (If a test market is exposed to both additional media weight and different creative executions, there would be no way to know which produced the incremental sales.) The following paragraphs describe possible objectives to test.

Complete Media Plan   A national media plan might be developed for a new product that has not been marketed before. The typical objective of the marketing part of a test for such a product is to learn a brand's sales or the market share that could be developed on a national scale. In addition, alternative forms of the national media plan can be tested to see which will best fulfill the brand's media needs.

Alternative Spending Levels   Testing can be used to help determine how much money should be spent on media. The following kinds of spending plans could be tested:

1. High spending versus current spending levels
2. Low spending versus current spending levels
3. High spending versus low spending levels
4. How much to allocate, either by dollars or gross rating points, to various geographic markets and/or media

In testing allocation weights, the tester might use various kinds of weighted BDIs and CDIs to help arrive at spending levels.

Planners should ensure that the difference between the test and control cells is large enough that the effect of the incremental weight will be noticeable. Experts believe the high-spending test cell should receive at least 50 percent more weight than the control.

Alternative Schedules   It is important to know whether a media plan should use flighting, continuity, or pulsing. Although experience provides planners with some basis for judgment, a test can sometimes provide more objective information.

Alternative Media Mixes   One could test the results obtained from any single medium or any combination—TV versus magazines, TV versus newspapers, national versus local media, etc. Testing of the media mix could also include comparing various dayparts in broadcast media—an exclusive daypart, such as prime time, or a combination of dayparts, such as daytime and early or late fringe. These are only a few of the possible combinations that could be tested.

Alternative Commercial Lengths or Ad Sizes   The media plan can also use many different combinations of commercial lengths and ad sizes. Any of these could be varied in test markets. For example, the research could test 60-second versus 30-second commercials, or 30-second versus 15-second (or 10-second) commercials, or half-page versus full-page print ads.

Requirements for Selecting Media Test Markets

A number of criteria for selecting test markets apply specifically to media. For example, enough media options should be available in the test markets to replicate the national media that will be used later. As a result, certain small markets are unsuitable for testing purposes. The following paragraphs address additional considerations.

Media Availability   A test market must have a balance of media alternatives available. For example, if television is to be part of a national media plan, then there should be at least four TV stations in the test market, because there probably will be at least four TV stations in major markets when the plan is implemented nationally. In the same manner, if radio is to be used in the national plan, then one radio station in the test market should not dominate the market. In a national marketing effort, few if any markets will be dominated by a single radio station.

Spill-in and Spill-out   One quality of a test-market medium is the degree to which it is isolated from other markets. Media from markets outside the test area often *spill into* the test market. That is, people in the test market are exposed to media originating from another market. Sometimes it works the other way; media from the test market *spill out* into adjacent markets.

The degree to which media in a test market spill out messages to markets outside the test area can be a serious problem. Spill-out is generally undesirable for a number of reasons. Consumers who live outside the test market might hear or see advertising for a product but be unable to buy it because it does not yet have national distribution. These consumers could become irritated at their inability to buy the advertised brand and might not respond to later advertising because of their annoyance at being unable to find the brand on store shelves during the testing period.

A marketer can attempt to avoid the problem by distributing the brand in the broader spill-out area, but this in turn could cause another problem: Will the supply of the brand be adequate? At times, only a limited amount of a brand is available for testing purposes, perhaps just enough for the test, but not for spill-out.

There is another way to get around the problem of poor distribution in spill-out areas: Print and broadcast advertisements can specifically tell consumers where to purchase the brand. This approach averts the animosity that could occur when there is no distribution in a spill-out area.

The reverse problem of spill-out is spill-in, which occurs when media originating in another market spill into the test market. The more that people in the test market are exposed to media from another market, the greater is the variation in the reach and frequency pattern from the pattern ordinarily expected.

Although spill-in and spill-out should still be considered, the growth of cable TV and satellite penetration to over 80 percent has reduced this problem. Viewers no longer need to tune to stations in adjacent markets in order to see popular programs that may not be available from local stations. Also, a test can minimize the effects of spill-in and spill-out by concentrating on local news programs that typically draw few viewers in neighboring markets. However, the need to minimize spill-out must be balanced against the need to faithfully duplicate a multi-daypart test.

Media Costs   When a market becomes known as a good test area, the local media sometimes raise their advertising rates to take advantage of their popularity. Some experts think that persons responsible for the media portion of testing should not worry about higher media costs in certain markets, because other considerations (spill-in, spill-out, quality, availability, etc.) are more important.

In translating a national media plan to a test market, the objective should not be to translate costs downward from a national plan, but to translate the delivery (e.g., reach and frequency) into the test market, regardless of the cost. If a test market cannot generate the necessary levels of reach and frequency, then some other market should be selected.

Test Area Coverage   When test markets are being selected for media planning, enough DMAs should be used to cover at least 95 percent of the sales district, territory, etc., that is being used for the test. This assumes that the test is being made to correspond to a specific company's sales area. At times, this correspondence is not necessary, depending on what the client wants to learn from the test.

Planners must be careful in identifying the DMAs needed to cover Nielsen's Scantrack or IRI's InfoScan markets since these areas do not clearly match DMA boundaries.

Network Delivery   Another consideration for test market selection, especially when the test is supposed to represent the entire United States, is that the daypart usage in the test market should closely match the planned national daypart usage of television or radio.

Cable Penetration   Penetration of cable and alternate delivery systems (satellites, etc.) should be comparable to the total United States, that is, about 80 to 85 percent.

Number of Markets   As discussed previously, the number of markets used in testing should be more than two or three. Despite consensus that as many as five, six, or more are desirable, often only one is used. When testing uses a single market, that one is assumed to be a Little U.S.A. market (to be discussed in the next section). Dangers of projecting from one market are well recognized.

Types of Markets   Some advertisers find it advantageous to test in large markets such as New York, Los Angeles, or Chicago. This preference assumes that these markets are more representative of the United States than smaller markets. A marketer might also try a test in an entire geographic region, such as the West

Coast, where a number of various-sized population centers exist. The regional approach could be much easier to use than a single isolated market, because the planner can more easily simulate the national media plan in the area. Regional editions of national magazines may be available, whereas there may be no local editions of a national magazine for a single market. The regional test would be less likely to be affected by local strikes, bad weather, or high competitive reactions to the test. Sometimes network buys in a region such as the West Coast are relatively inexpensive and flexible, but regional network buys are difficult to find, if available at all, especially with the advent of satellite-delivered network programs to affiliates.

Other reasons why regional test markets are preferred to individual and isolated markets are that it is easier to obtain distribution in a region, as well as easier to compare market data with media coverage. Finally, in auditing sales, it is easier and less costly to audit sales in large regions than in isolated markets.

On the other hand, there are three good reasons for not using regional tests. First, the cost might be prohibitive. Second, there could be a large amount of wasted media impressions because not everyone in the region is being tested. Finally, a regional test is not really a laboratory or sample test, but a small-scale introduction. The testing procedure does not eliminate the risks of large-scale failure if the product is not well accepted.

Sometimes media considerations are not an important part of test marketing. As one media planner noted, "Our client was interested only in finding out if he could sell the product to the trade. In this instance, the actual media schedules were not important."[5]

MEDIA TRANSLATIONS

As defined earlier, media translation is a process of simulating the effects of expensive national media plans in relatively inexpensive local test markets. This is an adjustment technique, and there are several ways to make such adjustments. Each technique is based on a different philosophy of operations.

---

5. B. G. Yavovich, "Quality of Local Markets Can Be a Determining Factor," *Advertising Age* (February 4, 1980): S-2.

Little U.S.A. Versus "As It Falls" Philosophy

There are at least two philosophies regarding media translations in test marketing: the Little U.S.A. concept and the As It Falls concept. The most commonly used is the Little U.S.A. concept, which is based on the idea that some test markets are so much like the country as a whole that these markets can easily be projected to the national market. Suppose a media plan calls for one prime-time network :30 per week with an 8 national rating. The test-market translation would be an 8 rating on some local program or a number of spot commercials with 8 gross rating points in that market, regardless of the local rating for that network vehicle in the test market. Another way to use the Little U.S.A. concept would be to translate it in direct proportion to the weight that would be delivered on a national basis. The measurement could be the average number of impressions to be delivered per household nationally, translated to a proportion the local market should have received.

In the As It Falls concept, the local market receives the exact media weight it would get from the national plan. Using the same example as before, with a prime-time network program rated 8, the planner might find that this program delivers a higher or lower rating in the test market, because national media deliver varying levels of advertising weight from market to market. If the prime-time program happens to deliver a 6 rating in the chosen test market, then 6 GRPs should be purchased in the test market.

The choice between Little U.S.A. and As It Falls generally depends on how representative the test area is relative to the national plan. If the As It Falls translation method would result in delivering an abnormally high (or low) level of media weight, some adjustment toward the Little U.S.A. is desirable.

Exhibit 14-4 shows how a Little U.S.A. media translation would be made. The example is based on a national media plan in which network and spot television and national magazines would be the only media. The spot television plan covers markets that include 60 percent of U.S. households. To make a Little U.S.A. translation, average delivery is scheduled in local test markets as shown in Exhibit 14-4.

Using the same data, the As It Falls translation first requires the planner to determine how many GRPs would go into individual markets. Whereas the Little U.S.A. technique used the average delivery, this technique requires much

EXHIBIT 14-4

National Media Plan: Little U.S.A. Method

MEDIA USED	SPOT MARKETS (WOMEN GRPs)	TOTAL U.S. (WOMEN GRPs)	TEST-MARKET TRANSLATION (WOMEN GRPs)
Network TV		400	400
Magazines		100	100
Spot TV (60% of U.S. covered)			
Average spot*	100	60†	60 (national average)
Total		560	560

*A markets received 150 GRPs, B markets 100 GRPs, and C markets 50 GRPs, but the average for all markets is 100.

†Average calculations are as follows: 100 GRPs in 60% of U.S. = 60

                                                        0 GRPs in 40% of U.S. =   0

                                      Weighted average = 60

EXHIBIT 14-5

National Media Plan: As It Falls Method

MEDIA USED	SPOT MARKETS (WOMEN GRPs)	TOTAL U.S. (WOMEN GRPs)	TEST-MARKET TRANSLATION (WOMEN GRPs)
Network TV		400	380
Magazines		100	120
Spot TV (60% of U.S. covered)			
Average spot*	100	100	
A markets	150		
B markets	100		
C markets*	50		50
Total		600	550

*The GRPs of C markets were used because test markets were C markets in character.

more detailed planning and estimation of local delivery. In making this translation, it might not be possible to buy GRPs precisely as planned, so some media get more and others less than the national plan, as shown in Exhibit 14-5.

Under the As It Falls approach, only 380 GRPs were purchased in network TV while 120 GRPs were purchased in magazines in the test market. The reason is that this combination of national media delivers the desired levels of GRPs in the test market. Although the difference between the two translation techniques might seem insignificant, it is the difference between average and actual plan delivery in the test market.

Translations in Radio and Television

There are a number of ways to execute the translation of a national media plan into local radio and television. One way is the *cut-in,* in which the broadcaster inserts a local commercial in a network or syndicated program in place of some other commercial originally scheduled in a market for the same advertiser. This is possible when the client already has purchased a commercial on a network and simply replaces it with the test-market commercial by cutting in only in the test market. The rest of the country would see the national commercial. A cut-in is considered an excellent way to translate for broadcast media because it keeps the program environments the same as in the national plan, and it provides the exact national weight in a local market.

Cut-ins do have drawbacks, however. Local stations charge high fees for mechanically inserting substitute commercials. Also, national advertising for some other product might suffer if it is replaced with the cut-in. Finally, cutting over cable telecasts is problematic because many systems serve a given market. Each system would have to execute the cut-in.

If a cut-in is not feasible, then the planner will have to substitute local announcements for the network commercials. This could be a problem, because the spot announcement times chosen must provide the same kind of target audience and the same audience sizes that the network program in that market would provide. With spot television, the only times available at a reasonable cost might be fringe times. Although fringe time spots produce lower ratings than prime-time network programs, planners might add GRPs to those of the theoretical plan level as a form of compensation. When a prime-time spot is used (instead of a prime-time network program), the additional GRP compensation might be less than the amount of compensation used with fringe spot. Each advertiser relies on research experience to determine the degree of additional spot weight over the theoretical plan level. There is no single set of industry standards that applies to such translation methods. However, any decisions about compensation should consider two factors: compensation for loss of reach and compensation for loss of program environment. Presumably, any spots used will aim for a selected target audience.

Compensations will vary among markets, depending on the relationship of audience sizes between prime time and fringe times. In fact, daytime spots can be used in lieu of daytime network programs without any compensation, because they can be purchased either within or next to the kinds of network programs used in the national media plan.

When a national media plan calls for spot television, no compensation is necessary. Spots are simply scheduled in the same number, same number of gross rating points, length, placement, reach, and frequency called for in the national plan.

In translating network radio, the method is identical to that used for translating daytime network television. For spot radio, the translation method would be identical to spot television.

Translations in Print

Translation of newspapers is direct and simple, because the national media plan spells out all details for local markets. Magazines might or might not require special translations. If there are regional, metropolitan, or special test-market editions of a magazine, then making a translation is simple. But if a national magazine has none of these editions, three alternatives exist for translation:

1. Using Sunday supplements adjusted to deliver the same number of impressions in a local market that a national magazine would have delivered
2. Using local magazines that are similar to those in the national plan, and adjusting differences through compensation
3. Using ROP color in newspapers with some kind of compensation

EXHIBIT 14-6

Translation of National Magazine Impressions to Sunday Supplements

Problem: How many Sunday supplement ads are needed to deliver the same number of national magazine impressions that would be delivered by a national magazine in test market X?

Solution: 1. Find the number of target audience members of a national magazine delivered into test market X (either from published data or by estimate). Suppose the magazine delivers 100,000 readers in market X.

2. Assume that the national media plan called for six national ads in that market for a year. Find the total number of impressions in market X: 100,000 impressions × 6 ads = 600,000.

3. Find the number of target audience members delivered by one ad in a Sunday supplement in market X. Assume it would be 75,000 readers.

4. Calculate the number of Sunday supplement ads that would be needed to deliver 600,000 target impressions: 600,000 ÷ 75,000 = 8 ads.

5. If the media planner judges that supplements have a lower "value" than magazines, the number of insertions needed in the test market can be increased to compensate (e.g., scheduling 9 or 10 insertions in supplements, rather than 8).

The third alternative might be the poorest choice, because the reproduction of ROP color in newspaper advertisements is not the same as color printed in most national magazines. But it would be possible to make some kind of compensation for the differences if that were the only viable alternative.

The use of Sunday supplements in lieu of national magazines is relatively easy to translate. An example of how this could be done appears in Exhibit 14-6. If the data on target audience delivery are not known in any given market, the planner could arrive at an estimate by working from known data. Usually the publisher can provide the number of copies delivered into Market X, as well as the national number of readers per copy of the magazine. The circulation times the number of readers per copy gives the number of readers in Market X. However, the amount would be total audience readers, not target audience members. The same type of calculation would estimate readers of Sunday supplements or similar magazines, and a translation then could be worked out.

If a national media plan calls for Sunday supplements in a select group of test markets, then translation is easily done by using the local supplement or test insertions in the nationally syndicated supplements. On the other hand, if there is no Sunday supplement in a given market, then the planner could buy ROP color ads in the local newspaper. The latter situation would require some form of compensation. In some markets, syndicated national supplements make test-market breakouts available.

In summary, whenever a direct translation is possible, it is preferable to simulating a national medium in a local market. Almost any simulation will require some kind of compensation, which at times must be based on arbitrary rather than empirical means.

Glossary

A Counties As defined by Nielsen Media Research, all counties belonging to the 25 largest Metropolitan Statistical Areas (MSAs). These MSAs include the largest cities and consolidated areas in the United States.

ABC See *Audit Bureau of Circulations.*

Accumulation A method of counting audiences wherein each person exposed to a vehicle is counted once, either in a given time period such as four weeks for broadcast, or in one issue for print. (See also *Reach.*)

ADI (Area of Dominant Influence) Obsolete—a television market coverage area as defined by the Arbitron Company until 1992 when it stopped producing television ratings. Since then, Nielsen Media Research has been the only company producing local market television ratings. Its comparable area is the Designated Market Area (DMA).

Adjacencies The specific time periods, usually two minutes long, that precede and follow regular television programming. These are commercial break positions available for local or spot advertisers. There is no such thing as a network adjacency; only spot adjacencies are available.

Adnorm A term used by Daniel Starch & Associates to indicate readership averages by publication, by space size and color, and by type of product for ads studied by Starch in a two-year period. It is used to provide a standard of comparison for individual ads against averages of similar types of ads.

Advertising Allowance Money paid under contract by a manufacturer or its representative to a wholesaler or a retailer for spending to advertise a specified product, brand, or line of the manufacturer. Usually used for consumer advertising.

Advertising Appropriation A company's estimated dollar figure for an advertising effort of a short-term flight, seasonal campaign, and/or total marketing year. Usually refers to the combined budget for working media, production, promotion, and reserve and is based on projected business volume.

Advertising Checking Bureau (ACB) A service organization that supplies advertisers and agencies with tearsheets of advertisements run in publications and with other information used by clients to assess the impact of their advertising and competitors' advertising.

Advertising Impression One person or home exposed to a single advertisement; on a gross basis, the sum of all impressions to the ads in a schedule. This includes duplication, for some of those exposed may have been exposed more than once. In some instances, advertising impression refers to persons or homes exposed to a media vehicle (magazine, television show, etc.); the result of multiplying the audience of each vehicle (on a household or person basis) by the number of advertisements or commercials carried by each vehicle and obtaining the total. In other cases, it refers to the number of persons or homes exposed to an advertisement or commercial within the carrier. In these cases, data on ad/commercial exposure are applied to the carrier audiences.

Advertising Weight A general term for the amount of advertising planned for, or used by, a brand. Although it is not limited to a particular measurement, it is most frequently stated in terms of the number of gross rating points or gross impressions delivered or the number of broadcasts or insertions placed over a period of time.

Affidavit of Performance A notarized statement from a television or radio station that verifies that a media schedule ran as ordered.

Afternoon Drive Radio daypart between 3:00 P.M. and 7:00 P.M.

Agency Commission A commission that an advertising agency receives for media it has placed. Traditionally, this is received as a 15 percent discount on the cost of ad space or time that is offered by the media to recognized advertising agencies. However, this form of agency compensation is being reevaluated by many in the industry, and some are now billing clients on a straight-fee basis, assigning a set fee to each agency function.

Agency of Record An agency that purchases media time or space for another agency or a group of agencies serving the same client.

Aided Recall A measurement technique in which an interviewer provides clues to help respondents remember portions or all of ads. (See *Unaided Recall.*)

Alternate Week Sponsor An advertiser who purchases full or participating sponsorship every other week of a network program for a full 52-week broadcast year. Each sponsor purchasing at least two minutes in a given program episode will receive billboard commercial time on its week of sponsorship.

Announcement A commercial message between or within programs. Announcements may be live, or recorded, or a combination of both. Common lengths in television are 60, 30, 20, 15, and 10 seconds.

Annual Discount A discount given to an advertiser by a media carrier based on the number of advertising insertions or units run during an established contract year.

Arbitron A radio rating service that measures the listening audience to local radio stations and national networks (see *RADAR*).

As It Falls Concept In test marketing, a translation method that executes a national media plan exactly as it would appear in the local test market. This method accurately reflects the market-to-market differences that would occur in an actual buy, but may complicate interpretation of the results if network delivery in a given test market is abnormally above or below average.

Associated Business Publications A trade association of business (industrial, trade, and technical) publications. (See www.abpi.net.)

Audience The number of people or households exposed to a medium. Exposure measurements indicate nothing about whether audiences saw, heard, or read either the advertisements or editorial contents of the medium.

Audience Composition The demographic makeup of people represented in the audience to a media vehicle with respect to income group, age, sex, geography, etc. Percent of a vehicle's audience.

Audience Duplication In broadcast, a measurement of the number of listeners or viewers reached by one program or station that is also reached by another program or station. In print, the measurement of the overlap of potential exposure between different issues of the same magazine or among issues of different magazines.

Audience Flow A measure of changes in audience between broadcast programs. May be reported on a minute-by-minute basis, by five-minute intervals, or from show to show.

Audience Holding Index A measurement of the retentive power or audience loyalty of a given program. Nielsen Media Research, for 30-minute programs, uses an index based on the percentage of homes tuned to the same program 25 minutes after the first measurement. It is a simple measure of the ratio of average audience rating to total audience rating of a given program. Also called *audience turnover*.

Audience, Potential In broadcasting, the number of sets in use in the time period to be studied, or the number of set owners. In print, the total audience of an issue.

Audience, Primary In print, all readers who live in households where someone subscribes to or purchases the magazine. May be called *primary readership*.

Audience Profile The characteristics of the people who make up the audience of a magazine, TV show, newspaper, radio show, etc., in terms of age, family size, location, education, income, and other factors.

Audience, Secondary Pass-along readers who read a publication they did not purchase. These readers should be taken into account in determining the total number of readers of a particular publication.

Audience Turnover See *Audience Holding Index*.

Audilog The diary that members of Nielsen's local rating panels fill out to show what they are viewing on television. It is the basis for demographic information about local television viewing in all 210 DMAs.

Audimeter An electronic device, developed by Nielsen Media Research, that records set usage and tuning on a minute-by-minute basis. This passive TV set information is integrated with demographic information from Audilog to provide local market ratings in 53 "meter" markets. Ratings in the remaining 157 DMAs are based on the Audilog diary alone.

Audit Bureau of Circulations (ABC) A tripartite, nonprofit, self-regulatory organization of advertisers, agencies, and magazine and newspaper publishers, which verifies the circulation figures of publishers and members and reports these data to advertiser and agency members.

Availability A specific period of broadcast commercial time offered for sale by a station or network for sponsorship.

Average Audience (AA) In broadcasting, the number of homes/persons tuned in to a TV program for an average minute (a Nielsen network TV measurement). In print, the number of persons who read or looked into an average issue of a publication.

Average Frequency The number of times the average home (or person) reached by a media schedule is exposed to the advertising. This is measured over a specific period of time, for example, four weeks in broadcast media.

Average Net Paid Average circulation per issue. To calculate, divide the total paid circulation for all the issues of the audit period by the total number of issues.

B Counties As defined by Nielsen Media Research, all counties that are not A Counties and are either over 150,000 population or in a metro area over 150,000 population according to the latest census.

Back of Book The section of a magazine following the main editorial section.

Back-to-Back Scheduling Two or more commercials run one immediately following the other.

Banner Advertising A unit of advertising space that runs above a number of columns of advertising or editorial material.

BAR (Broadcast Advertiser's Reports) An organization that monitored network and spot TV competitive activity. BAR has been replaced by MediaWatch™, a service of CMR.

Barter Acquisition by an advertiser of sizable quantities of spot time or free mentions at rates lower than card rates from broadcast stations in exchange for operating capital or merchandise. Although direct negotiation between the advertiser and station is possible, it is more common for barter to be arranged through a middleman, a barter agency, or a film producer or distributor, who may have procured the time through an exchange of film or taped shows.

Base A demographic group, such as total women or men aged 35–49.

Base Rate See *Open Rate*.

BehaviorScan A test market service of Information Resources, Inc., for measuring product and brand purchased through use of Universal Product Code at checkout counters.

Billboard (a) An identifying announcement of sponsorship at the beginning, end, or breaks of radio and television sponsored programs. Billboards are not sold, but usually are a bonus, based on the advertiser's volume or commitment with the program or the broadcaster. Usually 5 to 10 seconds in length. (b) An outdoor poster.

Billing (a) A charge made to an advertiser by an advertising agency, based on the listed or gross charges of the media from which space or time has been purchased, along with any other charges and fees incurred by the agency that are passed on to the advertiser. (b) Loosely, the money spent by an advertiser through an agency. (c) The actual charge made by a medium of communication to an advertising agency; the gross charge less the agency discount.

Blanket Coverage Total coverage by television and radio of a given geographic area.

Bleed An advertisement in which part or all of the illustration or copy runs past the usual margins out to the edge of a page. Bleed insertions are generally sold at a premium price, usually 15 percent over the basic rate.

Bonus Circulation Circulation delivered by a publication beyond the circulation on which an advertiser's rate is based.

Brand Development Index (BDI) The number of cases, units, or dollar volume of a brand sold per 1,000 population. To calculate BDI, divide the percentage of sales in a market by the population percentage in the same market.

Broadcast Calendar A calendar that is used for accounting purposes in the radio and TV industry and that contains months of four or five whole weeks, ending on the last Sunday of each month. Each quarter in the broadcast calendar contains 13 weeks.

Bulk Circulation Sales in quantity lots of an issue of a magazine or newspaper. The purchases are made by individuals or concerns, and the copies are usually directed to lists of names supplied by the purchasers. In the ABC report, bulk circulation is listed separately from single-copy sales.

Bulk Sales Sales of copies of a publication in quantity to one purchaser for the purchaser to give to others free. Many advertisers do not consider bulk sales to be a valuable part of a publication's circulation.

Business Building Test A test run by a specific brand and designed to determine whether a change in a marketing or advertising plan will produce enough additional business for the brand to pay the required costs of the change.

Business Paper A publication directed to a particular industry, trade, profession, or vocation. A horizontal business paper is designed to reach all groups in a broad trade or industry, regardless of location or occupational title. A vertical publication is for a specific profession, trade, or occupational level within or across various industries.

Business Press Audit (BPA) A company that verifies the circulation of free circulation magazines and newspapers—primarily industrial trade publications—that are delivered at no cost to readers.

Buyout A one-time payment to television or radio talent for all rights to performance.

C Counties As defined by Nielsen Media Research, all counties that are not A or B Counties and that either have over 40,000 population or are in a metropolitan area of over 40,000 population according to the latest census.

Cable TV A system of broadcasting television whereby programs are first tuned in by a community antenna and then distributed to individual homes by cables. Cable operators often receive programs transmitted by satellites and then transmit by cable to their subscribers.

Cancellation Date The last date on which it is possible to cancel advertising. Such dates occur for print, outdoor, and broadcasting.

Card Rate The cost of time and space quoted on a rate card.

Case Allowance An allowance or discount a manufacturer or wholesaler gives to a retailer on each case of product purchased, in return for which the retailer is to use the money to advertise the product.

Cash Discount A deduction allowed by print media (usually 2 percent of the net) for prompt payment (e.g., within 15 to 30 days), generally passed along by the agency to the advertiser to encourage collections.

Cash Refund Offer A type of mail-in offer, used by a brand or group of brands, that offers cash to the consumer upon providing proof of purchase.

Category Development Index (CDI) A Market Development Index. Essentially, a market's percent of total U.S. sales of a product category divided by the population percent in that market.

Center Spread An advertisement appearing on the two facing pages in the center of a publication.

Chain Break (a) The time between network programs during which a station identifies itself. (b) A commercial appearing in a chain break.

Checking Copy A copy of a publication sent to an advertiser and agency as proof that the advertisement appeared as ordered.

Circulation (a) In print, the number of copies of a vehicle distributed, based on an average of a number of issues. (b) In broadcast, the number of television or radio households that tune in to a station a minimum number of times within a specified time period (such as once a week or once a day). (c) In outdoor, the total number of people who have an opportunity to see a given showing of billboards within a specified time, such as a 24-hour period.

City Zone A geographic area that includes the corporate limits of the central city of the market plus any contiguous areas that have substantially the same built-up characteristics of the central city. This provides a method of reporting newspaper circulation according to the Audit Bureau of Circulations' standards.

Class A, B, C Rates Rates for television time, categorized by desirability of the time period. Class A rates are charged for the most desirable and costly television time, usually between

6 P.M. and 11 P.M. The next most costly level of rates is Class B; Class C is still less costly (and desirable). Each station sets its own time classifications. This system is seldom used today.

Class Magazine A publication that reaches select high-income readers, in contrast to magazines with larger circulations, generally referred to as *mass magazines.*

Clear Time Process used by an advertiser to reserve a time period with a local station and by a network to check with its affiliates on the availability of a time period.

Clearance Obtaining a time period for a program or commercial on a station or obtaining approval to use advertising from clients, legal and/or medical counsel, or network continuity departments.

Clipping Bureau An organization that examines newspapers and magazines and clips articles from them. It sends clients articles with references and allusions of interest to them.

Closing Date The final date to commit contractually for the purchase of advertising space, also called the *space closing date.* Generally, cancellations are not accepted after the closing date, although some publications have a separate cancellation date, which may fall earlier than this date. The *materials closing date* is the last date advertisers can supply production material to the publication.

Clutter Excessive amounts of advertising or nonprogram/editorial material carried by media vehicles, both print and broadcast. The amount may be excessive both in terms of the total amount of advertising time and space and in terms of its scheduling—long strings of consecutive commercials for broadcasting and solid banks of advertisements in print.

Column Inch A measurement of newspaper space that is one column wide and one inch deep. The standard unit of measurement for newspaper pricing.

Combination Rate A discounted rate offered to encourage use of two or more stations, newspapers, magazines, etc., having common ownership. Occasionally, an advertiser has no choice but to buy the combination, as space or time may not be sold separately.

Commercial Audience The audience for a specific commercial as determined by a survey that elicits information about what program viewers were watching just before, during, and after the commercial. The commercial audience is operationally defined as those people who were physically present in the room with the TV set at the time the commercial was on.

Commercial Break In broadcasting, an interruption of programming during which commercials are broadcast.

Commercial Delivery The part of the audience that is actually exposed to a particular commercial.

Commercial Pool The selection of television or radio commercials that an advertiser has available for airing at any one time.

Commercial Protection The amount of time that a network or station provides between the scheduling of competitive commercials.

Commission Compensation to a salesperson, agency, etc., as a percent of the person's or agency's sales.

Competitive Parity Method A method of establishing a marketing or media budget based on matching anticipated competitive expenditures.

Composition The percent of a media vehicle's audience that is within an advertiser's target. For example, if 10 million women read Magazine A and 5 million of them are aged 18–34, then the composition is 50 percent. This contrasts with *coverage*, which is the percent of the target exposed to the vehicle. In this example, since there are 30.6 million women aged 18–34 living in the United States, Magazine A's coverage is 16.3 percent (5/30.6).

Concentration Campaign An advertising campaign that uses a small number of media vehicles to carry a relatively heavy amount of advertising.

Confirmation Broadcast media statement that a requested time slot is available to a prospective client.

Consecutive Weeks Discount A discount granted to an advertiser who uses a minimum number of weeks of advertising on a station or network without interruption.

Consumer Magazine A magazine whose editorial content appeals to the general public, or a specific segment or layer of the public. The term is used to differentiate these magazines from trade or business magazines.

Continuity A method of scheduling advertising so that audiences have an opportunity to see ads at regular intervals. Many patterns are possible, from advertising once each day of the year to once a month.

Controlled-Circulation Publications Publications that confine or restrict their distribution to special groups on a free basis. Some controlled circulation is solicited, although most is nonsolicited.

Cooperative Advertising Advertising run by a local advertiser in conjunction with a national advertiser. The national advertiser usually provides the copy and/or printing material and also shares the cost with the local retailer. In return, the national advertiser receives local promotion for its product. The name of the local advertiser and its address appear in the ad.

Co-Sponsorship The participation of two or more sponsors in a single broadcast program where each advertiser pays a proportionate share of the cost.

Cost-Efficiency The effectiveness of media as measured by a comparison of audience, either potential or actual, with cost and expressed as a cost per thousand (CPM).

Cost per Rating Point (CPP) In broadcast, the cost of one household or demographic rating point in a given market. Used in media planning and evaluation, it is calculated by dividing the cost per spot by the rating. In the case of a number of spots, the CPP is their total cost divided by the total ratings or gross rating points.

Cost per Thousand (CPM)   The cost to deliver 1,000 people or homes. Used in comparing or evaluating the cost-efficiency of media vehicles, it is calculated by dividing the cost by the audience delivery, then multiplying the quotient by 1,000.

Cost Ratio   An adjustment, in magazine readership analysis by Daniel Starch & Associates, made to the score obtained on each readership measure. Based on the magazine's reported primary circulation and the cost of the ad in terms of size, color, etc., Starch translates the score into per-dollar terms, then states it as a percentage of the average per-dollar scores of all ads studied in the same issue. (See *Noted; Starch Method.*)

Counterprogramming   A technique used by networks to regulate audience flow by offering a program of a different type from that broadcast by a strong competitor in the same time period.

Coverage   A definition of a medium's geographical potential. In newspapers, coverage is the number of copies of a paper divided by the number of households in a given area. In magazines, it is the percentage of a given demographic market reached by a magazine. In radio and television, it is the percentage of television households that can tune in to a station (or stations) because they are in the signal area. In outdoor, coverage is the percentage of adults who pass a given showing and are exposed in a 30-day period. In previous years, coverage meant the same as reach. Today, the meaning depends on which medium is being discussed.

Cover Positions   Premium-priced cover space for magazine or business publication advertisements. Cover positions are numbered: 1st cover is the outside front cover; 2nd cover is the inside front cover; 3rd cover is the inside back cover; 4th cover is the outside back cover. The first cover of consumer publications is seldom used for advertising.

Cume   A broadcast term that is Nielsen's shorthand for net cumulative audience of a program or of a spot schedule (radio or TV) in four weeks' time. The figure is based on total number of unduplicated TV homes or people reached.

Cumulative Audience   The net unduplicated audience of a campaign, either in one medium or in a combination of media. Sometimes called *reach* or *cume.*

Cut-In   Different broadcast copy or format that is used to replace an originating commercial in a network program in a specific market or region. Frequently used in test markets.

Cycle   (a) An interval within a contract year at the end of which, upon proper notice, an advertiser may cancel network stations and/or facilities. Weekly and multiweekly program cycles usually last 13 weeks, while cosponsored program cycles usually encompass 13 major broadcasts. (b) A 13-week period used as a base for paying talent and use fees.

D Counties   Essentially rural counties in the Nielsen Media Research classification system of A, B, C, D counties.

Daily Rate   The rate a newspaper charges for space in its weekday editions, as opposed to the rate for the Sunday or weekend editions.

Day-After Recall Probably the most common method used to test television commercials. Test commercials are shown on the air in the normal fashion. Approximately 24 hours later, interviewers telephone people and ask about their previous day's viewing. Only those who viewed the program carrying the test commercial are questioned further. The test score consists of the proportion of the commercial audience who are able to provide specific correct audio or video details from the test commercial (See *Commercial Audience*.)

Daypart A part of the broadcast day, so designated for analytical purposes. In TV, the dayparts are usually daytime (morning and afternoon), early fringe, prime time, and late fringe. In radio, they are morning drive, daytime, afternoon drive, and evening.

Demographic Characteristics Physical characteristics, such as sex, age, education, occupation, used to describe a population. Standard definitions, established by the 4As (American Association of Advertising Agencies), are used by many research companies.

Demographic Edition An edition of a national publication circulated only to individuals with known demographic characteristics. Usually these editions differ from the national edition only in their advertisements.

Designated Market Area (DMA) Nonoverlapping TV market coverage as defined by Nielsen Media Research. Generally speaking, a DMA consists of all the counties that spend the plurality of viewing hours tuned to the TV stations in a given market.

Diary Method A research technique in which a sample of respondents record in diaries specific behavior within a given period of time. This method is commonly used to measure the consumption of both media and products.

Differential (Newspaper) The difference in newspaper rates charged to local and national advertisers. Most newspapers charge higher rates to national advertisers than to retailers with a local street address.

Discount A reduction from regular rates when an advertiser contracts to use quantities of advertising. Discounts in print may consider amount of space bought and frequency of insertion. Discounts in network broadcasting may be based upon number of dayparts used, frequency or weight, and length of contract. In local broadcasting, discounts will consider number of spots per week, length of contract, or purchase of plans or packages.

Drive Time The times of day (both morning and afternoon) when most people drive to or from work (about 6 to 10 A.M. and 3 to 7 P.M.).

Duplication (a) The number or percentage of people in one vehicle's audience who also are exposed to another vehicle. (b) Audiences who are counted more than once in measurements, such as those who view the same TV program more than once a month (also called *audience duplication*).

Earned Rate The rate that an advertiser has earned, based on volume or frequency of space or time used to obtain a discount.

Effective Frequency   The amount of frequency (or repetition) the planner judges to be necessary for advertisements to be effective in communicating.

Effective Reach   The percent of the target audience exposed at the frequency level that is effective in the planner's judgment.

Eight-Sheet Poster   See *Junior Panel.*

Exclusivity   Freedom from competing advertising that one advertiser enjoys within a given communications medium; requires major purchases of space or time.

Expansion Plan   An outline of the media to be used and timing thereof for a brand that plans to apply a theoretical national plan to portions of the country after testing and before actual national application. The expansion areas are the geographical units in which the product is to be sold.

Exposure   Open eyes facing a medium. Practically, measurements are based on respondents who either say with assurance that they have read or looked into a given magazine during the most recent publication period (day, week, month, etc.). In broadcast, the measurement counts those who classify themselves as "watching" a television program or "listening" to a radio station, either by pushing a button on a people meter or by reporting exposure in a diary.

Exposure, Depth of   The value credited to an increased number of broadcast commercials or multipage spreads in the form of heightened consciousness of an advertisement. While the audience for such media usage generally does not increase proportionally with the amount of additional investment, the depth of exposure tends to provide adequate compensation.

Exposure, Opportunity of   The degree to which an audience may reasonably be expected to see or hear an advertising message.

Fifteen and Two   The financial terms on which advertising media are ordered by advertising agencies for their clients. Shorthand for saying a 15 percent commission is allowed by the media on the gross cost, with a 2 percent discount on the net amount for prompt payment.

Fifty-Fifty Plan   In cooperative advertising, the equal sharing by a manufacturer and a dealer of the cost of a manufacturer's advertisement appearing over a dealer's name.

Fixed Position   A specific period of station broadcasting time reserved for an advertiser and sold at a premium rate.

Fixed Rate   Station's price for a time slot that guarantees the advertiser's announcement will run in that position without preemption. Seldom used today—advertisers assume their announcements will run as ordered for the price they agreed to pay.

Flat Rate   An advertisement rate that does not include any discounts.

Flighting   A method of scheduling advertising for a period of time, followed by a hiatus period of no advertising, followed by a resumption of advertising.

Flowchart A system-analysis tool, either computerized or manual, that provides a graphical presentation of a procedure. In media plans, a flowchart is typically a one-year calendar, delineated by weeks and months, which shows all planned media activity. This includes publication dates, ad sizes, TV dayparts, weekly GRP levels, reach/frequency, budget, and any other information that might be needed by an advertiser.

Food & Drug Index A service of A. C. Nielsen that uses store audits to collect data on retail sales movement.

Forced Combination Morning and evening newspapers owned by the same publisher and sold to national advertisers only in combination. Some forced combinations are morning and evening editions of the same newspapers.

Four-Color Process A halftone printing process that uses the colors magenta (red), cyan (blue), yellow, and black. This is the standard process used for color magazine ads.

Fourth Cover The outside back cover of a magazine.

Fractional Showing In outdoor, a showing of less than 25, offered in certain areas.

Franchise Position A specified position in a publication (e.g., back cover, inside front cover) that an advertiser has the right of first refusal to continue using as long as needed. If the advertiser does not use a given position one year, the right usually must be renegotiated for the advertiser to regain it.

Free Publication A publication sent without cost to a selected list of readers. Its circulation may or may not be audited by BPA or VAC, and the publication cannot qualify for ABC audit unless at least 70 percent of circulation is paid.

Frequency The average number of times an audience member is exposed to a commercial. Usually referred to as *average frequency*.

Frequency Discount A discount given for running a certain number of insertions, irrespective of size of advertisement, within a contract year. In broadcasting, similar discounts may be of two types: frequency per week and total number of announcements in a contract year.

Frequency Distribution An array of reach according to the level of frequency delivered to each group.

Frequency-of-Reading Technique The most commonly used method for determining the number of people who read a magazine. Respondents are asked to record the number of copies of each magazine they have read out of the last four issues—one out of four, two out of four, and so on.

Fringe Time Time periods preceding and following peak set-usage periods and adjacent network programming blocks. For television, usually classified as *early fringe* (4:00 to 7:30 P.M.) and *late fringe* (after 11 P.M. EST).

Full Position Preferred position for a newspaper advertisement, generally following and next to reading matter, or top of column next to reading matter. When specifically ordered, it costs more than a run-of-paper (ROP) position.

Full-Program Sponsorship A regular program sponsored by only one advertiser.

Full Showing In car card advertising, usually denotes one card in each car of a line in which space is bought. In New York subways, a full showing consists of two cards in each car; a half showing is two cards in every other car. In outdoor poster advertising, a full or 100-intensity showing indicates use of a specified number of panels in a particular market.

Gatefold A special space unit in magazines, usually consisting of one full page plus an additional page or part of page that is an extension of the outer edge of the original page and folds outward from the center of the magazine as a gate.

General Editorial Magazine A consumer magazine not classified as to specific audience.

Geographic Market Weighting The practice of giving extra consideration to one or more markets that have more varying sales potential—because of location or demographics or other reasons—than other markets.

Geographic Split Run A split run where one ad is placed in all of the circulation that falls within a specified geographic area and another ad is placed in other geographic areas or the balance of the country.

Grade A and B Contours Areas in a television station's coverage pattern in which the transmission signal should have specific levels of strength according to Federal Communications Commission requirements. Grade A service is defined as providing a picture expected to be satisfactory to the median (average) observer at least 90 percent of the time in at least 70 percent of the receiving locations within the contour, in the absence of interfering co-channel and adjacent-channel signals. Grade B service is satisfactory at least 90 percent of the time in at least 50 percent of the receiving locations.

Grid Card A rate card in which a broadcast station's spots are priced individually, with charges related to the audience delivered. This is seldom used today.

Gross Audience The combined audience of a combination of media or a campaign in a single medium. For example, if Medium A and Medium B have audiences of 7 million and 6 million, respectively, their gross audience is 13 million. To go from gross audience to net audience, one must subtract all duplicated audiences. The same as *gross impressions*.

Gross Impressions The duplicated sum of audiences of all vehicles used in a media plan. This number represents the message weight of a media plan. The number is sometimes called the "tonnage" of the plan, because it is so large. (See *Gross Audience*.)

Gross Rate The published rate for space or time quoted by an advertising medium, including agency commission, cash discount, and any other discounts.

Gross Rating Point (GRP) A measure of the total gross weight delivered by a vehicle (or vehicles). It is the sum of the ratings for all of the individual announcements or programs. Also calculated as gross impressions divided by the population base times 100. Gross rating points are duplicated ratings. Also, reach × frequency = GRPs.

Guaranteed Circulation   The circulation level of a print vehicle; the basis for the advertising space rate. Similar to rate base circulation, except that an advertiser is assured of an adjustment if the circulation level is not achieved.

Half-Page Spread   An advertisement composed of two half-pages facing each other in a publication.

Half Run   (a) In transportation advertising, a car card placed in every other car of the transit system used; also called a *half service*. (b) For certain publications, advertising in half of the publication's circulation.

Half Showing   One half of a full showing of cards; a 50-intensity showing of outdoor posters or panels.

Hall's Magazine Reports (www.hallsreports.com)   A study of the number of editorial pages a magazine devotes to various categories of product interest over a period of time (e.g., the number of pages a magazine devotes to articles on food, home furnishings, fiction, news). This information is frequently used in analyzing the editorial content of a magazine before advertising is placed in it.

Hiatus   A period of time during which there is no advertising activity.

Holding Power   The degree to which a program retains its audience throughout a broadcast. This percentage equals the average audience divided by the total audience. (See *Audience Holding Index*; *Turnover*.)

Holdover Audience   The audience a program acquires from listeners or viewers who tuned to the preceding program on the station and remained with the station.

Home Service Magazine   A publication with editorial content keyed to the home and home living. Examples are *Better Homes & Gardens* and *House Beautiful*.

Horizontal Cume   The cumulative audience rating for two programs in the same time period on different days.

Horizontal Half Page   A half-page advertisement running horizontally across the page. (See *Vertical Half Page*.)

Horizontal Trade Publications   A business publication editorially designed to be of interest to a variety of businesses or business functions.

Households Using TV (HUT)   A term used by Nielsen Media Research that refers to the total number of TV households using their television sets during a given time period. Can be used for the total United States or a local market.

Hyping   Intense activity on the part of a broadcaster to increase rating during a rating survey.

ID   Any short-length "identification" commercial on radio or TV (e.g., a 10-second ID).

Impressions   See *Gross Impressions*.

Impression Studies   Studies of print ads and TV commercials conducted by Daniel Starch & Associates and called, respectively, *Starch Reader Impression Studies* and *Starch Viewer Im-*

pression Studies; studies that try to determine the actual meanings readers take away from an advertisement, hence, whether the ad's message is being effectively communicated.

Imprint In cooperative poster advertising programs, the local dealer's name, placed on the bottom portion of the poster design (about 20 percent of the total copy area) to identify that store as the place to buy the product advertised. Sometimes the local dealer pays a portion of the cost of the poster space, and the parent company pays the remaining portion.

Index The ratio of a percentage to a base as a way to show what is above average (101 or greater), average (100), or below average (99 or less).

Industrial Advertising Advertising of capital goods, supplies, and services directed mainly to industrial or professional firms that require them in the course of manufacturing.

Inherited Audience On a radio or television station, the carryover of a portion of one program's audience to the next program. (See *Holdover Audience*.)

In-Home Audience The portion of media exposure (reading, listening, or viewing) that occurs in the home.

Insertion Order Authorization from an advertiser or agency to a publisher to print an advertisement of specified size on a given date or dates at a definite rate. Copy instructions and printing materials may accompany the order or be sent later.

Instantaneous Rating The size of a broadcast audience at a given instant, expressed as a percentage of some base.

In-Store Media Print or broadcast ads that appear in stores. Print options include shopping cart, billboards, shelf talkers, and aisle posters. TV options include end-of-aisle monitors and shopping cart and checkout monitors.

Integrated Commercial A commercial that features more than one product or service in the form of a single commercial message.

Integration (or Origination or Networking) Charge An extra charge to an advertiser by a TV network for the integration of a commercial into a program and for the distribution of the commercial from origination and other points, including the preparation of prints for delayed broadcast. Technology has eliminated this manual process, but the charge continues.

Intensity In outdoor advertising, the strength of combinations of poster locations throughout a city in terms of coverage or repetition opportunities. A 100 showing has a 100 intensity. A 100 showing (therefore, a 100 intensity) varies from city to city.

Interim Statement Sworn circulation statement of a publisher made quarterly to the Audit Bureau of Circulations at the publisher's option and issued unaudited but subject to audit. A situation that might call for an interim statement would occur when a community served by more than one newspaper loses one of them through consolidation or discontinuance and its circulation is absorbed by the other newspaper. (See *Publisher's Statement*.)

Intermedia Comparison In the planning process, a comparison among different media—such as among TV, radio, and magazines.

Internet A network of computer networks, derived from the Defense Department system for scientific communication and considered by many to be the freest and most flexible form of communication that exists today. A complete glossary of Internet terms can be found at www.matisse.net/files/glossary.html. This site is operated by Matisse Enzer, an Internet consultant in San Francisco.

Intramedia Comparison In the planning process, comparisons among media vehicles in the same class, such as among three magazines.

Island Position A newspaper or magazine advertisement entirely surrounded by editorial matter or margin.

Isolated 30 A 30-second commercial surrounded only by programming.

Issue Life The time during which a publication accrues its total readership. For a weekly, this is generally five weeks; for a monthly, three months.

Junior Page In print, a page size that permits an advertiser to use the same printing materials for small- and large-page publications. The advertisement is prepared as a full-page unit in the smaller publication, and in the larger publication as a junior page with editorial around it.

Junior Panel A small-scale version of the 30-sheet poster. Also called an *eight-sheet poster*.

Junior Spread A print advertisement that appears on two facing pages and occupies only part of each page.

Keying an Advertisement Identification within an advertisement or coupon that permits inquiries or requests to be traced to a specific advertisement.

Keyline An assembly of all elements of a print ad pasted on a board. This camera-ready art is photographed to make the negative that in turn is used to make the printing plate. Also called a *mechanical*.

Lead-In (a) Words spoken by announcer or narrator at the beginning of some shows to perform a scene-setting or recapitulation function. (b) A broadcast program positioned before another program.

Lead-Out In relation to audience flow, the program following an advertiser's program on the same station.

Lifestyle Targeting A target audience classification system that categorizes people based on their activities, interests, and opinions.

Linage (a) A newspaper term denoting the number of (agate) lines in an ad or an ad schedule. (b) The amount of total space run by a publication in certain categories (e.g., retail grocery linage). Newspaper line rates have been replaced by column inch rates.

List Broker In direct-mail advertising, an agent who rents prospect lists from the advertiser that compiled the data, and sells those lists to another advertiser. The agent receives a commission for these services.

Listener Diary Method of TV or radio research whereby the audience keeps a continuing record of viewing or listening in a diary.

Listening Area The geographic area covered by a station's signal, usually divided into primary and secondary areas.

Little U.S.A. Concept In test marketing, a media plan translation method that executes a national media plan in a small market that has the same demographics and product usage habits as the entire country. Contrast with *As It Falls Concept.*

Live Time The time that the actual performance of a program is transmitted by interconnected facilities directly to the receiving stations at the moment of performance.

Live-Time Delay A delay that coincides with the local live time. Usually occurs when the station is noninterconnected and thus unable to take a live feed.

Local Advertising Advertising by local retailers (as opposed to national advertisers advertising in local markets), usually at a lower rate than that charged national advertisers.

Local-Channel Station A radio station that is allowed just enough power to be heard near its point of transmission and is assigned a radio channel set aside for low-power local-channel stations (usually 250 watts).

Locally Edited Supplement Sunday magazine supplement similar in character to syndicated magazine supplements but owned and edited by the newspaper distributing it. Such supplements are available in most of the largest cities throughout the United States. Some of them have banded together into groups for purposes of soliciting of national advertising more efficiently, and they offer group rates to advertisers who buy all the papers.

Local Media Media whose coverage and circulation are confined to or concentrated in their market of origin. Usually, they offer different sets of rates to the national advertiser and the local advertiser.

Local Rate Rate charged by a medium to the local retail trade.

Local Time Availabilities or times of broadcasting quoted in terms of local time rather than eastern standard time.

Loyalty Index Frequency of listenership to a particular station.

Magazine Supplement A magazine section of a Sunday or daily newspaper distributed either locally or nationally.

Mail-In Premium A premium offered at the point of sale in a retail store to be obtained by the consumer by mailing a box top, coin, or label to the manufacturer.

Mail Survey Map A broadcast coverage map prepared by tabulating cumulative, unsolicited mail received during a certain period or by tabulating listener response to a special order or contest run during a certain period.

Makegood An announcement or advertisement run as a replacement for one that was scheduled but did not run, or that ran incorrectly. Also, no-charge units given to honor audience delivery guarantees.

Market The geographic area that can receive the program; can range from the entire United States down to a local market.

Market-by-Market Allocation (MBM) A system of media/marketing planning that allocates a brand's total available advertising dollars against current and/or potential business on the basis of each individual TV market. MBM spends all advertising dollars (national and local) available in each market in proportion to current and/or anticipated business in the market. The result of MBM planning is spending more accurately against anticipated sales and thereby generating greater business for a brand.

Market Development Index See *Category Development Index; Market Index.*

Market Index The factor chosen to measure relative sales opportunities in different geographic or territorial units. Any quantitative information that makes estimation of such opportunities possible might be used as a market index. A general market index is a factor that influences the purchase of a specific product or groups of related products. Sometimes called a *market development index* or *category development index.*

Marketing Mix A group of elements used to sell a product or service: product, place (or distribution), price, and promotion.

Market Outline The measurement of the share of market based on total purchases of a particular brand or groups of similar brands with a product category during a specific time period.

Market Pattern The pattern of a product's sales in terms of the relation between the volume and concentration either by total market or by individual market. A thick market pattern is one in which a high portion of all people are prospects for a product. A thin market pattern is one in which a low portion of all people are prospects for a product.

Market Potential The portion of a market that a company can hope to capture for its own product.

Market Profile A demographic description of the people or the households in a product's market. The description may also include economic and retailing information about a territory.

Market Segmentation A strategy of implementing different kinds of marketing programs to various segments of the total consumer market based on demographic or lifestyle characteristics.

Market Share A product's share of an industry's sales volume.

"Marriage" Split Ad placement that occurs when more than one advertiser buys the total circulation of a magazine and each of the advertisers runs its ad in only a portion of that circulation. For example, an advertiser with distribution in the western United States and one with distribution in the eastern United States may split an ad in a magazine that permits this. In this case, the advertiser with distribution in the West would use only the part of the magazine's circulation that reaches the West, and the other advertiser would use the remainder.

Masked-Recognition Test   A method of assessing an ad's effectiveness by finding the percentage of respondents who can identify the advertiser or brand when all identifying marks are concealed.

Mass Magazine   A magazine of a general nature that appeals to all types of people in all localities.

Mechanical   See *Keyline.*

Mechanical Requirements   The physical specifications of a publication that advertising material must meet in order to be reproduced in the publication. Such requirements are brought about by the physical requirements of the vehicle and the characteristics of its printing process. Broadcast media have similar requirements governing the physical characteristics of material acceptable for broadcast.

Media Consortia   A group of advertisers or advertising agencies that pool their media budgets to obtain maximum buying discounts through their greater combined negotiating leverage.

Mediamark Research Inc. (MRI)   A company that uses a single sample to measure product usage, media audiences, and consumer behavior.

Media Objectives   The goals a media plan is expected to accomplish.

Media Plan   The blueprint for how the advertising message will be delivered to the target audience. The plan also serves as a persuasive document that communicates the rationale behind a recommendation to spend significant amounts of money. Generally includes the media objectives, competitive analysis, target audience analysis and media habits, media strategy, time line, flowchart, and budget.

Media Records   A detailed report of advertising volume by selected brands in selected daily and Sunday newspapers in selected cities. Today this has been replaced by CMR National Newspaper Service.

Media Strategy Statement   A document prepared by an agency and outlining the specific media that the agency believes will best accomplish the brand's marketing objectives (as outlined in the market strategy statement) with the funds available.

Media Translation   (a) The process of reducing a national advertising media plan to local level in order to test a product or campaign inexpensively. (b) The expansion of a local advertising campaign to a national level.

Media Value   The judgment that a given medium has been found, through experience, to be more effective for a brand and its creative message, thus justifying more frequency in that medium.

Media Weight   The total impact of an advertising campaign in terms of number of commercials, impressions, GRPs, insertions, reach and frequency, advertising dollars, etc.

Medium   Any media class used to convey an advertising message to the public; includes newspapers, magazines, direct mail, radio, television, the Internet, and billboards.

Message Dispersion   A measure indicating how widely a message is received in a target universe. Reach is a measure of message dispersion.

Message Weight   The gross number of advertising messages delivered by a vehicle or a group of vehicles in a schedule.

Metro Area   A county or group of counties comprising the central core of a geographical market (usually based on governmental lines).

Metropolitan Statistical Area (MSA)   An area that consists of one or more entire counties meeting specified criteria pertaining to population, metropolitan character, and economic and social integration between outlying counties and the central county, determined by the Bureau of the Budget with the advice of the Federal Committee on Standard Metropolitan Areas composed of representatives of major federal government statistical agencies.

Middle Break   Station identification at about the halfway point of a show.

Milline Rate   A means of comparing rates of newspapers; the cost of one agate line per million circulation. The milline rate is computed by multiplying the line rate by 1 million, then dividing by the circulation. The factor of 1 million is used merely to provide an answer in convenient terms of dollars and cents, rather than in fractions of a cent. Today the line rate has been replaced by the inch rate in Standard Advertising Units (SAU).

Minimum Depth   At most newspapers, a requirement for the minimum size of advertisements—generally that an ad must be at least one inch high for every column it is wide. For example, if an advertiser wants to run an ad that is eight columns wide, the ad must be at least eight inches high.

Minute-by-Minute Profile   Nielsen data measuring the minute-by-minute program audience. Used to study audience gains and losses during specific minutes of the program and to aid in placing commercials at times when they receive maximum audiences.

Morning Drive   Radio daypart from 6:00 to 10:00 A.M.

Multistation Lineup   Purchase of commercial time on more than one station in a market.

NAB Codes   Radio and television codes promulgated by the National Association of Broadcasters to help its members meet their obligation to serve the American public. The codes include both program and advertising standards. Included in the advertising standards are sections dealing with presentation techniques, contests, premiums and offers, and time standards. These codes are extended by other documents providing interpretations and guidelines (e.g., Children's Television Advertising Guidelines and Alcoholic Beverage Advertising Guidelines). Discontinued in 1982.

Narrowcasting   Service by a cable system to a small community; the delivery of programming that addresses a specific need or audience.

National Advertising Rates   Rates for newspaper space charged to a national advertiser, as distinguished from local rates applying to local retailers. National advertising rates are generally higher than local rates.

National Media   Media that are national in scope.

National Plan   A media plan that is national in scope, as opposed to a local plan covering less than the entire United States.

National Rating   A rating of all households or individuals tuned in to a program on a national base. Sometimes the base is all television or radio households in the country. Other times, the base is only those households that can tune in to the program because they are served by a cable system carrying the program.

Net Controlled Circulation   The number of purchased and unpurchased copies of a controlled-circulation publication that are actually distributed to its intended readership.

Net Paid Circulation   A term used by ABC audit reports and publisher's statements referring to circulation that has been paid for at not less than 50 percent of the basic newsstand or subscription price. In 2001 this definition was changed to include publications that received any money (at least one penny) for a subscription. Audit reports show buyers how many copies are sold at each price point.

Net Plus   The net cost of a print ad, commercial, or program with an earned discount added on.

Net Unduplicated Audience   The combined cumulative audience for a single issue of a group of magazines or broadcasts.

Net Weekly Audience   In broadcast research, the number of families tuned in at least once to a program aired more than once a week.

Network   Two or more stations contractually united to broadcast programs (e.g., network programs).

Network Affiliate   A broadcast station that is part of a network and therefore offers network programs.

Network Franchise   A brand's right to retain the sponsorship of a program at the sponsoring brand's discretion. Advertisers acquire this right by agreeing to sponsor a program on a continuing basis.

Network Identification   Acknowledgment of a network affiliation at the end of a network broadcast.

Network Option Time   Time on network affiliates for which the network has selling priority.

Newspaper-Distributed Magazine   A supplement inserted into a Sunday newspaper.

Newspaper Syndicate   A business concern that sells special material (columns, photographs, comic strips) for simultaneous publication in a number of newspapers.

Newsstand Circulation Copies of publications purchased at outlets selling copies. These outlets may include hotels, vending machines, street vendors, drugstores, and supermarkets, in addition to the traditional newsstand or kiosk.

Nielsen Shorthand for two research organizations that were part of the same company before the mid-1990s, then split, and in 2001 became separate divisions of VNU, an international media and information company. A. C. Nielsen (ACN) provides market research data on products sold in grocery, drug, and mass-merchandise retail stores. Nielsen Media Research (NMR) provides television audience ratings for network, cable, and syndicated national broadcasts, as well as local television viewing in 210 DMAs. To avoid confusion, planners are cautioned to specify which company (i.e., ACN or NMR) is being referred to in reports and other communications.

Nielsen Clearing House (NCH) A company that handles the administrative work associated with processing coupons.

Nielsen Rating See *Rating*.

Nielsen Station Index (NSI) The local television rating service of Nielsen Media Research.

Ninety-Day Cancellation For all poster advertising, a policy that the advertising may be cancelled on 90 days' notice to the plant. This means that the advertiser or agency must notify the poster plant owner of cancellation 90 days before the contract posting date.

Noted The basic measure in the Starch method for testing print ads. This score represents the percentage of respondents (claimed readers of the issue) who say they saw the ad when they first read or looked into the magazine issue. In other words, they claimed recognition of the ad.

Obtained Score A Gallup & Robinson term for the actual percentage of respondents who prove recall of a print ad before the score is adjusted for color and size or converted to an index score. It is the basis for the final score.

Off Card Using a special rate not covered by a rate card.

Offensive Spending Advertising activity intended to secure new business.

On-Air Test A test of a commercial that uses a real broadcast response before the advertiser uses that commercial on a larger scale. An on-air test measures audience response to the creative executions, such as recall, attitude, or purchase interest for that product.

One-Time Rate The highest rate charged by a medium not subject to discounts. Sometimes called *open rate*.

Open End A broadcast that leaves the commercial spots blank to be filled in locally.

Open-End Transcription A recorded program usually sold on a syndicated basis in various cities and produced so that local commercial announcements may be inserted at various points throughout the show.

Open Rate In print, the highest rate charged to an advertiser, on which all discounts are based. Also called *base rate* or *one-time rate*.

Opportunities Marketing facts that exist and, without much money or effort, sell the product naturally.

Option Time (a) Time reserved by the networks in contract with their affiliates and for which the network has prior call under certain conditions for sponsored network programs; called network option time. (b) Time reserved by the local stations for local and national spot shows; called station option time.

Orbit A scheduling method in which stations rotate an advertiser's commercial among different programs and/or time periods—typically in prime time.

OTO One time only, describing a spot that runs only once. An OTO spot may be bought outright or provided as a makegood.

Outdoor Advertising Display advertising (billboards, posters, signs, etc.) placed out-of-doors, along highways and railroads, or on walls and roofs of buildings.

Out-of-Home Audience (a) Listeners to auto and battery-operated radios outside their homes. (b) The audience of a publication derived from exposure that occurred outside the reader's own home. (See *In-Home Audience.*)

Overlapping Circulation Duplication of circulation when advertising is placed in two or more media reaching the same prospects. Overlapping circulation is sometimes desirable to give additional impact to advertising.

Overnights Nielsen household ratings and shares provided to clients the morning following the day or evening of telecast.

Package (a) A combination of programs or commercials offered by a network for sponsorship at one price. Spot TV is sometimes sold as a package. (b) A program property in which all elements from script to finished production are owned and controlled by an individual or organization, commonly known as a *packager.*

Package Insert Separate advertising material included in packaged goods.

Package Plan A plan by which an advertiser purchases a certain number of TV or radio announcements per week, in return for which the station gives the advertiser a lower rate per announcement. The advertiser agrees to run the specific number of announcements each week and cannot split them up over a period of time.

Package Plan Discount In spot television, a price discount based upon frequency within a week, for example, "5-plan," "10-plan."

Packaged Goods Mostly food, soap, and household products that are marketed in the manufacturer's package, wrapper, or container.

Packager An individual or company producing a broadcast program or series of programs that are sold as complete units.

Painted Bulletin A billboard that is approximately 48 feet long by 14 feet high, with the copy message painted on the face of this structure, as contrasted to the poster panel that is composed of preprinted sheets that are pasted up like wallpaper.

Painted Display   See *Painted Bulletin.*

Painted Wall   An outdoor advertising unit, purchased individually, usually situated on a high-traffic artery or in a neighborhood shopping area.

Panel   (a) A fixed sample of respondents or stores selected to participate in a research project in which they report periodically on their knowledge, attitudes, and activities. This sampling technique is in contrast to the technique of using fresh samples each time. (b) A master TV or radio control board, usually in a master control room.

Panels   Regular and illuminated units of outdoor advertising. A regular panel is a billboard that is not lighted at night. An illuminated panel is a billboard that is lighted from dusk until midnight.

Pantry Audit   A consumer survey to tabulate brands, items, and varieties of grocery store products in the home.

Parallel Location   An outdoor advertising location in which the poster panel is parallel to the road.

Participation   An announcement inside the context of a program, as opposed to sponsorship or to chain or station breaks placed between programs. A station or network may program a segment of time to carry participation announcements, which it sells to various advertisers for commercial use. The announcements are usually 10, 30, or 60 seconds long, but may be longer.

Participation Program   (a) A commercial program cosponsored by a number of advertisers. (b) A program in which the audience participates (e.g., a quiz show).

Pass-Along Reader   A person who reads a publication not purchased by the person or a member of his or her family. These readers must be included in determining the total numbers of readers of a particular issue or a particular publication. (See *Audience, Secondary.*)

Pay Cable   Any of a number of program services for which cable subscribers pay a monthly charge in addition to the basic cable subscription fee.

Penalty Costs   In test market and expansion operation, the premium paid for local replacement media, compared with the national media that the brand uses for its national plan.

Penetration   The percentage of total homes or people in a specified area who are physically able to be exposed to a medium or who purchase a given product or service.

People Meter   An electronic device that measures viewership of TV programs. Present meters require members of a sample household to push their designated button when they consider themselves to be "watching" television. This information is sent via telephone lines to the computers of Nielsen Media Research, which tally the number of viewers watching each program.

Percent Composition   See *Composition.*

Percent Coverage   See *Coverage.*

Per Inquiry Advertising (PI Advertising) An agreement between a media owner and an advertiser in which the owner agrees to accept payment for advertising on the basis of the number of inquiries or completed sales resulting from advertising, soliciting inquiries, or direct sales.

Persons Using Radio (PUR) The percentage of an area's population (over age 12) listening to a radio at any given time.

P4C Abbreviation for "page/four-color," meaning a full-page ad printed in the four-color process. Other abbreviations include P2C (page/two-color), PB&W (page/black and white), 3/5P4C (3/5 page/four-color), 2C (second cover), and BC (back cover).

Piggyback The back-to-back scheduling of two or more brand commercials of one advertiser in network or spot positions.

Plan Rate The rate paid by an advertiser who purchased a TV or radio package plan. The rates are lower than if the spots were purchased individually, since the advertiser agreed to run a specific number of spots each week.

Pod A bank of consecutive commercials within a television program.

Position An advertisement's place on a page and the location of the page in the publication. A preferred position is an especially desirable position obtained by paying an extra charge or granted to an advertiser that has placed a heavy schedule in a publication. Publications occasionally rotate preferred positions among advertisers that have contracted for space above a specified minimum.

Poster A product sign intended to be displayed on a store window or on an inside wall, large enough to be legible at a reasonable distance.

Poster Panel A standard surface on which outdoor advertisements are mounted. The poster panel is the most widely used form of outdoor advertising. The standard panel measures 12 feet by 25 feet and is usually made of steel with a wood, fiberglass, or metal molding around the outer edges. The 24-sheet poster is posted on this structure.

Poster Showing Poster advertising is sold in packages called *showings*. It is possible to buy #25, #50, #75, #100, and #200 showings. A showing equals the percent of the market's population passing one or more of the boards each day and is sometimes referred to as *daily GRPS*. This is based on the Traffic Audit Bureau's count of cars passing each site multiplied by an estimated number of persons per car. So a #50 showing equals 50 GRPs per day or 1,500 GRPs per month. The #100 showing is designed to provide more intense coverage of practically all major streets in the market. The #200 showing is one designed for maximum impact. Each poster plant owner decides how many panels will constitute a #50 showing or a #100 showing in his or her city.

Posttest Study of the response to finished advertising after it has been published and telecast in media. Posttests rely on normal patterns of behavior to expose respondents to advertising.

Potential Audience See *Audience, Potential.*

Preemptible Spot A spot announcement sold at a reduced rate because the station has the option to sell that same spot to another advertiser willing to pay full rate.

Preemption Recapture by the station network of an advertiser's time in order to substitute a special program of universal value. For example, when the President speaks, the show regularly scheduled at that time is preempted.

Preferred Position A position in a magazine or newspaper that is regarded as excellent in terms of its ability to generate a large readership. Preferred position is usually located next to editorial material that has a high interest among the publication's readers.

Preprint A reproduction of an advertisement before it appears in a publication.

Pretest Study of advertisements or commercials prior to distribution via regular media channels. Advertising may be studied in rough or finished form. Pretesting relies on some special means of exposing respondents to the advertisement other than the regular media planned—portfolios, dummy magazines, etc.

Primary Audience See *Audience, Primary.*

Primary Households Households into which a publication has been introduced by purchase, either at the newsstand or by subscription, rather than by pass-along.

Primary Readers The readers of a publication who reside in primary households.

Primary Research Research conducted for a specific client or to meet a specific agency need.

Primary Service Area In AM or standard broadcasting, the area in which a station signal is strongest and steadiest. Defined by Federal Communications Commission rules as the area in which the ground wave (the primary wave for broadcast transmission) is not subject to objectionable interference or objectionable fading. No similar term is officially used in TV broadcasting, although television engineering standards recognize three zones of signal service existing in concentric rings from the transmitting tower: City Grade Service, A Contour, B Contour.

Prime Time The period of peak television set usage—between 8:00 and 11 P.M. in the eastern and Pacific time zones and between 7:00 and 10 P.M. in the central and mountain time zones. On Sundays, prime time begins an hour earlier.

Prime Time Access Rule (PTAR) A Federal Communications Commission rule that allows television stations to put on a specified amount of their own local programming during prime time. Under this rule, regular network programming starts at 8 P.M. eastern standard time Monday through Saturday and 7 P.M. on Sunday. The period from 7:30 to 8:00 P.M. is generally referred to as *prime access time.*

Product Protection Protection that an advertiser wants and sometimes gets against being positioned adjacent to a competitive product.

Program Coverage The number (or percentage) of television households that can receive a program over one or more stations because they are in the signal area of some station carrying the program.

Program Lineup A listing of stations carrying a program on either a live or delayed basis. The information on the list may be supplied by the network or received directly from their affiliates.

Program Station Rating A rating that is based on the television homes located in the area in which a program was telecast. This type of rating permits an unbiased comparison of different programs regardless of variation in the number of homes capable of receiving the programs.

Promotion Allowance Money received by a wholesaler or a retailer from a manufacturer or its representative for sales promotion other than advertising. (See *Advertising Allowance*.)

Psychographic A term that describes consumers or audience members on the basis of some psychological trait, characteristic of behavior, or lifestyle.

Public Access Federal Communications Commission rule that requires any cable system with 3,500 or more subscribers to have at least one noncommercial channel available to the public on a first-come nondiscriminatory basis.

Public Service Announcement (PSA) Promotional material for a nonprofit cause, usually prepared at no cost to the service advertised, and carried by vehicles at no cost.

Publishers Information Bureau (PIB) PIB is a membership organization that tracks the amount and type of advertising carried by consumer magazines. It accounts for about 85 percent of consumer magazine ad volume. Data is reported monthly by the CMR/PIB Magazine Service, which is designed to give convenient summaries of national magazine expenditures by advertiser and by publication.

Publisher's Statement A notarized statement made by a publisher regarding total circulation, geographic distribution, methods of securing subscriptions, etc. These statements are often issued between audited statements, especially when market conditions have changed.

Pulsing A media scheduling technique in which periods of heavy activity alternate with lower-activity periods.

Pure Program Ratings A measurement of audience size in which estimates exclude program preemptions that occurred during the survey period.

Qualified Issue Reader A respondent who qualifies to be interviewed about advertisements in a magazine on the basis of having read the study issue of a magazine. Requirements for such qualification vary. For Daniel Starch & Associates interviews, readers merely have to claim they looked into the issue when shown the cover. For Gallup & Robinson studies, respondents must prove reading by correctly describing some article when shown the issue's cover and table of contents.

Qualified Viewer Respondent who has demonstrated viewing of a TV program (on the basis of recall of at least one part of the episode), thus becoming eligible or qualified for interview about commercials aired on that show.

Quantity Discount (a) A graduated discount on quantity purchases scaled to the number of cases in a single order. (b) A periodic refund based upon the value of purchases over a period of time.

Quintile The division of any sample of respondents into five equal-sized groups ranging from the heaviest to the lightest amount of exposure to the medium. Samples may also be divided into tertiles (thirds), quartiles (fourths), deciles (tenths), etc.

Quota A predetermined media goal in a market. Goals can be established in terms of dollars spent, number of spots to be purchased, or GRPs to be achieved. The agency's time buyer uses quotas in implementing a media plan.

RADAR (Radio's All Dimension Audience Research) The network radio rating service provided by the National Radio Services division of Arbitron Company. It is set up to service national customers such as radio networks, syndicators, representative firms, public radio and satellite radio companies.

Rate Base The circulation level of a print vehicle, used in setting rates for advertising space.

Rate Card A medium's listing of advertising costs, mechanical requirements, issue dates, closing dates, cancellation dates, and circulation data. Rate cards are issued by both print and broadcast media.

Rate Class In broadcast media, the time charge in effect at a specified time.

Rate Differential Among newspapers, the difference between the national and the local rates.

Rate Holder (a) A minimum-sized advertisement placed in a publication during a contract period to hold a time or quantity discount rate. (b) An ID spot bought by the advertiser for the same reason.

Rate Protection A guarantee that an advertiser's rate under the old rate card will be protected for a period, usually from three to six months, should a new rate be introduced.

Rating In television or radio, the percent of the target audience in a market that is tuned in to a program or a daypart. In national television, ratings refer to the average minute. In local TV and radio, ratings refer to the average quarter hour.

Reach The number of different persons or homes exposed to a specific media vehicle or schedule at least once. Usually measured over a specific period of time (e.g., four weeks). Also known as *cume, cumulative, unduplicated,* or *net audience.*

Reader Impression Studies See *Impression Studies.*

Reader Interest (a) Expression of interest by readers in advertisements they have read. Sometimes evaluated by unsolicited mail. Sometimes evaluated by the numbers of people who can remember having read material with interest. (b) An evaluation of the relative level of general interest in different types of products.

Reader Traffic The movement from page to page by readers of a publication.

Readers People who are exposed to a print vehicle.

Readers per Copy The average number of readers of a magazine per copy of circulation. When multiplied by a magazine's circulation, the result equals its audience.

Readership or Audience The average number of persons who are exposed to a publication as distinguished from the circulation or number of copies distributed.

Read Most As defined by Daniel Starch & Associates for measurement of ad readership, magazine or newspaper readers who read 50 percent or more of the copy of a specific advertisement.

Rebate A refund that reduces the contract price for merchandise. The term is frequently used for advertising allowances. Also given to advertisers by a certain media vehicle as a result of an advertiser's exceeding the contract minimum and earning a greater discount.

Recent-Reading Technique In measurement of magazine readership, a technique in which survey respondents read a list of magazines and check the names of magazines they are sure they have read in the most recent publication period (week, month, quarter, etc.).

Recognition A technique used to determine whether a person saw or heard a given print advertisement or broadcast commercial; the researcher shows (or plays) the ad or commercial and inquires whether the person saw or heard it at a previous date in a specific medium. This technique was pioneered and is still being used by Daniel Starch & Associates.

Regional Edition A geographical section of a national magazine's circulation that an advertiser can purchase without having to purchase the rest of the magazine's circulation (as is required in a split run). The magazine usually charges a higher premium for regional editions and demographic editions.

Regional Network A network of stations serving a limited geographic area.

Regular Panel See *Panels.*

Remnant Space Magazine space sold at reduced price to help fill out regional editions.

Renewals (a) In print, magazine or newspaper subscriptions that people extend past their expiration dates. (b) In outdoor advertising, extra posters over and above the quantity actually needed to post the exact number of panels in a showing. They are shipped to the plant operator, and if one of the posters on display is damaged, the plant operator has a complete poster design on hand to replace the damaged poster immediately.

Repetition A measure indicating to what extent audience members were exposed to the same vehicle or group of vehicles. Frequency is a measure of repetition.

Replacement Media Local media that are being used to offset deficiencies in national media delivery in a test market or expansion area (e.g., local rotogravure supplements, comic sections, black-and-white daily newspapers).

Representative (or Rep) A general term used to describe sales representatives for media vehicles. A representative firm usually handles several vehicles, serving as their sales agent and taking commissions on the sales they make; salespersons may also be directly employed by stations or publications.

Response Function A table that quantifies differences in a target's response to advertising after varying numbers of exposures.

Retail Trading Zone The area beyond the city zone whose residents regularly trade to an important degree with retail merchants in the city zone. These are defined by the Audit Bureau of Circulations.

Returns per Thousand Circulation A gauge of the effectiveness of media used in support of promotions; computed by dividing the total number of returns by the circulation of the publication to which the returns are attributable. (See *Keying an Advertisement*.)

Rollout A marketing strategy technique in which a brand is introduced in a limited geographical area. If the brand succeeds in that area, it is then introduced in adjacent areas and, if successful, in other adjacent areas until the entire country is covered.

Roster Recall Method of research in which a list of radio or TV programs is submitted to respondents for recall.

Rotating Painted Bulletins Moving the advertiser's copy from one painted bulletin to another, usually every 60 days. This service, available in most major cities, offers advertisers an opportunity to cover a large area or a given market (over a long period of time) with a limited number of painted bulletins.

Rotation (a) The process of continuing a series of advertisements over and over again in a regular order. (b) The practice in store management of moving the older stock forward when restocking shelves or cases. (c) The practice, in retail advertising, of scheduling a branded product or group of products to be featured at intervals throughout the year to maintain a desired stock balance.

Run of Press (ROP) (a) A newspaper advertisement for which a definite position is not specified, but which usually appears in the general news sections. Also called *run of book*. (b) In connection with color newspaper advertising, color advertising in the main portion of the paper, as distinguished from that placed in the magazine section (Sunday supplement).

Run of Schedule (ROS) A broadcast commercial for which a definite time is not specified. For example, a nighttime commercial during prime time may be run at any time during this period. The time at which an announcement runs may also vary from week to week, depending upon other requirements.

Runs In television film syndication, the number of times a film has been telecast in a given area. The number of times a film may be run according to an advertiser's lease. A rerun among television film syndicators is an available program previously telecast in an area.

Russell Hall See *Hall's Magazine Reports*.

Sales Promotion Sales activities that supplement personal selling and advertising, coordinate the two, and help to make them effective; for example, sales incentives.

Saturation A level of advertising weight several times above normal reach and frequency levels standard for the market or product involved. Saturation implies simultaneous achievement of high reach and frequency designed to achieve maximum impact.

Saturation Showing In outdoor, a showing of maximum intensity, designed to surpass complete coverage (the 100 showing) with repeat impressions. Often a 200 showing.

Scatter Market The purchase of network or cable TV time on a quarterly basis, after the "up-front" selling season.

Scatter Plan The placing of announcements in a number of different network TV programs.

Schedule (a) A list of media to be used during an advertising campaign. (b) A list of a product's advertising to be included in a media vehicle during a specific time. (c) A chronological list of programs broadcast by a station. Also called a *flowchart*.

Secondary Audience See *Audience, Secondary.*

Secondary Research Research information gathered from a published study conducted by another person or group. (See *Syndicated Research*.)

Secondary Service Area The distant area in which a broadcast station's signal is subject to interference or fading but can still be received.

Sectional Magazine A magazine that is distributed only sectionally and not nationally (such as *Sunset*, which is confined to the western states). Also called a *regional magazine*.

Selective Magazine A magazine that, because of its nature and editorial content, appeals only to a certain type of audience.

Sets in Use The total number of sets tuned in to some program at a given time of day and day of week. At one time, "sets in use" was equivalent to HUT, but today, its meaning is limited to sets, not households. (See *Households Using TV.*)

Share, or Share of Audience The audience for a program as a percentage of all households using television (HUT) at the time of the program's broadcast.

Share of Market The percentage of the total sales of a specified class of products that is held by or attributed to a particular brand at a given time.

Share of Mind The percentage of relevant population (or sample of that population) who indicate awareness of, or preference for, the various brands within a product group. The specific meaning varies considerably with the method of measurement. It may be a test of salience or a test of total recall, aided or unaided. The term usually refers to consumer awareness of brands relative to like measures of awareness for competing brands.

Share of Voice A brand's share of the total advertising dollars or impressions for a product or commodity classification.

Shelter Magazines Magazines dealing editorially with the home, covering topics such as decorating, maintenance, and gardening. Additionally, these magazines carry a considerable amount of food editorial matter. An example is *Better Homes & Gardens*.

Shopper A newspaper that is published in a local community and containing mainly local news, shopping hints and suggestions, and advertisements. Sometimes called a *shopping newspaper*.

Short Rate The additional charge incurred when an advertiser fails to use enough media time or space to earn the contract discount envisaged at the time of the original order.

Showing (a) In outdoor advertising, the number of posters offered as a unit in terms of 100 GRPs per day and variations thereof. (b) In transit advertising, the number of cards included in a unit of sale. (See *Poster Showing.*)

Significantly Viewed As defined by the Federal Communications Commission, describing a station in a given county if (a) it is a network affiliate and achieves among noncable households a share of total viewing hours of at least 3 percent and a net weekly circulation of at least 25 percent; or (b) it is an independent station and achieves among noncable households a share of total viewing hours of at least 2 percent and a net weekly circulation of at least 5 percent. A station that is significantly viewed becomes "local" for regulatory purposes. It therefore can demand carriage on cable systems, and the systems need not delete the duplicate programming of a significantly viewed station at the request of a higher-priority (local) station.

Simmons Data Data on print and broadcast media audience exposure and product usage reported by the Simmons Market Research Bureau.

Simmons Market Research Bureau (SMRB) A media and marketing research firm that uses a single sample to measure product usage, media audience, and consumer behavior. Separate studies cover adults, teens, children, Hispanics, consumer online users, and computer professionals.

Single-Source Data Data on product usage and media behavior gathered from a single sample. This technique makes the results more reliable and avoids the need to match samples that have different characteristics.

Situation Analysis Research prepared in document format to provide background for a media planner. The analysis includes history of the market, distribution channels, consumer analysis, product analysis, and advertising and media analysis.

Sliding Rate A space or time rate in a medium that is reduced as the volume purchased increases over a period of time.

Space Position Value In outdoor, an estimate of the effectiveness of a particular poster location. The factors considered are the length of approach, the speed of travel, the angle of the panel to its circulation, and the relation of the panel to adjacent panels.

Space Schedule A schedule that the agency sends to the advertiser, showing the media to be used, dates on which advertising is to appear, size of advertisements, and cost of space.

Special A one-time TV show generally employing known talent and usually running an hour or longer. Also called a *spectacular*.

Spill-In (or Spill-Out) The degree to which programming is viewed in adjacent television markets. Depending on the perspective, this is either spill-in or spill-out. Milwaukee television programming spills out of the Milwaukee DMA and spills into the Madison, Wisconsin, area, and vice versa.

Spinoff A line extension of a magazine on a short-term basis. Also called a *"one-shot" annual edition.*

Split Run The running of two or more versions of an advertisement in every other copy of the same magazine or newspaper. In a variation of split runs, one version of the ad appears in newsstand copies, and another in mail subscription copies. Splits may also occur geographically.

Split-Run Test Research designed to test the effectiveness of various copy elements, prices, or types of offers by placing them in alternative copies of an issue. The researchers evaluate various forms of the advertisements by means of coupon or inquiry returns, or by orders placed for trial offers.

Sponsor Identification (SI) The extent to which a program's sponsor is identified or its product or service remembered. The percentage of listeners or viewers who correctly associate a program with the sponsor of his product is the Sponsor Identification Index (SII).

Sponsor Relief The process whereby an advertiser who has contracted for broadcast time that is no longer needed is granted relief by having another advertiser purchase the unneeded time.

Sponsorship The purchase of more than one announcement in a program (usually a majority of commercials) by one advertiser.

Spot (a) A time period filled entirely by a commercial or public service message and sold separately from the adjacent time periods. Such announcements may be placed between network programs or within local programs. (b) To buy time (programs and/or announcements) on a market-by-market basis from stations through their representatives.

Spot Announcement Commercial placed on individual radio and TV stations.

Spot Programming The process by which an advertiser secures the rights to a television program and places the program on stations in selected markets without regard to network affiliation. The advertiser may own the television program outright, have rights to the program for a specific length of time, or have rights to the program in only a certain part of the country.

Spot Radio The use of stations in selected markets without regard to network affiliation. May involve spot announcements or complete programs.

Spot Schedule A local spot announcement buy or a standard form that agencies submit showing specific times, adjacencies, etc., of a brand's current spot announcements in a market.

Spot Television The use of stations in selected markets without regard to network affiliation. May involve spot announcements or complete local programs.

Spread An advertisement appearing on any two facing pages of a publication.

SRDS (formerly Standard Rate & Data Service) A service that publishes the rates and discount structures of all major media. It also publishes marketing research studies, often on media or market areas. Its website is www.srds.com.

Staggered Schedule Several advertisements scheduled in two or more publications, arranged so as to alternate or rotate the dates of insertion.

Standard Advertising Unit (SAU) The 56 advertising units in broadsheet and 33 units in tabloid newspapers that are fixed sizes in depth and width and are measured in standard column inches.

Standby Space An order accepted by some magazines to run an advertisement whenever and wherever they wish, at an extra discount. The advertiser forwards print production materials with the order. This practice helps magazines fill odd pages or spaces.

Starch Method The recognition method used by Daniel Starch & Associates in the company's studies of advertising readership.

Station Break A time period between two programs when a station announces its call letters and channel number, and also broadcasts commercials.

Station Log The official, chronological listing of a radio or television station's programming and commercial announcements throughout the day.

Station Rep A sales organization or person representing individual stations to national advertisers. Short for *station representative.*

Store-Distributed Magazine Any one of several magazines (e.g., *Family Circle, Woman's Day*) whose primary channel of distribution was retail grocery stores. In recent years these "store books" have shifted to more than 60 percent of subscription sales.

Store Panel A selected sample of stores used repeatedly for marketing research to collect data on retail sales movement (e.g., A. C. Nielsen's food store panel). (See *Panel.*)

Strip Programming (a) Running of a television or radio series at the same hour on each weekday. (b) Similar but different programs telecast at the same time throughout the week. (c) The same program, but different episodes, broadcast several times weekly at the same time.

Sunday Newspaper Supplement Any printed matter that is inserted in a Sunday edition of a newspaper on a continuing basis and is not part of the newspaper itself. Two main publications fitting into this category are magazine supplements and comic sections. A supplement may be either syndicated nationally or edited locally. (See *Syndicated Sunday Magazine Supplement.*)

Sweeps Periods during which Nielsen surveys all local television markets. Sweeps are conducted four times yearly (November, February, May, and July), so these months are called *sweep months.*

Syndicated Program A method of selling a TV or radio program on a market-by-market (station-by-station) basis, as opposed to a network of affiliated stations.

Syndicated Research Research that is available for general purchase, as contrasted with custom research for a single advertiser or user. Examples include MRI, Nielsen Media Research, Arbitron, and CMR.

Syndicated Sunday Magazine Supplement A magazine supplement that is distributed through a group of newspapers and is owned by a single publisher. The distributing newspapers pay the publisher for the privilege of distributing the supplement, which in turn helps to build circulation for the distributing newspapers. There are only two nationally syndicated supplements: *Parade* and *USA Weekend.*

Tabloid A smaller than standard-sized newspaper, with five columns and about 1,000 lines per page.

Tag Line A final line of a dramatic scene or act that is treated to give point or impact to the preceding dialogue.

Target Audience The desired or intended audience for advertising, as described or determined by the advertiser. Usually defined in terms of specific demographic (age, sex, income, etc.), purchase, or ownership characteristics.

Targetcasting Another term for narrowcasting, where cable programming is created to meet the interests of a special demographic audience.

Tear Sheets Actual pages of advertising as they appear in an issue of any publication, used to serve as proofs of insertion.

Telecast A broadcast, program, or show on television.

Telemarketing The sale of goods and services through the use of a telephone. There are two classes of telemarketing: in-bound telemarketing—consumers initiate the call to ask questions or order a product; and out-bound telemarketing—calls are initiated by a telemarketing firm to consumers' homes.

Telephone Coincidental Survey In research, the interview method in which telephone calls are made while a particular activity, usually a broadcast program, is in progress.

Test Market A given marketing area, usually a metropolitan census region, in which a market test is conducted. Sometimes used as a verb to refer to introduction of a new product.

Test-Market Translation The use of local media that are available in a specific market to represent the national media included in a brand's national plan. The theoretical national plan must be reproduced as carefully and as accurately as possible in the test market, since company management will use sales results to determine whether the product should be expanded to national distribution. (See *Little U.S.A. Concept* and *As It Falls Concept.*)

Thirty-Sheet Poster An outdoor poster that is about 12 feet by 25 feet. In the early days of advertising, the poster consisted of 24 individual panels pasted together to form an ad. Today about 10 to 12 panels are used, depending on the type of artwork and copy.

Through-the-Book A technique of determining a print medium's audience size by having respondents go through a stripped-down issue with an interviewer to learn which articles are most interesting. After this preliminary examination, respondents are asked whether they are sure they looked into the magazine. Only those who answer positively are counted as readers. No longer used because of the limited number of magazines that can be carried by interviewers.

Tie-In A retail outlet's newspaper advertisement referring to or associating with another ad in the same newspaper. Tie-ins are paid for by the retail outlets that run them.

Time Shifting The practice of recording a program off the air and playing it back at a different time.

Total Audience The total number of unduplicated readers of a magazine.

Total Audience Rating The percent of households tuning to all or to any portion of a program for at least five minutes.

Total Net Paid The total of all classes of a publication's circulation for which the ultimate purchasers have paid in accordance with the standards set by the Audit Bureau of Circulations' rules. Includes single-copy sales, mail subscriptions, and specials.

TPT (Total Prime Time) A television research project of Gallup & Robinson evaluating all paid commercials aired during the evening period when national network programming is shown, i.e., both program commercials and station breaks. Offers data on percentage of commercial audience able to recall the commercial, plus an estimate of actual audience in station coverage. TPT has been replaced by other G & R services. See www.gallup-robinson.com.

Traceable Expenditures Published reports on advertising expenditures by media for different advertisers. Currently, traceable expenditures are available for consumer magazines, Sunday supplements, local newspapers, national newspapers, spot TV, network TV, cable TV, syndication TV, outdoor, network radio, and spot radio.

Trade Advertising Advertisements of consumer items directed to wholesalers and retailers in the distribution channel.

Trade Magazine See *Business Paper.*

Trade Paper Publication covering the commercial activities of wholesale and retail outlets, but many reach the sales departments of manufacturers. Trade papers include all publications that offer a manufacturer the opportunity to reach those who will sell the product for the company, at either the retail or wholesale level.

Trading Area The area surrounding a city as defined by the Audit Bureau of Circulations whose residents would normally be expected to use the city as their trading center.

Traffic Audit Bureau (TAB) An organization sponsored by outdoor advertising plants, advertising companies, and national advertisers for the purpose of authenticating circulation as related to outdoor advertising. See www.tabonline.com.

Traffic Count The evaluation of outdoor poster circulation by an actual count of traffic passing the poster.

Traffic Flow Map (Outdoor) An outline map of a market's streets scaled to indicate the relative densities of traffic.

Traffic Pattern Comparisons of customer count to establish averages. Behavior of customers in terms of shopping time, hour of day, day of week, frequency.

Transit Advertising Advertising on transportation vehicles such as buses, subways, and streetcars. Uses poster-type ads.

Turnover The ratio of a single telecast rating to a four-week reach. This ratio serves as an indication of the relative degree to which a program's audience changes. The greater the turnover in the audience, the higher the ratio. Also the ratio of total viewers of a telecast divided by the average minute rating.

Two-Sheet Posters Outdoor posters placed at transit or train stops and measuring 60 inches by 46 inches.

Unaided Recall The process of determining whether a person saw or heard a given ad or commercial sometime after exposure with only minimal cueing such as mention of product class (not brand).

Universe The estimated number of actual households or people from which the sample will be taken and to which data from the sample will be projected.

Upscale A general description of a medium's audience indicating membership in an upper socioeconomic class.

Vehicle A particular component of a media class, such as a particular magazine or broadcast program.

Vertical Cume In broadcast research, a cumulative rating for two or more programs broadcast on the same day.

Vertical Half Page A half-page ad where the long dimension of the ad is vertical. (See *Horizontal Half Page*.)

Vertical Publication A business publication that serves a specific trade, industry, business, or profession.

Viewer Impression Studies See *Impression Studies.*

Viewers per Set (VPS) The average number of persons watching or listening to a program in each home.

Viewers per Viewing Household (VPVH) "Estimated number of viewers, usually classified by age and sex, comprising the audience within those households viewing a given station or program or using television during a particular time period. Also called *Viewers per Tuning Household* (VPTH)." (Source: Nielsen Media Research.)

Volume Discount A discount that a publisher gives an advertiser in exchange for running ads in a certain volume of space in the publication. An advertiser might use many small insertions to make up the required number of pages.

Waste Circulation (a) The audience members of a magazine or newspaper who are not prospects for a particular advertised product. (b) Circulation in an area where an advertiser does not have distribution of its product.

Women's Service Magazine Magazine appealing to women (homemakers specifically), and whose editorial contents are designed to further their knowledge as homemakers.

Working Media Budget The portion of the budget set aside for the purchase of advertising space and time, as distinguished from other advertising-related expenses such as commercial production, talent payments, tapes, shipping, etc.

World Wide Web The organized storehouse of billions of pages of alphanumeric and multimedia content that is made available to worldwide users who have access to the Internet.

Yesterday-Reading Technique Research technique that asks respondents in a selected sample which newspapers they read yesterday; similar to recent-reading magazine technique.

Zapping Using a remote-control device to change television channels from across the room, especially to avoid viewing commercials.

Zipping Using a remote-control device to skip ahead of any portion of a television or VCR program, especially to skip over commercials.

Index

About the Authors

Jack Z. Sissors spent more than 40 years teaching and working in media at Northwestern University before retiring with the rank of professor emeritus. He created and edited *The Journal of Media Planning* and directed various media symposia for media planners. He worked on the Advertising Research Foundation's committees on single-source data, effective frequency, and media model building. Before working in academia, he held positions with Leo Burnett and other advertising companies.

Roger B. Baron is senior vice president, director of media research at Foote, Cone & Belding in Chicago. He received a BA in communications and public policy from the University of California, Berkeley, and an MA in telecommunications from the University of Southern California. Following graduate school he spent three years on active duty in the navy, retiring with the rank of captain in the naval reserve.

His professional experience includes five years at Leo Burnett in media research and as a media planner and supervisor on the Kellogg cereal account. He then spent 12 years at D'Arcy Masius Benton & Bowles in San Francisco—the last four as VP/media director. He returned to Chicago in 1987.

Mr. Baron is active in the Advertising Research Foundation. He is also a past president of the Media Research Club of Chicago. Baron is an accomplished computer programmer and has developed several computer models for media planning.

He is married and has two adult sons. In his spare time he reads, works around the house, and is an opera and (beginning) Civil War buff.